AFFLUENCE
AND AUTHORITY

AFFLUENCE
AND AUTHORITY

A Social History of
Twentieth-Century Britain

John Benson

Hodder Arnold

A MEMBER OF THE HODDER HEADLINE GROUP

First published in Great Britain in 2005 by
Hodder Education, a member of the Hodder Headline Group,
338 Euston Road, London NW1 3BH

http://www.hoddereducation.co.uk

Distributed in the United States of America by
Oxford University Press Inc.
198 Madison Avenue, New York, NY10016

The advice and information in this book are believed to be true and accurate
at the date of going to press, but neither the author nor the publisher can
accept any legal responsibility or liability for any errors or omissions.

British Library Cataloguing in Publication Data
A catalogue record for this book is available from the British Library

Library of Congress Cataloging-in-Publication Data
A catalog record for this book is available from the Library of Congress

ISBN-10: 0 340 76367 1
ISBN-13: 978 0 340 76367 4

1 2 3 4 5 6 7 8 9 10

Typeset in 10/12 pt Garamond by Charon Tec Pvt. Ltd, Chennai, India
www.charontec.com
Printed and bound in Great Britain by CPI Bath

What do you think about this book? Or any other Hodder Education title?
Please send your comments to the feedback section on www.hoddereducation.co.uk

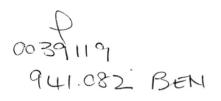

CONTENTS

LIST OF FIGURES

LIST OF TABLES

ACKNOWLEDGEMENTS

I am pleased to take this opportunity to thank those who have helped to make this book possible. At Hodder Arnold, Christopher Wheeler commissioned my original proposal, Christina Wipf Perry took an interest in its progress, and Michael Strang helped in a number of ways, including arranging for three anonymous readers to comment upon an early draft of the manuscript. I have also received a great deal of assistance from friends, colleagues and former colleagues. I am grateful to Karen Egan-Banks for undertaking research in the national press, and to Samantha Badger, Paula Bartley, Kristina Bennert, Hugh Bowen, Matthew Brannan, John Buckley, Martin Dangerfield, Mike Haynes, Andrew MacLennan, Barbara Massam, Steve Tolliday, Malcolm Wanklyn and Harvey Woolf for providing me with advice and information on a number of important issues. I am particularly indebted to Dariusz Galasinski, Martin Gorsky, Paul Henderson and Laura Ugolini all of whom took time from their own work to comment, most helpfully, on early drafts of many of the chapters. However, my greatest debt is to Carol Volante who for eighteen months worked with me enthusiastically, critically and constructively to improve a preliminary – and often strikingly underdeveloped – version of this social history of twentieth-century Britain.

I am grateful to the Black and Ethnic Minority Experience, University of Wolverhampton (infor@light-house.co.uk); to D. Brace, Assistant Keeper, Museum of Edinburgh, City of Edinburgh Museums and Galleries; and to M. Rudddock, Archivist, Museum of Welsh Life, Cardiff for permission to quote from material contained in their collections.

John Benson
July 2004

Note: Place of publication in footnotes is London unless otherwise stated.

INTRODUCTION

REFLECTIONS, RETROSPECTIVES AND REASSESSMENTS

The turn of the millennium spawned, not surprisingly, a plethora of reflections, retrospectives and reassessments examining the state of the nation and the ways in which life in Britain had changed over the centuries. What would it be like to have lived a hundred, a thousand or two thousand years ago? How had the world changed between the birth of Christ and the start of the twenty-first century? Would those living a thousand years ago recognize the world in which we found ourselves at the beginning of the third millennium? To what extent had day-to-day life changed during the course of the twentieth century? Were the British people more or less contented than they had been a hundred years before? Journalists, broadcasters, commentators and academics vied with one another to provide answers that would amuse and instruct. 'Big books are called for', claimed one historian. 'The 20th century demands an autopsy before its particular malaise eludes us, and a new millennium's resolutions must be fashioned on the basis of what the entrails reveal.'[1]

The millennium celebrations were scarcely over when the media turned its attention to commemorating the one hundredth birthday of Queen Elizabeth, the Queen Mother. The summer of 2000 provided the occasion, once more, for any number of reflections on the changes that had taken place during the course of the twentieth century, a period that corresponded, we were constantly reminded, with the lifetime of 'Britain's favourite grandmother'. Attention was drawn time and time again to the scale of the transformation through which she and her contemporaries had lived. The commentator Paul Johnson, captured the mood.

> The span of historical events covered by the life of the Queen Mother is awesome. When she was born on August 4, 1900, the British empire was still expanding ... the Labour party was five months old; aspirin had recently been invented; the first London motor bus had taken to the roads; Oscar Wilde was still alive; Johann Strauss, the 'king of waltz' had just died; Tolstoy was still writing and Kipling, Conrad and Chekov were in full spate. Much of the mental furniture of the modern world was not yet in existence. Einstein, totally unknown, was still working on his theory of relativity and Freud had only just published his intepretation of Dreams.[2]

There was much less less agreement, of course, as to whether these, and the many other, changes occurring during the Queen Mother's lifetime had worked to the advantage or disadvantage of her family's subjects. Was it true that the growth of mass prosperity had compensated in some way for the loss of empire and what many saw as

---

[1] S. Carruthers, 'Small corners of a century's killing fields', *The Times Higher Education Supplement*, 21 January 2000.

[2] P. Johnson, 'A century of empire spirit', *The Sunday Times*, 16 July 2000. See also 'A celebration of enduring values', *Daily Mail*, 20 July 2000.

the disintegration of family, neighbourhood and community ties? How was it that those in power had been able to maintain their authority in the face of economic depression, two world wars, the rise of labour, the growth of the women's movement and the emergence of the so-called permissive society? How were people able to make sense of the massive changes that they and their families had experienced during the course of the century? To what extent was it possible for those living in the early twenty-first century to take a detached and reasonably objective view of the hundred years during which they, their parents and grandparents had lived?

One thing at least seemed certain. It was accepted without qualification that this was a century that had witnessed a major, indeed an unprecedented, improvement in material conditions. In a textbook published early in 2000, Jeremy Black concluded, with proper scholarly caution, that,

> twentieth-century Britain witnessed very positive advances, although they were not such as to make Britain distinctive or a leading power. Relative economic (especially industrial) decline, symbolised by the fate of British companies in car manufacture, has to be set against improving living standards for all, including the poor. Most notably in the last quarter of the century, these brought levels of consumption to the majority of the population that would have been inconceivable to the generations born in the early part of the century.[3]

However, this was not the end of the matter. Whatever the conceptual awareness and statistical sophistication underpinning such conclusions, they were unable to conceal a palpable state of national anxiety. There remained a deep-seated feeling that economic improvement had failed to be matched by comparable advances in other aspects of national life. Something, it seemed, had gone wrong. When the Archbishop of Canterbury, Dr George Carey, addressed the Queen Mother at the service of celebration and thanksgiving in honour of her one hundredth birthday, he began conventionally enough. 'The world of the early 20th century, into which you, Ma'am, were born as Elizabeth Bowes-Lyon would be largely unrecognizable to the child of today.' Reflecting on the changes through which she and her contemporaries had lived, he went on to set improved communications and medical advances against political excesses and military catastrophes:

> You will be grateful, I imagine, for not having to travel around the country in a Model A Ford or fly round the world courtesy of the Wright brothers. Neither will you hanker greatly after the medical and dental treatment of another age. But the 100 years we celebrate so joyously with your approaching birthday has hardly been a century of unbroken advance. Our capacity to denigrate and destroy has sometimes threatened to lay waste the good and the life-giving. Evil dictatorships and terrible bloodshed have been too much a part of your lifetime.[4]

---

[3] J. Black, *Modern British History since 1900* (Basingstoke: Macmillan, 2000), p. 357. See also P. Clarke, *Hope and Glory: Britain 1900–1990* (Penguin, 1996), p. 4; P. Waldron, ' "The barbarians have not come": Europe's Twentieth Century', *History Today*, June 2000; A. Rosen, *The Transformation of British Life 1950–2000: A Social History* (Manchester: Manchester University Press, 2003), pp. 11–27.

[4] *Daily Telegraph*, 12 July 2000. See also J. Elliott and V. Groskop, 'Happy daze', *The Sunday Times*, 19 January 2003; G. Easterbrook, 'What money can't buy', *The Sunday Times*, 28 December 2003.

The sense that something had gone wrong was not confined to the spiritual, political and economic elite. We're 'much better off than we used to be', concluded a 61-year-old Coventry woman. 'But I think we've lost something along the way. Mostly, it's a sense of caring for other people. The world may be a much more comfortable place in material terms. But it's a much tougher place too.'[5] Others agreed. 'We may have solved the material questions of the Edwardian era', concluded a consumer consultant, 'but we are still grappling with political and spiritual issues that they would recognize.'[6] There remained a widespread, deep-seated and frequently expressed feeling that the country's potential has not been realized. Economic gains had not been matched by comparable advances in other aspects of national life. Economic gains, to adapt the old adage, had to be set against social, cultural and community losses.[7]

Insofar as opinion was divided, it was not about whether something had gone wrong. It was about what had gone wrong. Those on the right were in little doubt how to strike the balance between material improvement and other aspects of national life. They welcomed economic growth and rising standards of living, but they deplored the loss of the British Empire and the decline in the country's economic, military and diplomatic power. They bemoaned the demise of organized religion, the growth of lawlessness and the failure of working people to take a pride in their work. They disparaged women's growing economic and social independence, the influx of immigrants and asylum-seekers, and what they regarded as the decline of the nuclear family and the break-up of the United Kingdom.[8] Indeed, on the day I drafted this paragraph, the correspondence page of my local newspaper carried a letter articulating many of these concerns about the direction in which the country was heading.

Since the First World War, and more so since the Second World War, successive governments have, in their infinite wisdom, eroded the English way of life and created a multi-cultural society in which being English has become offensive in a way that we cannot do anything that will offend our ethnic neighbours ... The do-gooders down the years have restricted discipline and we were fed the garbage of 'it is better to take part than to win'. So our youth is left without direction and indulges in alcohol and drugs in search of solace. Perhaps hooliganism is a real cry for help. It is one way that they can take a stand together, channelling their anger and frustration and hitting back at the oppressors who, often, is our own kind – namely, the Government.[9]

Those on the left appeared equally certain about what had gone wrong. They welcomed the economic advances that had been made, but they regretted Britain's inability to shake itself free of its imperial past and abandon its predilection for posturing on the international stage. They deplored the country's economic, social

---

[5] *Daily Mail*, 20 July 2000.

[6] *The Sunday Times*, 26 December 1999.

[7] My local newspaper, the Wolverhampton, *Express and Star*, was packed with such views. See, for example, W. Hodgkiss, 'We shared it altogether', 29 December 2000. Cf. 'We're a great little country', 23 June 2001.

[8] N. Tebbit, 'Watch out for the Central Office saboteurs, Mr Howard', *The Guardian*, 1 November 2003; R. Honeyford, 'Is the multicultural madness over? You must be joking ...', *Daily Mail*, 12 April 2004.

[9] J. Simcox to *Express and Star*, 20 July 2000.

and cultural inequalities which, they believed, continued to disadvantage the elderly, women, working people and those from ethnic minorities. It was such inequalities, they maintained, that went far towards explaining the incidence and distribution of ill health, lawlessness and other forms of anti-social behaviour. They were appalled at the weakening of class ties, and people's persistent, and seemingly unthinking, acceptance of existing sources of power and authority. When Roy Hattersley, the former deputy leader of the Labour Party, looked back at the end of the century, he disliked much of what he saw:

> The peace of the traditional British Sunday was being shattered by petty thieves, vandals, ram-raiders and ill-named 'joy-riders' – many of whom had consumed Dutch courage in the public houses which, thanks to 'more liberal' licensing laws, were often open all day. The notion that crime is frequently the product of poverty – although documented and demonstrated to the satisfaction of anyone who took a serious interest in the subject – was dismissed out of hand, since it was incompatible with the individualistic spirit of the age.[10]

PROBLEMS, PERSPECTIVES AND HYPOTHESES

It is the aim of this book to subject these – and related – issues to the serious and sustained scrutiny which they deserve. It must be emphasized, of course, that it does not, and cannot, make any claim to objectivity. This is one person's view of what happened, one person's judgement of what was important, and one person's interpretation of how best to account for the key developments that are identified as worthy of discussion. As a reviewer in the *Journal of Japanese Studies* remarked several years ago, 'When I read a book on Japanese society I ask myself where the author is sitting as he writes. Each observation post has its long views and blind spots.'[11] In writing *Affluence and Authority*, I have done my best to recognize my own, and other commentators' 'long views and blind spots'.

Certainly, the book's focus upon the twentieth century presents difficulties as well as advantages. The assumption that the hundred years between 1900 and 2000 represents an appropriate period for study is clear, convenient and conventional. However, periodization in history is rarely as straightforward as it may seem. In this case, it must be conceded, clarity, convenience and convention come at something of a cost. The decision to focus on the twentieth century begs as many questions as it answers and, unless one is very careful, can preclude genuinely open-minded analysis of the issues in which one is interested.

There are two obvious complications. The first, and most obvious, is that it is difficult to decide whether 1900 (rather than 1880, 1901, 1914 or some other year) provides the best starting point for a study such as this. Moreover, it is impossible, writing in 2004, to know whether 2000 (rather than 1980, 2001, 2014 or some other year) will prove a sensible date at which to bring the analysis to a close. It will be seen, for instance, that many of the key developments in economic growth, patterns of

[10] R. Hattersley, *Fifty Years On: A Prejudiced History of Britain since the War* (Abacus, 1997), pp. 383–4.
[11] D.W. Plath in *Journal of Japanese Studies*, 12, 1986, p. 156.

consumptions, policing strategies, educational policy and class formation had their origins in the late nineteenth century rather than the early twentieth century. It will be seen too that there are reasons for supposing that the late twentieth-century acceleration of workplace insecurity, state regulation and family restructuring, with which we are all familiar, will seem less striking – and less important – to future generations than it does to those who have just lived through it.

The second, perhaps less obvious, difficulty is to avoid attributing to the twentieth century – or whatever other period is selected for analysis – an appealing and seemingly convincing coherence and homogeneity. This is particularly important when studying the social history of twentieth-century Britain. It will be seen at various points in the book that the middle of the century marked a significant turning point in standards of living, levels of health, patterns of migration and attitudes towards the state. It will be seen too that the 1980s marked a decisive turning point – or point of acceleration – in consumption patterns, leisure preferences, family relationships and class attitudes.

In all events, it is believed that the book has some claim to originality. For one thing, this is history with a context. For while it is common to pay lip-service to the perils of studying social history in isolation, there have been few attempts to interpret the social history of twentieth-century Britain in the light of the broader economic, political, cultural, demographic and ideological developments that were taking place. Moreover, this is history with ambitions towards inclusivity. For although it is not unusual to acknowledge the importance of considering all groups in society, there have been few studies that attempt, let alone manage, to capture the experiences even of the major groups that made up the population. This book will do its best to pay proper attention to men, women and children; young adults, the middle-aged and the elderly; the rich, the comfortably off and the poor; the upper class, the middle class and the working class; the English, the Welsh and the Scots; those who were born in this country and those who came here from overseas.

Accordingly, it is the aim of the book to provide a wide-ranging, well-informed and accessible interpretation of British social history during a period of profound, and almost certainly unprecedented, economic, political, cultural, demographic and ideological change. It is intended, more specifically, to consider the changing material conditions of everyday life, the ways in which authority was maintained, and the ways in which people made sense of the many changes with which they found themselves confronted.

It will lay particular emphasis upon material conditions in accounting for the underlying stability of British society during the course of this turbulent and troubled century. This, it must be stressed, is not a plea for the excavation of a long interred Whig historiography or for the revival of a more recently abandoned economic determinism. It will be suggested, however, that despite the impact of the economic cycle and the fact that many groups shared only haltingly and uncertainly in the benefits of economic growth, it was the long-term improvement in the standard of living that provides the single most important key to understanding the social history of twentieth-century Britain.

The book will also pay particular attention to the balance between economic and social developments. Indeed, it is one of the central purposes of this study to challenge, or at least modify, the view that economic gains were undermined by social losses, that the British people failed for some reason to respond as constructively as they should have to the economic improvements that they enjoyed. This, it must be stressed again, will not entail adopting a Whiggish stance to the many deleterious social changes that have occurred during the course of the century. Rather it will involve showing how easy it is to be blinded by nostalgia, to be lured into adopting an approach whereby, in Pat Thane's telling phrase, 'a half-understood present is contrasted with an idealised past'.[12]

---

[12] P. Thane, *Old Age in English History: Past Experiences, Present Issues* (Oxford: Oxford University Press, 2000), p. 12.

PART ONE
THE GROWTH OF PROSPERITY

1 WEALTH, COMFORT AND POVERTY

CLAIMS AND COMPLICATIONS

There is no denying the growing prosperity of the British people. Statistical analysis confirms what common sense suggests. The signs are all around us. Whenever we watch a period drama, consult a scholarly text, read a historical novel or visit one of the country's many heritage sites, we see the material improvements that have taken place during the past hundred years. Those brought up at the beginning of the twentieth century, we are reminded, earned lower incomes, possessed less wealth, were less healthy, lived shorter lives, were less well educated, enjoyed fewer choices, and had access to a vastly inferior range of goods and services than their grandchildren and great-grandchildren lucky enough to live at the end of the century. Prosperity may have its disadvantages, but few of us would be prepared to exchange late twentieth-century affluence for early twentieth-century poverty, anxiety and discomfort. 'Materialism', it has been pointed out, 'is most comfortably deprecated with your hand round a large Pimm's.'[1]

Indeed, it is the central tenet of the book that growing prosperity provides the single most important key to understanding the changes that took place during the course of the twentieth century. It was the interaction of income, wealth and the cost of living that determined people's economic power. It was economic power, together with the ways in which it was secured, that affected virtually every aspect of people's lives: the standard of living they enjoyed; the pursuits in which they participated; the people with whom they spent their time; the values and attitudes which they adopted; and the ways in which they responded to the world round about them.

However, this argument can easily be traduced. It is important to make clear again that this is a plea neither for a monocausal explanation of complex developments, nor for a Whiggish view of the past – nor indeed for the resurrection of an outmoded economic determinism that precludes individual agency and individual action. The argument here is much simpler. It is a plea to recognize the importance of the relationship, confused and confusing though it could be, that existed between economic circumstances, patterns of thought and patterns of behaviour. The wealth, comfort or poverty in which people existed exercised a profound effect upon every aspect of the ways in which they lived their lives.

Unfortunately, there is no denying the difficulties of measuring precisely the growth of prosperity. The problems are at once conceptual, methodological and empirical. It is hard to define wealth, comfort and poverty. It is a challenge to know whether to

---

[1] S. Hogg, 'The economics of happiness don't always add up', *Independent*, 7 August 2000. See also N.F.R. Crafts, 'Is Economic Growth Good for Us?' (London School of Economics, 2003), p. 1.

concentrate upon individual, family or household circumstances; it is difficult to decide how best to balance changes in income against changes in wealth and changes in the cost of living; and it is not easy to take account of age, gender, ethnicity, class and so on. Indeed, whatever procedures are adopted, it is invariably more frustrating than one would wish to come up with the evidence that is required to pursue the questions in which one is interested.

Accordingly, this chapter is divided into two. The first section examines the rising incomes and burgeoning wealth of the people as a whole. It will use both conventional economic accounting and more recently developed indicators of 'human development' to establish the scale, timing – and something of the significance – of the unprecedented prosperity that developed during the course of the twentieth century. The second section of the chapter examines the extent to which this picture of growing national well-being needs to be modified when one considers the experience, not of the population as a whole, but of some of the major social groups within it. It will show, not surprisingly, that there were losers as well as winners, that age, gender, ethnicity and class all need to be taken into account when attempting to reconstruct the British experience of wealth, comfort and poverty.

WEALTH, INCOME AND THE COST OF LIVING

Those interested in changes in economic well-being have until recently concentrated their attention upon wealth, income and the cost of living. Although this narrow, statistical approach has not always proved entirely helpful, there is no doubt that it provides the essential foundations from which any subsequent analysis must proceed. Whatever the conceptual and empirical limitations of their research, economic historians have identified the broad pattern of material change during the course of the century. They have established beyond reasonable doubt the scale, speed and contours of the country's growing prosperity.[2]

They have shown that the population was becoming increasingly wealthy. This can be seen most strikingly in the enormous growth in the volume and value of personal savings, and in the number of people who bought (or were in the process of buying) their own homes. Firm figures for the number of owner-occupiers during the first third of the century are unavailable (although 10 per cent seems a reasonable estimate).[3] Table 1.1 shows that the proportion of homeowners increased gradually to 31 per cent in 1951, and (encouraged by tax relief on mortgage interest payments and the sale of council housing) 67 per cent in 1991. It was a remarkable transformation and one, it will be shown, that was influential in both reflecting and reinforcing significant popular patterns of thought and behaviour.[4]

Increasing wealth was associated with rising incomes. Of course, wealth and income were by no means synonymous. We all know of old people who are asset-rich but

---

[2] The essential statistics are set out in volumes such as P. Deane and W.A. Cole, *British Economic Growth 1688–1959: Trends and Structure* (Cambridge: Cambridge University Press, 1969); and A.H. Halsey (ed.), *Twentieth-Century British Social Trends* (Basingstoke: Macmillan, 2000).

[3] J. Benson, *The Working Class in Britain, 1850–1939* (Harlow: Longman, 1989), p. 73.

[4] See, for example, M. Swenarton and S. Taylor, 'The scale and nature of the growth of owner-occupation in Britain between the wars', *Economic History Review*, xxxviii, 1985.

TABLE 1.1 OWNER-OCCUPIED ACCOMMODATION
AS A PROPORTION OF ALL ACCOMMODATION,
ENGLAND AND WALES, 1901–96

Year	Percentage
1901	c.10
1938	32
1951	31
1961	44
1971	52
1981	58
1991	67
1996	67

Source: Based on A. Holmans, 'Housing', in A.H. Halsey (ed.),
Twentieth-Century British Social Trends (Basingstoke:
Macmillan, 2000), pp. 487–8.

income-poor: those who own large houses but exist on modest pensions.[5] Nonetheless, a person's wealth does provide an indication of the economic power at his or her disposal because assets, in the form of savings, investments, possessions and pension rights, can be drawn upon to supplement, or replace, other sources of income. It was suggested many years ago that, 'other things being equal, an increase in wealth will lead to more spending and so to less saving'.[6]

This correlation between wealth and income is of the utmost importance when attempting to measure changes in economic power. It is not just that wage rates – as distinct from wage earnings and salaries – provide an imperfect guide to take-home pay. It is also that take-home pay provides an imperfect guide to aggregate income. To take but one example, the way in which a married couple made their living was almost certain to change during the course of their lives. When they were first married, their parents might help them with the cost of setting up home; when they had a young family, the children might do odd jobs and the wife take on part-time work she could do from home; when the children were older, she might decide to go out to work full-time for a wage or salary; when their parents died, they might inherit furniture, savings or even a house; and when they themselves grew old, they would almost certainly draw on their savings, receive the state pension – and perhaps an occupational one too if they had been able to join such a scheme. Few families, this means, were likely to depend throughout their lives solely upon the one or two jobs that they reported to the census enumerators when they called at the house every ten years.[7]

---

[5] 'Facing the difficulties of life on a pension', *Daily Mail*, 4 September 1950.

[6] We all know – or know of – those who are asset-rich and income-rich, but time poor. R. Stone, 'Private saving in Britain, past, present and future', *Manchester School of Economic and Social Studies*, 32, 1967, p. 80.

[7] For example, Museum of Welsh Life, RS6, pp. 54, 61; Northumbria County Record Office, T301/95/61C2 (ii), 1985. See also B.S. Rowntree, *Poverty: A Study of Town Life* (Macmillan, 1902), pp. 136–8; J. Benson, *Working Class*, Ch. 2.

TABLE 1.2 INCOME (£) PER HEAD (BEFORE TAXATION)
FROM EMPLOYMENT, SELF-EMPLOYMENT AND WELFARE,
UNITED KINGDOM, 1900/1–95 (1997 PRICES)

Year	Employment	Self-employment	Welfare
1900/1	1326	471	n.a
1910/1	1299	416	n.a
1920/1	1727	376	79
1930/1	1867	463	174
1950/1	2846	518	251
1960/1	3664	484	359
1970/1	4668	633	599
1980/1	5763	759	1063
1990/1	6808	1273	1366
1995	6816	1221	1868

Source: Based on A. Dilnot and C. Emmerson, 'The Economic Environment',
and J. Webb, 'Social Security', in A.H. Halsey (ed.), *Twentieth-Century British
Social Trends* (Basingstoke: Macmillan, 2000), pp. 326, 571–2, 712.

The problem then is to find a way of identifying, quantifying and combining these
various sources of income in order to construct an index that can be used to plot the ways
in which individual and/or family incomes changed during the course of the century.
This is not easily done. Although Table 1.2 brings together the best evidence that is
available, it is not without its limitations. It refers to the United Kingdom; it contains no
figures at all for certain years; and the figures which it does contain consist, of course, of
official measures of activities which were often carried out intermittently, surreptitiously
or illegally. Not all those working for themselves or claiming social security benefits were
as scrupulous as they should have been in declaring the sources of their income or the
extent of their wealth. As the compilers of some of the statistics used in this chapter
warned rather soberly, 'Until 1941, estimates of national income were based almost
entirely on data of individual incomes obtained from the Inland Revenue.'[8]

Nevertheless, Table 1.2 represents a considerable advance on – or supplement to –
many existing indices of individual and family income. It is valuable in that it provides
an indication of the ways in which income per head, in real terms, from employment,
self-employment and welfare transfers grew during the course of the century. Whatever the problems of fraud and other forms of misrepresentation, it provides statistical
support for the claim that was made above about take-home pay providing an imperfect
guide to aggregate income. It shows, for example, that although work opportunities and practices changed in significant, and sometimes unexpected ways, self-
employment was always more important than many people recognize. Moreover, it
confirms that however important self-employment remained, spending on welfare –
in the form of pensions, sickness payments, unemployment benefit and so on –
expanded enormously during the course of the century. The years between 1900 and

---

[8] R. Bacon *et al.*, 'The Economic Environment', in A.H. Halsey (ed.), *Trends in British Society Since 1900*
(Basingstoke: Macmillan, 1972), p. 69.

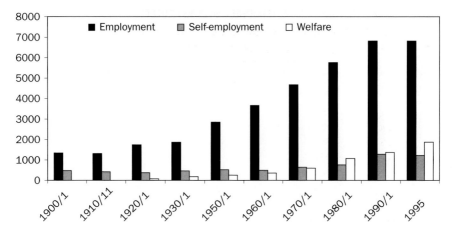

Figure 1.1 Income (£) per head (before taxation) from employment, self-employment and welfare, United Kingdom, 1900/1–95 (1997 prices)
Source: Based on A. Dilnot and C. Emmerson, 'The Economic Environment', and J. Webb, 'Social Security', in A.H. Halsey (ed.), *Twentieth-Century British Social Trends* (Basingstoke: Macmillan, 2000), pp. 326, 571–2, 712.

2000 saw, it must be emphasized, not only a major rise in real income per head but also significant changes in the ways that such incomes were put together.

The changes set out in Table 1.2 can be seen more clearly still in Figure 1.1. The latter reveals vividly the ways in which the balance between income derived from wage earnings and salaries, earnings from self-employment and income in the form of welfare benefits changed during the course of the century. These are changes that one should try to keep constantly in mind as one seeks to understand the material bases of many of the developments considered later in the volume. When this is done, it will be possible, it is hoped, to begin to understand attitudes and behaviour that might otherwise appear irretrievably opaque.

The rise in money incomes is well known; the changing balance between wage earnings and salaries, income from self-employment and welfare benefits much less so. When this fuller picture is available, it can be tempting to conclude that as incomes rose, people worked less hard, became less enterprising and tended to be sucked more and more into a culture of dependency. It is a temptation that needs to be resisted. For one thing, money incomes, no matter how carefully they are calculated, need to be adjusted for the cost of living before they can reveal anything helpful about economic well-being – let alone about economic behaviour or about cultural attitudes. We all know that the cost of goods and services has changed over time. Indeed, once people reach a certain age, they fall prey, it seems, to an apparently overwhelming desire to look back with nostalgia to a time when food and drink were cheap and small luxuries within the reach of those on even the most modest of incomes. It used to be possible, we have all heard it said, to enjoy a good night out and still have change from a shilling, a pound, or a £5 note.[9]

[9] W.P. Pearson to *Daily Mail*, 4 July 1970.

TABLE 1.3 RETAIL PRICE INDEX, UNITED
KINGDOM, 1900–97

Year	Prices
1900	100
1910	106
1920	274
1930	174
1940	201
1950	318
1960	474
1970	706
1980	2548
1990	4805
1997	6002

Source: Based on A.H. Halsey (ed.), *Twentieth-Century
British Social Trends* (Basingstoke: Macmillan, 2000), p. 712.

In fact, efforts to plot changes in the cost of living, the final component of conventional attempts to analyse economic well-being, are as fraught with difficulty as attempts to reconstruct the scale and components of aggregate income. As John Burnett has pointed out,

> [the] major difficulty for any student of the history of the cost of living is the paucity of data on past prices. Although scattered references to prices are to be found in almost any contemporary source – from household books and accounts to diaries, journals, letters and autobiographies – they usually relate to a particular place at a particular time only … What the historian would like are long series of retail prices of goods of a known and standard description, bought at various places at frequent and regular intervals, but these are almost non-existent …[10]

This is not the end of the matter. Even when it is possible to unearth reliable, long-run statistics of retail prices, there remains the problem of knowing how to bring them together into a single index. It is always exceptionally difficult to decide how to combine the evidence available in a way that takes account of changing patterns of individual and family consumption. As the compilers of many of the statistics used in this section of the chapter concluded rather wearily,

> it is doubtful whether any single index, however weighted, can adequately reflect changes in the cost-of-living. Given wide variations in expenditure patterns according to such factors as family size, income level, and social habits, and given variations in the extent to which the prices of different goods and services change, then an index number which measures the average change in the cost-of-living may not be relevant for particular individuals or groups because their pattern of expenditure differs from that assumed in the index.[11]

[10] J. Burnett, *A History of the Cost of Living* (Penguin, 1969), pp. 11–13.

[11] G. Sayer *et al.*, 'The Labour Force', in Halsey (ed.), *Trends*, p. 109. See also N.F.R. Crafts, 'Is Economic Growth Good for Us?', pp. 3–5.

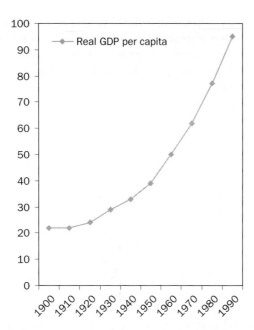

Figure 1.2 Real GDP per capita, United Kingdom, 1900–95 (1995 = 100)
Source: Based on A. Dilnot and C. Emmerson, 'The Economic Environment', and J. Webb, 'Social
Security', in A.H. Halsey (ed.), *Twentieth-Century British Social Trends*, (Basingstoke: Macmillan, 2000),
pp. 326, 571–2, 712.

It has been decided not to pursue further the complexities of compiling the 'basket
of goods' that is needed to make possible the construction of a credible cost of living
index. Nonetheless, it is believed that Table 1.3 provides a serviceable enough guide to
changes in the level of retail prices during the course of the twentieth century. It shows
that prices rose more than 58 times during the period, with major increases occurring
in the 1910s and the 1970s.

It is possible, finally, to plot the rise of real GDP (gross domestic product) per head
over the course of the century. The results are most instructive. For although one might
look suspiciously at some of the short-term changes suggested by Figure 1.2, there is no
doubting the long-term trend that it reveals. It shows, and shows incontrovertibly, that
real GDP per head expanded powerfully during the period covered by this book, with
growth particularly strong in the years following the Second World War.

HUMAN DEVELOPMENT

However, there is no denying that conventional economic analysis cannot – indeed
does not seek to – capture all aspects of economic well-being. 'There is widespread
agreement', pointed out one the country's leading econometric historians in 1997,
'that real GDP per head or real wage rates capture important components, but are not
comprehensive measures, of economic welfare.'[12] What then is to be done? Should one

---

[12] N.F.R. Crafts, 'Some dimensions of the "quality of life" during the British Industrial Revolution',
Economic History Review, L, 1997, p. 618.

widen the concept of economic welfare (what we have called economic well-being) so as to include quality of life? If quality of life is to be included, how is one to incorporate into the analysis factors as seemingly unquantifiable as leisure, health, education, political representation and workplace rights, let alone the risk or fear of crime, and the quality of the environment?[13]

Development economists have led the way in devising strategies for capturing factors such as these in statistical terms. In the early 1990s, the United Nations' first *Human Development Report* argued that the primary purpose of development was not economic growth but a widening of the choices open to the people of the world. 'Human development', it insisted, 'is development *of* the people *for* the people *by* the people.' The *Report* also introduced a new yardstick for measuring human progress, the so-called human development index (or HDI). By combining conventional measures of real purchasing power with less used indicators of quality of life such as health and education, it provided a guide to living standards which was a great deal more comprehensive than existing indices of economic well-being.[14]

Sara Horrell has taken up the challenge. By combining the most recent human development index with an index compiled by Partha Dasgupta and Martin Weale, she has undertaken a new and highly sophisticated investigation of economic well-being in twentieth-century Britain. Her aim, she explains, 'is to take an eclectic view of living standards and evaluate the evolution of the six components: income and leisure, wealth and income security, health, education, political and workplace rights, and living conditions'. Her conclusion is firmly optimistic. She shows, for example, that the twentieth century saw 'dramatic improvements' in infant mortality and life expectancy. She stresses the extension of free, compulsory education and the fact that by the end of the century, 'a university education is no longer the privilege of a small minority'. She emphasizes the increasing ability of ordinary people to influence the course of government policy: 'The electorate was widened in 20th century Britain and the proportion of the adult population with the right to vote in elections measures this aspect of political rights.' Indeed, the state played a key role, she believes, both in enhancing prosperity and in extending opportunities.

> The progress made over the 20th century should not be understated. Areas of health, education, income inequality and gender inequality have shown significant improvements along with growth in national income and wealth. The conception and development of the welfare state have been behind much of the improvement.[15]

However, Horrell's optimism is neither unquestioning nor unqualified. She goes on immediately to warn, for example, against the dangers of generalizing solely upon the basis of decennial, aggregate indicators. The reassuring picture of growing national

---

[13] See N.F.R. Crafts, 'Is Economic Growth Good for Us?'. See also T. Scitovsky, *The Joyless Economy: An Inquiry into Human Satisfaction and Consumer Dissatisfaction* (Oxford: Oxford University Press, 1976).

[14] For example, United Nations Development Programme, *Human Development Report* (Oxford: Oxford University Press, 1993), overview.

[15] S. Horrell, 'Living standards in Britain 1900–2000: Women's century?', *National Institute Economic Review*, 172, 2000, pp. 63, 73. See also N.F.R. Crafts, 'Is Economic Growth Good for Us?' p. 1.

prosperity needs to be modified, she points out, when one considers short-term disruptions or the experiences, not of the population as a whole, but of the major groups within it. Horrell's particular concern is with gender differences:

> there is no room for complacency, some of the reversals seen in the 1980s and 1990s demonstrate that the gains are not immutable and need to be protected. Furthermore, women's position has improved if the end of the century is compared with the beginning, but little progress has been made in changing women's position relative to men over the last few decades on the dimensions considered here.[16]

The message is clear. In considering the material conditions of people in Britain, it must be borne constantly in mind that there were losers as well as winners, that gender – not to mention age, ethnicity and class – needs to be taken into account when attempting to reconstruct the country's growing experience of prosperity.

CHILDHOOD, ADOLESCENCE, MIDDLE AGE AND OLD AGE

Age most certainly needs to be taken into account when attempting to reconstruct the British experience of prosperity – or indeed any other aspect of the country's economic and social history. Age needs to be set alongside, and sometimes even perhaps above, gender, ethnicity, class, region, religion, and so on when attempting to describe and explain the way in which people lived and the way in which society developed. For, as a moment's reflection will confirm, it makes no sense at all to discuss the people of Britain – or anywhere else – as if they were a single, ageless, homogeneous mass. They moved, we hardly need reminding, from childhood, through adolescence, to adulthood, middle age and old age.

The growth of children's economic power became increasingly recognized towards the end of the century. The fact that children represented a declining proportion both of the population and of the workforce was balanced – and more than balanced – by the coalescence of a number of economic, demographic and cultural developments. It was not just that as parents became more prosperous they were able to be more generous to their children. According to K.D. Brown,

> Another important contribution to purchasing power was made by the tendency for families to become smaller, which simultaneously encouraged the greater indulgence of children and realised more disposable income for them. The enormous increase in the number of married women entering the labour force after 1945 also served to raise the general level of family income and may have encouraged the buying gifts as a form of compensation.[17]

Moreover, as families became more prosperous, children were able to exercise more influence over economic decision-making. It was estimated in 1970, for instance, that school-age children had a say in some 15 per cent of family food purchases. Thirty years later, it was found that, 'Children have greater power and influence than ever

---

[16] Horrell , 'Living standards', p. 73.

[17] K.D. Brown, *The British Toy Business: A History since 1700* (Hambledon, 1996), p. 225.

before': a survey of 950 families carried out by Abbey National suggested that 42 per cent of children helped to decide whether to move house, 65 per cent were involved in choosing the family's holiday destination, and 90 per cent decided what should be cooked for the family's evening meal.[18]

The growth of adolescent economic power was rarely overlooked – and was almost never underestimated. Generation upon generation of adults bemoaned the economic power of young adults, parents finding it difficult to cope when their children asked them for money, and difficult too when they began to be financially independent. As an article in the *British Medical Journal* explained in 1949, 'many a father found his dignity and authority as the main support of a family replaced by a sense of ignominious dependence on the earnings of children who sometimes resented the burden of the maintenance of their parents' home'.[19]

At first sight, it must be said, the burgeoning economic power of young adults appears somewhat surprising. Adolescents represented a declining proportion of the population, were increasingly likely to stay at school into their late teens and when they did begin work were unlikely to accumulate very much in the way of assets. There is no doubt, however, that adolescent purchasing power increased substantially between the wars, and increased again in the years following 1945. Teenagers benefited indirectly from the improvements generally in incomes that were discussed earlier in the chapter, and directly from the improvements that were taking place in their own incomes. It has been found, for example, that whereas adult wages rose by some 25 per cent between 1938 and 1958, adolescent wages increased by 50 per cent during the same 20-year period.[20]

Moreover, adolescents managed to retain a growing proportion of their growing incomes. Families were increasingly likely to regard wage earnings as belonging, not to the family as a whole, but to the person who earned them. The change occurred, it seems, some time during the Second World War. Before the war, working-class teenagers were normally allowed to keep only a small proportion of their earnings: perhaps a penny in the shilling, or a shilling in the pound (a practice that many seemingly accepted with good grace). Within a few years of the war ending, they were able to retain a good deal more: in the East End of London, for example, a 'boy aged about 16 would get £6 or £7 of which he would give his mother £2, leaving £4 or £5 for himself, while a 20-year-old earning £12 would give his mother £3 or £4, leaving himself £8 or £9'.[21] Indeed, a 'wealth of the nation' survey carried out by Halifax Share Dealing at the end

---

[18] 'Pester Power is Good News for Families', The Future Foundation Survey for Abbey National, 31 July 2001; see also R. Scott, *The Female Consumer* (Associated Business Programmes, 1976), pp. 43–4; J. Benson, *The Rise of Consumer Society in Britain, 1880–1980* (Harlow: Longman,1994), p. 70; *Regional Trends*, 34, 1999, p. 108.

[19] A.P. Thompson, 'Problems of ageing and chronic sickness', *British Medical Journal*, 30 July 1949. See also G. Pearson, *Hooligan: A History of Respectable Fears* (Basingstoke: Macmillan, 1983).

[20] D. Fowler, 'Teenage Consumers? Young Wage-Earners and Leisure in Manchester, 1919–1939', in A. Davies and S. Fielding (eds), *Workers' Worlds: Cultures and Communities in Manchester and Salford, 1880–1939* (Manchester: Manchester University Press, 1992); Benson, *Consumer Society*, pp. 17–18.

[21] P. Wilmott, *Adolescent Boys of East London* (Routledge & Kegan Paul, 1975), p. 21; E. Roberts, *A Woman's Place: An Oral History of Working-Class Women* (Oxford: Blackwell, 1984), p. 43; Benson, *Consumer Society*, p. 18.

of the century suggested that 88 per cent of those under 24 had some savings 'put aside for a rainy day'.[22]

The economic power of the middle-aged, on the other hand, has been curiously overlooked. The middle-aged constituted a growing proportion of the population, shared (for most of the century) in the growing prosperity enjoyed by the nation as a whole and were increasingly likely to inherit housing, savings and other assets from their parents. However, the prosperity of the middle-aged became a matter for comment only just before it began to be undercut by the economic downturn of the 1980s and 1990s.[23] Until the 1960s and 1970s, the middle-aged shared in the material improvements taking place among the population as a whole, but thereafter they failed to benefit to the same extent as those from other age groups.[24]

Nevertheless, the standard of living enjoyed by middle-aged households was always likely to be higher than in those headed by young adults or the elderly. Middle-aged incomes tended to be higher than those of the population as a whole, and the expenses of the late middle-aged tended to be lower than those of families with children and teenagers to provide for. The result, not surprisingly, was that the resources at the disposal of late middle-aged households tended to be considerably greater than those at earlier and later stages of the life course. When market researchers rediscovered the middle-aged market in the 1980s, they were at pains to emphasize that, 'people in the ten or fifteen years before retirement are not only physically and economically very active; they also have greater discretionary spending power, since their mortgages are paid off and their children grown up'.[25] Asked to compare conditions in middle age and young adulthood, a West Midlands woman who was born in 1928 remarked simply: 'Good because you was getting on your feet. You'd reared your children hadn't you?'[26]

The economic power of the elderly, much more than that of the middle-aged, became an issue of lively public debate towards the end of the century. The elderly, it was constantly stressed, represented a growing proportion of the population. 'In 1900 about 7 per cent of the population of the United Kingdom was aged 65 or above; in 2000 about 18 per cent.' The elderly, it was sometimes emphasized, were also growing wealthier. Wealth, of course, tended to increase up to a certain age, since most people accumulated property, possessions, pension rights and other assets during the course of their working lives. 'House purchase is usually completed by the age of 60 or 65, and savings tend to peak at the time of retirement – and to diminish thereafter as they are drawn upon in order to finance expenditure.'[27]

---

[22] *Sunday Telegraph*, 1 April 2001.

[23] '50,000 executives at the head of the jobless queue', *Daily Mail*, 2 January 1970.

[24] J. Benson, *Prime Time: A History of the Middle Aged in Twentieth-Century Britain* (Harlow: Longman, 1997), pp. 62–70.

[25] H. Lind, 'Media research and the affluent middle aged', *ADMAP*, February 1981, p. 66. See also *The Times*, 15 July 1999; Benson, *Prime Time*, pp. 72–3.

[26] Wolverhampton Oral History Project, Interview 19, p. 7. See also p. 13.

[27] *Royal Commission on the Distribution of Income and Wealth, Report No. 1*, 1975, pp. 110, 115; L. Hannah, *Inventing Retirement: The Development of Occupational Pensions in Britain* (Cambridge: Cambridge University Press, 1986), p. 125; Benson, *Consumer Society*, p. 19; P. Thane, *Old Age in English History: Past Experiences, Present Issues* (Oxford: Oxford University Press, 2000), p. 1; R. Dyson, 'Why today's pensioners are sitting pretty', *Daily Express*, 16 August 2000.

However, the incomes of the elderly did not increase to the same extent as their wealth. For one thing, old people did not necessarily find it either easy or desirable to use their property and possessions to generate income on a day-to-day basis.[28] For another, it became a great deal less common for old people to continue in paid employment. Whereas during the late nineteenth century, two-thirds of men and women in the workforce continued to work beyond the age of 65, by the 1920s this figure had fallen to less than 50 per cent, and by the 1980s to no more than 10 per cent.[29]

Nonetheless, the economic power of the elderly grew very significantly. The increasing tendency for old people to retire from wage labour was offset, in many cases, by the increasing likelihood of their qualifying for the state pension or for payments from an occupational scheme. It is sometimes easy to underestimate the transformation brought about by the introduction of state pensions. 'A century ago,' explained one end-of-millennium review, 'most people worked until they died or became so unwell that they became a "burden" on their families or ended up as "guests" of the Poor Law Commissioners.' Lloyd George's non-contributory scheme of 1908 was therefore of enormous significance. As Pat Thane points out,

> The state pension, low and means-tested though it was, gave a regular and secure income to a higher proportion of old people than the poor relief system had ever done. It rescued some of them from painful and degrading labour, enabled more of them to keep independent households, and assisted families to support ageing relatives. It even stimulated saving among older people.[30]

The spread of occupational pension schemes also did a good deal to enhance elderly incomes. The proportion of the workforce protected in this way increased from just 5 per cent in 1900, to 13 per cent in 1956, and nearly 50 per cent in 1980. It was a development that reinforced, and accentuated, the economic heterogeneity of the elderly. It was pointed out at the end of the century:

> Old Age is not synonymous with poverty any more. Over the past 20 years, pensioners have done twice as well as the general population. But while share-owning and occupational personal pensions have underpinned a 60 per cent growth in income, the divide between rich and poor has widened dramatically. Affluent older people are the volunteers – the cancer-shop workers or meals-on-wheels deliverers – who see the poverty among those of their peers who get the worst NHS treatment, a pitiful pension and a life of isolation imposed, in part, by an abysmal transport system.[31]

Age stereotyping is always to be avoided. Pat Thane stresses the particular dangers of regarding old people as an undifferentiated mass: 'The age group which is most

---

[28] *Daily Mail*, 4 September 1950.

[29] Thane, *Old Age*, pp. 283, 307, 327; *Birmingham Mail*, 11 April 1995; Hannah, *Inventing Retirement*, pp. 122–3, 154, 188.

[30] T. Levine, 'Lloyd George knew my father's needs', *The Guardian*, 18 December 1999; Thane, *Old Age*, p. 308.

[31] M. Riddell, 'Sing if you're glad to be grey', *The Times*, reference mislaid. See P. Mullan, *The Imaginary Time Bomb: Why an Ageing Population is Not a Social Problem* (Tauris, 2001).

generalized about in fact incorporates a greater variety of ages, of social, economic and physical conditions than any other age group and that variety has increased over the twentieth century.'[32] 'We're happy being retired', reported a professional couple in the early 1970s. But 'People on a State pension must find it dreadfully difficult. What is it – £5 for a single person? Well, my weekly housekeeping comes to more than that and we grow all our own vegetables which saves us a lot … As it is, with our savings we're going on an educational cruise in November around the Mediterranean.'[33]

However, age stereotyping is not the same as age awareness. Age awareness is essential. It is simply not possible to reconstruct – let alone understand – the material conditions of the British people without paying due attention to age, to the distinct and often divergent experiences of children, adolescents, young adults, the middle-aged and the elderly.

MEN AND WOMEN

Nor is it possible to understand the material conditions of people in Britain without paying proper attention to gender, to the fact that men and women frequently – many would say invariably – shared unequally in the country's growing prosperity. Sara Horrell concludes, it will be recalled, that, 'Women's position has improved if the end of the century is compared to its beginning, but there has been little change in women's position relative to men's over the last few decades.'[34]

There is no doubt that gender inequality was deeply embedded in Britain's economic, social and cultural life. It must never be forgotten, for example, that although women constituted the majority of Britain's population, they owned only a minority of its wealth. However, it is important to stress too that this maldistribution became less acute during the course of the century: whereas in the late 1920s women held 33 per cent of the personal wealth in England and Wales, by the early 1970s they held very nearly 40 per cent.[35]

It must not be forgotten either that women's incomes tended to be much lower than men's. It has been found, to take but one example, that 'Women's earnings in manufacturing as a proportion of male remained remarkably stable from pre-war years until 1970, fluctuating gently around the 50% mark, with a light rise in wartime and a subsequent return to the pre-war level.' However, it is important to stress too that this aspect of gender maldistribution also became less acute, especially during the final third of the century. According to Horrell,

> The extra 10 per cent of total income that women have gained since 1965 has been acquired both through gains in relative pay brought about by equal opportunities legislation and more hours devoted to the labour market.[36]

---

[32] Thane, *Old* Age, p. 15. Also Hannah, *Inventing Retirement*, pp. 16–17; Benson, *Consumer Society*, p. 20.

[33] *Age Concern on Pensioner Incomes* (HMSO, 1971), p. 10.

[34] Horrell, 'Living standards', p. 62.

[35] Benson, *Consumer Society*, p. 21.

[36] Horrell, 'Living standards', p. 73. See also S. Pollard, *The Development of the British Economy* (Arnold, 1983), pp. 321–2.

Nonetheless, neither wealth nor income necessarily provides an accurate indication of women's economic well-being or economic power. What mattered too was their ability to influence the deployment of the wealth and income which were at the family's disposal. These internal dynamics are, of course, extremely difficult to disentangle. It is easy enough to point out that consumption provided women with an important vehicle for the exercise of economic power; it is great deal more difficult to assess changes in the scale, shape and impact of that power. There is the temptation, it seems, to exaggerate both the dependence of women at the beginning of the century and the independence of their granddaughters and great-granddaughters at the end of it.

It is easily overlooked that early twentieth-century women of all classes exercised considerable power within the domestic economy. Those from the aristocracy were expected to exercise overall control over the management of their households. Those from the middle class were expected to exercise day-to-day, as well as overall, control. For example, when Violet Markham took over the running of the family home in 1912, she discovered that her mother had not only kept scrupulous domestic accounts but had also drawn up a detailed timetable describing the work that each of the household's nine servants was required to carry out on a daily and a weekly basis.[37]

It is not so easily overlooked that women from the working class were required to exercise day-to-day, if not hour-to-hour, responsibility for household management. It was widely accepted in the early years of the century that while it was the husband's duty to provide his family with as high and steady an income as he could, it was the wife's job to make it stretch as far as possible. Such assumptions have probably helped to encourage the view that women exercised less power than their contribution to the household economy entitled them to. According to Laura Oren, many working-class wives during the first half of the century did not know how much their husbands earned, had to make do with inadequate housekeeping allowances and chose, or felt compelled, to consume less food than their partners. Even 'Higher wages and greater prosperity', she believes, '... did not eliminate the uneven distribution of incomes between husbands and wives.'[38] In 1970, the Labour MP for Newark, Ted Bishop, suggested making it compulsory for wives to countersign their husbands' income tax returns. Local officials of the engineers' and transport workers' unions were not slow to make known their objections: 'Few husbands are happy to have to trot home with their wages and hand them over unopened to their wives ... The men reckon their wage packet is their own business.'[39]

However, the gendered distribution of family responsibilities meant too that women enjoyed a good deal more financial influence – and sometimes autonomy – than their contribution to the household economy 'deserved'. Elizabeth Roberts concludes from her oral investigation of Preston, Lancaster and Barrow-in-Furness

---

[37] J. Lewis, *Women in England 1870–1950: Sexual Divisions and Social Change* (Brighton: Wheatsheaf, 1984), p. 115.

[38] L. Oren, 'The Welfare of Women in Laboring Families: England, 1860–1950', in M.S. Hartman and L. Banner (eds), *Clio's Consciousness Raised: New Perspectives on the History of Women* (Harper & Row, 1974), p. 236. See also C. Glendinning and J. Millar (eds), *Women and Poverty in Britain* (Brighton: Wheatsheaf, 1987).

[39] *Daily Mail*, 5 January 1970.

between 1890 and 1940 that, 'in the majority of working-class marriages it would appear to be misleading and inaccurate to see the wife as downtrodden, bullied and dependent'. Such stereotyping, she believes, needs almost to be reversed. 'She was much more likely to be respected and highly regarded, [the] financial and household manager, and the arbiter of familial and indeed neighbourhood standards.'[40]

Carl Chinn goes further still. He opens his book on the urban poor between 1880 and 1939 with a quotation from Helen Bosanquet's 1915 study, *The Family*: 'the wise man recognizes that the real acting authority in daily life is that of the woman.' He goes on to assert the crucial role played by lower working-class women in the management of the domestic economy:

> what distinguished all mothers of the poor, whether they worked or not, was their total command of the family finances in every respect, except for the money retained by a husband for his own pleasure ... She it was who paid the rent, who bought the clothes, who purchased the food and who applied for credit at the local corner shop. It was she who conducted all financial negotiations and it was upon her generalship that the family relied to supply it with a meal.[41]

However, considerable caution is necessary. It is as easy to exaggerate the financial independence of late twentieth-century women, as it is the dependence of their early twentieth-century predecessors. The economic power that women were able to command certainly changed during the course of the century, but it did not do so in the straightforward, unambiguously advantageous way that one sometimes tends to suppose.

On the one hand, women increased their economic power by working more outside the home, spending more on the family's food, household goods and consumer durables, and spending more too on the medical, fashion and beauty products which they purchased for themselves. On the other hand, they abrogated some of their power because they rarely kept back all their earnings for personal consumption, because the money they spent on food and household goods constituted a declining proportion of household expenditure, and because the money that the family spent on consumer durables began to attract the interest – and influence – of husbands and children.[42]

Women of all classes tended to retain control over those aspects of domestic consumption that were regarded as 'feminine', routine or in some way unappealing. Even when husbands and children took an interest in what was bought, helped to carry the shopping or went to the shops on their own, shopping remained, as it always had been, essentially the woman's responsibility. 'Does Your Wife Know How to Choose a Toothbrush?' wondered the manufacturer Wisdom in 1950.[43] According to Rosemary Scott, husbands in the mid-1970s exercised considerable influence over the purchase of such 'masculine' goods as record players and motor cars:

> there will be more family involvement, particularly by the husband, in those purchase decisions where the product is perceived of as important to the family

[40] Roberts, *A Woman's Place*, p. 124.

[41] C. Chinn, *They Worked All Their Lives: Women of the Urban Poor in England, 1880–1939* (Manchester: Manchester University Press, 1988), pp. 51–2.

[42] Benson, *Consumer Society*, pp. 181–7.

[43] *Daily Mail*, 5 April 1950.

as a whole, or is more expensive and less frequently purchased. There will be more housewife influence operating on those products which are small, inexpensive and more frequently purchased which the family tends to take for granted, for example, food and household goods.[44]

Scott's careful balancing of the arguments confirms how difficult it was – and still is – to measure women's consumer power. In fact, the proliferation of oral, social survey and other evidence about household arrangements that became available during the second half of the century served to complicate as well as clarify the analysis. According to Ben Fine and Ellen Leopold, 'With the major exception of the motor car, consumerism has always been heavily associated with the female, particularly in its early forms when tied to luxury, display and distinction.' However, as they immediately go on to point out, 'The gendering of consumerism has also occurred in the modern world but, for quite the opposite reason, i.e., because of the close identification of women in the household, serving as mundane and unobserved providers (and purchasers).'[45]

Certainly, the danger of gender stereotyping is never far away. Women, it should go without saying, were no more homogeneous than any other group in society. However, it is a point that apparently does need to be laboured. Women were divided, we have seen, by differences in age; and they were divided, we shall see, by differences in ethnicity and social class (as well as in regional background, religious affiliation, political persuasion and so on). Moreover, as a moment's thought will confirm, even women sharing the same age, ethnicity or social class did not necessarily share the same regional background, religious affiliation, political persuasion, marital status or family circumstances.

Not all women married, not all women who married stayed married, and not all women who married or stayed married had children. Indeed, it is not always recognized that those who were single, divorced or widowed comprised a substantial, albeit declining, proportion of the female population. In 1901, they accounted for fully 50 per cent (56 per cent in Scotland) of all women over the age of 15. Although the proportion of the female population in these categories declined thereafter, they remained a substantial, if easily overlooked, minority. The single, widowed and divorced accounted for 47 per cent (53 per cent in Scotland) of adult women in 1931 and 36 per cent (41 per cent) in 1961. The 'problem' of unmarried women, if problem it was, was certainly not confined to the early years of the century.[46]

Single women tended to be young; divorcees and widows tended increasingly to be middle-aged and elderly. For instance, the proportion of widows aged 65 and over increased from 47 per cent in 1931 to 60 per cent in 1951 and 67 per cent in 1961. Such demographic patterns and developments had important economic repercussions. Single women, divorcees and widows tended not only to have lower incomes and possess less wealth than married women but also had to budget alone for the expenses that married couples were able to share between them. Seebohm Rowntree reported that in early twentieth-century York, 45 per cent of 'the poorest people in the city' were widows; and A.H. Halsey suggested in the mid-1980s that, 'There are now three-quarters of a million one-parent families with dependent

[44] Scott, *Female Consumer*, p. 124.

[45] B. Fine and E. Leopold, *The World of Consumption* (Routledge, 1993), pp. 68–9.

[46] C. Rollett and J. Parker, 'Population and Family', in Halsey (ed.), *Trends*, pp. 41–2.

children. The woman left to raise children alone is among the most pathetic casualties of an affluent society.'[47]

Gender stereotyping, however sensitive and sympathetic, can lead all too quickly to misinformation and misunderstanding. Thus there is no doubt that women shared unequally in Britain's growing prosperity. However, there is no doubt either that women did not share equally in their inequality. What is needed is an awareness both of the economic (and other) disadvantages that women shared and of the economic (and other) differences that divided them. Only then will it be possible to understand properly men's and women's experience of twentieth-century prosperity and the impact that it had on other aspects of their lives.

MINORITIES AND MAJORITIES

Whatever the sensitivities of gender history, they are as nothing compared to the complications waiting to ensnare those attempting to reconstruct and understand the experiences of Britain's minority ethnic communities. However, no account of twentieth-century social history can make even the most modest claim to inclusivity and comprehensiveness without a consideration of the country's major ethnic minorities, and the relationships they enjoyed – or endured – with other groups in society.

It is not easy even to decide which minorities to discuss. It has become customary, of course, to associate ethnic minorities with non-white immigration. However, this is not the association that was normally made during the first half of the century. Of the major groups of immigrants entering the country before the Second World War, only one, the Jews whose emigration from Germany, Poland and Russian began from the 1880s onwards, could possibly be described as 'non-white'. Other substantial groups included the Irish who came in large numbers in the wake of the famine of the 1840s, and those from the 'Old Commonwealth' who moved to the 'mother country' in small numbers throughout the twentieth century. It was only in the years following the Second World War that those from the 'New Commonwealth' began to enter the country in significant numbers, going on, with their children and grandchildren, to form what were to become known as ethnic minorities.[48]

Table 1.4 is most revealing. It not only provides certain, basic demographic data but can also be used to begin unravelling the discrepancy that existed between the demography and the demonology of immigration. It shows that those born in Ireland and the New Commonwealth – two of the most visible and discriminated against groups – comprised a very small minority of the population: under 2 per cent at the start of the century, less than 4 per cent in 1960/1, just over 7 per cent in 1970/1, and well under 5 per cent in 1990/1.

[47] Rowntree, *Poverty*, pp. 45, 47; A.H. Halsey, *Change in British Society* (Oxford: Oxford University Press, 1986), p. 110. See also K. Dayus, *All My Days* (Virago, 1988), pp. 74–5; 'Plight of the lonely,' *News of the World*, 19 May 1974; also National Council for the Unmarried Mother and Her Child, *Housing for Unsupported Mothers* (1967), p. 2.

[48] R. Miles and J. Solomos, 'Migration and the State in Britain: A Historical Overview', in C. Husband (ed.), *'Race' in Britain: Continuity and Change* (Hutchinson, 1987), pp. 76–91; T. Modood and R. Berthoud, *Ethnic Minorities in Britain: Diversity and Disadvantage* (Policy Studies Institute, 1997), pp. 12–17.

TABLE 1.4 IRISH- AND NEW COMMONWEALTH-BORN POPULATION, ENGLAND AND
WALES, 1900–91 (000s)

	Irish-born	New Commonwealth-born	Irish and New Commonwealth-born as percentage of total
1900/1	427	N/A	–
1910/11	375	187	1.6
1920/1	365	225	1.6
1931/1	521	223	1.9
1950/1	627	241	2.0
1960/1	871	741	3.5
1970/1	892	2672	7.3
1980/1	789	2062	5.7
1990/1	569	1645	4.3

Source: Based on D. Coleman and J. Salt, *British Population Trends* (Oxford: Oxford University Press, 1992), p. 482; Office of Population Censuses and Surveys, *Census: 1991 General Report, Great Britain*, Vol. 1 (HMSO, 1991).

However, aggregate data can always be misleading. It is important to acknowledge therefore that Irish, Jewish and New Commonwealth immigrants all tended to settle in a relatively small number of cities and conurbations. The Irish congregated in London, Lancashire and the west of Scotland; the Jews in London, Glasgow, Leeds, Birmingham and Manchester; and those from the New Commonwealth in London, Yorkshire, Lancashire and the West Midlands. In the mid-1960s, for instance, those born in the West Indies, India and Pakistan comprised just over 1 per cent of the population of England and Wales, but nearly 2 per cent of those living in West Yorkshire, and more than 3 per cent of those living in the West Midlands and Greater London. Thirty years later, ethnic minorities accounted for 7 per cent of the population of England and Wales, but 10 per cent of those living in the West Midlands and 26 per cent of those living in London.[49]

Robert Miles and John Solomos explain carefully and dispassionately how such residential concentration became associated with the idea of the 'enemy within'. It was a process which, fanned by insecurity, prejudice and certain sections of the media, acquired a seemingly unstoppable momentum.

> The image of inner city areas becoming 'black enclaves' where British law and order could not be easily enforced, leading to the emergence of 'alien values' within these areas, was seen as a potential threat to the 'way of life' and culture of white residents.[50]

---

[49] J. Cheetham, 'Immigration', in Halsey (ed.), *Trends*, p. 497; *Regional Trends*, 34, 1999, p. 48; R. Skellington with P. Morris, *'Race' in Britain Today* (Sage/Open University Press, 1996), pp. 52–6.

[50] Miles and Solomos, 'Migration and the State', p. 101. Such demonization had a long history, with similar accusations being made against the Jews at the beginning of the century. See, for example, *Royal Commission on Alien Immigration*, Vol. 1, 1903–4.

The image of black and Irish 'enclaves' was reinforced by the age, gender and class characteristics they often displayed. It is well known that when immigrant groups first arrived, they tended to be young, male and economically disadvantaged; but that in time they were likely to assume age, gender and economic profiles closer to those of the populations in which they settled.[51] However, this does not mean that the experiences of those from Ireland and the New Commonwealth – let alone from different parts of the New Commonwealth – should be conflated. Such spurious homogeneity can be highly misleading and impede, rather than facilitate, the understanding of developments that are likely anyway to be highly contentious.

Although Irish immigration was very well established by the end of the nineteenth century, the Irish in Britain remained for many years disproportionately young and disproportionately poor. They were able to find work during the 1930s, but only because of their willingness to travel, to work long hours and to take on the heaviest and most unpleasant jobs. It was not until the Second World War that their employment prospects began to improve.

> Whereas before the war Irish were mostly employed in building, labouring and domestic service, opportunities now existed in various industrial occupations, transport and catering. Immediately after the war Irish were recruited for nursing, the mines, agriculture and metal manufacture and many firms, hotels and hospitals continue [in 1972] to advertise their vacancies in the Irish press.[52]

The Welsh too faced less discrimination after the war. In 1930s' Weston-super-Mare, for example, advertisements in the local press decreed that 'Welsh need not apply.' But '[t]hat was before the war. They were jolly glad of them after.'[53]

Those from the New Commonwealth began to arrive in Britain at the very time that the Irish were beginning to broaden their employment opportunities. This was of crucial importance. In fact, it was claimed in the late 1980s that, 'Many of those Irish who have been in Britain since the 1940s and 1950s openly acknowledge the fact that the arrival of the New Commonwealth immigrants, and their subsequent racialisation, were the best things to happen to the Irish, reducing the pressures of prejudice and intolerance.'[54]

---

[51] The number of Irish females and males coming to Britain has been roughly equal. See M. Kells,' "I'm Myself and Nobody Else": Gender and Ethnicity among Young Middle-Class Irish Women in London', in P. O'Sullivan, (ed.), *The Irish World Wide Series: History, Heritage, Identity, Irish Women and Irish Migration*, Vol. 4 (Labour Publishing Co., Leicester: Leicester University Press, 1995), p. 201. Jews tended to migrate in family groups: D. Baines, *Emigration from Europe, 1815–1930* (Cambridge: Cambridge University Press, 1995), p. 40.

[52] Cheetham, 'Immigration', p. 474.

[53] Museum of Welsh Life, RS3, p. 28.

[54] C. Peach, V. Robinson, J. Maxted and J. Chance, 'Immigration and Ethnicity', in A.H. Halsey (ed.), *British Social Trends: A Guide to the Changing Social Structure of Britain* (Basingstoke: Macmillan, 1988), p. 575.

New Commonwealth immigrants ended the twentieth century much as Irish immigrants had ended the nineteenth century: young and poor.[55] Certainly, the age structure of minority ethnic communities was often strikingly different from that of the population as a whole, particularly during the early stages of settlement. It was pointed out, for example, that in the late 1980s, 59 per cent of the West Indian population 'were aged 29 or under compared with 42 per cent of the white population', and that 'only 2 per cent were of retirement age compared with 18 per cent of the white population'.[56]

The gender balance of ethnic minorities also tended to set them apart, particularly (again) when they first came to the country. Even those seeking to emphasize the growing demographic maturity of New Commonwealth minorities were unable to conceal their continuing distinctiveness. For example, it was reported, with apparent approval, in 1988 that all South Asian groups 'now record more balanced sex ratios'. What this meant, it was explained, was that, 'between 1971 and 1981 the number of men per 100 women fell from 125 to 105 for Indians and from 210 to 121 for Pakistanis and Bangladeshis'.[57]

It is scarcely surprising to discover therefore that those from the New Commonwealth shared only very slowly and uncertainly in the growing prosperity of the country. Whatever skills they brought to Britain, they found themselves confined overwhelmingly to a narrow range of unskilled, insecure, low paying jobs. Tariq Modood puts it extremely soberly:

> despite a long-term trend in the reduction of differences in job-levels achieved, there is a more or less constant 'ethnic penalty' paid by non-white people measured in terms of the jobs that similarly qualified people achieve ... That is to say, ethnic minorities may be getting better jobs, but they are still doing so to a lesser extent than white people with the same qualifications.[58]

During the first half of the century, discrimination was more or less open and overt. Respondents recall, for instance, how difficult it was for school-leavers to secure apprenticeships: 'He was talking to the other person on the phone, saying I've got this Indian boy here – the first 3 or 4 said we don't want Indians.'[59] Even at the very end of the century, those from ethnic minority communities remained particularly prone to unemployment, and when in employment to poor pay – and thus inevitably to economic disadvantage (and social exclusion). *Social Trends* recorded in some detail – and with some dismay – the income and wealth of the ethnic minority population at

---

[55] Some Indian and Ugandan Asian immigrants were well off when they arrived in the country. *Manchester Guardian*, 24 June 1948; I. Conveny and J. Welshman, 'Migration, "Multi-Occupation", and Medical Officers of Health: Housing the "South Asian Worker"', Association of Business Historians, University of Reading, June 2002.

[56] Peach *et al.*, 'Immigration', p. 578. Also *Social Trends*, 28, 1998, p. 34; Cheetham, 'Immigration', p. 499; E. Royle, *Modern Britain: A Social History 1750–1997*, rev. edn (Arnold, 1997), p. 79.

[57] Peach *et al.*, 'Immigration', p. 590.

[58] T. Modood, 'Employment', in Modood and Berthoud (eds), *Ethnic Minorities*, p. 84. See also M. Luthra, *Britain's Black Population: Social Change, Public Policy and Agenda* (Aldershot: Arena, 1997), p. 368.

[59] Black and Ethnic Minority Project, DX-624/6/1–2. Also Museum of Welsh Life, RS3.

the turn of the millennium. Defining low income as '60 per cent of median equivalised household disposable income', it confirmed that those from minority ethnic communities were over-represented among low-income households. 'Nearly two-thirds of Pakistani and Bangladeshi people live in low income households, compared with over a quarter of Black, Indian and people from other ethnic minority groups and only 17 per cent of White people.'[60]

SOCIAL CLASS

If there were few scholars at the beginning of the twenty-first century who denied the role of ethnicity in determining economic (and other) life chances, there were a growing number seeking to devalue the importance of social class. Their challenge was part of a much wider, and fiercely acrimonious, debate concerning the merits and demerits of postmodernism. It is a debate which raises profound questions for those writing, reading and studying social history – not least when attempting to assess the significance of economic factors in explaining social, cultural and political developments. Historians such as Patrick Joyce and Keith Jenkins have led the attack upon conventional, class-based analysis.[61] 'Embracing the new poststructuralist concern with texts and languages, they argued that only if texts articulated a clear and explicit sense of class, and class division, in their discourse, could it be claimed that class existed in any useful or meaningful way.'[62]

The author of this book takes a more conventional approach. He continues to believe, along with many other scholars (by no means all of them Marxist), that an awareness of class divisions remains fundamental to the proper analysis of Britain's (and many other countries') social and economic history. Mike Savage and Andrew Miles put it like this in their 1994 study, *The Remaking of the British Working Class, 1840–1940*:

> Although politicians and commentators alike are wont to stress the declining
> salience of class in our own times, we should be cautious about projecting
> current scepticism back onto the historical record … For so long as we live in
> an unequal society, in which some people exploit others, class divisions are
> likely to have profound political [and other] ramifications.[63]

That said, it is exceptionally difficult to define the class identity of any individual or group, let alone to assess the impact that class identity had upon other aspects of economic, social, cultural and political life. Class, it has been pointed out, 'is the most

---

[60] *Social Trends*, 30, 2000, pp. 93–4. Also R. Berthoud, 'Income and Standards of Living', in Modood and Berthoud (eds), *Ethnic Minorities*, esp. pp. 168–78.

[61] See, for example, P. Joyce, 'Refabricating labour history; or from labour history to the history of labour', *Labour History Review*, 62, 1997; K. Jenkins, *On 'What Is History?' From Carr and Elton to Rorty and White* (Routledge, 1995).

[62] M. Savage and A. Miles, *The Remaking of the British Working Class, 1840–1940* (Routledge, 1994), p. 14. See also R.J. Evans, *In Defence of History* (Granta, 1997).

[63] Savage and Miles, *Remaking*, p. 90. See also Evans, *Defence*, pp. 184–6.

contested category in the whole lexicon of the social sciences. We all know class and classes exist, but it and they elude both scientific definition and enumeration.'[64]

It is difficult to decide whether class should be defined by economic criteria (such as occupation, income and relationship to the means of production); by social and cultural criteria (such as behaviour, status, power, attitudes and relationships with other groups); or by some elusive combination of them all. However, even those who believe that class is best defined by social and cultural criteria concede that very often there is no real alternative to measuring it by means of economic indicators. 'Although it is unlikely that any two sociologists would ever agree about a definition of social class, there would be fairly widespread concurrence ... that occupation is one of the major – perhaps the major – determinant of social class.'[65]

It has been decided therefore to divide British society, conventionally, into three broad classes. There was a tiny, but highly influential upper class (or aristocracy) which derived its wealth and income primarily from the ownership of land. There was a substantial, and growing, middle class (or bourgeoisie) which derived its wealth and income primarily from the ownership of finance and property other than land, and from their employment in non-manual labour. There was finally a working class (or proletariat) which, though always the largest of the three, accounted for a declining proportion of the population. Those in the working class derived their income, as one would expect, primarily from their employment in manual (and service) labour.[66]

The economic, social and cultural power of the aristocracy was eroded, though not of course eliminated, during the course of the century. There were three major challenges to its hegemony: Lloyd George's 'People's Budget' of 1909; the imposition ten years later of 40 per cent death duty on estates worth more than £2 million; and the introduction during the 1960s and 1970s of capital gains tax and capital transfer tax. An increasing number of aristocrats found themselves in straitened circumstances – during the 1960s, for instance, the fifth Lord Redesdale, whose family had once owned 30,000 acres in Northumberland, was reduced to running a laundry and dry-cleaning business.[67] But neither impecuniosity, insouciance nor irresponsibility undermined their appeal to the local and national press. The grandfather of the Countess of Cardigan, it was reported wonderingly in 1936, 'still walked half a mile a day at the age of 102'.[68]

By contrast, the economic and cultural power of the middle class grew very substantially during the course of the century. It was not just that the number (and proportion) of the population who can be identified as middle class increased from just over 9 million (25 per cent) at the beginning of the century to well over 22 million

[64] J. White, *The Worst Street in North London: Campbell Bunk, Islington, Between the Wars* (Routledge & Kegan Paul, 1986), p. 27.

[65] Burnett, *Cost of Living*, p. 292.

[66] See, for example, D. Cannadine, *The Decline and Fall of the British Aristocracy* (Yale University Press, 1989); A. Light, *Forever England: Femininity, Literature and Conservatism Between the Wars* (Routledge, 1991), pp. 12–13; J. Raynor, *The Middle Class* (Harlow: Longman, 1969); Benson, *Working Class*, pp. 3–4.

[67] J.V. Beckett, *The Aristocracy in England 1660–1914* (Oxford: Blackwell, 1986); Cannadine, *Decline and Fall*; F.M.L. Thompson, 'English landed society in the twentieth century: I, property: collapse and survival', *Transactions of the Royal Historical Society*, 40, 1990.

[68] *Express and Star*, 12 December 1936.

(40 per cent) at the beginning of the 1980s. It was also that those who can be identified as middle class were amassing increasing amounts of wealth. Between 1923 and 1976, for example, the richest 20 per cent of the population (excluding the very richest 2 per cent) increased the proportion of marketable wealth which they held by more than a half, from 33 per cent to 52 per cent of the total.[69]

The middle class were also earning higher, and generally more secure, incomes. It has been calculated, for instance, that salary earners' share of national income grew from just under 12 per cent in 1913, to 20 per cent in 1951, and over 26 per cent in 1973. There were signs indeed that the 'lower' middle class was narrowing the gap that existed between itself and the 'upper' middle class. It has been suggested that between 1910 and 1960, for example, the income, in real terms, of the typical doctor/general practitioner grew by just over 50 per cent, whereas the earnings of a male bank clerk improved, again in real terms, by practically 75 per cent.[70] When Mass-Observation carried out an investigation into popular attitudes in 1938, it discovered that, 'A large number of lower middle class people are pretty satisfied with their present standard of living and are not ambitious to change it.'[71]

Not that the gap always appeared to be narrowing. When Andrew Burn looks back on his childhood, he recalls that,

> For the upper middle classes and the middle classes in the 1930s life was perhaps more similar to that in 1890 than in today's world. Our household in the 1920s included two full time gardeners and four living-in domestic servants. There was a lot of formality and on every evening except Sunday the family dressed for dinner – and this meant dinner jackets – and we as children had to do the same once we had graduated from nursery. The kitchen, scullery and pantry were not parts of the house that we went into often.[72]

Towards the end of the century, there erupted the furore over so-called 'fat cats'. A survey carried out in 2000 revealed, for instance, that the salaries of the directors of FTSE 100 companies were increasing four times faster than those of their employees. Neither trade unionists, politicians nor journalists were slow to voice their objections:

> with the average chief executive's salary and bonus package worth 18 times the average worker's, according to one Warwick University study, the usual excuses for why they are worth their weight in gold are wearing a bit threadbare. (For any chief executive earning more than half a million and weighing in at less than 14 stone, that statistic is literally true.)[73]

---

[69] D. Metcalf and R. Richardson, 'Labour', in A.R. Prest and D.J. Coppock (eds), *The UK Economy: A Manual of Applied Economics* (Weidenfeld & Nicolson, 1980), p. 259.

[70] R.C.O. Mathews, C.H. Feinstein and J.C Odling-Smee, *British Economic Growth 1856–1973* (Oxford: Clarendon, 1982), p. 164; Burnett, *Cost of Living*, pp. 298–9. The 1980s saw growing economic inequality. Indeed, the proportion of households without any assets whatsoever doubled between 1979 and 1996: *The Guardian*, 7 March 2001.

[71] Mass-Observation, A10, 1938, p. 2.

[72] A. Burn, *May The Fathers Tell Their Children – The Adventures of a Desert Rat, 1940–1946* (Bristol: L'Mont Publications, 2003), p. 32.

[73] C. Denny, '1 chief executive = 5 roadsweepers', *The Guardian*, 5 July 2000.

Nevertheless, working-class economic and social – and perhaps even cultural – power was growing apace. This was due in part simply to the growth in the number of working people: over 27 million (74 per cent of the population) in 1901, just over 36 million (69 per cent) in 1951 and just over 33 million (59 per cent) in 1981. The growth of working-class economic power also owed a little – though not a great deal – to the expansion of wealth-holding. After the Second World War, nearly two-thirds of the population possessed private capital worth less than £100. Indeed, even at the end of the century, 39 per cent of people in Britain possessed less than £1,000 – and a further 18 per cent less than £5,000 – in cash savings and equity investments.[74] But the growth of working-class owner-occupation was of considerable importance. Tax relief on mortgage interest payments (and the sale of council housing) benefited working people along with (and more than) those from other classes. The popular press trumpeted the advantages of council house purchase. 'Eight years ago,' reported *The Sun* in 1988, 'Jim Welsh and his wife bought their council house in Camden, North London, for £15,700. They took pride in their home and kept it spick and span. Now they have sold it for £180,000. Don't envy them – follow them.'[75]

The growth of working-class economic power was due much more to improvements in working-class incomes. Although wage earners comprised a declining proportion of the population, they retained a constant 40 per cent or so of national income. It has been calculated, for instance, that during the first 80 years of the century, the weekly wage earnings of manual workers increased by well over 400 per cent.[76] It seems too that the semi-skilled and unskilled benefited more than the skilled. Guy Routh has estimated that between 1913–14 and 1978, the rise in the earnings of unskilled workers exceeded that of skilled workers by just over a third.[77]

It seems extraordinary therefore to deny the role that social class has played in determining economic, social and cultural (and other life) chances. The logic is inescapable. Social class needs to be set alongside, and often above, age, gender and ethnicity when attempting to explain social, cultural and political developments.

CONCLUSIONS AND IMPLICATIONS

At this point, it is worth reiterating the central tenets both of this chapter and of the book as a whole. It has been shown in this chapter that the twentieth century witnessed unprecedented national prosperity but that, as one would expect, there were losers as well as winners. Age, gender, ethnicity and social class, it has been suggested, all need to be taken into account when reconstructing the British experience of prosperity. It will be argued in the rest of the book that it was this growing prosperity – however one may qualify it – which provides the single most important key to understanding the social, cultural and political changes that took place during the course of the century. It is not for nothing that governments do their best to synchronize the economic cycle with the electoral cycle.

---

[74] J. Stevenson, *British Society 1914–45* (Penguin, 1984), p. 331; Benson, *Consumer Society*, p. 26; *Sunday Telegraph*, 15 April 2001.

[75] *Sun*, 14 April 1988.

[76] Mass-Observation, 3089, 'Notes on the Cost of Living', 1949, p. 6.

[77] G. Routh, *Occupation and Pay in Great Britain 1906–79* (Basingstoke: Macmillan, 1980), p. 125; see also Pollard, *British Economy*, p. 188.

2 SPENDING AND SAVING

CONSUMPTION AND CONSUMER SOCIETY

In recent years, the study of living standards and the quality of life has been strengthened – it sometimes seems superseded – by the study of consumption, consumer attitudes and consumer behaviour.[1] Historians of twentieth-century Britain have joined historians of other periods and other countries – along with scholars from other disciplines – in focusing upon the ways in which goods and services were consumed as well as the ways in which they were produced. Paul Johnson commented in the late 1980s, for example, on the historiographical shift that he saw taking place around him:

> After many years studying the role of production and supply in the economic development of Britain, historians have belatedly turned their attention to demand, and have been discovering, or rediscovering, the history of consumption.[2]

Indeed, some historians of twentieth-century Britain became so enamoured of studying consumption that they saw it as a way not just of describing, but also of explaining, the changes that took place during the course of the century. 'My argument', explained Daniel Miller, in 1995, 'is that consumption has become the vanguard of history.'[3] Something of a new consensus seemed to be emerging. Britain, it was suggested, has undergone a consumer revolution and developed into a 'consumer society', manifesting all of the signs of a recognizable 'consumer culture'. Edward Royle's *Modern Britain: A Social History 1750–1997* is one of the best-known guides to nineteenth- and twentieth-century developments, and in it he refers time and again to late twentieth-century Britain as a consumer society:

> The lubricant to make the consumer society function smoothly was advertising, which was made all the easier by the advent of television … Though society is no longer divided between the leisured and the non-leisured, and though the circumstances of almost all families have much improved during the second half

---

[1] This section draws heavily upon J. Benson, *The Rise of the Consumer Society in Britain, 1880–1980* (Harlow: Longman, 1994).

[2] P. Johnson, 'Conspicuous consumption and the working class in late Victorian and Edwardian Britain', *Transactions of the Royal Historical Society*, 38, 1988, p. 27.

[3] D. Miller, 'Consumption as the Vanguard of History: A Polemic by Way of Introduction', in D. Miller (ed.), *Acknowledging Consumption: A Review of New Studies* (Routledge, 1995).

of the twentieth century, in a consumer society those with most money have remained clearly differentiated from those with least.[4]

However, the new consensus that late twentieth-century Britain was a consumer society did not extend to agreeing whether or not this was a good thing or a bad thing. On the one hand, there were those, primarily on the right, who believed that living in a consumer society brought benefits to virtually all sections of the community. Conservative MP Teresa Gorman claimed, for example, that, 'Women actually have enormous power in this country because they're the people who do the shopping, who spend most of the household budget … A duchess's £5 is worth the same in Marks & Spencer as a pensioner's.'[5] Others took the argument further still. According to leading New Right thinker Arthur Seldon,

> Ordinary people haven't done well out of democracy as it is operated. The market offers you one-man, one-vote every day. Politics offers you one-man, one-vote every thousand days. Purchasing power is to own a vote. A man doesn't have to know anyone with influence. He doesn't have to explain why he wants to do things. All he needs is coins.[6]

On the other hand, there were those, primarily on the left, who disagreed profoundly with this benign view of consumer culture. They believed that living in the new consumer society of late twentieth-century Britain bred frustration, perpetuated the subordination of women and ethnic minorities, and widened economic and social inequalities. Fred Hirsch, for instance, argued that affluence inevitably led to frustration: however prosperous we became, we could not all enjoy solitary possession of the world's finest beaches; the more we moved to the suburbs, the less attractive suburban life would become.[7] Others developed the argument. Tony Sewell suggested that youth culture, with its emphasis on money and consumer goods, was more harmful than racism to black pupils' prospects of educational success.[8] Susie Orbach claimed that anorexia nervosa and other eating disorders were 'a metaphor' for the times: millions of women refused to consume the food they needed in a revolt against the conflicting demands that consumer capitalism placed upon them.[9] Ursula Huws pointed to the fact that consumption entailed commodification, a process that resulted in the replacement of public ownership by private ownership.

> Instead of simply paying for the use of a service, it is now necessary to pay the capital costs of providing it … As a higher and higher proportion of the

---

[4] E. Royle, *Modern Britain: A Social History 1750–1997* rev. edn (Arnold, 1997), pp. 286, 288. See also M. Hilton, 'The fable of the sheep, or, private virtues, public vices: The consumer revolution of the twentieth century', *Past and Present*, 176, 2002.

[5] Cited in G. Bedell, 'The woman least likely', *The Guardian*, 16 December 1990.

[6] Cited in P. Hennessy, 'Market "The measure of democracy" ', *The Times*, 24 December 1990.

[7] F. Hirsch, *Social Limits to Growth* (Routledge & Kegan Paul, 1978), pp. 37–9. See also T. Scitovsky, *The Joyless Economy: An Inquiry into Human Satisfaction and Consumer Dissatisfaction* (Oxford: Oxford University Press, 1976).

[8] T. Sewell, *Black Masculinities and Schooling: How Black Boys Survive Modern Schooling* (Stoke-on-Trent: Trentham Books, 1997).

[9] S. Orbach, *Hunger Strike: The Anorexic's Struggle as a Metaphor for our Age* (Faber and Faber, 1986).

population became owners of these things, then the public provision of the service which they replace atrophies or becomes prohibitively expensive because the economies of scale have been lost ... The gap between the haves and have-nots is intensified.[10]

Accordingly, it is the aim of this chapter to examine the ways in which the people of Britain spent – and saved – the growing income which they had at their disposal. This chapter, like the last, is divided into two parts, the first examining the experience of the population as a whole, the second the experiences of some of the major social groups that went to make it up. It will be suggested, and suggested most strongly, that while there is no doubt that consumption became more important during the course of the century, this certainly does not mean that Britain became a consumer society.

THE GROWTH OF CONSUMPTION

It will come as no surprise to learn that as people's incomes rose, so too did their spending. Indeed, such a claim may seem little more than a truism of the most weary and predictable kind. People worked in order to earn, and they earned in order to spend. As I have suggested elsewhere (in a study of the working class), when real incomes rose,

> the first priority was to obtain enough food to eat and adequate accommodation in which to live. But once these basic needs had been met, priorities began to alter. The better off wished to enjoy some of the trappings of their new-found, if often insecure, prosperity. They wanted to eat a more varied diet and wear more fashionable clothes; they planned to live in a more comfortable and better furnished home; and they expected to enjoy some at least of the new forms of leisure that were becoming available to those with the money to pay for them.[11]

It is clearly true that consumer spending grew, and grew substantially, during the course of the century. Table 2.1 shows that it increased nearly five times in real terms: from just under £100 billion (at 1997 prices) in 1900, to almost £180 billion in 1950, just over £270 billion in 1970, and £473 billion in 1995. Those living in the early 1950s spent 50 per cent more than their parents and grandparents at the beginning of the century; those living at the end of the century spent two-and-a-half times as much as their parents and grandparents in the early 1950s – and nearly five times as much as their grandparents and great-grandparents at the beginning of the century. This growth of consumer spending (and the growth of income upon which it depended) constituted a crucially important feature of twentieth-century economic, social, cultural and political life, and one to which we shall return time and time and again during the course of the book.

It is also true that consumer spending grew broadly in line with personal incomes. However, the relationship between spending and income was by no means as straightforward as one might imagine. Figure 2.1 brings together the statistics of

---

[10] U. Huws, 'Consuming fashions', *New Statesman and Society*, 19 August 1988.

[11] J. Benson, *The Working Class in Britain, 1850–1939* (Harlow: Longman, 1989), p. 146.

TABLE 2.1 CONSUMER SPENDING (£ BILLIONS) AND
INDEX, UNITED KINGDOM, 1900–95

Year	Consumer expenditure	Index
1900	99	100
1910	107	109
1920	110	112
1930	136	138
1940	143	146
1950	179	182
1960	215	219
1970	273	278
1980	327	332
1990	434	442
1995	473	481

Source: Based on A. Dilnot and C. Emmerson, 'Economic Environment',
in A.H. Halsey (ed.), *Twentieth-Century British Social Trends*
(Basingstoke: Macmillan, 2000), p. 330.

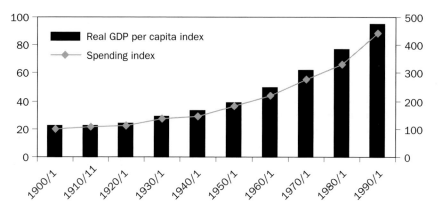

**Figure 2.1 Consumer spending and real GDP per capita indices, United Kingdom,
1900/1–1990/1**
Source: Based on A. Dilnot and C. Emmerson, 'The Economic Environment', in A.H. Halsey (ed.),
Twentieth-Century British Social Trends (Basingstoke: Macmillan, 2000), pp. 326–7, 330, 571.

consumer spending that were set out in Table 2.1 with the statistics of GDP that were
discussed in the previous chapter. The juxtaposition of income and spending confirms
the truth of John Maynard Keynes's suggestion that, 'men are disposed, as a rule and
on the average, to increase their consumption as their income increases, but not by as
much as the increase in their income'.[12]

Rising incomes and growing consumer spending were accompanied by changes in
the goods and services on which people spent their money. Figures 2.2 and 2.3 reveal

---

[12] Benson, *Consumer Society*, p. 61.

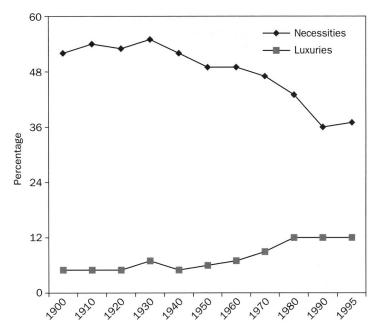

Figure 2.2 Spending on 'necessities' and 'luxuries' as a proportion of all consumer expenditure, United Kingdom, 1900–95

Source: Based on A. Dilnot and C. Emmerson, 'Economic Environment', in A.H. Halsey (ed.), *Twentieth-Century British Social Trends* (Basingstoke: Macmillan, 2000), pp. 342–3.

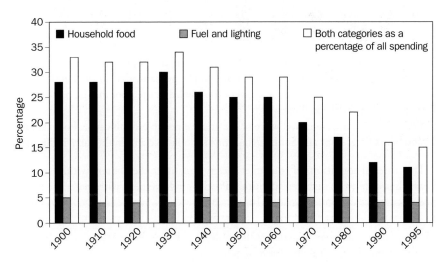

Figure 2.3 Household spending on food, fuel and lighting as a percentage of all consumer expenditure, United Kingdom, 1900–95

Source: Based on A. Dilnot and C. Emmerson, 'Economic Environment', in A.H. Halsey (ed.), *Twentieth-Century British Social Trends* (Basingstoke: Macmillan, 2000), pp. 342–3.

something of the transformation that took place. They show, most obviously, that there was a long-term decline in the proportion of consumer spending devoted to 'necessities' such as food and clothing; and a long-term increase in the proportion spent on 'luxuries' such as travel and communications, and running a car. There was little change during the first half of the century. Thereafter, however, the pace of change quickened appreciably: during the second half of the century, the proportion of consumer spending devoted to food and clothing declined very significantly, while the proportion allocated to travel and running a car increased very significantly.

The declining significance of food spending raises a number of important issues. As Andrew Dilnot and Carl Emmerson commented in a recent analysis of long-term economic change, 'Perhaps the most striking illustration of increased affluence, especially in the post-war period, has been the declining share of spending on household food, which accounted for one-third of consumer spending in the 1920s, compared with little more than 10 per cent now.'[13] The declining significance of food spending in household budgets suggests that there was an inverse relationship between income level and food consumption; it suggests, in other words, that food had a backward-sloping demand curve. It was a development that led Ernest Engel to suggest many years ago that as income rises, so the proportion spent on food tends to decline.[14]

Nor was this all. The declining significance of food spending was associated with changes in the type of food that people purchased. As incomes rose, shoppers tended to reduce their consumption of staple products like bread and potatoes, and to increase their consumption of more expensive products such as meat, fruit and vegetables.[15] So, just as there was an inverse relationship between income level and food consumption, so there tended to exist a similar relationship between income level and staple food consumption. Staple foods, like food generally, had a backward-sloping demand curve. As incomes rose in twentieth-century Britain, so the proportion spent on staple foods tended to fall.[16]

It is developments such as these that form the basis for claims that by the end of the century Britain had undergone a consumer revolution and become a consumer society. The people of Britain, it is pointed out, grew more prosperous, spent more of their growing prosperity on goods and services, and developed new and distinctive patterns of consumption. It was a sign of the times, perhaps, that in the late 1980s, a male nurse shot dead an intruder who went for a swim in the pool that he had built in the garden of his home in Tonypandy.[17]

These changes, it is suggested, were of the greatest possible significance. For example, psychologists Peter Lunt and Sonia Livingstone felt able to claim in the early 1990s that,

The material conditions of consumer society constitute the context within which people work out their identities. People's involvement with material

---

[13] A. Dilnot and C. Emmerson, 'Economic Environment', in A.H. Halsey (ed.), *Twentieth-Century British Social Trends* (Basingstoke: Macmillan, 2000), p. 341.

[14] W. Minchinton, 'Patterns of Demand 1750–1914', in C.M. Cipolla (ed.), *The Fontana Economic History of Europe: The Industrial Revolution* (Glasgow: Fontana, 1973), p. 115.

[15] A. Hook, *The Workers' Share* (1924).

[16] Minchinton, 'Patterns of Demand', p. 82.

[17] *Daily Mail*, 3 April 1990.

culture is such that mass consumption infiltrates everyday life not only at the levels of economic processes, social activities and household structures, but also at the level of meaningful psychological experience – affecting the construction of identities, the formation of relationships, the framing of events.[18]

The growth of consumption is not in doubt. What is in doubt is whether, and to what extent, mass consumption infiltrated everyday life, influencing identity construction, relationship formation and the framing of events in the way that Lunt and Livingstone suggest. How 'mass' was mass consumption? How can one show that it was consumption – 'mass' or otherwise – that influenced economic processes, social relationships, household structures and psychological experiences? Could it not be that the relationship operated in the reverse direction – that economic processes, social relationships, household structures and psychological experiences influenced consumption? Could it not be that the state, education, religion, the mass media, work, and so on played a role as great as, if not greater than, consumption in identity construction, relationship formation and the framing of events?

The remainder of the chapter will examine such issues by investigating the extent to which people's experience of consumption varied with – and/or depended upon – age, gender, ethnicity and social class. It will be shown that people's experience of consumption certainly varied with – and often depended upon – their age, gender, ethnic and class position. Indeed, it will be suggested that the persistence of these variations is of such significance that it deals a fatal blow to claims that by the end of the century Britain had become a consumer society.

AGE, SAVING AND SPENDING

It goes almost without saying that consumption varied with age. Nobody, presumably, would ever suppose that children, adolescents, young adults, the middle-aged and the elderly enjoyed the same purchasing power, or that they put the purchasing power they enjoyed to the same, or even similar, ends. Indeed, it was shown in the previous chapter that as families became more prosperous, children and adolescents were able to exercise increasing power over economic decision-making; and it was established too that the economic power of the middle-aged and the elderly became a matter of increasing public debate. How then did the different age groups use their economic power? How far did the balance between spending and saving change over the life course?

There was certainly increasing concern about childhood consumption. Children's purchasing power was growing, growing fast and needed, many believed, to be curtailed. What was seen at the beginning of the century as the pleasing product of growing national prosperity was sometimes regarded by the end of it as both cause and consequence of parental indulgence and childhood selfishness.[19] Generational and class prejudice often converged. A 1940 survey of urban life reported not only that, 'schoolchildren in the poorer districts had far more pocket-money than those of the

[18] P.K. Lunt and S.M. Livingstone, *Mass Consumption and Personal Identity: Everyday Economic Experience* (Buckingham: Open University Press, 1992), p. 24.
[19] J. Turner, 'The over-indulged child should be seen off and not played with', *The Times*, 6 September 2003.

better class', but also that they spent it 'largely on sweets, ice-creams and comics'. If that were not bad enough, it went on, the sweets were 'often of the most wretched quality' and the comics 'poor to a degree'.[20] Generational and parental solidarities too often coalesced. There was a belief by the early 1990s – and no doubt before – that it was the caring parent who was most likely to give into his or her children's demands.

> I think that when you have children and they are growing and you also want to see them having, I am not saying the same as everybody else, but if a child is different at school in some way, that child perhaps get picked upon, and it must be very hard to be a parent under those circumstances.[21]

Such fears were not unfounded. The twentieth century undoubtedly saw a shift in the balance of economic – and other – power between parents and children. A working-class mother from the East End of London explained in the early 1950s that, 'When I was a kid Dad always had the best of everything. Now it's the children who get the best of it. If there's one pork chop left, the kiddy gets it.'[22] By the end of the century, the inter-generational contract between parents and children – and between adults and young people more broadly – had changed for all to see. One commentator concluded:

> We live in an increasingly child-centred world. Every other pub serves chicken nuggets and has a play area, stately homes have bouncy castles dotted around the park land, supermarkets have ball ponds and garden centres offer face painting.[23]

The inter-generational contract between adults and adolescents changed less than that between adults and children. This was because adults had always been intensely concerned about adolescent consumption – as about most other aspects of adolescent behaviour. In the early 1980s, Geoffrey Pearson published a fascinating study of the relationship between adolescence, hooliganism and what he described as the myth of the British way of life. There was nothing new, he showed, about the belief in adolescents' unconscionable behaviour. Britain, he explained, had been plagued for a century and more by the same, or very similar, anxieties:

> successive generations have voiced identical fears of social breakdown and moral degeneration, whether directed against the 'garotters' and original 'Hooligan' gangs of late Victorian London, or the 'muggers' of the contemporary urban streets.[24]

---

[20] H. Cunningham, *Children and Childhood in Western Society since 1500* (Harlow: Longman, 1995), p. 183. See too 'Children are over-fussed', *Daily Mail*, 5 September 1950.

[21] Lunt and Livingstone, *Mass Consumption*, pp. 41–2.

[22] Cunningham, *Children*, pp. 182–3.

[23] M. Ingram, 'Why mother knows best', *The Times*, 1 August 2000. See also Abbey National, 'Pester Power is Good News for Families' (Abbey National, 2000).

[24] G. Pearson, *Hooligan: A History of Respectable Fear* (Basingstoke: Macmillan, 1983), p. ix and dust jacket.

Nor was there anything new about young people using consumption as a means of expressing their distinctiveness from adult society. Students, street gangs and other groups all used consumption – and non-consumption – to distinguish themselves from the children's world they were leaving and the adult world they were entering. During the post-war years, recalls Roy Hattersley, he and his fellow students at Hull University, 'believed – from the depth of our duffle-coats, corduroy trousers and long, striped scarves – that sartorial rebellion was the hallmark of integrity'.[25] At the same time, 'Teddy boys' adopted – and of course adapted – Edwardian upper-class clothing, horrifying the majority of the adult population with their tight 'drainpipe' trousers, drape jackets with velvet collars, bootlace ties, brightly coloured socks and thick crepe-soled shoes or 'brothel-creepers'.[26]

However, it was not only self-consciously recalcitrant groups such as these that used consumption to delineate themselves from adult society. So too did the great majority of young people who rebelled much more carefully and much more cautiously. It was common – one is tempted to say normal – for young people throughout the century to resist attempts at family outings, argue with their parents over what clothes to buy, and go with their friends to the local market, high street or shopping centre on a Saturday afternoon.

In a perceptive study of north London between the wars, Jerry White provides several examples of working-class girls quarrelling with their mothers over what clothes to purchase. May Purslowe, for instance, hated giving her mother her hard-earned wages so that she could buy her second-hand clothes.

> And this one particular day I said to her, 'I'm not giving you all my money, I'm gonna buy my own clothes.' And we went to Chapel Street, Islington market, and I bought a velvet skirt and a blouse. And when I came home, washed myself, dressed to go out, she says to me, 'And where do you think *you're* going?' I said, 'Well, I'm going out.' So she says, 'Oh are you?' And she said no more, she tore all these clothes off me.[27]

Others remember similar, albeit more sedate, altercations taking place 20, 30 and 40 years later. A South Wales man recalls trying to emulate 1950s' stars like Bill Haley:

> I remember buying a suit ... and it had like a metallic thread all the way through it, see, it was £5 this suit, and when my parents saw it they said, 'Oh yeah'. But when I went out it all lit up, the sunlight would hit it and oh![28]

It was a situation with which generation upon generation of young people will surely be able to empathize.

---

[25] Benson, *Consumer Society*, p. 166.

[26] S. Chibnall, 'Whistle and zoot: The changing meaning of a suit of clothes', *History Workshop*, 20, 1985.

[27] J. White, *The Worst Street in North London: Campbell Bunk, Islington, Between the Wars* (Routledge & Kegan Paul, 1986), p. 202.

[28] Museum of Welsh Life, 8203/1. See also S. Pixner, 'The Oyster and the Shadow', in L. Heron (ed.), *Truth, Dare or Promise: Girls Growing Up in the Fifties* (Virago, 1985); B. Tolley, ' "Let's Talk about Girls": Young Women and Consumption in the 1960s and early 1970s', University of Wolverhampton MA, 2001, pp. 40–3.

While there was nothing new about adult-adolescent acrimony, there was a significant increase in the material resources that young people were able to bring to the struggle. It was seen in the previous chapter that adolescent purchasing power increased between the wars, and increased again during the second half of the century. David Fowler points to the changes that occurred during the inter-war years. It appears, he argues, 'that a distinctive teenage culture, based largely upon access to commercialised leisure and the conspicuous consumption of leisure products and services aimed at the young, was in evidence in British towns and cities by the 1930s'.[29] However, it is more commonly accepted that the crucial changes took place in the years following, rather than preceding, the Second World War. In his classic study, *Teenage Consumer Spending in 1959*, Mark Abrams concluded that,

> the quite large amount of money at the disposal of Britain's average teenager is spent mainly on dress and on goods which form the nexus of teenage gregariousness outside the home. In other words, this is distinctive teenage spending for distinctive teenage ends in a distinctive teenage world.[30]

However, one should not make too much of adult–adolescent acrimony. Sometimes parents' views and children's views coincided – or at least converged – reasonably closely. By the end of the century, mobile phones were 'the latest fashion accessory in the school play-ground. Whilst youngsters consider mobiles a status symbol to rank alongside the latest training shoe, parents view them as a safety measure to help them keep track of their children.'[31]

Middle-aged and elderly spending also became a matter of public debate. Statisticians and market researchers interested in consumer behaviour began to investigate the material circumstances of the middle-aged (and other age groups). In a pioneering study of the relationship between age, income, saving and wealth, Harold Lydall concluded that, 'As people pass from youth to middle-age, and thence to old age and senility, their economic behaviour passes through various phases. The pattern of these changes is sufficiently stable in any one country to warrant our dignifying it with the title of an "economic life cycle".'[32]

When market researchers rediscovered the middle-aged market in the 1980s, they were struck by the fact that 'people in the ten or fifteen years before retirement are not only physically and economically very active; they also have greater discretionary spending power, since their mortgages are paid off and their children grown up'.[33] The trouble, from the market researchers' point of view, was that the middle-aged seemed inclined to use their new-found spending power for saving rather than for spending.[34]

---

[29] D. Fowler, *The First Teenagers: The Lifestyle of Young Wage-Earners in Interwar Britain* (Woburn Press, 1995), p. 110.

[30] M. Abrams, *Teenage Consumer Spending in 1959 (Part II): Middle Class and Working Class Boys and Girls* (London Press Exchange, 1961), p. 5. 'Good ale and hearty men', *Daily Mail*, 5 April 1950.

[31] *Daily Mail*, 6 January 2000.

[32] H. Lydall, 'The life cycle in income, saving, and asset ownership', *Economica*, 23, 1955, pp. 132–3. See also J. Benson, *Prime Time: A History of the Middle Aged in Twentieth-Century Britain* (Harlow: Longman, 1997), Ch. 4. S.B. Rowntree had drawn attention to the working-class life cycle in *Poverty: A Study of Town Life* (Macmillan, 1902).

[33] H. Lind, 'Media research and the affluent middle aged', *ADMAP*, February 1981, p. 66.

[34] S.F. Buck, 'The affluent middle aged: Spending and saving patterns', *ADMAP*, March 1981, p. 129.

In truth, the middle-aged used their surplus income both for saving and for spending. Concerned about their long-term financial security, they decided, many of them, to do what they could to build up assets that they would be able to draw upon in their old age. It was reported in the early 1980s, for instance, that those in their late forties and early fifties possessed building society savings almost 10 per cent higher than those of the population as a whole – while those in their late fifties and early sixties had savings almost 80 per cent greater than those of the population as a whole.[35]

Concerned not to forgo their short-term pleasures, the middle-aged also decided, many of them, to do what they could to acquire the goods and services which they had been unable to afford in the past, and which they would probably be unable to afford in the future. It was a response that was founded upon the growing material prosperity that occurred during the second half of the century.[36] A report published in the late 1990s, suggested, according to *The Times*, that,

> today's 40-year-olds are refusing to grow old gracefully, frequently behaving like overgrown teenagers. Despite family and professional commitments, they are more likely to spend spare money on a foreign holiday than on their house and more likely to buy casual clothes from Gap than Marks & Spencer.[37]

This was not entirely journalistic hyperbole. Those born around the middle of the century recognised the shift that was taking place. 'Since we've been in our forties and fifties', explained a supply teacher from the West Midlands, 'and particularly since the boys have been to university and so forth, we've been able to go on holiday on our own and have better holidays in nice hotels.'[38] A 60-year-old widow whose husband died in 1988 concluded:

> Middle age is the best time of my life. Having sort of reared a family, struggled financially at the beginning of the marriage and being in a comfortable position … I suppose at the moment I feel at times I can feel a bit selfish 'cause there's only me and I spoil myself and I do what I want to do.[39]

The elderly too displayed distinctive patterns of spending and saving. Indeed, commentators frequently found it difficult to avoid stereotypical images of frailty, incapacity and introspection when considering the economic and social impact of an ageing population. It would mean, predicted the demographer David Glass in the mid-1930s, 'that fewer toys would be wanted; but on the other hand it may result in a greater demand for armchairs and slippers; and it may mean an increase in the amount spent on pensions, but also a decrease in the aggregate cost of education'.[40] It would mean, concluded the sociologist Mark Abrams at the end of the Second World War,

---

[35] M. Hughes, 'Selling savings products to the older investor', *ADMAP*, April 1981. See also Benson, *Prime Time*, p. 73; *Social Trends*, 12, 1982, p. 113.

[36] But see, for example, Arbiter, 'Fashions for Men', *Observer*, 10 March 1912.

[37] *The Times*, 15 July 1999.

[38] Wolverhampton Oral History Project, Interview 20.

[39] Wolverhampton Oral History Project, Interview 48.

[40] Cited in P. Thane, *Old Age in English History: Past Experiences, Present Issues* (Oxford: Oxford University Press, 2000), p. 339.

that 'nurses and undertakers, slipper and armchair manufacturers would do well, but that more "essential" forms of production were likely to wither'.[41]

Stereotyping aside, it is easier to generalize about the consumer behaviour of the elderly than of those at earlier stages of the life course. This may seem somewhat surprising, since it was seen in the previous chapter how important it is to avoid regarding old people as an undifferentiated mass.[42] Nevertheless, the heterogeneity of the elderly had less impact than one would expect upon their spending and saving. It is true that the 1960s and 1970s saw the emergence of a growing minority of old people who, as homeowners and recipients of occupational pensions, were able to live their final years in security and comfort. It was a development so striking that it led some commentators to reassess the relationship between age, spending and saving.

> The one-time commonplace of economic theory that older people are dissavers has not survived scrutiny; indeed they may save more than younger groups, not least because of the uncertain length of life ahead of them. Age in itself has little effect upon consumer demand once account is taken of differences in income and household composition.[43]

However, this is to push the argument too far. There is the danger of conflating the experiences of a minority with those of the majority. The prosperous minority used their resources, as they always had, to remain independent, live comfortably and travel extensively. It was reported in the early 1980s, for instance, that this favoured few 'spent much of their additional money on better housing (which they usually own), on transport and vehicles (primarily on running a car) and on services (mainly hotel and holiday expenses)'.[44]

The less prosperous majority deployed their resources, as they always had, in efforts to keep warm, eat adequately and stay healthy. Poverty and poor mobility meant that old people, like poor people generally, continued to devote a high proportion of their spending to the purchase of fuel and food. Even in the early 1980s, those living in 'elderly' households remained 'over-spenders' on food and fuel, their expenditure on these two items alone accounting for 33 per cent of their budgets, compared to 27 per cent of 'non-elderly' budgets.[45] Old people continued to purchase such basic necessities more frequently, more expensively, and from a narrower range of outlets than those who were younger and/or more mobile and more affluent.

Conventional stereotyping of the elderly tends therefore to impede, rather than promote, our understanding of the relationship between age, spending and saving. Old age should be associated not so much with frailty and incapacity as with poverty. Old people were less likely to spend their declining years worrying about which slippers to wear and which armchair to sit in than about how to keep warm and how to get enough to eat.

---

[41] Cited in J. Macnicol, *The Politics of Retirement in Britain, 1878–1948* (Cambridge: Cambridge University Press, 1998), p. 262. See also, 'The old in the gold', *Daily Mail*, 6 September 1950.

[42] Thane, *Old Age*, p. 15.

[43] Thane, *Old Age*, p. 490.

[44] M. Abrams, 'Some background facts', *Journal of the Market Research Society*, 251, 1983, p. 222. Also *Age Concern on Pensioner Incomes* (HMSO, 1971).

[45] Abrams, 'Background facts', pp. 219–20.

GENDER, SAVING AND SPENDING

It goes without saying too that consumption varied according to gender. Nobody, presumably, would suggest that men and women enjoyed the same economic power, or that they used the economic power they possessed to purchase the same goods and services. Indeed, it will be recalled from the previous chapter that Sara Horrell concluded that, 'Women's position has improved if the end of the century is compared to its beginning, but there has been little change in women's position relative to men's over the last few decades.'[46] Accordingly, it is the aim of this section of the chapter to explore the use that men and women made of the – unequal – economic resources that they had at their disposal. It will suggest that while changes in consumption offered women new economic power, new social possibilities and new opportunities for improving their social status, it did so within limits that reinforced, rather than challenged, their conventional, subordinate position in society.

There is no denying that women's control of consumption changed significantly during the course of the century. However, it was seen in the previous chapter that it is easy to exaggerate the scale of the change. It can be tempting, in particular, to overestimate the dependence of early twentieth-century women and the independence of their late twentieth-century successors. It is a temptation that needs to be avoided. Recent research reveals the power that many early twentieth-century women of all classes exercised over domestic management, family behaviour and neighbourhood values.[47] Contemporary and near-contemporary investigation confirms the subordinate position in which many late twentieth-century women of all ages and all classes continued to find themselves whether they were at home, in the workplace or active in the wider world.[48]

Even when this misleading dichotomy is avoided, it remains difficult to identify and evaluate changes in women's power over consumption. There were a number of contradictory developments. Women maintained, and in some respects increased, the power they exercised with regard to the purchase of food and household goods. They retained their autonomy because, despite going out to work, the challenges of feminism and the introduction of equal pay legislation, the family division of labour remained fundamentally unaltered. Even when husbands, partners and children took an interest in what was bought, helped to carry the shopping or went to the shops on their own, the purchase of household necessities remained overwhelmingly a female responsibility. It was women, not men, who bought the family's baking powder, scouring pads and toilet cleaners. Here then was a crucial paradox. It was continuing inequality in the distribution of domestic responsibilities that sustained women's power over certain key aspects of the family economy.[49]

---

[46] S. Horrell, 'Living standards in Britain 1900–2000: Women's century?', *National Institute Economic Review*, 172, 2000, p. 62.

[47] See, for example, Lord Northcliffe's tribute to female newspaper readers in the *Observer*, 3 November 1912.

[48] See, for example, C. Chinn, *They Worked All Their Lives: Women of the Urban Poor in England, 1880–1939* (Manchester: Manchester University Press, 1988); E. Roberts, *A Woman's Place: An Oral History of Working-Class Women 1890–1940* (Oxford: Blackwell, 1984).

[49] Benson, *Consumer Society*, pp. 68–71, 182–3.

Women increased their power for the very obvious reason that spending on food and basic household goods increased significantly during the course of the century. Spending (at 1997 prices) on household food virtually doubled between 1900 and 1995, spending on fuel and lighting grew nearly four times – and spending on housing increased more than seven times. However, the power that women enjoyed by virtue of their control over these aspects of consumption did not go unchallenged. It was weakened by the operation of Engel's Law which suggested, it will be recalled, that as incomes rose, the proportion (as opposed to the amount) of family income spent on food tended to fall. This, it was seen earlier in the chapter, was exactly what happened. The proportion of consumer expenditure devoted to food declined, from 28–30 per cent during the first 30 years of the century, to 25 per cent in 1950 and 1960, 17 per cent in 1980, and barely 10 per cent by the end of the century.

Women's power was weakened too because as incomes rose, shopping became less burdensome and other family members began to take more of an interest in consumption. They made their likes and dislikes increasingly clear, and involved themselves more and more actively at the point of purchase. It was claimed in the late 1960s, for instance, that 'husbands helped with shopping in 8 per cent of cases every day or most days and helped "regularly" with shopping 35 per cent of the time'.[50] Fifteen years later, it was calculated that a quarter of all husbands were sent out occasionally to buy groceries, and that over a third of young husbands regularly accompanied their wives on major, grocery-buying expeditions.[51] Thus women shoppers found themselves in a double bind. They retained control over household consumption so long as economic constraints rendered it worrying, time-consuming and potentially embarrassing. They began to share responsibility with other family members as rising incomes, improving personal mobility and new forms of retailing made it easier to cope with the demands imposed by this aspect of domestic management. The so-called 'new man', insofar as he existed, had his roots in economic change as well as, if not more than, in ideological revelation.[52]

Moreover, when women went shopping for consumer durables and for medical, beauty and fashion products, they found themselves caught, once again, in something of a double bind. On the one hand, women of all ages and all classes turned with apparent enthusiasm to the growing volume and variety of household appliances, clothing, footwear, cosmetics, slimming aids and medical products that were targeted at them. Women increased their spending on traditionally 'female' products like toiletries, beauty aids and fashion goods. They were also able to bring considerable influence to bear upon the purchase of 'domestic' durables such as curtains, carpets, vacuum cleaners, washing machines and dishwashers. Indeed, some of the younger and better off began to play a more or less autonomous role in the purchase of 'masculine' and/or gender-free products such as cigarettes, alcohol, holidays and motor cars. 'A very few dual-income, high-earner couples', it was reported in 1992,

[50] R. Scott, *The Female Consumer* (Associated Business Programmes, 1976), p. 78.

[51] P. Davies, 'The shape of retail trading policies', *Retail & Distribution Management*, September–October 1982, p. 8.

[52] L. Ugolini, 'Ready-to-wear or made-to-measure? Consumer choice in the British menswear trade, 1900–1939', *Textile History*, 34, 2003.

'have been identified as employing independent control over their separate incomes.'[53]

This was always the exception rather than the rule. Indeed, women were never able to exercise much influence over the purchase of more 'masculine', more costly and less overtly 'domestic' products such as motor cycles, motor cars, television sets and video recorders. Whatever their income and however determined they were, women found it difficult – and for many years impossible – to secure credit on acceptable terms.[54] It is no surprise therefore to find it reported in 1976 that there was 'more family involvement, particularly by the husband, in those purchase decisions where the product is perceived of as important to the family as a whole, or is more expensive and less frequently purchased'.[55]

Moreover, it is surprising how many married women were able to purchase medical, beauty, fashion and other products only with the approval and/or financial support of their husbands. It remained more common than some commentators suppose for women to have to ask their husbands whenever they wished to spend money on anything for themselves. Even when middle-class couples operated shared bank accounts, it was often the husband who remained firmly in control. A Lancaster woman recalls that during the 1950s her husband had his salary paid straight into their joint account, an arrangement which did not cause her any difficulties because, she explained, 'whatever I wanted, I just asked and I got it'.[56]

There was surprisingly little change during the following 40–50 years. A number of studies published in the late 1980s, for instance, revealed the resilience of long-standing attitudes and practices. One investigation showed that women often paid for child care entirely out of their own earnings; another reported that even though women referred to the importance of having control over their 'own money', their earnings tended to end up in the overall family budget. Jane Lewis found it difficult to contain her indignation:

> The fact that women have both a differential access to resources entering the
> household and a differential command over them is given graphic illustration
> by the repeated finding that many battered wives find themselves better off
> drawing state benefits than living with their husbands.[57]

ETHNICITY, SAVING AND SPENDING

Ethnicity was just as important, and often just as visible, as gender. Indeed, as one would expect, contemporaries remarked time, time and time again on the fact that

---

[53] J. Lewis, *Women in Britain since 1945: Women, Family, Work and the State in the Post-War Years* (Oxford: Blackwell, 1992), p. 102.

[54] For example, *Observer*, 9 March, 5 October 1924; T. Thompson, *Edwardian Childhoods* (Routledge & Kegan Paul, 1981), p. 24; S. Badger, 'Consumption and the Emancipation of Women? Household Appliances and Working-Class Women: The Black Country', University of Wolverhampton MA, 1997, pp. 29–30.

[55] Scott, *Female Consumer*, pp. 123–4, 144.

[56] University of Lancaster, 'Social and Family Life in Preston', Lancaster and Barrow, Mrs A4L, p. 54.

[57] Lewis, *Women in Britain*, p. 102.

those from minority ethnic communities were characterized, *inter alia*, by their distinctive – not to say disturbing – patterns of consumption. They dressed differently, they ate differently, and they had different tastes in music.

First impressions frequently concentrated upon dress. 'I don't think I ever saw a Jew until we moved to Bacon Street', recalls East Ender Arthur Harding. 'Suddenly you saw them everywhere. Hundreds of thousands had come to England in the 1890s and you would still see them coming from the London docks: they came in horse brakes and some of them had white sheepskin coats.'[58] Fifty years later, *Punch* reported on the early years of large-scale West Indian immigration. It concluded that although the coloured man

> has put his original costume behind him and adopted the main lines of European dress, the clothes he actually wears have a style of their own which have only a remote resemblance to that of Savile Row. In England, of course, this divergence is more marked than it would be in the United States, for most coloured men wear adaptations not of English, but of American clothes; but even those they wear with a difference, and that difference is not due to ignorance but to deliberate intention.[59]

The judgements passed on minority groups when they became more settled tended, not unnaturally, to combine an appraisal of consumption with a broader assessment of income, status, attitudes and behaviour. When a Lancashire miner described the community in which he worked during the 1920s, he recalled that many families 'had lodgers, mainly young Irishmen – single men who'd come over for seasonal work, and stayed. Many of these men are now assimilated in the area. They're married and they're all Lancashire men in effect.'[60] When a Bristol woman complained in the mid-1960s about the deterioration of the council estate on which she lived, she remarked that,

> The old nice neighbours have gone and they put anyone up here now. People keep the fronts of their houses so bad. I don't mind immigrants; they have got to live somewhere. The lady down the road is a very nice person, keeps her children nice. They are much better than some of these English; they know their manners.[61]

Nonetheless, there was one group that the majority population always tended to assess very much in terms of their consumption. Tony Sewell suggested, it will be recalled, that by the end of the century, youth culture, with its emphasis on consumption goods, was more harmful than racism to black pupils' prospects of educational success.[62] His views were taken up and given considerable prominence. 'Returning to the important points made by Tony Sewell,' concluded an *Independent* columnist in

---

[58] R. Samuel, *East End Underworld: Chapters in the Life of Arthur Harding* (Routledge & Kegan Paul, 1981), p. 125.

[59] Chibnall, 'Whistle and zoot', p. 80.

[60] C. Forman, *Industrial Town: Self Portrait of St Helens in the 1920s* (Paladin, 1979), p. 33.

[61] A.H. Richmond, *Migration and Race Relations in an English City: A Study in Bristol* (Oxford: Oxford University Press, 1973), p. 159.

[62] Sewell, *Black Masculinities*.

2000, 'it is interesting to note that he pinpoints money and consumer goods as black youth's overriding interests.' 'Is it a paradox or a truism that those at the bottom of the capitalist pyramid are the ones most exclusively focused on their role as consumers and least concerned with developing their role as creators?'[63] Others chose to put the relationship between youth, ethnicity and consumption more positively: 'from boardroom levels young black Brits are seen to be "punching above their weight" in the marketplace: why? Because they are regarded as style gurus when it comes to fashion.'[64]

Whatever the validity of such stereotyping, it is important – once again – to avoid confusing the experiences of the young and visible with those of the older and less visible. It is true that ethnic communities were disproportionately young. But they were also disproportionately poor: and if we are to generalize about ethnic minority consumption, it can only be done by recognizing the realities of day-to-day life. The consumption behaviour of Britain's immigrant communities was shaped less by style and fashion than it was by uncertainty, insecurity and poverty.[65] It was seen in the previous chapter that, even at the end of the century, those from ethnic minority communities remained particularly prone to unemployment, and when in employment to low levels of pay – as well as, of course, to other forms of economic, social and cultural disadvantage. It is not surprising therefore that such groups, like the poor generally, were less likely than other sections of society to apply their resources to saving, and more likely to use them for the purchase of basic necessities.

Those from ethnic minority communities certainly saved less than those from the majority population. Even among settled immigrants, such as Italians in the 1920s, very few were sufficiently well off to be able to save, and of those who could few kept their savings in banks.[66] Anthony Richmond's investigation of race relations in Bristol during the mid-1960s confirmed not only that immigrants were less likely to save than the English-born, but also that their lack of thrift was due primarily to the economic circumstances in which they found themselves. However, he drew a sharp distinction between the Irish and those from India, Pakistan and the West Indies. Many of the former, he reported, earned relatively high incomes, sent money home and saved a substantial proportion of their earnings. Many of the latter 'were in unskilled occupations, working shifts and paying high rents. Out of their earnings they were sending substantial sums of money back to their former countries and also, in many cases, trying to save money.'[67]

When *Social Trends* began to collect information about ethnic minority expenditure at the end of the century, it found that those from the Indian subcontinent, in particular, were 'under-spenders' on 'luxuries' and 'over-spenders' on 'necessities'.

[63] D. Orr, 'The culture consuming us all', *Independent*, 22 August 2000.

[64] C. Arnot, 'Altered images', *The Guardian*, 31 October 2001.

[65] R. Glasser, *Growing Up in the Gorbals* (Glasgow: Chatto & Windus, 1986), p. 47. Also Museum of Welsh Life, 5958, p. 15.

[66] C.A. Volante, 'Identities and Perceptions: Gender, Generation and Ethnicity in the Italian Quarter, Birmingham, c1891–1938', University of Wolverhampton PhD, 2001, p. 110.

[67] Richmond, *Migration*, p. 94. See also M. Phillips and T. Phillips, *Windrush: The Irresistible Rise of Multi-Racial Britain* (HarperCollins, 1999), pp. 97, 99; S. Patterson, *Dark Strangers: A Study of West Indians in London* (Pelican, 1965), p. 312.

Using material from the Office for National Statistics' family expenditure survey, it revealed that between 1997 and 1999, Pakistani and Bangladeshi households spent less than half as much as other households on leisure goods and services, but practically a quarter more on the purchase of food.[68]

CLASS, SAVING AND SPENDING

The discussion of poverty, saving and spending leads inevitably to a consideration of the relationship between class, saving and spending. It was argued in the previous chapter, it will be recalled, that an awareness of class divisions remains fundamental to the proper understanding of Britain's twentieth-century social history. It seems almost perverse, it was concluded, to deny the role that social class played – and continues to play – in determining people's economic, social and cultural life chances.

In all events, it can be shown that there was a clear correlation between class and saving. However, it was a relationship that displayed signs both of convergence and of diversity. On the one hand, the middle class and working class both recognized the need for saving, both began to save with some of the same institutions, and both began to set aside more and more of their income in anticipation of their future needs. On the other hand, the middle class and the working class continued to save in different ways and, of course, to save on very different scales. The working class, their 'betters' always felt, needed to be taught the virtues of thrift and foresight. Poor Law Guardian, the Countess of Carlisle warned in 1906, 'should not promote the love of finery, which prevailed too much among [working-class] girls'.[69]

Certainly, it was hard to make saving exciting. As a *Sunday Times* columnist pointed out in 1997, 'As headlines go, "Consumers indulge in an orgy of saving" does not quite have the ring to it.'[70] As Marcel van der Linden explained in a scholarly volume on mutual benefit societies published in the previous year, it was remarkable how labour historians had 'virtually overlooked an essential aspect of workers' lives: their constant struggle for protection from threats to their way of life, such as illness, unemployment, disability, and old age'.[71]

Nonetheless, the middle class and the working class both realized the desirability of saving.[72] By the time they reached middle age, if not before, most people, whatever their class background, recognized the need for financial security and stability.[73] In a 1920s' study of how 'working-men's wives', coped with low or irregular housekeeping income, Mrs B revealed that, 'it is very difficult, well-nigh impossible, to *save* for the future, but I still hope for the best always, and perhaps when the children are able to

[68] *Social Trends*, 2000, p. 100. See also R. Lennox, J. Carter and L. Henderson, *Housing Association Tenants: A Survey of Current and Recent Tenants (in England)* (HMSO, 1991), p. 204.

[69] *Observer*, 5 August 1906. Also *Newcastle Evening Chronicle,* 10 September 1905; *Royal Commission on Income Tax*, 1919, pp. 106–7.

[70] D. Smith, 'Save, save, save: The cry of sensible Britain', *The Sunday Times*, 14 September 1997.

[71] M. van der Linden (ed.), *Social Security Mutualism: The Comparative History of Mutual Benefit Societies* (Berne: Peter Lang, 1996), p. 11.

[72] There were regional differences. Mass-Observation, 3089, 'Notes on the Cost of Living', 1949, p. 3.

[73] Benson, *Prime Time*, p. 149.

help later on, it won't be so hard'.[74] By the end of the century, most people were only too well aware that the state was unlikely to provide the security and stability they were looking for. 'I suppose I'm one of the great crowd that keeps putting it off', observed an early middle-aged architect. But 'it's something that I'm beginning to … think about.'[75] A cleaner in her early fifties agreed.

> I should imagine people you know that are coming up to retirement age that are worried if they haven't made enough provisions. But as I say when we was younger and my husband was twenty-two or even when he was forty he did take another pension scheme out, to provide so we've always got this – we want to live in the lifestyle that we've been used to living in when we get older.[76]

Nor is it always appreciated that both the middle class and the working class made do and mended. A Newcastle-upon-Tyne woman working as a domestic servant in the 1920s was surprised that her employers had their clothes repaired. 'You'd think they['d] just get new ones, but they didn't.'[77] Both the middle class and the working class also began to place their savings with some of the same institutions. The convergence can be seen most clearly in the rapid expansion of the building society movement. The number of building society share accounts grew from half a million at the beginning of the century to 30 million in the 1990s[78] – an expansion which simply could not have taken place were it not for the societies' popularity across all major sections of society. It was found during the late 1970s, for example, that just under 20 per cent of those from social classes A and B, and just over 20 per cent of those from social classes D and E, possessed building society accounts.[79] A key feature of the Staffordshire Building Society, claimed its official historian in the late 1970s,

> is that it has many more account holders for its assets than most other societies. This is because of the tradition of dealing more with the man in the street, who needs a convenient place for his small savings, than concentrating on attracting money solely from the relatively wealthy members of the community.[80]

This does not mean, however, that claims about a correlation between class and saving should be disregarded. Convergence should certainly not be mistaken for homogeneity. The middle class and the working class continued to save in distinctively different ways. Such differences had obvious historical antecedents. 'In the years before the First World War,' explains Charles More, 'Britain had evolved mechanisms of great sophistication for mobilising the savings of middle-class investors and placing them in fixed-interest securities.'[81] The problem was that it took the country's

---

[74] P. Pollock (ed.), *Working Days* (Cape, 1926), p. 263.

[75] Wolverhampton Oral History Project, Interview 30.

[76] Wolverhampton Oral History Project, Interview 23.

[77] Northumbria County Record Office, T.84.

[78] A.B. Atkinson, 'Distribution of Income and Wealth', in Halsey (ed.), *British Social Trends*, p. 359.

[79] *Social Trends*, 1982, p. 113.

[80] J. Hunter, *The First £100 Million: A History of the Staffordshire Building Society* (Wolverhampton: Staffordshire Building Society, c. 1978), p. 69. Cf. S. Regan, 'Saving grace', *The Guardian*, 7 March 2001.

[81] C. More, *The Industrial Age: Economy and Society in Britain 1750–1985* (Harlow: Longman, 1989), p. 312.

mainstream financial institutions many years to develop mechanisms capable of mobilizing working-class savings to anything like the same extent.[82]

Critics of the financial services industry complained constantly about its failure to cater for small savers – and spokespeople for the industry complained constantly about the government's failure to set an appropriate fiscal framework. The debate rumbled on. In the late 1990s, for example, the director of the Low Pay Unit criticized the industry for offering poor families less choice and less value than it did its better-off customers, and the Institute of Fiscal Studies reported that only 1 per cent of lone parents were in possession of a TESSA (tax exempt savings account). The savings director of Abbey National responded by urging the government 'to target substantial tax relief to lower income families through their pay packets'. If this were done, he predicted, 'then these new accounts could become a huge phenomenon'.[83]

It is not surprising therefore that when working people decided to save, they continued for many years to do so in distinctively working-class ways, using distinctively working-class institutions.[84] 'Now what about the worker's ways of saving?' wondered Ferdynand Zweig in his 1952 study of *The British Worker*. The British working man, he had no doubt, liked to save communally. 'He prefers saving through a friendly society, trade union, or club to saving alone at home, and still less than in a bank or Post Office. He likes to know that he is supported in his saving by his fellows, and that he helps them in his turn.'[85]

The class nature of saving remained resolutely impervious to broader economic, social and cultural developments. The same report that revealed the building societies' cross-class popularity in the late 1970s stressed too the persistence of class differences.

> The type of savings held varies with social class. Unit trusts, stocks and shares were the most popular form of savings by adults in households where the head of the household was in a higher or intermediate management or professional occupation; whereas Trustee Savings Bank accounts were the most popular type of holding in households headed by a semi-skilled, unskilled, or casual manual worker, state pensioner, or widow.[86]

Such differences persisted. 'Nearly all people in class AB have a bank account compared with only two-thirds of those in class DE', concluded *Social Trends* in 1993. 'The difference is even more marked for unit and investment trusts; people in class AB are nearly ten times more likely to hold them than people in class DE.'[87] Three years later, the Weinberg Committee reported that 22 per cent of the population possessed less than £500 in savings – a sum not much more than a single week's income for a man on average full-time earnings.[88]

---

[82] *Observer*, 21 August 1927; 22 February 1930.

[83] T. Hunter, 'New savings plans could be popular in name only', *The Guardian*, 4 July 1997.

[84] Museum of Welsh Life, 8203/1.

[85] F. Zweig, *The British Worker* (Penguin, 1952), p. 172. Also *Observer*, 18 November 1921; 21 August 1927. Cf. R. Lewis and A. Maude, *The English Middle Classes* (Penguin, 1953), p. 173.

[86] *Social Trends*, 1982, p. 113.

[87] *Social Trends*, 1993, p. 90.

[88] A. Garrett, 'Future fear makes us all squirrels now', *Observer*, 14 September 1997; Regan, 'Saving grace'.

The class nature of saving becomes more visible still when we switch our attention from the well-known, formal, readily quantifiable indicators of savings held in building societies, savings banks, trade unions, pension schemes, stocks, shares, TESSAs and other financial vehicles. Many working people pursued a series of less well-known, less formal, and much less quantifiable strategies for setting aside resources against their future needs.[89] They saved in ways which can elude all but the most perceptive of commentators. During the early years of the century, the poor often practised what has been dubbed 'thrift in reverse', buying 'luxury items like furniture, clothing, domestic utensils and ornaments in the summer, which they pawned off one by one in the winter to help tide over bad times'.[90] When they shopped at the Co-op, the better-off members of the working class sometimes used their dividends to build up share accounts held by the society. 'Members tended to look upon withdrawable shares in much the same light as a savings bank account and to draw upon them when needing cash.'[91] They accumulated considerable sums. In 1911, Co-operative Society members held £33.2 million of share capital, a sum equivalent to £12.60 per member, and £3.70 per working-class household.[92]

Rather than attempting to put money aside for the long term, working people of all kinds tended to look to short-term, more immediately realizable objectives. In his mid-century study of working-class life, Ferdynand Zweig claimed, for example, that young men's most frequent reasons for saving were to get married, to buy clothes, to go on holiday and to prepare for Christmas. 'For a married man with a home of his own the most popular objects for saving are again: clothes, holidays, Christmas, things for the children, and things for the house; and that never comes to an end.'[93]

Rather than depositing their money in the post office or letting their dividends accumulate, many working-class savers hid what money they had under the mattress or among their underwear.[94] 'Life is very much a week-by-week affair, with little likelihood of saving a lump sum to "fall back on" ', confirmed Richard Hoggart in his celebrated recreation of working-class culture between the wars. 'There may be a tin box on the mantelpiece in which savings for the holiday are put, but this is not usual.'[95] Even those who were saving for the medium and long term, frequently did so

---

[89] See, for instance, P. Johnson, *Saving and Spending: The Working-Class Economy in Britain 1870–1939* (Oxford: Clarendon Press, 1985); J. Benson, 'Working-class consumption, saving, and investment in England and Wales, 1851–1911', *Journal of Design History*, 9, 1996.

[90] Cited in Benson, 'Working-class consumption', p. 88. See also V. Nicolson and S. Smith, *Spend, Spend, Spend* (Fontana, 1978), pp. 143, 153; W. Woodruff, *The Road to Nab End: An Extraordinary Northern Childhood* (Abacus Press, 2002), pp. 44–5; J. Benson, 'Coalminers and Consumption: The Cannock Chase Coalfield, 1893 and 1926', in A. Knotter, B. Altena and D. Damsma (eds), *Labour, Social Policy, and the Welfare State* (Amsterdam: Stichting beheer IISG, 1997), p. 69.

[91] Mass-Observation, 2460, 'Co-operative Users in London', 1946, p. 10; P.H.J.H. Gosden, *Self-Help: Voluntary Associations in Nineteenth-Century Britain* (Batsford, 1973), p. 197.

[92] Benson, 'Working-class Consumption', p. 89. See also Roberts, *A Woman's Place*, p. 164.

[93] Zweig, *British Worker*, p. 170.

[94] *Observer*, 16 August, 1903; 3 February 1924.

[95] R. Hoggart, *The Uses of Literacy: Aspects of Working-Class Life with Special Reference to Publications and Entertainments* (Penguin, 1957), p. 44.

by hiding cash somewhere about the house.[96] Indeed, one continues to be struck by the fact that when old people are burgled, they are often robbed of substantial savings because they, like so many working-class people before them, have hidden their money in the bedroom or in a vase on the mantelpiece.[97]

There was an equally close correlation between class and spending. It was a relationship that displayed, once again, signs both of convergence and of diversity. On the one hand, the middle class and the working class both valued consumption, both devoted increasing resources to it, and both began to purchase similar products, in similar ways from similar suppliers. On the other hand, the middle class and working class continued to devote unequal resources to consumption, and continued to consume in their own ways, displaying an unyielding determination to patronize the suppliers that they preferred.

There never seemed much doubt about the cross-class inclination to consume. The problem, most observers believed, was that while the working class were only too keen on consumption, they never learned to do so with intelligence and discretion. This disdain for popular consumption is most revealing. The literary critic John Carey has produced a highly effective dissection of early twentieth-century intellectual attitudes towards the 'masses'. The purpose of modernist writing, he argued, was to preserve the intellectuals' seclusion from ordinary people, with their absurd liking for suburban homes, tabloid newspapers, tinned food and plastic toys.[98] The late twentieth-century press was unable to contain its contempt for soccer players, football pools winners and National Lottery winners without the breeding or education to know how to spend their new-found riches.[99]

It was widely believed that such class animosity – and class anxiety – was grounded in economic convergence, and that economic convergence exercised a profound impact upon consumption behaviour. 'Although many of the upper classes are as wealthy as ever,' explained a *Daily Express* columnist in 2001, 'the working and middle classes have increased their own wealth, relatively, far more.' The result, he went on, was that,

> As many toffs can be found among the saboteurs as among the hunt. Cruising on the Heath has become smarter than cruising on a ship, now deemed deeply middle-class. Toffs are no longer arbiters of correct form. Power has shifted from hereditary to celebrity. The girl in pearls has been replaced by the girl in the altogether. If the Beckhams think it good taste to celebrate their wedding astride a gold throne, then no one will dare tell them otherwise.[100]

There was a large grain of truth amidst the journalistic hyperbole. Consumers, both middle class and working class, began to shop in the same stores, began to buy the same clothes, and began to acquire similar consumer durables. The process was already under way at the beginning of the century, with department stores, for instance,

---

[96] Roberts, *A Woman's Place*, p. 164; *Express and Star*, 18 May 1995.

[97] *Express and Star*, 1 January 1993; *Wolverhampton Ad News*, 3 May 2001.

[98] J. Carey, *The Intellectuals and the Masses: Pride and Prejudice Among the Literary Intelligentsia, 1880–1939* (Faber and Faber, 1992), esp. Preface, pp. 6–10, 21–2.

[99] Cf. 'Peer v Pensioner', *Daily Mail*, 1 April 2000.

[100] J. Gerard, 'The ins and outs of a new social revolution', *Daily Express*, 31 January 2001.

catering for a broader spectrum of customers than is sometimes supposed.[101] Between the wars, multiple stores based their entire business strategy upon targeting the working-class and lower middle-class market. 'The multiple shop was an innovation of the days of my youth,' recalls a Sheffield engineering worker: 'whereas previously the rich man had a tailor and the poor man bought his clothes off the peg, it became possible for Jack to be as well dressed as his Master, or very nearly.'[102]

The process accelerated from the 1950s onwards. 'The motor car, once a middle-class status symbol, now became a leveller, as ownership extended yearly to lower income groups', explains Sidney Pollard. Indeed, he goes on to argue that the levelling effect of car ownership was reinforced by the increasing ownership of a range of products: 'radio and television sets, by other electric and gas appliances, by furniture and furnishings in the home and even by clothes and fashion goods, particularly among the young'.[103] So it was that when John Goldthorpe and his collaborators studied the 'affluent workers' of Luton in the early 1960s, they concluded that consumption played a crucial role in concealing, if not dissolving, class distinctions.

> In the sphere of domestic consumption, at least, there was little evidence at all of any restricting influence being exerted by traditional working-class norms. Considering, for example, refrigerators and cars – two high-cost and characteristically 'middle-class' possessions – the extent of ownership proved to be roughly comparable between our manual and nonmanual samples: 58% of the former as against 56% of the latter had refrigerators and 45% as against 52% owned cars.[104]

This so-called embourgeoisement thesis has become a standard feature of many attempts to understand the social history of late twentieth-century Britain. It is now firmly embedded in a number of social history and sociology texts. Edward Royle states unequivocally in his *Modern Britain: A Social History 1750–1997* that, 'Since the late 1960s, when Goldthorpe's team published their findings, events have borne out their conclusions.'[105] What is significant, concludes James Obelkevich in *Understanding Post-War British Society*, was not so much that the working class was catching up with the middle class, but that, 'people in all classes were getting their first fridge or washing machine at much the same time. Affluence did not eliminate class differences: but it significantly reduced them. What the middle classes had, the working classes wanted, and often got.'[106]

---

[101] G. Crossick and S. Jaumain, 'The World of the Department Stores: Distribution, Culture and Social Change', in G. Crossick and S. Jaumain (eds), *Cathedrals of Consumption: The European Department Store, 1850–1939* (Aldershot: Ashgate, 1999), p. 25.

[102] S.R. Davey, *Recollections* (Sheffield: Sheffield Women's Printing, n.d.), p. 25. See also G. Orwell, *The Road to Wigan Pier* (Penguin, 1937), p. 79.

[103] S. Pollard, *The Development of the British Economy 1914–1980* (Arnold, 1983), p. 324. For the effect of the war, see Imperial War Museum, 009598/06, S. Fisher. Rationing ended in 1954.

[104] J. Goldthorpe, D. Lockwood, F. Bechhofer and J. Platt, *The Affluent Worker in the Class Structure* (Cambridge: Cambridge University Press, 1969), p. 39.

[105] Royle, *Modern Britain*, p. 153.

[106] J. Obelkevich, 'Consumption', in J. Obelkevich and P. Catterall (eds), *Understanding Post-War British Society* (Routledge, 1994), p. 149.

Obelkevich is correct. The reduction of class differences should not be mistaken for their elimination. Only somebody who never went shopping, never moved house, never took a holiday, never took an interest in sport, and never went out for a drink could doubt the relationship between class and consumption. Class identity, class anxiety and class aspiration continued to play an important, and sometimes decisive, role in determining the ways in which the people of Britain consumed the goods and services available to them.

The upper class, of course, were proud of the class character of their consumption. They knew perfectly well that their country houses, their shopping habits, their sporting interests, their 'seasons' in London and their holidays abroad all sent out signals about their wealth, power and status, and thus about their economic, social and cultural distance from the rest of the population. 'She was fortunate in acquiring by marriage or inheritance two houses admirably suited to her talents', explained the obituary of Anne, Countess of Rosse in 1992. Both her houses had 'a stage-set or film-set quality'.[107]

The middle class were just as proud of – albeit a good deal more anxious about – the class character of their consumption. They too recognized that the houses in which they lived, the sports they enjoyed, the holidays they took, the stores where they shopped, the clothes that they wore and the cars that they drove all sent out powerful signs about their taste, about their status and, not least, about their class identity.[108] 'Are you picnicking at Glyndebourne or shooting off to Bisley?' wondered a *Times* columnist in the spring of 1981. The well-to-do, he explained, 'use the longer daylight hours to extend the bounds of sociability'.[109]

Middle-class consumers were aware of – and sometimes became obsessed with – shopping in ways that reflected their class identity and/or the identity to which they and their families aspired. Some declined to shop at all. 'I haven't been in a shop for ten years', boasted one of Britain's 'truly wealthy' in the early 1970s: 'it's something I have never gone in for and I've always had someone to do it for me.'[110] But most middle-class consumers were only too happy to venture into the market place, where they long regarded chain stores and mail order selling with disapproval, enjoyed the deference they were shown at specialist shops, and were careful to discriminate between the various departments stores, supermarkets and superstores vying for their custom.

They knew that mail order and chain stores – especially the Co-op – catered primarily for the working class and lower middle class. Source after source reveals the skill with which middle-class shoppers appraised the acceptability of the outlets they were considering patronizing. 'What she decides depends on many things', explained a trade guide published in 1963: 'her age and social class, the importance of the

---

[107] H. Massingfield, (ed.), *The Daily Telegraph Fifth Book of Obituaries* (Pan Books, 1999), p. 170. See also Benson, *Consumer Society*, p. 205.

[108] So too did the ways in which they obtained credit. See P. Scott, 'The twilight world of interwar British hire purchase', *Past and Present*, 177, 2002. See the advertisement for the *Evening Standard* in the *Observer*, 21 December 1924.

[109] N. Wapshott, 'Are you picnicking at Glyndebourne or shooting off to Bisley?' *The Times*, 6 June 1981.

[110] R. Costello, 'The middle class planners' guide to wealth or how to reach the "As" ', *ADMAP*, June 1973, p. 185.

purchase, proximity to another centre, the pull of particular shops, even the mood of the moment.'[111] Price, the guide stressed time and again, was by no means the only factor that was taken into consideration.

> If the theory were not valid there would, for instance, be only one type of restaurant, i.e. the cheapest whereas, as we all realize, when a restaurant meal is sought the prospective client thinks not only in terms of price but also in terms of the other amenities which are on offer such as comfort, convenience, prestige and even snobbery.[112]

Department store managers knew what they were up against. Faced with the burgeoning competition of the multiples during the 1930s, they responded, some of them, by raising, not lowering, their prices. When a new general manager took over a store in Shrewsbury in 1934, he instructed his buyers to counter the chain store threat by spending half their budgets 'on high-grade merchandise which gave a good profit'.[113] As a spokesman for a leading Chester store explained five years later, 'People in this city are rather particular, and they do not like it to be known that they buy cheap stuff from the chains.'[114]

Specialist shops offered the necessary reassurance. Their combination of expert advice, long opening hours, free home delivery, generous credit facilities and obsequious service helped to confirm the class identity – and class superiority – of their customers. W. MacQueen Pope looked back nostalgically to the beginning of the century. It was a time, he recalled, when competition compelled shopkeepers to display as much obsequiousness as was humanly possible. 'On moving to a new district, or when a couple of newly wed Middle Class young people entered their home, there was a state of siege. Tradesmen of all kinds came to their door, begging their custom.'[115] A Brighton man recalls that when he started working at his parents' butcher's shop in the late 1930s, he was trained to be punctilious even when dealing with the working-class employees of middle-class customers. At the servants' entrance,

> I had to go to the door, knock and shout 'Butcher' – as they opened the door, always touch my forehead with no hat on or touch the peak of my cap. And this is how to address them: 'Good morning madam, is there anything you'd like this morning, would you like any steak, any chops, any part of meat, anything for the animals, and when would you like me to bring it back?'[116]

Middle-class shoppers remained careful to discriminate between the specialist stores, department stores, supermarkets, superstores and other outlets seeking their custom.[117]

---

[111] L.M. Harris, *Buyer's Market: How to Prepare for the New Era in Retailing* (Business Publications, 1963), p. 77.

[112] Harris, *Buyer's Market*, p. 151.

[113] *Smallwares and Accessories*, March 1939.

[114] *Smallwares and Accessories*, March 1939.

[115] Cited in M.J. Winstanley, *The Shopkeeper's World 1830–1914* (Manchester: Manchester University Press, 1983), p. 54.

[116] N. Griffiths, *Shops Book: Brighton 1900–1930* (Brighton: Queens Park Books, n.d.), p. 14.

[117] Ugolini, 'Ready-to-wear'.

I can see now that during the late 1950s and 1960s, my mother believed firmly that shopping at department stores like Stones of Romford and Roomes of Upminster helped to confirm our family's highly prized lower middle-class identity. By the end of the century, virtually everybody knew that Safeway was superior to Tesco, and Tesco more acceptable than Kwik Save. But Sainsbury stood supreme. Indeed, the ritual of the Friday-evening trip to Sainsbury seemed, in a curious way, to epitomise the 'companionable', dual-income, car-owning, middle-class family of late twentieth-century Britain.[118]

Working-class people too were aware of the relationship between class and consumption. They knew that consumption sent out powerful signals about their wealth, income, taste, status and class identity. They did their best therefore to shop in ways that felt safe and/or desirable – in ways, in other words, that befitted their class identity and/or aspirations. They avoided specialist shops, and for many years they tended to regard department stores and even supermarkets with a certain amount of suspicion. It was better, many felt, to pay more at 'working-class' stores where they felt comfortable than to risk embarrassment at 'middle-class' stores where they were not known and would not feel sure how to behave.[119]

Corner shops, Co-ops and chain stores all catered specifically for working-class shoppers. It is easy to be cynical about the accessibility, intimacy and warmth of the traditional corner shop as it is recreated so lovingly in contemporary comedy and soap opera. However, such nostalgia is not entirely a dramatic device. Corner shops were often run by families with backgrounds the same as, or similar to, those of their customers. Indeed, as Peter Mathias has pointed out, 'a working-class background and consciousness could be a precious asset. Such men knew their future markets instinctively and innately.'[120] By opening long hours, selling small quantities and offering credit, they retained an important, if unquantifiable, role in the domestic economy of a large number of working-class families. Richard Hoggart recalls:

> Many housewives remember how obliging their grocer was during the
> depression: he knew they had not enough money to pay off the bill each week,
> that he might have to wait for months; but if he did not serve them there would
> have been no customers, so he kept on and weathered it, or shut up shop after a
> time. Now he goes on providing an almost seven-days-a-week service, with
> Sunday morning as one of the busiest; and if you do find him shut, you can go
> round to the house-door.[121]

Such service survived rationing and the vicissitudes of the Second World War. A Wolverhampton woman recalls her grandmother making ice cream on Saturdays, the

---

[118] B. Fine, 'From Political Economy to Consumption', in Miller (ed.), *Acknowledging Consumption*, p. 148; G. Davies, 'Positioning, image and the marketing of multiple retailers', *International Review of Retail, Distribution and Consumer Research*, 2, 1992.

[119] M. Tebbutt, *Making Ends Meet: Pawnbroking and Working-Class Credit* (Leicester: Leicester University Press, 1983), p. 194.

[120] P. Mathias, *Retailing Revolution: A History of Multiple Retailing in the Food Trades Based on the Allied Suppliers Group of Companies* (Longman, Green and Co., 1967), p. 106.

[121] Hoggart, *Uses of Literacy*, p. 61.

day after her customers were paid: she 'used to charge at her own discretion, guessing the amount they had had and what the customer could afford'.[122] A Scottish woman looks back with regret to the 1950s:

> The service was very good: in the corner shop you always got a very friendly reception because you knew the person, because you were maybe in quite a lot. The shops in those days did not change hands as much as they do now, therefore you very often knew who owned the shop. Also, their assistants wouldn't chop and change as much as now.[123]

Co-ops too had been established by, and for, working-class people, and they too retained wide popularity until the middle of the century. In 1939, for example, the movement's 8.5 million members were responsible for over 20 per cent of all purchases of groceries and provisions in the country, and eight years later a Mass-Observation report revealed that 60 per cent of skilled workers in London still used the stores on a regular basis.[124] Thereafter, however, the movement tended to stagnate, so that by the mid-1990s the societies' turnover of nearly £8 billion accounted for only 4 per cent of the country's retail trade.[125]

The multiples expanded as the Co-ops declined. Already in existence at the beginning of the century, the chains of multiples opened almost a thousand new branches between the wars. Their efforts to target the working-class consumer were hugely successful. Indeed, some of the statistical evidence collected during the 1930s almost defies belief. Seebohm Rowntree and his collaborators conducted a census of those visiting Woolworth's, Marks & Spencer, and British Home Stores in York one June weekend in 1936. They concluded that the 'great majority' of those visiting the stores were 'working people' and that the Saturday figure of 46,000 visitors was 'equal to almost one-half of the total population of the city'.[126] These, and similar stores, provided easy access, cheap goods, attractive displays – and no pressure to buy. As a respondent explained to Mass-Observation in the early 1940s, 'They are a good system for the working class pocket. Their stuff is not for rich people's standards, but for the working man's family they make the money go further.'[127]

Even towards the end of the century, the poor consumed in ways that continued to distinguish them from the remainder of the population. A large-scale survey of shopping habits in Cardiff during the early 1980s confirmed, for instance, that those

---

[122] Black Country Museum, Shopping Survey, 1993, Mrs G.G. I owe this reference to Samantha Badger.

[123] P. Lyon, A. Colquhoun and D. Kinney, 'Food Shopping in the 1950s: The Social Construction of Customer Loyalty', CHORD Conference, University of Wolverhampton, September, 2002.

[124] Mass-Observation, 2460, 'A Report on People and the Co-op', 1947, pp. 3, 5, 40; J. Burnett, *Plenty and Want: A Social History of Food in England from 1815 to the Present Day* (Routledge, 1989), p. 260.

[125] J. Birchall, *The International Cooperative Movement* (Manchester: Manchester University Press, 1997), p. 84. Also L. Sparks, 'Consumer co-operation in the United Kingdom, 1945–1993', *Journal of Cooperative Studies*, 1994; J. Perkins and C. Freedman, 'Organisational forms and retailing development: The department and the chain store', *Service Industries Journal*, 19, 1999.

[126] B.S. Rowntree, *Poverty and Progress: A Second Social Survey of York* (Longman, Green and Co., 1941), pp. 218–19.

[127] Mass-Observation, 1532, 'Report on Shopping Habits (Part III)', 1942, p. 20.

living in 'retired' households were less likely than other groups to use supermarkets and superstores, and more likely to patronize nearby co-operative and independent stores. 'Price competition', it concluded, 'has allowed savings to be made by consumers who can use the larger stores, but has increased the relative disadvantage for those who depend upon smaller grocery outlets.'[128] *Social Trends* provided further statistical confirmation of the consumption paradox. It reported in 1995, for instance, that on the one hand, 'higher social groups spent a smaller proportion of their expenditure on food and fuel than those in the lower social groups but a larger proportion on housing'; and that on the other hand, 'Households headed by a retired or unoccupied person spent more than twice the proportion of their total household expenditure on fuel, light and power than those headed by a professional.'[129] It carried a report the following year on the class background of those buying tickets for the newly established National Lottery. 'The amount spent varied between the different social classes', it concluded: 'households headed by a skilled manual worker spent the most at an average of £3.13 a week.'[130] The Lottery, like many retail outlets, operated regressively. The Lottery redirected resources from those who needed them most to those who needed them least. Retail outlets, all too often, offered the greatest savings to those who needed them least, and the least savings to those who needed them most.

SPENDING, SAVING AND CONSUMER SOCIETY

It was seen at the beginning of the chapter how common it has become to turn to consumption as a means of describing and explaining many of the most crucial changes occurring in the social history of late twentieth-century Britain. It is not difficult to see why. There is no doubting that consumption became more important during the course of the century, and no doubting either that most groups in society set increasing store by their spending on goods and services, and by the status that they believed their purchases afforded them. This does not mean, however, that Britain became a consumer society. It has been seen, in particular, that spending and saving can be difficult to distinguish, and seen too that age, gender, ethnicity and social class continued to exercise a powerful influence upon people's experiences of consumption. It is doubtful, therefore, whether the use of an age, gender, ethnic and class-neutral term such as consumer society can possibly encompass the many complexities of modern British society. Britain is not, never has been – and probably never will be – best described as a consumer society.[131]

[128] C. Guy, 'The food and grocery shopping behaviour of disadvantaged consumers: Some results from the Cardiff Consumer Panel', *Transactions of the Institute of British Geographers*, 10, 1985, p. 181. Resale Price Maintenance was abolished in 1964.

[129] *Social Trends*, 1995, p. 104.

[130] *Social Trends*, 1996, p. 117.

[131] Benson, *Consumer Society*, pp. 233–5; J. Benson, 'Consumption and the consumer revolution', *Refresh*, 23, 1996, pp. 7–8.

3 HEALTH, ILL HEALTH AND GOOD HEALTH

HEALTH, FITNESS AND WELL-BEING

The study of health, like the study of consumption, has become increasingly popular in recent years. Spurred on by growing prosperity, advances in medical knowledge, the ageing of the 'baby boom' generation, the failings of the National Health Service and the munificence of the Wellcome Trust, students of twentieth-century Britain have begun to pay increasing attention to the social history of health. Turning their backs on the conventional 'history of medicine', with its celebratory accounts of sanitary progress and medical intervention, they are now examining the ways in which people's health has affected, and was affected by, broader social, cultural and economic developments. They have begun, in the words of F.B. Smith, 'to weigh the life chances of individuals, families and occupational sets by analysing variations in morbidity and mortality through time, and by attempting to reconstruct lay and professional notions of health and ill-health, the pursuit of the first and the acceptance and management of the latter'.[1] 'Health outcomes', concludes Rodney Lowe, 'can typically be better improved by expenditure on other services (e.g. the personal social services, housing).'[2]

Recognizing the validity of the adage that nothing is more important than one's health, a new generation of medical historians has attempted to reconstruct people's day-to-day experiences of health (ill health and good health). This raises more conceptual difficulties than one might imagine. Ideas about what it meant to be healthy or unhealthy not only varied between individuals and groups but also changed during the course of the century. Indeed, as the title of this chapter suggests, it has become increasingly common to distinguish between health, ill health and good health, the latter a category which often incorporates within it notions of fitness and well-being. At the beginning of the century, death rates were high and health was defined negatively, but not inappropriately, as 'the absence of disease and infirmity'. By the end of the century, health was routinely defined, in the words of the World Health Organization, as 'physical, mental, and social well-being, and not merely the absence of disease and infirmity'.[3]

---

[1] F.B. Smith, 'Health', in J. Benson (ed.), *The Working Class in England 1875–1914* (Croom Helm, 1984), p. 37. See also H. Jones, *Health and Society in Twentieth-Century Britain* (Harlow: Longman, 1994), p. 2.

[2] R. Lowe, *Financing Health Care in Britain Since 1939*, www.historyandpolicy.org/main/policy-paper-08.html. The classic statement remains T. McKeown, *The Modern Rise of Population* (Arnold, 1976).

[3] R. Fitzpatrick and T. Chandola, 'Health', in A.H. Halsey (ed.), *Twentieth-Century British Social Trends* (Basingstoke: Macmillan, 2000), p. 94.

Of course, it is recognized almost without exception that health (however defined) has improved immensely during the course of the twentieth century. 'The expansion of definitions and expectations of health that has occurred in recent years', explain Ray Fitzpatrick and Tarani Chandola, 'in many ways is the most striking testament to the improvements in health status that have taken place in Britain and other Western societies in the last 100 years.'[4] 'The changes to people's lives that have come about as a result of new medical technology', concludes Peter Waldron, 'have dealt effectively with one of Beveridge's five giants', the scourge of disease.[5] Even those suspicious of such medically-driven optimism would almost certainly concede the scale and significance of the improvement that has taken place. Few of us today would wish to go back to the days before the invention of antibiotics or the introduction of a vaccination against poliomyelitis; few of us today would know how to cope with a world in which one child in eight died in infancy, and both men and women could expect to die before they reached the age of 50.[6]

Nevertheless, neither increasing longevity, nor medical advances could conceal deep-seated anxieties about the nation's health. Improvements in life expectancy towards the beginning of the century coincided with concerns about the state of the 'race'; the establishment of the National Health Service in 1947 unleashed a torrent of pent-up demand for medical care.[7] There emerged by the end of the century a powerful, and apparently growing, feeling that mortality statistics presented a misleadingly optimistic picture of national well-being. It was important, it was felt, to distinguish between health, ill health and good health; and when considering health, ill health and good health, it was necessary to take account of both physical and psychological circumstances. And when taking account of physical and psychological circumstances, it was essential to take account of the distinction between mortality and morbidity – between death and sickness. It was possible, after all, that although people were living longer, they were living less healthily.[8]

In examining these and similar issues, every effort will be made to distinguish between health, ill health and good health, and to pay proper attention to both physical and psychological factors. This chapter will identify, so far as is possible, the major changes that took place in the health of the population, the factors that made such changes possible, and the impact that such changes had upon other aspects of social, economic and cultural life. It will be suggested that while there can be no doubting the long-term improvement in the health of the country, there can be no doubting either the persistence of stark and deeply entrenched inequalities. National statistics and long-term trends must not be allowed to conceal the role that age,

---

[4] Fitzpatrick and Chandola, 'Health', p. 94.

[5] P. Waldron, ' "The barbarians have not come": Europe's twentieth century', *History Today*, June 2000, pp. 51–2.

[6] Jones, *Health*, p. 196. Cf. Fitzpatrick and Chandola, 'Health', pp. 95, 97. Also *The Guardian*, 4 July 1988; *Daily Telegraph*, 12 July 2000.

[7] A. Davin, 'Imperialism and motherhood', *History Workshop*, 5, 1978; C. Webster, 'The Elderly and the Early National Health Service', in M. Pelling and R.M. Smith (eds), *Life, Death and the Elderly: Historical Perspectives* (Routledge, 1991).

[8] A. Hardy, *Health and Medicine in Britain since 1860* (Basingstoke: Palgrave, 2001), 'Introduction'.

gender, ethnicity and class (as well, of course, as individual attitudes and behaviour) have played in determining health, ill health and good health.

CHILD MORTALITY AND LIFE EXPECTANCY

The health of people in Britain improved tremendously between 1900 and 2000. This can be illustrated in a number of ways, but most tellingly perhaps by considering child mortality and life expectancy. At the beginning of the century, one child in eight died before reaching their first birthday, and the death rate from childhood diseases such as measles, diphtheria, scarlet fever and whooping cough stood at over 2,500 per million of the under-15 population. A hundred years later, children's health had been transformed. Fewer than one child in a hundred died before reaching their first birthday, and the death rate from childhood diseases had fallen to just three per million.[9] 'Infant death comes into our lives nowadays like a blinding explosion', wrote Edward Shorter in 1975. 'Losing a small child is one of the terrible personal disasters of modern times, a scalding that leaves permanent scars.'[10]

It is life expectancy that provides the clearest and most incontrovertible evidence of rising health standards. The introduction of compulsory registration of deaths means that mortality statistics have now been available for well over 150 years. Table 3.1 uses the information collected in this way to reveal the scale of the transformation that has taken place. It shows that life expectancy increased by practically 50 per cent during the course of the twentieth century: children born between 1901 and 1910 could expect to live for less than 55 years; their great-grandchildren born during the mid-1990s could expect to live for well over 70 years.

TABLE 3.1 LIFE EXPECTANCY AT BIRTH, ENGLAND, WALES AND SCOTLAND, 1901–96

Year of birth	Males	Females	Year of birth	Males	Females
England and Wales			*Scotland*		
1901–1910	48.5	52.4	1890–1900	44.7	47.4
1910–1912	51.5	55.4	1910–1912	50.1	53.2
1920–1922	55.6	59.6	1920–1922	53.1	56.4
1930–1932	58.7	62.9	1930–1932	56.0	59.5
1950–1952	66.4	71.5	1942–1944	59.8	64.6
1960–1962	68.1	74.0	1950–1952	64.4	68.7
1970–1972	69.0	75.3	1960–1962	66.2	72.0
1980–1982	71.0	77.0	1970–1972	67.3	73.7
1990–1992	73.4	79.0	1980–1982	69.1	75.3
1993–1995	74.1	79.4	1990–1992	71.3	77.1
			1996	72.0	77.7

Source: R. Fitzpatrick and T. Chandola, 'Health', in A.H. Halsey (ed.), *Twentieth-Century British Social Trends* (Basingstoke: Macmillan, 2000), p. 95.

---

[9] Jones, *Health*, pp. 4–5, 196–7.

[10] E. Shorter, *The Making of the Modern Family* (Collins, 1977), p. 199.

The increase in life expectancy was well known, its consequences regarded, by the end of the century, with concern as well as with pleasure and satisfaction. When the Office for National Statistics published *Britain 2000* in late 1999 (in time for the millennium celebrations), its editor anticipated that it would be used 'as a source book for those who want to know what happened at the beginning of the century'. In reviewing the book, *The Guardian* drew particular attention to the demographic transformation it revealed.

> The most dramatic change they have identified is that the nation is in the midst of a serious ageing *problem* [my italics]. In 1901 the average man lived to 45 while women could expect to last until the ripe old age of 49. Ten decades later and the figures shot up to 74 and 79 respectively, with the proportion of the population aged 50 and over nearly doubling from one in six in 1901 to about one in three by 1998.[11]

What was much less widely recognized was the impact that the ageing of the population had upon other aspects of social, economic and cultural life. F.B. Smith was one of the first historians to point to the wide-ranging, long-term significance of the transformation of life expectancy. He drew attention to 'extensions in the span of active working lives; increases in production made possible by stronger, healthier (and more experienced – if set in their ways) workers; the steadily growing numbers of people retired or widowed, liable to the physical and social disabilities attendant upon ageing; and the belated social and official condonation of birth control'.[12] It constituted a formidable agenda for future research and policy-making, and provides an indication of the importance that this chapter will play in our attempts to understand the social history of twentieth-century Britain.

LIFE EXPECTANCY, PHYSICAL HEALTH AND PSYCHOLOGICAL HEALTH

But what of the possibility that although people were living longer, they were living less healthily? Is it really the case that mortality statistics present a misleadingly optimistic picture of the nation's health? If so, how is the misrepresentation to be rectified? In seeking to answer such questions it is essential both to distinguish between the incidence and the virulence of sickness, and to take account of the psychological as well as the physical determinants of the people's health. So it was that James C. Riley entitled his study of working men's health in the late nineteenth and early twentieth centuries *Sick, Not Dead*:

> The average life lengthened from 41.4 years for an infant male in England and Wales in the 1870s to 73.2 years in 1989–91 … Beginning in the 1870s and lasting at least into the 1930s, however, the average amount of sickness time increased at each age. Although people fell sick less often, their sickness lasted longer.[13]

---

[11] J. Wilson, 'End of century snapshot of nation', *The Guardian*, 12 November 1999.

[12] Smith, 'Health', p. 57. See also N.F.R. Crafts, 'Is Economic Growth Good for Us?' (London School of Economics, 2003), pp. 4, 7.

[13] J.C. Riley, *Sick, Not Dead: The Health of British Workingmen during the Mortality Decline* (Baltimore, MD: Johns Hopkins University Press, 1997), p. 209.

Unfortunately, sickness statistics have never been collected with the same consistency and reliability as mortality statistics. It was one thing, after all, to produce mortality statistics when the registration of deaths had been made compulsory by the state. It was another thing altogether to record the incidence, duration and severity of sickness when people's propensity to report their health problems depended upon the medical, financial and other incentives and disincentives for doing so.[14] There was a temptation for those who were insured against sickness to report any difficulties, however trivial or imaginary; there was little reason for those not entitled to medical treatment or financial compensation to report their difficulties, even when they were of considerable severity.[15]

It is possible, however, to discern major shifts in the causes, incidence and severity of sickness. It can be shown, for example, that work generally became less exhausting and less dangerous. Mechanization, trade-union pressure and state intervention combined to make manual work a great deal safer. In manufacturing, if not always in mining, mechanization reduced the sheer physical effort that was required. 'You see, the machines are so adjusted that there's little for a man to do except watch them', explained a car worker in the late 1930s. 'It's not that the job is hard work but the monotony of it gets you down.'[16] The qualitative and quantitative evidence tends to coalesce. 'Statistically,' concludes Arthur McIvor, 'the risk of death through a work-related injury had been three times higher in 1880 than it was in 1950.' Of course, he concedes, 'It is more difficult to be definitive about occupational health'. Nonetheless, he feels able to identify the causes and consequences of the major changes that took place:

> controls over poisonous substances, such as lead and phosphorus, and the
> reduction of dust inhalation at work indicate marked amelioration in
> 'traditional' hazards, though to some extent this was offset by new diseases
> (e.g. cancers) and exposure to toxic substances (such as asbestos).[17]

It can be shown too that life beyond the workplace became more healthy. Indeed, it has become something of a commonplace to point to the new pattern of health and ill health that developed in twentieth-century Britain (and most of the rest of the western world). But if it is a cliché, it is one that bears repeating. Infectious diseases such as typhus and tuberculosis tended to give way to 'degenerative' diseases such as cancer,

---

[14] N. Whiteside, 'Counting the cost: Sickness and disability among working people in an era of industrial recession, 1920–39', *Economic History Review*, XL, 1987, p. 232.

[15] D.G. Green, *Working-Class Patients and the Medical Establishment: Self-Help in Britain from the Mid-Nineteenth Century to 1948* (Gower/Maurice Temple Smith, 1985), pp. 189–200; Fitzpatrick and Chandola, 'Health', pp. 104–5.

[16] W. Greenwood, *How the Other Man Lives* (Labour Book Club, 1937), p. 94; J. Benson, *The Working Class in Britain, 1850–1939* (Harlow: Longman, 1989), p. 15.

[17] A.J. McIvor, *A History of Work in Britain, 1880–1950* (Basingstoke: Palgrave, 2001), p. 145. See also G. Tweedale and D.J. Jeremy, 'Compensating the workers: Industrial injury and compensation in the British asbestos industry, 1930s–60s', *Business History*, 41, 1999; R. Johnston and A. McIvor, ' "Dust to dust": Oral testimonies of asbestos-related disease on Clydeside', *Oral History*, 29, 2001; A. Fowler, *Lancashire Cotton Operatives and Work, 1900–1950: A Social History of Lancashire Cotton Operatives in the Twentieth Century* (Aldershot: Ashgate, 2003), Ch. 6.

strokes and heart disease.[18] At the beginning of the century, infectious diseases accounted for 20 per cent, and cancer for 7 per cent, of all deaths in the country. By the end of the century, the balance had been – more than – reversed, with infectious diseases accounting for less than 1 per cent, and cancer for more than 25 per cent, of all deaths. Diseases of poverty had been replaced by diseases of prosperity.[19]

However, as soon as one moves away from such mortality-driven indicators of health and ill health, a number of major qualifications need to be made. The relationship between longevity and health was not necessarily positive. Attention was drawn earlier in the chapter to the possibility that although people were living longer they might be living less healthily. It was a possibility that encouraged health statisticians to develop the concept of 'healthy life expectancy'. Armed with their new-found ability to distinguish life expectancy from healthy life expectancy (that is, life free of substantial health problems), they discovered that between the mid-1970s and the early 1990s, gains in life expectancy were not matched by gains in healthy life expectancy.[20]

The possibility that people were living longer but not necessarily living more healthily leads inevitably to a consideration of the relationship between physical and psychological well-being. Some people, of course, had always worried excessively. In 1927, to take but one example, a 47-year-old London man gassed himself because he thought he had cancer. 'It is most unfortunate', remarked the coroner, 'that people should have fear of cancer to such an extent that it becomes an obsession.'[21] However, it became increasingly common to draw attention to the paradox that improvements in health seemed to be accompanied by an increase, rather than a decrease, in health-related anxiety.[22] There was a causal connection, many believed.

> Anxiety over health seems to be increasing precisely at the time that technology is producing major medical advances. The two may be related. When there was negligible treatment available for most conditions, there was little value in worrying. Early detection wasn't relevant. Now, with the improved treatments, God forbid if that little ache is a warning sign as opposed to a fleeting nothing.'[23]

Whatever the statistical evidence of increasing longevity and improving physical health, many people believed that the pressures of late twentieth-century life were damaging their psychological and emotional well-being. 'More stress, less sex', proclaimed the headline over *The Guardian*'s report on a survey carried out by the Chartered Institute of Personnel and Development early in 2001. The report revealed that the partners of over half of people working more than 48 hours a week claimed

---

[18] McKeown, *Population*, Ch. 3.

[19] Smith, 'Health', pp. 51–2; Fitzpatrick and Chandola, 'Health', pp. 101, 104–16; A. Hardy, 'Reforming disease: Changing perceptions of tuberculosis in England and Wales, 1938–70', *Historical Research*, LXXVI, 2003.

[20] Fitzpatrick and Chandola, 'Health', pp. 108–9. For the first part of the century, see Riley, *Sick, Not Dead*.

[21] *Observer*, 17 April 1927.

[22] Whiteside, 'Counting the cost', p. 239.

[23] *Observer*, 4 March 2001. See also H. Hopkins, *The New Look: A Social History of the Forties and Fifties* (Readers Union/Secker & Warbug, 1964), pp. 140–2.

that their sex lives were affected. The survey also discovered that long working hours led, *inter alia*, to mistakes at work, relationship problems, children being neglected, 'as well as physical and mental health complaints'.[24]

There was a growing conviction that the increase in cancer was linked to the deterioration of the psychological, emotional – and environmental – circumstances in which people found themselves towards the end of the century. Nearly half of all women with breast cancer believed that stress was at least partly to blame for their illness. They were probably correct, believed the *Daily Express*:

> Professor Ian Fentiman of Guy's Hospital, London says there is emerging evidence that human breast cancer cells grow more quickly when exposed to high levels of prolactin – a hormone which builds up in the body when people feel stressed. 'What we can say is that it's quite possible that stress might speed up the growth of their breast cancer though it probably doesn't cause it.'[25]

The difficulty, of course, is to find a way of comparing the stress and anxiety experienced by those living at the end of the century with the problems and pressures that their predecessors had to cope with a hundred years before. John Humphries maintained in 2000:

> By any objective measurement the claim that people of my generation suffer greater stress than our parents or grandparents is not just absurd, it is obscene. Uncle Tom, Tommy's father had fought in the trenches of the Great War as a young man and had been gassed. When he was sent home from France the only work he could find was loading coal at Barry docks, the worst possible job for a workman whose lungs were already wrecked by mustard gas. Going on the dole or claiming incapacity benefit was not an option. There were the soup kitchens, but he had his pride. He could never lie down to sleep because his lungs would fill with fluid. He died an early, suffocating death.[26]

Nonetheless a survey of more than 40,000 people born in 1946, 1958 and 1970 revealed that 14 per cent of the men (and 20 per cent of the women) born in 1970 admitted to depression and anxiety in 2000, compared to 7 per cent (and 12 per cent) of the 1958 cohort in 1991.[27]

One way to approach the problem of comparing the impact of stress and anxiety at the beginning and end of the century is to consider changes in the incidence of suicide. The suicide rate, it must be admitted, is by no means a perfect measure of stress and depression. There were many reasons for attempting suicide, and attempting suicide was not the same as committing suicide. Moreover, attempting suicide was a crime before, but not after, 1961, and even following decriminalization it seems certain that a substantial, albeit unknown, proportion of suicides continued to be recorded as accidental deaths. Indeed, however scrupulously suicide statistics are

---

[24] *The Guardian*, 12 March 2001. See also 5 March 2001.

[25] *Daily Express*, 8 March 2001. See also 'Breast cancer deadlier for career women', *The Times*, 7 November 2003.

[26] J. Humphries in *The Sunday Times*, 3 September 2000.

[27] *The Guardian*, 22 February 2003.

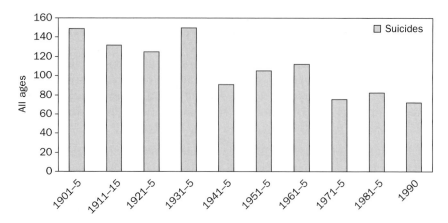

Figure 3.1 Standardized mortality ratios for suicide, England and Wales, 1901/5–90

Source: Based on R. Fitzpatrick and T. Chandola, 'Health', in A.H. Halsey (ed.), *Twentieth-Century British Social Trends* (Basingstoke: Macmillan, 2000), p. 105.

interpreted, they remain, it must be recognized, yet another mortality-based indicator of morbidity.[28]

Nonetheless, there are at least two reasons for believing Figure 3.1 to be of some value. First, it may be that the incidence of suicide reflects, albeit imperfectly, the incidence of severe depressive illness. Second, the statistics used to compile the table, flawed though they may be, have been collected since the earliest years of the century. Thus Figure 3.1 suggests that, insofar as suicide is a measure of severe depression, severe depressive illness leading to suicide became a great deal less common during the hundred years that form the subject of this book.

It goes without saying then that it remains exceptionally difficult to identify, combine and balance the many changes that took place between 1900 and 2000 so as to produce a single index covering all aspects of physical and psychological well-being. However, it is possible to turn, once again, to the human development approach that was used in the discussion of wealth, comfort and poverty in Chapter 1. It will be recalled that Sara Horrell combined the most recent human development index with the Dasgupta-Weale index in order to produce a new index plotting changes in economic well-being during the course of the century. The conclusion she reached was unqualified and apparently incontrovertible. The extension of state activity, 'along with improved public health, nutrition and accommodation, have led to an unambiguous improvement in the health environment over the century'.[29]

MEDICAL INTERVENTION

The difficulties of plotting the improvement in the nation's health are dwarfed by the complexities of identifying the factors that caused the improvement.[30] It used to be

---

[28] C.A.H. Watts to *British Medical Journal*, 5 July 1975; *British Medical Journal*, 23 July 1977.

[29] S. Horrell, 'Living standards in Britain 1900–2000: Women's century?', *National Institute Economic Review*, 172, 2000, p. 65.

[30] McKeown, *Population*, Ch. 1.

felt, so long as the 'conventional' history of medicine held sway, that the key to understanding the transformation of the nation's health during the nineteenth and twentieth centuries lay in individual initiative, sanitary progress and medical intervention. Contemporaries might caricature Edwin Chadwick, conceded Derek Fraser in 1973, 'but the historian can only marvel at the daunting range of … [his] conception of the problem of public health'.[31] The extension of statutory responsibility, claimed Maurice Bruce a decade or so earlier, was 'an essentially practical response to the problems and conditions of English society as it developed and became more self-conscious'. This practical approach, he concluded contentedly, was 'typically English'.[32]

Whatever one's reservations about this historiographical tradition, they do not mean that medical intervention and medical advances should be ignored. Indeed, it is sometimes difficult to avoid adopting a triumphalist, Whiggish approach to the history both of public health and of medical practice. The evidence that Sara Horrell produces in support of her claim about the 'unambiguous improvement in the health environment over the century' is truly remarkable. 'Real expenditure on health (hospitals and public health) has increased', she concludes, 'from 46p per capita in 1900 to some £189.67 per capita (in 1900 prices) by 1998.'[33] This means, it needs emphasizing, that expenditure on health increased nearly 400 times in less than 100 years.

The practice of medicine changed almost as dramatically. At the beginning of the century, patent medicines were extremely popular. Selling in huge quantities, Beecham's Pills alone claimed to be able to cure

> Constipation, Headache, Dizziness or Swimming in the Head, Wind, Pain, and Spasms at the Stomach, Pains in the Back, Restlessness, Insomnia, Indigestion, Want of Appetite, Fullness after Meals, Vomitings, Sickness of the Stomach, Bilious or Liver Complaints, Sick Headaches, Cold Chills, Flushings of Heat, Lowness of Spirits, and all Nervous Affections, Scurvy and Scorbutic Affections, Pimples and Blotches on the Skin, Bad Legs, Ulcers, Wounds, Maladies of Indiscretion, Kidney and Urinary Disorders, and Menstrual Derangements.[34]

The medical profession was not necessarily a great deal better informed. *The Practioner's Pocket Pharmacy and Formulary*, published in 1917, recommended administering chloroform – by gas, mouth or the rectum – as a treatment, *inter alia*, for asthma, cholera, colic, cough, croup, cystitis, flatulence, gall-stones, gout, herpes, hydrophobia, hysteria, inflammation of the testicle, lumbago, neuralgia, pneumonia, rheumatism, sea-sickness, strychnine poisoning, tonsillitis and typhoid.[35]

---

[31] D. Fraser, *The Evolution of the British Welfare State: A History of Social Policy since the Industrial Revolution* (Basingstoke: Macmillan, 1973), p. 66.

[32] M. Bruce, *The Coming of the Welfare State* (Batsford, 1961), p. 7.

[33] Horrell, 'Living Standards', p. 66.

[34] T. Richards, *The Commodity Culture of Victorian England: Advertising and Spectacle, 1851–1914* (Verso, 1991), p. 176. See, for example, 'Restored to a new life', *Daily Mail*, 3 January 1900.

[35] T. Dalrymple, 'When arsenic was the wonder drug', *Sunday Telegraph*, 12 December 1999. Also A. Digby, *Making a Medical Living: Doctors and Patients in the English Market for Medicine, 1720–1911* (Cambridge: Cambridge University Press, 1994); Jones, *Health*, pp. 20, 27.

The situation changed out of all recognition during the course of the century. The medical and pharmaceutical industries continued to market their products, but they changed the thrust of their advertising in response to the growing prosperity and rising expectations of their customers. For instance, at the beginning of the century, they offered to relieve women of basic gynaecological disorders; during the 1930s they promised them 'Radiant Health in Middle Age'; and by the 1980s companies like BUPA were promoting the facilities that they were able to provide for screening against breast cancer.[36]

The medical profession acquired the ability to treat – and treat successfully – a range of diseases that had wrought the most terrible damage at the beginning of the century. The use of antibiotics during the Second World War, and the introduction of large-scale programmes of immunization after it, massively reduced the death rate from infectious diseases. In fact, the post-war years witnessed important advances on a range of fronts. Developments in surgery meant that by the end of the century, hip replacement operations alone offered 50,000 patients a year relief from the pain and immobility of osteoarthritis. The discovery of insulin reduced deaths from diabetes, new drugs for hypertension benefited stroke victims, while advances in radiotherapy and chemotherapy did a great deal to improve the treatment of those suffering from such common cancers as leukaemia and Hodgkin's disease.[37]

It was never enough. Medical professionals complained that those most in need were often reluctant to seek help. An Edinburgh welfare worker recalled that in the late 1940s, her clients 'might live within ten yards of the ... clinic, but would they go there...?'[38] Patients complained that their doctors did not listen to them, that hospital waiting lists were too long, and that there were too many illnesses that modern medicine remained unable to treat. The Ministry of Health estimated in 1924 that general practitioners probably spent 20 minutes examining new cases, but only 5–6 minutes dealing with existing ones.[39] Patients recognized, but perhaps did not really value, the advances that had been made. 'Today's problem', it was pointed out at the very end of the century, 'is a thousand times more real to us than yesterday's solution, which is why discontent springs eternal in the human breast, no matter how much progress there has been.'[40]

PROSPERITY, CONSUMPTION AND HEALTH

In recent years, medical historians have begun to adopt a much broader perspective in their attempts to explain the changing health of the British people. The way to understand the health transformation occurring in the twentieth century, they now believe, is to focus less upon public health and medical intervention, and to look more to the growth of prosperity and the emergence of new patterns of consumption.[41]

---

[36] J. Benson, *The Rise of Consumer Society in Britain, 1880–1980* (Harlow: Longman, 1994), p. 48.

[37] Fitzpatrick and Chandola, 'Health', pp. 123–4.

[38] Museum of Edinburgh, T68/87.

[39] A. Digby and N. Bosanquet, 'Doctors and patients in an era of National Health Insurance and private practice, 1913–38', *Economic History Review*, XLI, 1988, p. 82.

[40] Dalrymple, 'When arsenic was the wonder drug'. Also Digby, *Making a Medical Living*, p. 299.

[41] McKeown, *Population*, Ch. 7.

It has been shown already that one of the key components of the twentieth-century transition was the displacement of diseases of poverty by diseases of prosperity. It was seen in the previous chapter that as incomes rose, shoppers tended to reduce their consumption of staple foods like bread and potatoes, and to increase their consumption of more expensive products such as fruit, meat and vegetables. Between the 1890s and the early 1930s, the average Briton increased his or her consumption of meat by almost a half; and during the following 50 years, increased his or her consumption of vegetables (other than potatoes) by 45 per cent.[42] 'Thus rising real incomes contributed to improved diet which in turn raised resistance to a wide range of serious infectious diseases as well as enhancing general health status.'[43] Material circumstances, it is now clear, constituted a key determinant of Britain's twentieth-century improvement in health, fitness and well-being.

However, the dietary changes that helped to raise resistance to infectious illnesses also tended to increase vulnerability to cardiovascular disease. The consumption of high saturated fats, in the form of butter and lard, began to increase in the 1930s, and then declined from the 1970s as the health risks of these and similar foods became more widely known. 'Too much fat, too much sugar or salt can be and are linked directly to heart disease, cancer, obesity and stroke, among other killer diseases', cautioned a United States Senate committee in 1977. Six years later, Britain's newly established National Advisory Council on Nutrition Education recommended that people reduce their consumption of fats by a quarter, their consumption of alcohol by a third, and their consumption of salt, sugar and saturated fats by a half.[44]

Even when people began to heed such advice, other changes they made to their diet tended to undermine their health, fitness and well-being. The increasing popularity of convenience and fast food combined with the decreasing popularity of – and need for – physical activity to produce a taller, broader and heavier population.[45] During the second half of the century, the average woman became about 15 kg heavier and saw her waist size expand by just over 10 per cent (from 65 cm to 72 cm).[46] Obesity, conclude Fitzpatrick and Chandola soberly, 'is an epidemiological risk factor in a wide range of diseases from heart diseases and diabetes through to osteoarthrisis.'[47]

The relationship between prosperity, consumption and ill health can be seen most clearly, of course, by reference to smoking. At the beginning of the century, men

---

[42] F. Capie, 'The Demand for Meat in England and Wales between the Two World Wars', in D.J. Oddy and D.S. Miller (eds), *Diet and Health in Modern Britain* (Croom Helm, 1985), p. 67; P. Atkins, 'The Production and Marketing of Fruit and Vegetables, 1850–1950', in Oddy and Miller (eds), *Diet and Health*, pp. 123–4; Benson, *Consumer Society*, p. 63.

[43] Fitzpatrick and Chandola, 'Health', p. 116. See also Benson, *Working Class*, pp. 60–1.

[44] J. Burnett, *Plenty and Want: A Social History of Food in England from 1815 to the Present Day* (Routledge, 1989), pp. 292, 326–7. See also Fitzpatrick and Chandola, 'Health', p. 118. Second World War rationing improved, it seems, the health of mothers and children.

[45] There were growing concerns, of course, about childhood obesity.

[46] J. Black, *Modern British History since 1900* (Basingstoke: Macmillan, 2000), p. 38.

[47] Fitzpatrick and Chandola, 'Health', p. 118. See also R. Passmore, 'Obesity and the Plumpness which Needs no Diet', in D. Anderson (ed.), *A Diet of Reason: Sense and Nonsense in the Healthy Eating Debate* (Social Affairs Unit, 1986), p. 100.

consumed an average of 0.5 kg of tobacco a year, a figure which by the 1940s had risen to 4.1 kg. Women began to smoke in substantial numbers during the 1920s, and by the late 1970s they consumed an average of 1.9 kg of tobacco a year.[48] The growing popularity of smoking was the product of a combination of rising prosperity, medical ignorance and ingenious advertising. During the First World War, for instance, there was reportedly a 'magnificent response' to Lady Hamilton's appeal for 'comforts' for the troops serving in the Dardanelles: 'boxes containing tobacco, pipes, lighters and cigarettes have been packed with evidence of loving care, and a little note of good wishes to the recipient has been enclosed'.[49] During the 1930s and 1940s, doctors recommended smoking as a treatment for asthma, and one well-known advertisement assured young women that it was easy for them to retain their figures: 'When tempted to over-indulge – to eat between meals, they say: "*No thanks, I'll smoke a Kensitas instead*"'.[50]

It was the middle of the century, again, that marked the decisive turning point in public knowledge, attitudes and behaviour. Once the link between smoking and lung cancer was established, the amount spent on tobacco began to decline: from £150 billion in 1965 to £80 billion 35 years later.[51] The impact upon the incidence of lung cancer was immediate and impressive. Sir Richard Doll was one of the first to establish the link between smoking and lung cancer, and 50 years later he and a colleague reviewed the changes which had taken place since his original investigation.

> Our 1950 study showed that smoking was a cause of most of the lung cancer in Britain at that time, and our new study shows that widespread cessation of smoking has halved the number of lung cancer deaths that would otherwise be occurring in Britain in 2000.[52]

The fact that health standards were related so closely to material conditions and patterns of consumption suggests that the improvement which took place was likely to be inconsistent and unequal. However, these inconsistencies and inequalities can be discussed with more confidence than one might imagine since health, fitness and well-being tended to depend less upon individual factors like personality and attitude and more upon impersonal, structural characteristics such as age, gender, ethnicity and class.[53]

AGE AND HEALTH

The health of all age groups improved substantially between 1900 and 2000. But it did so for different reasons, at different times, to different degrees and with different

---

[48] 'The boom in cigarettes', *Observer*, 13 March 1927.

[49] *Observer*, 18 November 1915.

[50] Benson, *Consumer Society*, p. 48; Dalrymple, 'When arsenic was the wonder drug'.

[51] For example, 'Smokers are puffing more', *Daily Mail*, 5 April 1990.

[52] K. Perry, 'Cancer warning halves deaths due to smoking', *The Guardian,* 3 August 2000. C. Hall, 'Levels of lung cancer halved', *The Times*, 3 August 2000. See also Fitzpatrick and Chandola, 'Health', pp. 118–20; R. Elliot, 'Growing up and giving up: Smoking in Paul Thompson's "100 Families"', *Oral History*, 29, 2001.

[53] L. Appleby, *A Medical Tour through the Whole Island of Great Britain* (Faber and Faber, 1994).

consequences. It is essential therefore to distinguish, as in previous chapters, between the experiences of children, adolescents, the middle-aged and the elderly.

Children were the first to benefit. At first sight, this might seem somewhat surprising. It was seen in the opening chapter that as families became more prosperous, children were able to exercise more power over economic decision-making; and it follows from the discussion in the previous chapter that some of the ways in which they exercised that power – by buying sweets and ice cream – were unlikely to improve the state of their health. In fact, children's influence over their health is easily exaggerated. The ways in which they spent their money may have ruined their teeth, but were unlikely to confine them to bed or place their lives at risk. However unwise children's spending, it paled into insignificance compared with the choices that their parents made with regard to food, clothing, heating, housing and other aspects of domestic management.[54] It paled into insignificance too when compared with the broader policy developments and structural changes associated with rising national prosperity.

It will be seen in the following chapter that the state intervened increasingly to try to ensure that young people were raised healthily. For instance, in 1907 local education authorities were required to inspect children's health, and four years later they were permitted to provide meals for poor pupils. The earlier the intervention the better, many believed. 'The contribution of the Maternity and Child Welfare Centres, supported out of public funds, to the safeguarding of the health of mothers and babies who attended them', it was argued in 1930, 'is everywhere recognised, and to their teaching is attributed a very considerable share of the credit for the halving of the infant death rate during the present century.'[55]

It was stressed earlier in this chapter – and it bears stressing again – that one of the keys to understanding the health transition of the twentieth century was the displacement of diseases of poverty by diseases of prosperity. At the beginning of the century, child poverty and ill health among children were endemic and often highly visible. In Birmingham, for example, ' 5,000, poor little street-bred children' were twice a year treated to a meal and an outing to the countryside, courtesy of local philanthropic groups. It was reported that they were watched by 'passers-by [who] must have been impressed not only with the magnitude of the gathering, but also with the appalling amount of poverty and wretchedness represented by the ragged and emaciated little ones'.[56] Gradually such searing poverty and ill health became – more or less – a thing of the past. As 'a student social worker' in the 1950s, recalled a Scottish woman, 'I was accustomed to seeing children running around in the slums of Glasgow with bare feet and what was called "sewn" into their clothes for the winter'. But, 'latterly … the thing I noticed particularly was that all children had socks and shoes, a great improvement on children's health and well-being'.[57]

---

[54] Nutrition during the first months of life was of crucial significance.

[55] 'Babies' clubs', *Observer*, 6 April 1930.

[56] 'Poor children in Sutton Park', *Birmingham Daily Post,* 11 August 1904. For reports on similar outings elsewhere, see 'Poor children's visit to the parks', Greater Manchester Police Museum, Police Orders 317–318, 30 July 1914; R. Glasser, *Growing Up in the Gorbals* (Chatto & Windus, 1986), pp. 54–5.

[57] Museum of Edinburgh, T68/87.

There was constant concern, of course, about adolescent consumption and the deleterious effects that it was likely to have, *inter alia*, upon young people's health. It was seen in Chapter 1 that teenage purchasing power increased substantially between the wars, and increased again in the years following 1945. It was shown in Chapter 2 that young people throughout the century used consumption as a way of distinguishing themselves both from the children's world they were leaving and from the adult world they were entering.[58] Some of the ways in which they did so, by eating unwisely, by smoking, drinking and taking drugs, had obvious health implications.[59] These were choices which, unlike those made by children, were likely, everybody recognized, to have an impact one way or another upon health, fitness and well-being. However, there was often an inverse relationship between the scale of public concern and the severity of the threat.

By the 1980s, teenage drug-taking had become an issue of major public anxiety.[60] 'The spread of drugs throughout Britain is now so wide', declared the *Daily Mail* in 2000, 'that as many as one in five 15-year-olds has been offered heroin, a report revealed yesterday. And one in four told researchers that they could readily find a source of the drug.'[61] Nonetheless, a survey of nearly 19,000 people carried out in the early 1990s revealed that fewer than 1 per cent of respondents aged between 16 and 24 reported ever having injected non-prescribed drugs. Even though this is virtually certain to be an underestimate, it does not suggest that teenage drug-injecting posed a major threat to young people's health.[62]

Teenage smoking had always provoked a degree of anxiety. Indeed, trying one's first cigarette behind the bicycle sheds – or anywhere else – constituted one of the most common and most commonly recognized rites of passage between childhood and adulthood.[63] The survey referred to above produced startling evidence about the extent of young people's smoking in the early 1990s. It showed that although those aged 16 to 24 were less likely than other age groups to smoke heavily, they were a great deal more likely to smoke 'lightly'. Smoking lightly meant that even after 20 years and more of anti-smoking propaganda, almost 23 per cent of young men, and more than 25 per cent of young women, smoked up to 14 cigarettes a day. It meant that over 15 per cent of young women, and almost 18 per cent of young men, smoked 15 and more a day. Smoking, the report noted somberly, 'is known to be causally related to a number of serious conditions including lung cancer, lung disease and heart disease'.[64]

Nevertheless, an increasing number of children and adolescents survived into adulthood, middle age and old age. It will be recalled from Chapter 1 that there was

---

[58] See, generally, Benson, *Consumer Society*, Ch. 7, 'The Creation of Youth Culture?'

[59] 'Women must eat wisely to look well', *Daily Mail*, 17 February 1920.

[60] Jones, *Health*, p. 164.

[61] 'Heroin is being offered to one in five 15-year-olds', *Daily Mail*, 5 April 2000. See also 'Agonies of Ecstasy', *Daily Mail*, 1 July 1995; 7 January 2000; Abbey National, 'Pester Power is Good News for Families' (Abbey National, 2000), p. 6.

[62] K. Wellings, J. Field, A. Johnson and J. Wadsworth, *Sexual Behaviour in Britain: The National Survey of Sexual Attitudes and Lifestyles* (Penguin, 1994), pp. 294–6.

[63] Glasser, *Growing Up*, pp. 77–8.

[64] Wellings *et al.*, *Sexual Behaviour*, pp. 282–3. See also 'Young women in lung cancer alert', *Daily Mail*, 5 January 2000.

an increase in both the number and the proportion of the population that was middle-aged and elderly. Between 1901 and 1995, the number of people in their forties and fifties all but doubled, and from the 1930s onwards they accounted for a quarter or so of the population.[65] Between 1901 and 1981, the number of people over 65 grew more than five-and-a-half times, so that by the 1980s they represented 15 per cent of the entire population.[66]

It is here that misunderstandings can arise. The fact that an increasing number of children and adolescents survived into adulthood, middle age and old age meant, in turn, that there were an increasing number of middle-aged and elderly people at risk from strokes, cancer, heart disease and similar life-threatening – and life-spoiling – illnesses. Improving material conditions and changing patterns of consumption tended to increase the middle-aged's susceptibility to the so-called diseases of prosperity. The president of the General Medical Council put it like this in 1968:

> The most difficult tasks which confront health education are those which apply
> to adults in middle age, when the aim of health education is to modify
> deleterious habits – cigarette smoking, over-indulgence in alcohol, over-eating,
> lack of exercise, and the like.[67]

However, improving material conditions and changing patterns of consumption also tended to improve the longevity of the middle-aged. Figure 3.2 shows, for example, that the death rate of men and women between 45 and 54 fell by more than a half between the beginning and the middle of the century, and continued to decline, albeit more slowly, between the early 1950s and the early 1990s. It shows too that the death rate of those in their late sixties and early seventies declined fairly consistently, and that men's rates improved towards the end of the century. Figure 3.2 shows, in other words, that the middle-aged and elderly shared, though later than other groups, in the more general improvement in health standards that was enjoyed by the population as a whole.[68]

However, as soon as one moves away from mortality-driven indicators of health and ill health, generalization becomes a good deal more complicated. It was possible, after all, for the middle-aged and elderly to live longer but to live less healthily.[69] It did not take much to disrupt their quality of life. 'Some old people have retired to bed

---

[65] J. Benson, *Prime Time: A History of the Middle Aged in Twentieth-Century Britain* (Harlow: Longman, 1997), pp. 33–4.

[66] J. Macnicol, *The Politics of Retirement in Britain, 1878–1948* (Cambridge: Cambridge University Press, 1998), p. 7. See also P. Coleman, J. Bond and S. Peace, 'Ageing in the Twentieth Century', in J. Bond, P. Coleman and S. Peace (eds), *Ageing in Society: An Introduction to Social Gerontology* (Sage, 1993), pp. 1–3.

[67] Benson, *Prime Time*, pp. 48–9.

[68] Smith, 'Health', p. 38; Benson, *Prime Time*, p. 49; M. Sidell, *Health in Old Age: Myth, Mystery and Management* (Buckingham: Open University Press, 1995), p. 36. There were suggestions, however, that health professionals discriminated against the elderly: *Daily Mail*, 3 April 2000.

[69] L. Boul, 'Male Midlife: An Investigation into Men's Experiences, Attitudes and Perceptions', University of Sheffield PhD, 2002.

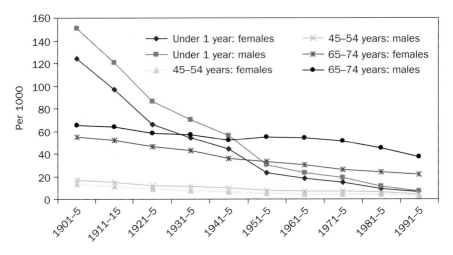

Figure 3.2 Death rates by sex and age, England and Wales, 1901/5–1991/5
Source: Based on R. Fitzpatrick and T. Chandola, 'Health', A.H. Halsey (ed.), *Twentieth-Century British Social Trends* (Basingstoke: Macmillan, 2000), p. 99. (Civilians only 1911–15, 1941–5.)

simply because they could not cut their own toenails. You can't grow old gracefully if your feet hurt.'[70] Thus health statisticians, it was seen earlier, developed the concept of 'healthy life expectancy', the period during which one could expect to live free of substantial health problems.[71] Yet informed opinion remained sharply polarized about the relationship between life expectancy and healthy life expectancy.[72]

On the one hand, the statistical evidence collected in the 1980s and 1990s suggested that the correlation between the two was weak. When *The Guardian* considered the *Social Trends* survey published in 1999, it headed its report, 'Life in old age gets longer but no healthier'. It explained that, 'Although the 1990s have seen enormous change in diets and lifestyles, government statisticians today report, older people still tend to be afflicted by debilitating health problems.' It went on to list some of them:

> By age 65–74, 52 per cent of men and 51 per cent of women say they suffer pain and discomfort. Over 75, 50 per cent of men and 60 per cent of women report difficulty getting about. The persistence of such complaints among older people has prompted conclusions that while life expectancy is improving constantly – it is now almost 75 for men and almost 80 for women – 'healthy life expectancy' has remained stuck for the past two decades.[73]

On the other hand, the combination of statistical and non-statistical evidence used by sociologists and social historians suggests that there was a much closer correlation

---

[70] *The Sunday Times,* 14 October 1960.

[71] Fitzpatrick and Chandola, 'Health', pp. 108–9.

[72] C.R. Victor, *Health and Health Care in Later Life* (Buckingham: Open University Press, 1991), pp. 42–3; Sidell, *Health in Old Age*, pp. 40–1.

[73] http://www.guardian.co.uk/Archive/Article/0,4273,3813640,00.html. See also Fitzpatrick and Chandola, 'Health', pp. 108–9.

between life expectancy and healthy life expectancy. John Macnicol, for example, is insistent that, 'By the 1990s most retired people were healthy, were leading independent lives and were contributing greatly to the informal economy by performing a multitude of unpaid but vitally important tasks for their own children, for neighbours or for the community.'[74] Pat Thane agrees:

> By the end of the twentieth century, although people are living longer, they are not making greater demands on medical care. A longer life does not mean a longer period of illness before death; rather as people live longer, the onset of serious ill-health occurs later in life, if at all, since most older people, including those who live to be very old, do not experience a period of protracted, serious ill-health before death.[75]

What happened, it seems, was that ill health became compressed into the final years of life – and this of course at the same time as life itself was getting longer. It was the chronology, rather than the severity, of ill health that changed.

GENDER AND HEALTH

The chronology of health, ill health and well-being depended, in large part, upon gendered patterns of economic power and consumer choice.[76] It was seen in the previous two chapters that although there is no doubt that gender inequality was embedded deeply in British society, it can prove remarkably difficult to identify the economic power that women were – and were not – able to exercise. It was suggested that they increased their power, *inter alia*, by working more outside the home and by maintaining, and increasing, their responsibility for many aspects of consumption (including food, drink and health care). It will therefore come as no surprise to discover that men and women had strikingly different experiences of, and attitudes towards, health, ill health and well-being.

However, the analysis of these differences is more difficult than one might expect. The complications arise largely from the contradictions that existed – yet again – between life expectancy and healthy life expectancy. 'In general', it is agreed, 'men experience higher death rates than women in every age group from birth through to old age, whilst women consistently record higher levels of illness than men.'[77] A detailed analysis of national health insurance statistics for 1921–2 found the 'average amount of sickness among unmarried women to be from 25 to 30 per cent more than

---

[74] Macnicol, *Politics of Retirement*, p. 16. See also M. Henderson, 'Getting old will be more fun than most of us think', *The Times*, 13 September 2003.

[75] P. Thane, *Old Age in English History: Past Experiences, Present Issues* (Oxford: Oxford University Press, 2000), p. 15.

[76] P. Thane, 'Gender, Welfare and Old Age in Britain 1870s–1940s', in A. Digby and J. Stewart (eds), *Gender, Health and Welfare* (Routledge, 1996), p. 189.

[77] J. Popay, ' "My Health is All Right, But I'm Just Tired All the Time": Women's Experience of Ill Health', in H. Roberts (ed.), *Women's Health Matters* (Routledge, 1992), p. 99. See also pp. 101–5; Victor, *Health and Health Care*, p. 73.

among men'.[78] A survey conducted in the mid-1950s revealed that women were 40 per cent more likely than men to go to their doctors with tumours, cancers and leukaemia, twice as likely to seek advice for mental disorders, and four times as likely to request treatment for diseases of the genito-urinary system. A similar survey carried out in the early 1990s revealed similar differences. Women, it discovered, were 50 per cent more likely than men to go to their doctors with tumours, cancers and leukaemia, nearly 90 per more likely to seek advice for mental disorders, and more than five times as likely to request treatment for diseases of the genito-urinary system.[79]

The tension between life expectancy and healthy life expectancy – between mortality-based indicators and non-mortality-based indicators – is fundamental to the analysis of gender, health and ill health. The mortality-based indicators are absolutely incontrovertible. Men experienced higher death rates than women: men's life expectancy improved from 45 to 74 between the beginning and the end of the century; women's increased from 49 to 79.[80] The importance of these differences was widely recognized, and not just by those responsible for economic and social policy-making. They were something that needed to be taken into account by anybody marrying a younger or older spouse, by any family with middle-aged or elderly parents to look after, by any husband and wife planning how to cope in their retirement.

Unfortunately, the non-mortality-based indicators of health and ill health are anything but incontrovertible. It is important, it has been seen, to recognize the possibility that although people were living longer, they were living less healthily. However, what also needs to be made clear at this point are the limitations of the non-mortality-based indicators that are used to exemplify, and explain, gender differences in morbidity. Indeed, some commentators believe that gender differences in morbidity were no more than what has been called 'an artefact of social structure'. They challenge, for example, the validity of morbidity statistics based upon GP consultations. They concede that women were more likely than men to consult a doctor. However, they believe that this was not because women were more prone to sickness, but because they were more prepared to seek medical advice. They were less likely to be employed in full-time work, and more likely to be accustomed to dealing with members of the medical profession. It was women, not men, who gave birth; and women, not men, who assumed primary responsibility for child care.[81]

The criticism of morbidity statistics based on GP consultations draws too upon dissatisfaction with the ways in which members of the medical profession regarded their female patients. Feminist scholars are scathing in their criticism. Health research has concentrated on men, complains Christina Lee:

This, together with linguistic traditions that equate 'man' with 'adult human' and regard 'woman' as a special case, has meant that the study of woman's

[78] A.W. Watson, 'National Health Insurance: A statistical review', *Journal of the Royal Statistical Society*, III, 1927, p. 451. National Health Insurance covered nearly 16 million people. Also Whiteside, 'Counting the Cost', p. 233.

[79] Fitzpatrick and Chandola, 'Health', p. 106.

[80] The two world wars, naturally, killed many more men than women. See J. Bourke, *Dismembering the Male: Men's Bodies, Britain and the Great War* (Reaktion Books, 1996).

[81] Victor, *Health and Health Care*, p. 73; Jones, *Health*, pp. 182–3; *The Guardian*, 18 January 1995.

health has until recently been restricted to obstetric and gynaecological issues, and has tended to assume that the only interesting thing about women's health is reproductive capacity.[82]

According to this view, doctors were prone to regard men as normal and women as abnormal. They therefore tended to diagnose their female patients as suffering from hormonal and/or mental health problems at every stage of the life course.[83] This, at least, was how it appeared to many female patients. A Birmingham woman recalls how, in the early 1960s, she was prescribed the drug Valium when she complained to her GP about persistent and severe pains in her shoulders, neck and head. It was not until many years later that arthritis of the spine was diagnosed.[84] Doctors believed that women were at increased risk of psychiatric illness immediately before their premenstrual periods, that there was a causal relationship between childbirth and depressive disorders, and that the menopause posed a grievous threat to women's physical and psychological well-being. As an editorial in *The Lancet* explained in 1975, the menopause not only caused short-term problems like hot flushes and long-term difficulties such as cancer and osteoporosis, but 'perhaps most important of all, the loss of femininity associated with progressive atrophy of the secondary sexual characteristics'.[85]

The medical profession's stereotyping of female patients is scarcely in doubt. It does not follow, however, that gender differences in morbidity were merely an artefact of social structure. They were not. Women really did experience more sickness than men. They faced obstetric and gynaecological difficulties that men did not, they assumed emotional and pastoral roles that men did not, and they had to contend with economic, social and cultural burdens that men did not.

Pregnancy and childbirth were the most obvious gender-specific threats to women's health. At the beginning of the century, over 3,000 women a year died of obstetric complications, a cull that led one 1930s' Labour Party activist to complain that, 'It is four times as dangerous to bear a child as to work in a mine, and mining is men's most dangerous trade.'[86] Thereafter, the situation improved dramatically, and by the end of the century, pregnancy and childbirth accounted for fewer than 50 deaths a year. Nevertheless, these remained difficult and stressful stages of the life course, and even in the early 1990s more than 2 per cent of all women – of all ages – felt it necessary to consult their GPs each year with complications arising from pregnancy and childbirth.[87]

---

[82] C. Lee, *Women's Health: Psychological and Social Perspectives* (Sage, 1998), p. 1. See also A. Digby and J. Stewart, 'Welfare in Context', in Digby and Stewart (eds), *Gender, Health and Welfare*; E.M. Goudsmit, 'All in Her Mind! Stereotypic Views and the Psychologisation of Women's Illness', in S. Wilkinson and C. Kitzinger (eds), *Women and Health: Feminist Perspectives* (Taylor & Francis, 1994).

[83] Lee, *Women's Health*, p. 15; Jones, *Health*, p. 183.

[84] Information from Mrs J. Volante.

[85] Benson, *Prime Time*, p. 13. Also Lee, *Women's Health*, pp. 22, 32; G. Greer, *The Change: Women, Ageing and the Menopause* (Penguin, 1992). For patients' views, see M. Blaxter and E. Paterson, *Mothers and Daughters: A Three-Generational Study of Health Attitudes and Behaviour* (Aldershot: Avebury, 1982), Ch. 14.

[86] Jones, *Health*, p. 68. See also *Observer*, 11 May 1930.

[87] S. Kitzinger, 'Birth and Violence Against Women: Generating Hypotheses from Women's Accounts of Unhappiness after Childbirth', in Roberts (ed.), *Women's Health Matters*; Fitzpatrick and Chandola, 'Health', pp. 104, 106.

Women's emotional and pastoral roles posed a less widely recognized threat to their physical and psychological well-being. The threat was real for all that. Women were responsible not only for their own health care, but also for seeing to the well-being of their husbands, their children, their parents, and sometimes their husbands' parents. It was a burden that bit particularly hard in middle age. A 1948 study of Wolverhampton revealed that a significant proportion of those who had elderly relatives living with them claimed that it placed them under considerable strain: 44 per cent of the sample found the old person difficult to deal with, 35 per cent felt that they had too much to do, 49 per cent reported that they were unable to go out as much as they wished, and 29 per cent complained that it was impossible for them to get away on holiday.[88]

Women were also sicker than men because they were poorer. Chapter 1 showed that women generally were less wealthy and earned lower incomes than men. It stressed too that married women frequently exercised less economic power than their contribution to the household economy 'entitled' them to. Laura Oren argued, it will be recalled, that even higher wages and growing prosperity failed to dislodge 'the uneven distribution of incomes between husbands and wives'.[89] Margery Spring Rice suggested in 1939 that, '3 inter-connected factors ... cause the life of the working-class housewife to be too difficult and strenuous. The first is poverty, the second ill-health and the third a lack of trained knowledge.'[90] Moreover, single women, divorcees and widows tended not only to possess less wealth than married women but also to have to budget alone for the expenses that married couples were able to share between them. A.H. Halsey pointed out, it will be remembered, that, 'The woman left to raise children alone is among the most pathetic casualties of an affluent society.'[91]

Women's poverty and women's poor health were intimately entwined. It is not always possible, it is true, to prove that poverty caused poor health – rather than poor health being the cause of poverty. Nonetheless, there were innumerable occasions when it can be shown that women's poverty impacted directly and adversely upon their physical and psychological well-being.[92] This can be seen most clearly, of course, when circumstances were at their most desperate. A survey of maternal mortality in Durham and South Wales during the Depression of the late 1920s found that mothers were severely malnourished and concluded that it was this malnutrition, rather than lack of medical care, that was the key factor in their high maternal mortality rates.[93]

Economic, social and cultural pressures coalesced. Even when women possessed the material resources and nutritional knowledge to provide their families with a balanced and healthy diet, they did not necessarily choose to do so.[94] A study carried out in

---

[88] Benson, *Prime Time*, pp. 112–13; Digby and Stewart, 'Welfare in Context', pp. 19–20.

[89] L. Oren, 'The Welfare of Women in Laboring Families: England, 1860–1950', in M.S. Hartman and L. Banner (eds), *Clio's Consciousness Raised: New Perspectives on the History of Women* (Harper & Row, 1974), p. 236.

[90] M. Spring Rice, *Working-Class Wives: Their Health and Conditions* (Pelican, 1939), p. 188. Also Whiteside, 'Counting the cost', pp. 242, 244.

[91] A.H. Halsey, *Change in British Society* (Oxford: Oxford University Press, 1986), p. 110.

[92] Benson, *Working Class*, pp. 61–2; Jones, *Health*, pp. 183–4.

[93] A. Digby, 'Poverty, Health and the Politics of Gender in Britain, 1870–1948', in Digby and Stewart (eds.), *Gender, Health and Welfare*, p. 70.

[94] For example, W. Hannington, *The Problem of the Distressed Areas* (Gollancz, 1937), Ch. v.

'a northern town' in the late 1970s revealed, for instance, that mothers typically replaced 'medically preferred methods' such as breastfeeding with mixed feeding by the time their babies were four months old. The report's author concluded that there was a conflict between what the medical profession recommended and what the mother's family was prepared to put up with: 'the women's culturally defined responsibilities for providing for the whole family and maintaining domestic harmony gave them "good" social reasons for 'bad' nutritional habits.'[95]

ETHNICITY AND HEALTH

The discussion of economic, social and cultural pressures leads to a consideration of the relationship between ethnicity and health. It is a relationship which has not yet attracted a great deal of interest;[96] and insofar as it has, the research produced has been disfigured, some specialists believe, by partiality, sexism and racism. One Afro-Caribbean health professional put it like this in 1992: 'Although there is a growing literature on the health experiences of black and minority ethnic women, research studies have been concerned primarily with experiences of maternity services. Much of the literature describes family organization and cultural practices to do with childbirth and child rearing, where black family patterns are described as deviating from white families.'[97]

Nonetheless, it does not follow, any more than in the case of women, that the health differences that were reported were merely an 'artefact of social structure'. The health of ethnic minorities was definitely worse than that of the majority population. It could scarcely be otherwise. It was shown in Chapter 1 that New Commonwealth immigrants ended the century much as Irish immigrants had started it. They remained prone to unemployment, and when in employment to poor pay – and of course to other forms of economic, social and cultural disadvantage. It was shown in Chapter 2 that those from ethnic minority communities, like the poor generally, were likely to apply a high proportion of what resources they had to the purchase of basic necessities such as food and accommodation.

Moreover, it has been suggested time and again in the course of this chapter that material conditions provide a key factor in explaining the health, ill health and well-being of Britain's population. It follows therefore that those from minority ethnic groups were likely to suffer worse health than those from the majority population.[98] This was precisely what happened. Nonetheless, there is the danger, it must be

[95] A. Murcott, 'Food and Nutrition in Post-War Britain', in J. Obelkevich and P. Catterall (eds), *Understanding Post-War British Society* (Routledge, 1994), pp. 162–3.
[96] For the problems of communication, see K. Gardner, *Age, Narrative and Migration: The Life Course and Life Histories of Bengali Elders in London* (Oxford: Berg, 2002), pp. 71–3.
[97] J. Douglas, 'Black Women's Health Matters: Putting Black Women on the Research Agenda', in Roberts (ed.), *Women's Health Matters*, p. 33. See also p. 34; L. Marks and M. Worboys, 'Introduction', in L. Marks and M. Worboys (eds), *Migrants, Minorities and Health: Historical and Contemporary Studies* (Routledge, 1997); J.Y. Nazroo, *The Health of Britain's Ethnic Minorities: Findings from a National Survey* (Policy Studies Institute, 1997), pp. 1–2.
[98] B. Benjamin, 'Variations of Mortality in the United Kingdom with Special Reference to Immigrants and Minority Groups', in D.A. Coleman (ed.), *Demography and Minority Groups in the United Kingdom* (Academic Press, 1982).

admitted, of overconfident generalization. It is essential to distinguish between the experiences of different ethnic groups, to allow for age, gender, class and other variables, and to avoid assuming that ethnicity necessarily provides the best, let alone the only, way of explaining the different health experiences of different ethnic groups.[99]

There is no denying, however, that ethnicity, economic circumstances and health were intimately related. The best evidence comes, as one would expect, from the end of the century. It has been seen already that the Bangladeshi community was particularly impoverished. In the early 1990s, nearly a quarter of Bangladeshi households (compared to under 0.5 per cent of all households in the country) lived more than 1.5 people to a room; nearly a quarter (compared to 19 per cent) had no central heating; and more than 60 per cent (compared to a third) did not own a car. The community, not surprisingly, was also very unhealthy. 'Perhaps as a reflection of these living conditions,' one group of experts concluded, 'a striking proportion of Bangladeshis are permanently sick: 9 per cent of men aged sixteen and over are in this position and 2 per cent of women. Nationally, 5 per cent of men and 3 per cent of women aged sixteen and over are permanently sick.'[100]

In 1997, the Policy Studies Institute and Social and Community Planning Research published the fourth in a series of surveys of Britain's ethnic minorities. A thorough and sophisticated study, it confirmed once again that those from ethnic minorities suffered poorer health than the rest of the population. However, it stressed too the importance of distinguishing between the experiences of different groups: the health of the survey's Chinese, Indian and African-Asian respondents was similar, it emphasized, to that of the white population; the health of Caribbeans, Pakistanis and Bangladeshis was significantly inferior.[101]

The survey examined a range of factors thought likely to play a part in determining the ethnic variations it had uncovered. It considered the ways in which the investigation had collected its data; the cultural, biological and genetic differences that distinguished particular ethnic groups; and the possible health-related selection of these groups as a result of the migration process. It found, however, that the health differences revealed by the survey were explained best by material factors. It examined a combination of social class, unemployment, and the lack of basic amenities such as hot water, a bathroom and central heating. It discovered that, 'Across all three of these dimensions of socio-economic status both the Chinese and African-Asian groups compared favourably to whites, Indians were similar to, but slightly worse off than, whites, and Caribbeans, Pakistanis and Bangladeshis were clearly worse off, with Bangladeshis the most disadvantaged.' Its conclusion was a model of academic restraint:

> The fact that variations in socio-economic status across ethnic groups follow the pattern for health, while the other explanatory factors do not, adds weight to the suggestion that this may, on prima facie grounds, be a fruitful avenue to explore.[102]

---

[99] L. Marks and L. Holder, 'Ethnic Advantage: Infant Survival among Jewish and Bengali Immigrants in East London, 1870–1990', in Marks and Worboys (eds), *Migrants, Minorities and Health*.

[100] C. Peach, A. Rogers, J. Chance and P. Daley, 'Immigration and Ethnicity', in Halsey (ed.), *British Social Trends*, pp. 154–5.

[101] J.Y. Nazroo, *The Health of Britains' Ethnic Minorities: Findings from a National Survey* (Policy Studies Institute, 1997), p. 82. See *Census 2001: National Report for England and Wales,* pp. 56–7, 130–1.

CLASS AND HEALTH

The discussion of socio-economic status leads finally to a consideration of the relationship between class and health. It is a relationship which, unlike that between ethnicity and health, stimulated political attention, academic investigation and public interest throughout the whole of the century. The difficulty therefore is not to unearth relevant evidence but to avoid selecting material that is unusual and persuasive rather than representative and possibly ambiguous. It was suggested in Chapter 1 that an awareness of class divisions remains fundamental to the proper analysis of Britain's social history. Certainly, the mortality-based indicators of health are compelling. Figure 3.3 reveals pronounced, persistent – indeed increasing – class differences in death rates. It shows that men from social class V suffered a death rate 54 per cent higher than those from social class I in 1910–12, 32 per cent higher in 1949–53 and 123 per cent higher in 1991–3.

Social class, it was argued earlier, needs to be set alongside, and often above, age, gender and ethnicity when attempting to explain the social, cultural and political history of the twentieth century. The upper class, we all know, were generally able to exercise greater economic power than the middle class, and the middle class greater economic power than the working class. It has also been shown that there existed a clear correlation between class, saving and spending. The upper class, the middle class and the working class, it was no surprise to learn, tended both to save and to spend in class-specific ways. Nor is this all. It has been suggested time and again in the course of this chapter that material conditions and patterns of consumption constituted a key determinant – not to say predictor – of health, ill health and well-being.

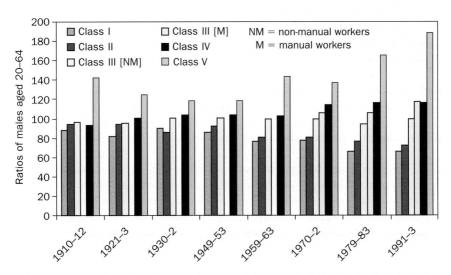

Figure 3.3 Standardized male mortality ratios by social class, England and Wales, 1910/12–1991/3

Source: Based on R. Fitzpatrick and T. Chandola, 'Health', in A.H. Halsey (ed.), *Twentieth-Century British Social Trends* (Basingstoke: Macmillan, 2000), p. 110.

[102] Nazroo, *Health*, p. 85. See also pp. 82–4.

Indeed, there is an abundance of evidence not yet cited about class differences in consumption. Food and tobacco are of crucial significance. During the First World War, it has been suggested, some working men enlisted partly in order to be able to eat 'meat every day'.[103] In the mid-1930s, Sir William Crawford led an investigation involving house-to-house interviews with 5,000 respondents from seven major cities. His findings revealed a clear correlation between (economically defined) social class and food spending. Fewer than 1 per cent of those in class B (earning £250–£499) failed to spend the British Medical Association-recommended minimum on food, whereas 17 per cent of those in class C (earning £125–£249) and 48 per cent of those in class D (earning under £125) failed to reach this level. Whether class C and class D spending was determined by poverty, ignorance, inertia, stupidity or poor domestic facilities is beside the point. The correlation between social class and food consumption was clear and apparently incontrovertible.[104]

The reports produced by the National Food Survey provide comparable information for the later years of the century. They confirmed that there continued to be a correlation between levels of income and spending on food. The survey published in 1987 revealed, for example, that those earning the highest incomes spent 46p a week on cheese, 69p on fish, £1.16 on fruit and fruit products, and £1.35 on vegetables. Those earning the lowest incomes spent far less: 26p a week on cheese, 36p on fish, 36p on fruit and fruit products, and £1.04 on vegetables. The continuities were as striking as the changes. For as John Burnett points out, 'There is much here which parallels the poverty of the 1930s, modified by the technological changes which now make frozen chips, fish fingers, and hamburgers convenient and relatively cheap substitutes for traditional dishes.'[105]

There were also class differences in smoking. Figures 3.4a and 3.4b show that during the final quarter of the century, those from Social Classes I and II smoked less than those from Social Classes IV and V; and this suggests of course that they responded more positively to the publicity that was being given to the dangers of the habit. There is other evidence besides. In 1982, Mildred Blaxter and Elizabeth Paterson published the results of a study of the health attitudes and behaviour of working-class women in 58 three-generation families living in an unnamed 'Scottish city'. In none of the three generations, they discovered, was there much evidence of anti-smoking propaganda having a great deal of impact.

> Despite an extremely high rate of bronchial disease in the group, almost all the women smoked. Although one or two paid lip-service to health education slogans about cigarettes being detrimental to health, most of the women claimed they were entirely unconvinced by the 'statistics' or 'rumours'; they readily quoted examples of acquaintances or kin who had smoked Woodbine

---

[103] G. Robb, *British Culture and the First World War* (Basingstoke: Palgrave, 2002), p. 71.

[104] Burnett, *Plenty and Want*, pp. 274–81. See also, for the beginning of the century, A. Hook, *The Worker's Share* (Labour Publishing Co.,1924), pp. 30–1; Glasser, *Growing Up*, p. 2.

[105] Burnett, *Plenty and Want*, pp. 324–5. Also J.P. Johnston, *A Hundred Years Eating: Food, Drink and the Daily Diet in Britain Since the Late Nineteenth Century* (Dublin: Gill & Macmillan, 1977), pp. 48–9.

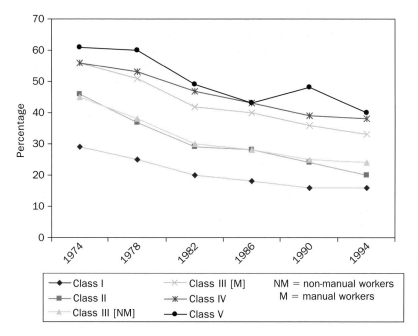

Figure 3.4a Male cigarette smokers by social class, Great Britain, 1974–94

Source: Based on R. Fitzpatrick and T. Chandola, 'Health', in A.H. Halsey (ed.), *Twentieth-Century British Social Trends* (Basingstoke: Macmillan, 2000), pp. 120–1.

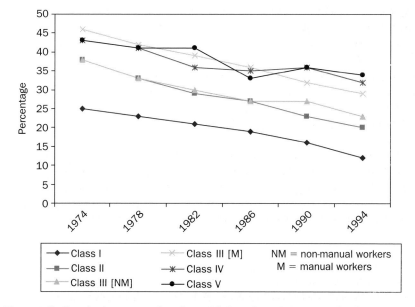

Figure 3.4b Female cigarette smokers by social class, Great Britain, 1974–94

Source: Based on R. Fitzpatrick and T. Chandola, 'Health', in A.H. Halsey (ed.), *Twentieth-Century British Social Trends* (Basingstoke: Macmillan, 2000), pp. 120–1.

all their lives and survived to a ripe old age, while non-smoking, non-drinking contemporaries died of cancer or heart disease in their 50s.[106]

There were also class differences in spending on, and access to, the health care that was available. When Lady Bell published her celebrated study of working-class life in early twentieth-century Middlesbrough, she made much of the impact that such differences had upon the health of those she was investigating. It is a passage that is worth quoting at some length.

> The well-to-do man may wake up one morning, it may be, not feeling as well as usual, simply remain in bed, take his own temperature, perhaps, and telephone for his doctor to come and see him ... But the workman has no telephone, and needless to say no thermometer; he subscribes, it is true, to the doctor belonging to the works, whose services he is entitled to use, but he probably does not know where to lay his hand on that doctor, and in many cases his idea of finding him is to wait until he casually meets him in the street. He goes out, therefore, as usual, no matter what the weather or how he is feeling, in order not to lose a day's work and a day's pay, and when he comes home it is not surprising if he is worse.[107]

Such differential access to health care continued. Household expenditure surveys carried out in the late 1930s suggested that as incomes rose, demand for medical care rose as well. It did so along class lines: middle-class households devoted 7–8 per cent, but working-class households less than 3 per cent, of their spending to health care (defined as expenditure on medicine, doctors, dentists and hospital care other than through the national insurance scheme). The poorest families, in particular, were much more likely to consult a local chemist than a local doctor.[108]

Nor did the establishment of the National Health Service in 1947 bring an end to class inequalities in health care. This is an issue which, as one would expect, continues to be shrouded in a good deal of political controversy. It is easy to assume that because the NHS was paid for chiefly out of general taxation, it meant that the middle class bore the brunt of the financial burden, while the working class reaped the bulk of the medical benefits.[109] In fact, the middle class benefited as much as, if not more than, the working class. For one thing, those from the middle class made greater use of preventative services such as immunization, antenatal care and cervical screening. For another, they were better informed and more confident in their dealings with the health care professionals with whom they came into contact. A study carried out in the 1970s revealed, for example, that middle-class patients' consultations with their GPs lasted, on average, over six minutes. Working-class consultations lasted under five minutes. Another study conducted during the 1970s concluded that working-class patients

---

[106] Blaxter and Paterson, *Mothers and Daughters*, p. 29. Also *The Guardian*, 7 April 1988; 22 February 2003.

[107] Lady Bell, *At the Works: A Study of a Manufacturing Town* (Virago, 1985), pp. 85–6.

[108] Digby and Bosanquet, 'Doctors and Patients', pp. 88–9. Also, A.M. Roberts, *Working Class Barrow and Lancaster 1890–1930* (Lancaster: University of Lancaster, 1976), p. 37; V. Nicolson and S. Smith, *Spend, Spend, Spend* (Fontana, 1978).

[109] Jones, *Health*, p. 173.

received less information and less explanation than middle-class patients, and that, not surprisingly, they expressed less satisfaction with the care which they received.[110]

Class remains central then to the analysis of health. Those from the upper and middle classes tended both to enjoy better health and to live longer than those from the working class.[111] Of course, the correlation between class and health did not always work in this way. Working people were protected, some argue, by the 'generosity' of the welfare state.[112] 'By the end of the 1930s, the social welfare system involved the transfer of £200–250 millions a year from those with incomes above, to those with incomes below, the £250 level.'[113] The better off tended to be at particular risk from the combination of cancer, hypertension, and cardiac and coronary problems that characterized the new twentieth-century distribution of disease and disability. Insofar as the upper class and middle class ate more, worried more, and exercised less than the working class, they put themselves more at risk.[114] Nearly always, however, the relationship between class and health worked to the advantage of the upper and middle classes and to the disadvantage of the working class. Income inequalities, unequal patterns of consumption and differential access to health care meant that it was the working class who tended to suffer from the poorest health and to die at a younger age than other social groups.[115] It is telling, of course, that the academic debate, unlike the political debate, focuses not upon whether class-based inequalities existed, but upon whether they were increasing or decreasing.[116]

The debate revolves, inevitably, around the analysis of mortality statistics. The evidence set out in Figure 3.3 provides little support for the view that rising prosperity and changing patterns of health care brought about a narrowing in class-based differentials. Rather the reverse. It shows not only that class differentials remained stubbornly persistent over the course of the century, but also that they widened, rather than narrowed, following the establishment of the National Health Service. 'In other words, for most of the second half of the century improvements in mortality were greater for individuals in Social Classes I and II than for individuals in Social Classes IV and V.'[117] The analysis of mortality statistics provides no comfort at all for those seeking to decry the relationship between class and health – or more broadly between class analysis and the social history of twentieth-century Britain.

HEALTH, INDIVIDUALS AND STRUCTURES

When discussing health, ill health and well-being, there will always be disagreement as to the balance that should be struck between individual factors such as attitudes,

---

[110] Jones, *Health*, pp. 173–4; Blaxter and Paterson, *Mothers and Daughters*, Ch. 14.

[111] For example, *Observer*, 8 January 1903.

[112] D.K. Benjamin and L.A. Kochin, 'Searching for an explanation of unemployment in interwar Britain', *Journal of Political Economy*, 87, 1979.

[113] Benson, *Working Class*, p. 51.

[114] Benson, *Prime Time*, p. 58; Benson, *Working Class*, pp. 97–8.

[115] Whiteside, 'Counting the cost', pp. 228, 236–7; D. Walker, 'What's your poison?', *The Guardian*, 5 March 2004.

[116] Victor, *Health and Health Care*, p. 55.

[117] Fitzpatrick and Chandola, 'Health', pp. 110–11.

preferences and presuppositions, and structural factors such as age, gender, ethnicity and social class. We are all inclined perhaps to favour individualist explanations. After all, there is a good deal we can do to modify the choices we make; there is nothing we can do to alter our age, gender or ethnicity, and not much most of us can do to change the social class in which we find ourselves. However, the arguments put forward in this chapter suggest that we, like our twentieth-century predecessors, are less likely to enjoy the health we think we deserve, than the health that we probably expect.

PART TWO
THE ACCEPTANCE OF AUTHORITY

4 THE COERCIVE POWER OF THE STATE

COERCION, POWER AND THE STATE

The study of power relations, like the study of consumption and the study of health, has proved increasingly popular in recent years. How was it, historians wonder, that the twentieth century saw so little challenge to the existing economic, social and political order? Why was it that those in power were able to maintain their authority in the face of economic inequality, social deprivation, the horrors of two world wars, the loss of empire, the rise of labour and the challenge of the feminist movement? Why was it that these and the many other changes that took place during the course of the century did not do more to undermine existing patterns of power and authority?

Such questions pose particular difficulties for those whose ideological views predispose them to emphasize the iniquities and inequalities of capitalist society. Left-wing historians bemoan the failure of working people to recognize, let alone attempt to remove, the disabilities under which they laboured. They despair at what they regard as the readiness of the mass of the population to acquiesce in its own subordination. Mike Savage and Andrew Miles point out:

> The problem for Marxist writers lay in explaining why it was that the British
> working class appeared more interested in going to the pub or winning the football
> pools than in setting up barricades and seizing political power. Why, despite the
> apparent solidarity and cohesiveness of working-class culture, despite the unique
> resilience and strength of the trade union movement, despite the entrenched class
> awareness evident in British society, was the working class apparently so unwilling
> to engage in radical political action to achieve a better society?[1]

The answer, left-wing scholars believe, lay partly in the coercive power of the state and partly in the manipulative power of the country's cultural institutions. On the one hand, they argue, the political, legal and law enforcement systems were effective in preventing overt, physical challenges to those who exercised traditional sources of power. On the other hand, they believe, the churches, the schools and the mass media were successful in persuading the great majority of the population that there was no reason for them to attempt to dislodge, or seriously undermine, the existing system of power relations.[2]

---

[1] M. Savage and A. Miles, *The Remaking of the British Working Class, 1840–1940* (Routledge, 1994), pp. 5–6. See also J. Benson, *The Working Class in Britain, 1850–1939* (Harlow: Longman, 1989), p. 141.

[2] See, for example, Savage and Miles, *Remaking*, Ch. 1.

The question of how those in authority managed to retain their power during a century of unprecedented political, economic, social and cultural change poses far fewer difficulties for those whose views incline them to accept and/or welcome the way in which society was organized. Regarding the power structure as natural and welcome, if not preordained, they point to the good sense of the British people in accepting the position that they enjoyed within a stable, increasingly democratic and ever more prosperous society. Eric Hopkins explains:

> Between 1979 and 1990 the working-class electorate was subjected to a constant bombardment of right-wing propaganda in favour of individual enterprise, the supremacy of market forces, the need for cost-effectiveness and the wickedness of the dependency culture … What effect all this had on the average working-class man or woman is hard to say, but perhaps it is not too fanciful to suppose that it became easier for those in work to forget the plight of the unemployed and others on social security. As long as the rent or mortgage repayments could be paid, the family fed, the car serviced and the holiday booked in Spain, all appeared to be well.[3]

This is all rather odd. It seems strange that scholars from opposite ends of the political spectrum should agree about the stability of British society, and stranger still that they should explain that stability in terms largely of the manipulative power of the country's political and cultural institutions. One would have thought, on the face of it, that the most obvious reason for the lack of challenge to the existing economic, social and political order was likely to lie not in the persuasive power of political and cultural institutions but in the coercive power of the state.

Accordingly, it is the aim of this chapter to consider the role and effectiveness of state agencies in preventing overt, physical challenges to the holders of political, economic, social and cultural power. This will be done, as in other chapters, by discussing developments affecting the population as a whole, and then moving on to examine the experiences of some of its major constituent groups: the young, middle-aged and the elderly; men and women; members of ethnic minorities; and those from the middle class and the working class. No group, it will be suggested was able to ignore the direct control of the state, much less evade the indirect influence that the authorities were able to bring to bear upon the conduct of their citizens.

THE NATIONAL STATE AND THE LOCAL STATE

Examining state power is a good deal easier said than done. There are two major complications. The first is that historians, like most people, are prone not only to pay more attention to some aspects of the state's activities than to others, but also to select some aspects for condonation and some for condemnation. Those from the left tend to welcome state intervention in economic planning, industrial relations and social policy. Those from the right are inclined to look favourably upon state involvement when it is directed at military affairs, the regulation of moral behaviour and the enforcement of law and order.

---

[3] E. Hopkins, *The Rise and Decline of the English Working Classes 1918–1990* (Weidenfeld & Nicolson, 1991), p. 277.

The second complication is that historians, like most other people, find it difficult to decide where exactly state power was located.[4] Often, of course, policy was set nationally, but implemented regionally or locally – and with a surprising degree of de facto, if not *de jure*, autonomy. Often too, there are problems in deciding which aspects of state power to include in the analysis that one undertakes. The armed forces, the legal system, the police force and the prison service all acted obviously, and more or less openly, as agents of state power.[5] A.J.P. Taylor claimed:

> Until August, 1914, a sensible, law-abiding, Englishman could pass through life and hardly notice the existence of the state, beyond the post office and the policemen. He could live where he liked and as he liked. He had no official number or identity card. He could travel abroad or leave his country for ever without a passport or any sort of official permission. He could exchange his money for any other currency without restriction or limit. He could buy goods from any country in the world on the same terms as he bought goods at home.[6]

Thereafter, the situation changed, and changed profoundly.[7] There were many other institutions – and individuals – whose role as agents of state power it remains very easy to overlook. Central government became increasingly active. By the end of the century, the Health and Safety Executive decided, for example, when, where, and under what conditions employers could take on labour; the Department of Social Security, the Child Support Agency and the War Pensions Agency decided between them who should and should not receive financial assistance at times of individual and family need.

Local government too assumed powers over an ever expanding, and sometimes bewildering, range of day-to-day activities. By the end of the century, council planning departments decided when, where, and in what form building development could take place; council housing departments decided who should and should not live in local authority-owned accommodation; and council 'parks, recreation and contract services' departments decided the terms upon which members of the public were allowed to make use of the open spaces, nature reserves and adventure playgrounds that they controlled.[8] One almost begins to understand how it was that some commentators sensed a deep-seated government conspiracy to dominate all aspects of civil society. Complained a *Daily Mail* columnist in 1980:

> It's all too easy to become a criminal in Britain. Every one of us is in danger of committing a crime without realising it … For experience shows that so long as stupid laws remain, there will always be the occasional – or bloody-minded – policeman or town councillor who will want to enforce them.[9]

---

[4] D. Garland, *The Culture of Control: Crime and Social Order in Contemporary Society* (Oxford: Oxford University Press, 2001), pp. 5–6.

[5] C. Emsley, *The English Police: A Political and Social History* (Harlow: Longman, 1991), pp. 1–2.

[6] A.J.P. Taylor, *English History, 1914–1945* (Penguin, 1975), p. 25.

[7] D. Garland, *Culture of Control*; J. Paxman, *The Political Animal: An Anatomy* (Penguin, 2003), pp. 194–5.

[8] For example, 'Carol singing illegal', *Observer*, 4 December 1921; 'Compulsory purchase orders – slum clearance', *Birmingham Mail*, 30 October 1934.

[9] F. Bresler, 'How many crimes will you commit today?', *Daily Mail*, 5 July 1980.

Even when it has been decided which agencies of state power to consider, it remains exceptionally difficult to know how best to judge their effectiveness or to decide what was cause and what was effect. However, it can certainly be shown that the state sought, at both national and local levels, to maintain law and order; it can be shown that, with certain exceptions, law and order were maintained; and it can be suggested, though it cannot be proved, that the former was, to some extent, the cause of the latter. Thus the case to be made in this chapter is that state coercion needs to be set alongside – and sometimes above – cultural and political persuasion when seeking to understand the roots of popular compliance with the demands of those who occupied positions of political, economic, social and cultural power.

COMPULSION AND COMPLIANCE

It is surprising how little attention historians pay to the role that the armed forces, the legal system, the police force and the prison service have played in the maintenance of law and order. It is true that certain left-wing commentators routinely ascribe the revolutionary failings of the British people to the machinations of the capitalist state and the venality of its ranks of 'non-commissioned officers'.[10] The problem, explains George Barnsby, is to understand 'the methods whereby the working class were controlled, the capitalist system consolidated, profits protected and the immense strength of the working class movement contained'. The explanation, he believes, is to be found in the tripartite analysis embedded in classic Marxist theory. He wrote in 1972,

> Today in the period of state monopoly capitalism Marxists discuss the
> dictatorship of the bourgeoisie in national terms as the domination of private
> owners of capital over the mass of the population by exploitation at the point of
> production, together with ownership or control of the mass media of
> propaganda and central control of the administration of the State, including the
> coercive apparatus of … armies, police, prisons and the like.[11]

Whatever their ideological presuppositions, historians considering the relationship between state power and public order tend – like Barnsby – to focus upon the nineteenth century, rather than the twentieth.[12] It was the nineteenth century, they believe, that saw the decisive turning point in the state's struggle against drunks, criminals, rioters, strikers and political activists who threatened, intentionally or not, to undermine the authorities' hold over public order. By the 1880s, concludes David Woods, there was a marked decline in drunkenness, common assault and assaults

---

[10] J. Melling, ' "Non-Commissioned Officers": British employers and their supervisory workers, 1880–1920', *Social History*, 5, 1980.

[11] G. Barnsby, *Dictatorship of the Bourgeoisie: Social Control in the Nineteenth Century Black Country* (History Group of the Communist Party, 1972), p. 1.

[12] See, for example, R. Quinault and J. Stevenson (eds), *Popular Protest and Public Order: Six Studies in British History 1790–1920* (Allen & Unwin, 1974); and E. Royle, *Modern Britain: A Social History 1750–1997*, rev. edn (Arnold, 1997), which devotes nineteen pages to 'law, order and restraint', but fewer than six of them to developments during the twentieth century.

on police officers, and this suggests, he believes, 'a substantial change in public order in most areas'.[13] Roger Hood and Andrew Roddam agree. 'As the twentieth century opened the number of crimes recorded by the police in England and Wales and the proportion per head of population were at their lowest point since the first national criminal statistics were published in 1857.'[14] Donald Richter comes to a similar conclusion. One of his aims in writing his book *Riotous Victorians*, he emphasizes, was to challenge 'the widely held belief in the public orderliness of Victorian society, at least (my italics) *in the eighteen-sixties, seventies, and eighties*'.[15] The historical consensus is clear: by the end of the nineteenth century, the struggle for law and order had been more or less won. Although there were threats to the status quo, Britain was spared the disorder and challenges that afflicted so many other countries around the world.

This was not the view taken by the politicians, chief constables, police officers, judges, JPs, lawyers and prison governors who had responsibility for the maintenance of law and order.[16] It is true of course that members of such groups had a vested interest in emphasizing – and all too often exaggerating – the dangers besetting the body politic, and true too that public rhetoric should never be accepted unquestioningly as a reflection of private beliefs.[17] Nonetheless, there is no escaping the conclusion that in the twentieth century, as in the nineteenth, the state and its agents were perfectly prepared to use force and the threat of force when they believed public order – or their own interests – to be seriously at risk.[18]

Those involved in coal mining disputes bore the brunt of state violence. In 1910, Winston Churchill sent mounted cavalry and 500 Metropolitan Police to reinforce the 600 officers already at the disposal of the chief constable of Glamorgan as he struggled to cope during the long and bitter Cambrian Combine strike that raged in the Aberdare and Rhondda valleys. 'It is entirely in the discretion of the police and military authorities', Churchill stressed, 'to say where and when and in what circumstances the constables can be most usefully employed to maintain order and to protect life and property.'[19] Eighty years later, the miners' strike of 1984–5 revived sights and memories that most people thought had disappeared forever. There were reports of troops disguising themselves in police uniforms; and of the police adopting tactics that were designed, according to their own guidelines, not only to 'disperse

---

[13] D. Woods, 'Community Violence', in J. Benson (ed.), *The Working Class in England* 1875–1914 (Croom Helm, 1984), p. 195.

[14] R. Hood and A. Roddam, 'Crime, Sentencing and Punishment', in A.H. Halsey (ed.), *Twentieth-Century British Social Trends* (Macmillan, 2000), p. 675.

[15] Donald C. Richter, *Riotous Victorians* (Athens, OH.: Ohio University Press, 1981), p. 163.

[16] See for example, Manchester Police Museum, Police Order 456, Vol. 8, 30 September 1919; 'Theft of 4 bananas, 3 Years for a Muswell Hill burglar', *Observer*, 25 September 1927.

[17] See, for instance, B. Porter, 'Secrecy and the Special Branch, 1880–1914', *Bulletin of the Society for the Study of Labour History*, 52, 1987.

[18] 'The Women's Conference at Manchester', *Observer*, 1 May 1921.

[19] D. Evans, *Labour Strife in the South Wales Coalfield 1910–1911* (Cardiff: Cymric Federation Press, 1911), p. 248. Also R.P. Arnot, *South Wales Miners Glowyr de Cymru: A History of the South Wales Miners' Federation (1898–1914)* (Allen & Unwin, 1967), Ch. vii.

and/or incapacitate' but also 'to create fear'.[20] These new tactics proved highly effective. Reported a Nottinghamshire striker:

> I never felt so frightened or so angry in my life … I could see … three or four … policemen kicking hell out of a youth … He managed to stagger to his feet and his face was covered in blood … and one of them … it was like one of those African executions, he got his stick out about a yard long and whacked him across the face with it and the ambulance man was angry and was effing and blinding to the police and they had to put that young lad on an oxygen tank for about 20 minutes before they moved him.[21]

The miners were not the only victims of police violence. Striking dockers, railwaymen, engineering workers and print workers all found themselves on the receiving end of intimidatory policing.[22] Sometimes, the state's tactics seem, at least in retrospect, to border almost on the absurd. When railway workers went on strike in 1919, the Lloyd George government responded by stationing troops in Hyde Park, and during the General Strike of 1926 the Baldwin administration took the decision to deploy battleships – and a submarine – off the South Wales coast.[23] It was more usual, however, for the authorities to react to the potential breakdown of public order with tactics that were intimidating – and were sometimes undeniably brutal. In 1919, for example, a 'general strike' in Glasgow culminated in a running battle between police and strikers; in 1932, the police baton-charged striking Lancashire weavers; and in 1968, three of the six pickets arrested at Stockport during a strike at the town's Roberts-Arundel factory appeared in court nursing severe bruises, broken noses and, in one case, a neck injury.[24]

It was not only strikers who found themselves victims of police violence. So sometimes did political activists and those who took part in protest marches and demonstrations. In 1901, the police launched a baton charge to clear the streets of Birmingham following a speech by Lloyd George in the town hall, an action that left one man dead, apparently the result of a truncheon blow. In 1920, a superintendent in the Metropolitan Police justified a baton charge against a procession of the unemployed on the grounds that the crowd was 'obviously composed of the lower class of alien Jews'.[25] In 1932, violence flared when 2,500 police confronted hunger marchers in Hyde Park: the special constables lost their nerve and attacked the crowd.[26] The 1950s saw a series of violent confrontations between the police and demonstrators supporting

[20] C. Lloyd, 'A National Riot Police: Britain's "Third Force"?', in B. Fine and R. Millar (eds), *Policing the Miners' Strike* (Lawrence & Wishart, 1985), p. 75; Emsley, *English Police*, pp. 184, 257.

[21] R. Samuel, 'Introduction', in R. Samuel, B. Bloomfield and G. Boanas (eds), *The Enemy Within: Pit Villages and the Miners' Strike of 1984–5* (Routledge & Kegan Paul, 1986), p. 16.

[22] R. Geary, *Policing Industrial Disputes: 1893 to 1985* (Methuen, 1985). See, for example, 'Strikers attack black-leg citadel. Police injured in Scottish riot', *Observer*, 16 June 1912.

[23] Samuel *et al.* (eds), *Enemy Within*, p. 2.

[24] Geary, *Policing Industrial Disputes*, pp. 49, 52, 69.

[25] Emsley, *English Police*, pp. 112, 138.

[26] B. Weinberger, *The Best Police in the World: An Oral History of English Policing from the 1930s to the 1960s* (Aldershot: Scolar, 1995), p. 172.

the Campaign for Nuclear Disarmament, opposing the war in Vietnam and protesting against the apartheid regime in South Africa.[27] Indeed, it has been suggested that, 'Since 1981 public order training has become, in effect, riot control training', and that this, together with new 'hardline' police attitudes, 'has played a significant part in escalating industrial confrontation beyond the pushing and shoving of the seventies to a new, more violent, level'.[28]

COMPULSION, COMPLIANCE AND ACCOUNTABILITY

It is an unsettling catalogue of violence, intimidation and intransigence. It most certainly presents a picture far removed from the comforting notion, which has still not entirely disappeared, of the avuncular British 'bobby', more honest, more caring, more decent and more approachable than his counterparts overseas. Whether or not the long-running television series *Dixon of Dock Green* reflected reality (or as *The Times* suggested, drew upon 'an indulgent tradition'), it set the standard against which police behaviour was often measured during the second half of the century. 'This was policing as people would have liked it to be, as they liked to remember it, as they hoped it had been.'[29]

However, this is not quite the point. The issue is less whether the police were violent or how often they were violent, but why they were violent, and what impact their violence had upon popular attitudes and behaviour. These are highly complex issues that raise fundamental questions not only about the ways in which the state wielded its power but also about the ways in which historians deal with issues of subjectivity, causation and evidence. The fact that police violence occurred does not mean that it was common, does not mean that it was state policy and certainly does not mean that it was effective in determining public attitudes and behaviour.

The leading historians of English policing acquit the service of charges of acting as the agent of state-inspired violence. 'Massed police operations in the context of large-scale demonstrations was not what the police relished or saw as their primary task', explains Barbara Weinberger. 'Instead, it was the routine maintenance of order on the beat by individual constables that the PC valued and saw as his central role.'[30] Clive Emsley too is insistent that when violence occurred, it resulted from the ineffectiveness, rather than the effectiveness, of internal lines of command. According to this analysis, the causes of indiscipline were environmental rather than ideological. Crowd control was most likely to turn brutal, he maintains, when, for example, the police were frightened, angry at losing a rest day and/or resentful at being away from home, a situation in which 'they might respond like soldiers in alien territory with little liking or respect for the local community'. Indeed, he concludes that of all the possible reasons that one might bring to bear to account for outbreaks of crowd-control violence, the argument that the police, 'were simply acting as the shock troops of capitalism when they broke heads is the least convincing'.[31]

---

[27] Emsley, *English Police*, p. 177.

[28] Geary, *Policing Industrial Disputes*, pp. 134–5. See also Emsley, *English Police*, p. 257.

[29] Weinberger, *Best Police in the World*, p. 205. See also Emsley, *English Police*, pp. xiii, 169–70.

[30] Weinberger, *Best Police in the World*, p. 183. See also, Emsley, *English Police*, p. 3.

[31] Emsley, *English Police*, p. 142.

Whether or not the police broke heads at the instigation of an uncompromising capitalist state, those in positions of political authority routinely obfuscated and/or defended the actions taken by officers in controlling crowds and demonstrations. When the Lloyd George Cabinet discussed police violence during the 1919 'general strike' in Glasgow, it was told that, 'foot and mounted police had charged the crowd in order to quell a riot', and was reassured by the Secretary for Scotland, that, 'it was more clear than ever that it was a misnomer to call the situation in Glasgow a strike – it was a Bolshevist rising'.[32] When an Independent Labour Party MP asked a question in the House of Commons in 1934 about police 'brutality' against unemployed demonstrators in Manchester and Sheffield, the Home Secretary replied that he had received reports from the chief constables in question and saw no need to take any action. As Lady Astor remarked, 'Is not the word of a chief constable better than that of a Communist?'[33]

It is not surprising perhaps that those with operational responsibility for the policing of disputes often continued to adopt a similarly dismissive approach when confronted with complaints about police behaviour. When shop stewards involved in the Roberts-Arundel strike of 1968 asked the superintendent charged with the control of picketing to exercise more restraint over his men, he retorted, 'Never mind that, there were three policemen injured last Thursday.'[34] Such attitudes persisted. During the 1980s, Roger Geary interviewed a number of senior officers as part of the research for a book on the policing of industrial disputes. Several of them conceded that constables who came face-to-face with pickets and strikers sometimes overreacted.

> So far as the senior officer knowing anything about it, I don't think they bother all that much because, it sounds awful, but if you've got a dog job to do, if you've got a dog, you've got to give it a lump of sugar now and again … It's a bit like Generals turning a blind eye to rape and pillaging in wartime.[35]

However, this, once again, is not quite the point. Whether police violence was concealed, criticized or condoned, there is no denying that it occurred. The police, even their most fervent admirers admit, were sometimes violent in their dealings with strikers, demonstrators, protesters and others perceived to pose a threat to industrial efficiency, political authority and public order. It was clear to anyone with eyes to see and ears to hear that in certain circumstances the police, one of the state's foremost agents of control, were prepared to use force in order to ensure that they controlled dissent and maintained an acceptable level of public order.

However, there is no denying either that police violence occurred only occasionally. Nor did it touch directly the great majority of the population who never went on strike, never joined a demonstration, never took part in a protest march – and never found themselves in police custody. It follows therefore that the great majority of the population were affected by state violence, if affected they were, not by what they

---

[32] I. McLean, 'Popular Protest and Public Order: Red Clydeside, 1915–1919', in Quinault and Stevenson (eds), *Popular Protest*, p. 231. See also Manchester Police Museum, Police Order 215, Vol. 8, 30 September 1920.

[33] Emsley, *English Police*, p. 143.

[34] Geary, *Policing Industrial Disputes*, p. 69.

[35] Geary, *Policing Industrial Disputes*, p. 114. See also P. Lawrence, 'The Police, Poverty and Criminality in France and England, 1850–1939', European Social Science History Conference, Humboldt University, 2004.

themselves saw and experienced, but by what they heard from friends and aquaintances, what they read in newspapers and magazines and what they saw at the cinema or on the television.

Such detachment compounds, rather than diminishes the problem of determining the extent to which the state maintained its power by the use of coercion as well as/instead of the use of persuasion. Accordingly, it is believed that the best way to proceed is, as in other chapters, to narrow the focus from the population as a whole to some of the major groups within it. This narrower focus should prove of considerable benefit. It will make it easier to consider agencies of state control other than the police. It will also make it possible to show beyond reasonable doubt that the state targeted some groups more than others, and that this targeting sometimes had consequences diametrically opposed to those that were intended.

AGE, ANXIETY AND SURVEILLANCE

Age marked out some groups for special attention. Those with a benign view of the state and its activities might be surprised by this, supposing that those in power did their best to be age-blind, or at least age-neutral in their formulation of policy. But this was far from the case. The state, its agencies and its agents believed that they needed to take account of the different circumstances of different age groups – an awareness that sometimes slipped into age stereotyping. The state and its agents assumed, along with most other sections of society, that children were in need of special treatment. They assumed too that if there was a threat to public order or political authority, it was likely to emanate from adolescents and young adults rather than the middle-aged or the elderly.[36] Age, it will be suggested, is as important to understanding state policy as it is most of the other aspects of twentieth-century history considered in this book.

The state intervened increasingly in the way that young people were brought up. This, again, may come as something of a surprise since it is often assumed that it was the nineteenth century, not the twentieth, that saw the key initiatives in the state's attempts to improve the lives of the nation's children. It is true that by the end of the nineteenth century informed opinion believed that children had rights, and that the state alone was in a position to enforce them.[37] Between 1870 and 1900, legislation was passed to ensure, it was hoped, that children were not ill-treated, that they attended school until the age of 12, and that when they left school they did not work more than a maximum number of hours a week in industries such as textiles, agriculture, coal mining and brick making. 'On the whole,' concludes Eric Hopkins, 'notable strides appear to have been made towards a more civilised treatment of children by the end of the nineteenth century.'[38]

---

[36] 'Police problems', *Daily Mail*, 6 February 1920; 'Grannies jailed for drug smuggling', *Daily Mail*, 1 April 1995.

[37] H. Cunningham, *Children and Childhood in Western Society Since 1500* (Harlow: Longman, 1995), p. 162.

[38] E. Hopkins, *Childhood Transformed: Working-Class Children in Nineteenth-Century England* (Manchester: Manchester University Press, 1994), p. 315. Also pp. 219–20; L. Rose, *The Erosion of Childhood: Child Oppression in Britain 1860–1918* (Routledge, 1991), p. 244.

But much remained to be done. Governments, both Labour and Conservative, continued to intervene to limit parental freedom of action in dealing with their children. They specified with increasing precision – and increasing effectiveness – how young people should spend their time, how they should be fed, how their health should be protected, and how they should be disciplined.[39] The education system provided the obvious vehicle for state intervention. The governments in power during the twentieth century raised by a third the age until which parents were required to keep their children in full-time education. They did so in stages, increasing the school-leaving age from 12 at the beginning of the century, to 14 in 1922, 15 in 1947, and 16 in 1972. The result was that between the mid-1960s and the mid-1990s, for example, the proportion of 15-year-olds attending school – with or without their parents' blessing – increased from well under two-thirds to getting on for 100 per cent.[40]

Many parents did not give their blessing. Indeed, the fact that the state felt it necessary to stipulate a school-leaving age suggests, of course, that not all families placed a high value on formal educational provision. 'Don't worry about your education', the wife of a Bristol bricklayer used to tell her children during the 1930s: '… as long as you can read and as long as you can write and as long as you know what's in your wage packet, that's all you need to know, the rest will come to you as you live your life.'[41] Working-class families continued to display a distrust of book-based learning, reported Richard Hoggart in the 1950s:

> Parents who refuse, as a few still do, to allow their children to take up
> scholarships are not always thinking of the fact that they would have to be fed
> and clothed for much longer; at the back is this vaguely formulated but strong
> doubt of the value of education.[42]

Those responsible for social policy also began to see to it that the nation's children received at least one square meal a day. Legislation passed in 1911 allowed local authorities to provide meals for poor children, an initiative which proved highly contentious because it involved 'public intervention in family life to take over what many considered an essential parental responsibility'.[43] In fact, the new legislation had little day-to-day impact until the 1930s.[44] But by the early 1970s, more than 5 million meals were served every day. Although this figure had fallen to 3.5 million by the mid-1990s, it represented a continuing and substantial incursion into parental autonomy. It meant that at the end of the century, after 100 years and more of economic growth and economic

---

[39] M.J. Wiener, *Reconstructing the Criminal: Culture, Law and Policy in England, 1830–1914* (Cambridge: Cambridge University Press, 1990), p. 375.

[40] G. Smith, 'Schools', in Halsey (ed.), *British Social Trends*, pp. 186, 194–5.

[41] Avon County Reference Library, Bristol People's Oral History Project, Transcript RO59, p. 4.

[42] R. Hoggart, *The Uses of Literacy: Aspects of Working-Class Life with Special Reference to Publications and Entertainments* (Penguin, 1957), p. 84.

[43] J. Parker and J. Webb, 'Social Services', in Halsey (ed.), *British Social Trends*, p. 534. See also D. Fraser, *The Evolution of the British Welfare State: A History of Social Policy Since the Industrial Revolution* (Basingstoke: Macmillan, 1973), p. 138.

[44] 'Sandwiches and dulled wits', *Observer*, 27 November 1927.

prosperity, the state provided meals for 45 per cent of its children – and fed nearly 20 per cent of them without charging because they came from low-income families.[45]

The state strove in other ways to bypass parents in the drive to improve the physical well-being of the nation's children. The establishment of the School Medical Service in 1907 imposed a duty on education authorities to inspect children, and legislation passed two years later enabled them to recover the costs of treating children whose parents gave their consent and were able to pay.[46] Between 1910 and 1935, the number of school clinics increased from 30 to 2,037, the number of school dentists from 27 to 852, and the number of school nurses from 436 to 3,429.[47] The 'nit nurse' became widely recognized – widely resented and widely ridiculed – in the nation's struggle against head lice.[48]

However, the state did not confine itself to attaching a series of specialist child-welfare agencies to the formal educational system. It also intervened directly in the parent–child relationship, stipulating with more and more precision how parents were to treat their children, whether children should be allowed to marry without parental consent – and eventually giving children the right to start legal proceedings against their parents.[49] Such changes, it goes without saying, constituted a remarkable realignment of the formal, legal relationship between parents and children, between one generation and the next.

There was a whole raft of child welfare legislation. The Children's Act of 1908 consolidated the state's nineteenth-century efforts to protect the young: it required, *inter alia*, that local authorities monitor foster children under the age of 7, and that the Poor Law authorities supervise children who, at home or in care, had been the subject of cruelty proceedings.[50] The Children Act of 1948 compelled local authorities to set up specialist committees with professional officers with a view to establishing a secure family environment for children in care.[51] The Children and Young Persons Act of 1969 attempted to remove responsibility for juvenile offenders from the police, magistrates and prison department and place it instead in the hands of local authorities and the Department of Health and Social Security.[52] Finally in 1989, new legislation allowed children, for the first time, to instruct a solicitor to start proceedings on family matters which were of concern to them. It was a radical departure. 'There is a sense in which the law is entering uncharted waters here', concludes Jeremy Roche: 'adult society does not know the kinds of issues that will be brought before the courts.'[53]

---

[45] Parker and Webb, 'Social Services', pp. 534–5.

[46] Rose, *Erosion*, p. 159.

[47] Cunningham, *Children and Childhood*, p. 168.

[48] Personal recollection.

[49] 'Parents over-ruled', *Observer*, 13 March 1927.

[50] Hopkins, *Childhood Transformed*, p. 203. Also J. Briggs, C. Harrison, A. McInnes and D. Vincent, *Crime and Punishment in England: An Introductory History* (UCL Press, 1996), p. 236.

[51] Fraser, *Evolution of the British Welfare State*, pp. 217–18. See Women's Group on Public Welfare, *The Neglected Child and His Family: A Study Made in 1946–7* (Oxford: Oxford University Press, 1948).

[52] J. Roche, 'Children's Rights: Participation and Dialogue', in J. Roche and S. Tucker (eds), *Youth in Society: Contemporary Theory, Policy and Practice* (Buckingham: Open University, 1997), p. 134.

[53] Roche, 'Children's Rights', p. 51.

The law, as everybody recognized, did not necessarily develop in line with public opinion. Some parents seemed only too pleased to beat their children, and most were prepared to slap, smack or hit them when their patience snapped or they had tried everything else that they could think of. Nor, it must be stressed, were such attitudes confined to the beginning of the century or found only among families that were poor and ill educated. The author of this book recalls, for example, how common corporal punishment was in the lower-middle-class suburb of London in which he was brought up during the 1950s and early 1960s.[54] A survey carried out on behalf of the Scottish Law Commission in 1992 revealed that two-thirds of parents approved of smacking 15-year-olds.[55] Six years later, a Scottish teacher was prosecuted for pulling down his 8-year-old daughter's pants and trousers and smacking her when she became hysterical on a visit to the dentist. It was a case that split public opinion – yet again – between those who believed that the state had a responsibility to protect the most vulnerable members of society and those who believed that state interference in family life had gone too far.[56]

There was also some divergence between state policy and public opinion when it came to the treatment of adolescents. There was widespread agreement that teenagers needed disciplining, and that the state had a key role to play in doing so. There was a feeling by the beginning of the century that parents – primarily, of course, working-class parents – were either 'too lenient for the public good or too savage for the good of the erring child'. Many felt therefore that, 'the work of the police and the courts was bound to increase'.[57] And increase it did, as the power of the state was brought to bear upon those in their teens and early twenties. Legislation was passed, policing targeted and sentencing strengthened. However, there was a widespread feeling that the police and the courts were far too lenient in their treatment of juvenile offenders.[58]

It is not always appreciated by those not directly affected how much legislation was – and remains – explicitly age-specific. For example, the Children Act of 1908 made it 'the duty of a constable and a park keeper being in uniform, to seize any cigarettes or cigarette papers in the possession of any person apparently under the age of sixteen whom he finds smoking in any street or public place'. The Children and Young Persons Act of 1933 decreed that, 'If a child is found in the bar of any licensed premises during the permitted hours, the holder of the licence shall be deemed to have committed an offence under this section unless he shows that he had used due diligence to prevent the child from being admitted to the bar or that the child had apparently attained the age of fourteen years.'[59] The age of criminal responsibility was

---

[54] Personal recollection.

[55] B. Corby, 'The Mistreatment of Young People', in Roche and Tucker (eds), *Youth in Society*, p. 209.

[56] *The Guardian*, 10 September 2001. The authorities were less prepared to intervene in other forms of domestic violence. 'The good old law', *Observer*, 13 February 1921; 18 December 1927. See, for example, Manchester Police Museum, *Chief Constable of Manchester Police Annual Report*, 1935, p. iii; Warrington Library and Museum, *Warrington County Borough Juvenile Court Panel, Chairman's Annual Report*, 1971–2, PS13, p. 1.

[57] Briggs *et al., Crime and Punishment*, p. 181. See, for example, 'Girl thief of 12', *Daily Mail*, 20 February 1920. Also Wiener, *Reconstructing the Criminal*, p. 275.

[58] J. Mattinson and C. Mirrlees-Black, *Attitudes to Crime and Criminal Justice: Findings from the 1998 British Crime Survey* (Home Office Research, Development and Statistics Directorate, 2000), p. 1.

[59] Children's Act 1908 (8 Edw. 7), Ch. 67, no. 40. Children and Young Persons Act 1933 (23 Geo.5), Ch. 12, no. 6. I am grateful to Mike Haynes for these references.

raised from 7 to 8 in 1933, and from 8 to 10 during the early 1960s.[60] The age of consent for heterosexual intercourse has been fixed at 16 since 1885,[61] but when homosexual intercourse was made legal in 1967, the age of consent was set at 21.[62]

The result was that by the end of the century, 16- and 17-year-olds were subject to a substantial, but inchoate, conglomeration of controls and constraints. They could marry, but only with their parents' consent. They could buy cigarettes, but not drink in a pub. They were legally responsible for the crimes they committed, but they were not able to sign legal contracts (including tenancy agreements) unless they lived in Scotland. They were entitled to receive medical advice and treatment without their parents' knowledge or consent, but only if their GP considered that they were mature enough to understand the importance of the decisions that they were making.[63]

It is much more widely recognized that when it came to the enforcement of legislation (whether or not it was age-specific), a great deal depended upon public perceptions, policing policy, the attitudes of the men on the beat, and the resources that they had at their disposal.[64] Indeed, any attempt to draw conclusions about the relationship between policing and criminality is bedevilled by the intractable difficulties of distinguishing between cause and effect.[65] Thus the statistics that are available show that young people were more likely than those from other age groups to be stopped, arrested, prosecuted, found guilty or cautioned. What these statistics cannot tell us is whether this means that young people were less law-abiding than those from other age groups or that they were more likely to be singled out for special attention.

It is clear, nevertheless, that the police always tended to look with particular suspicion on the 'independent youth culture which they saw on the street'.[66] They did not like young people congregating on street corners, gathering together in larger groups or, naturally enough, causing any kind of trouble.[67] However, constables on the beat enjoyed more discretion when dealing with young people than they did when they came into contact with those from other age groups. The way they reacted depended to a considerable degree upon local custom and local circumstances: Barbara Weinberger suggests that for most of the century, 'The balance between the proper use of police discretion and their proper role as law enforcers remained uneasy, with no one prepared to condemn outright the preventive work of juvenile liaison officers, but no one prepared to insist that they became part of the set up in every force.'[68]

---

[60] R. Hood and A. Roddam, 'Crime, Sentencing and Punishment', in Halsey (ed.), *British Social Trends*, p. 679.

[61] Briggs *et al.*, *Crime and Punishment*, p. 200.

[62] K. Wellings, J. Field, A. Johnson and J. Wadsworth, *Sexual Behaviour in Britain: The National Survey of Sexual Attitudes and Lifestyles* (Penguin, 1994), pp. 199, 236.

[63] B. Coles, 'Welfare Services for Young People', in Roche and Tucker (eds), *Youth in Society*, pp. 98–9.

[64] Manchester Police Museum, Greater Manchester Police Constable Pocket Book, A121, April, 1938. Hood and Roddam, 'Crime, Sentencing and Punishment', p. 678.

[65] See, for instance, D. Charles, *Britain Since 1939: Progress and Decline* (Basingstoke: Palgrave, 2002), pp. 15–16.

[66] P. Thompson, *The Edwardians: The Remaking of British Society* (Paladin, 1977), p. 70.

[67] See, for example, Warrington Library and Museum, Warrington County Borough Juvenile Court Panel, Chairman's Annual Report, 1971–2, p. 2.

[68] Weinberger, *Best Police in the World*, p. 153.

During the second half of the century, the situation was complicated – and politicized – by the controversies that raged around the policing of 'black' youth. It is an issue that will be considered at some length later in the chapter. For the moment, what needs to be stressed is that from the Second World War onwards, new concerns about large-scale, non-white immigration began to coalesce with long-standing anxieties about the threat posed by the indigenous adolescent population. The appearance of Teddy boys in the 1950s, the battles between mods and rockers in the 1960s, the panic about mugging in the 1970s, the 'race' riots of the early 1980s, and the football hooliganism of the 1980s and 1990s all seemed to point, in their different ways, to the breakdown both of inter-generational relations and of the contract between the governors and the governed. Those in authority knew who to blame.[69] 'Parents, of this time, unfortunately, do not take sufficient care in bringing up their children', complained the Recorder of Bradford in 1951.[70] 'Parental negligence in responsibility is a significant factor in delinquent behaviour', explained the chairman of Warrington Juvenile Court in the early 1970s.[71] It was parental failings that were responsible for the riots of 1981, agreed the Chief Constable of Manchester:

> What in the name of goodness are these young people doing on the streets indulging in this behaviour and at this time of night? Is there no discipline that can be brought to bear on these young people? Are the parents not interested in the futures of these young people?[72]

If parents would not discipline the nation's children, the state would have to step in. There was a constant tension, as might be expected, between those who advocated the support and rehabilitation of young offenders and those who saw no alternative to punishment and incarceration. It was the latter who eventually won the day.[73] It was a long and complex debate, but something of the change in official thinking can be seen by comparing a White Paper from the late 1960s with ministerial pronouncements made in the early 1990s. The 1968 White Paper, *Children in Trouble*, suggested that youth crime should be regarded as an indication of immaturity, maladjustment or damaged personality, and needed to be treated therefore in much the same way as an illness or a disease.[74] Twenty-five years later, state intervention was defined very firmly in terms of punishment rather than rehabilitation. The Conservative Prime Minister, John Major, proclaimed that, 'we should understand less and condemn more', while the Home Secretary, Michael Howard, insisting time and again that 'prison works', proposed the establishment of ten American-style 'boot camps' to give juvenile offenders a taste of 'shock' incarceration.[75]

---

[69] 'Teaching her child to steal', *Observer*, 11 February 1906.

[70] G. Pearson, *Hooligan: A History of Respectable Fears* (Basingstoke: Macmillan, 1983), pp. 21–2.

[71] Warrington Library and Museum, Warrington Juvenile Court, Annual Report, 1955, PS13, p. 1.

[72] E. Cashmore and E. McLaughlin (eds), *Out of Order: Policing Black People* (Routledge, 1991), pp. 54–5.

[73] Garland, *Culture of Control*, pp. 8–9, 14. See also Manchester Police Museum, *Chief Constable of Manchester Police Annual Report*, 1935, p. ii; Warrington Library and Museum, Warrington County Borough Juvenile Court Panel, Chairman's Annual Report, 1971–2, p. 5.

[74] J. Muncie, 'Shifting Sands: Care, Community and Custody in Justice Discourse', in Roche and Tucker (eds), *Youth in Society*, p. 133.

[75] J. Muncie, 'Shifting Sands', pp. 139–40. See also Garland, *Culture of Control*, pp. 13–14.

GENDER, INVISIBILITY AND VISIBILITY

It was an analysis from which the female half of the adolescent population was effectively
excluded. In this respect, if no other, the way that those in power viewed young
people was indicative of the way in which they regarded the population as a whole.
Insofar as they perceived any overt, physical challenge to their authority, they believed
that it was gender-specific, that it emanated from men rather than from women.

This is not to say that those in power saw no need for women to be taught to think
and behave in ways that, by happy coincidence, were held to be both gender-
appropriate and conducive to the needs of the family, the demands of the economy,
the stability of the social system and the maintenance of public order. Indeed, this is
one of the themes to be examined in detail in the chapter which follows. What needs
to be stressed here is the commonly held belief that the sexes needed to be treated in
different ways. Those in power felt that girls and women could probably be persuaded
relatively easily to accept conventional patterns of power and authority.[76] They feared,
however, that boys and men might possibly challenge the existing economic, social
and political order. They needed to be reminded therefore that the authorities were
prepared to use the threat of force – and force itself – to bring them into line.

When politicians, policy-makers, the police, the press and other commentators
discussed what to do about strikers, protestors, demonstrators, football hooligans,
criminals and other potential threats to the social order, they generally assumed that
they were dealing with the male half of the population. The history of the term
'hooligan' is instructive. Thanks to Geoffrey Pearson, we know a good deal about its
provenance and usage: the term, he explains, dates from the late nineteenth century,
and was probably popularized by a music hall song:

> Oh, the Hooligans! Oh, the Hooligans!
> Always on the riot,
> Cannot keep them quiet,
> Oh, the Hooligans! Oh, the Hooligans!
> They are the boys
> To make a noise
> In our backyard.[77]

He cites many further examples of the gender assumptions embedded in discussions
of teenagers and their delinquent behaviour. In the early 1950s, he reminds us, Richard
Hoggart identified a group known as the 'juke box boys', young men, 'between fifteen
and twenty, with drape-suits, picture ties, and an American slouch'.[78] Ten years later,
the British Medical Association published its views about *The Adolescent*. 'Looked at
in his worst light the adolescent can take on an alarming aspect', it warned: 'he has
learned no definite moral standards from his parents, is contemptuous of the law,

[76] For example, *Newcastle Evening Chronicle*, 10 September 1905; *Observer*, 11 December 1906.
[77] Pearson, *Hooligan*, p. 75.
[78] Pearson, *Hooligan*, p. 19.

easily bored.'[79] Pearson himself puts it rather neatly: 'It was always assumed … in these hooligan discourses, that "the adolescent" was a boy: when the other sex figures at all it is as mothers, usually neglectful ones.'[80]

It was assumed too that the adult criminal was likely to be a man. Prostitution and shoplifting aside, crime was seen as a male phenomenon. Respectable women, it was believed, came to court only as victims or as witnesses.[81] Indeed, it has been suggested that the fact that men committed more crime than women is the first thing that any theory of criminality should seek to accommodate.[82] The second thing it would need to take on board was the fact that men were much more likely than women to commit violent crimes such as murder and assault.[83] It must be said though that towards the end of the century, there developed 'something of a moral panic created about the allegations that women's share of crime was rising faster than that of men and rising particularly fast in unfeminine and untypical offences such as robbery and violence'.[84] 'Having a baby won't save women from jail', reported the *Daily Mail* in 1990. 'The warning came from the controversial Judge Pickles after he had sent a teenage single mother to jail for six months.'[85]

It is true, it bears repeating, that women were less likely than men to work in strike-prone industries such as coal mining and building, less likely to attend football matches, and less likely perhaps to feel the need to turn to crime as a means of making a living. However, it must be recognized too that gender-based analyses of crime contained within them elements both of circularity and of self-fulfilling prophecy. The authorities believed that men were more likely than women to indulge in disruptive behaviour, they expected to find men engaging in such behaviour, they looked for men engaging in such behaviour, they found men engaging in such behaviour – and they prosecuted them for it. Accordingly, it is well known that criminal statistics are notoriously

> difficult to interpret when used as a barometer of changing morality or respect for the law. This is because the extent to which events are reported as criminal victimizations and reported to the police, the extent to which they are recorded as crimes of various types by the police, the extent to which such crimes are cleared up, and the use by police and prosecutors of their discretionary powers to bring offenders to justice, are all affected by the very moral and social changes, which the statistics seek to illuminate.[86]

---

[79] Pearson, *Hooligan*, p. 17. See also S. Hall, C. Critcher, T. Jefferson, J. Clarke and B. Roberts, *Policing the Crisis: Mugging, the State, and Law and Order* (Basingstoke: Macmillan, 1978).

[80] Pearson, *Hooligan*, p. 17.

[81] M. Meyers, *News Coverage of Violence Against Women: Engendering Blame* (Sage, 1997); Briggs *et al.*, *Crime and Punishment*, p. 183. But see, for example, 'Psychology of women', *Observer*, 19 December 1909; 'The policewoman', *Observer*, 28 March 1915.

[82] S. Walklate, *Gender, Crime and Criminal Justice* (Cullompton: Willan, 2001), p. 1.

[83] Walklate, *Gender*, pp. 5–6. See also 'Women turn to violent crime in hunt for thrills', *Daily Mail*, 1 September 1996.

[84] F. Heidensohn, *Women and Crime* (Basingstoke: Macmillan, 1985), p. 6.

[85] 'Having a baby won't save women from jail', *Daily Mail*, 3 January 1990.

[86] Hood and Roddam, 'Crime, Sentencing and Punishment', p. 676.

Nevertheless, those in power were right in the gender assumptions that they made. Although there were protestors and demonstrators of both sexes,[87] not many women became involved in activities that challenged public order and threatened established authority. There were few female strikers. Industrial disputes were virtually unknown in industries such as retailing and domestic service where women predominated;[88] and when women did get involved, as they did for example in the miners' strike of 1984–5, it became a matter of public comment and debate.[89] Nor were there many women involved in football hooliganism, a form of disorder which has been described, correctly enough, as a form of 'lad culture'.[90] 'Oxford Boys we are here,' the hooligans chanted, 'shag your women, drink your beer.'[91]

Women's contribution to criminality was also limited, notes Frances Heidensohn. 'Indeed this is an area of public achievement where women hardly compete with men.'[92] Certainly, the criminal statistics, for all the reservations one has about them, offer consistent and convincing support for the authorities' gendered reading of crime, dissent and disorder. The statistics collected from 1930 onwards show, in Figure 4.1, that for the following three-quarters of a century, six times more men than women were found guilty or cautioned for indictable offences.[93] Other statistics collected

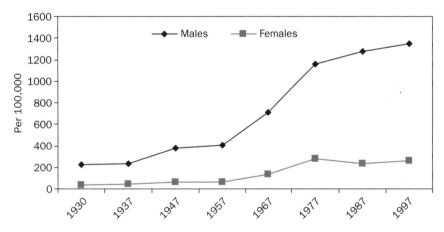

Figure 4.1 Males and females 21 years and over found guilty or cautioned, England and Wales, 1930–97
Source: Based on R. Hood and A. Roddam, 'Crime, Sentencing and Punishment', in A.H. Halsey (ed.), *Twentieth-Century British Social Trends* (Basingstoke: Macmillan, 2000), p. 689.

---

[87] 'Women rioters to stay in prison', *Observer*, 24 April 1927.

[88] J. Benson, *The Working Class in Britain, 1850–1939* (Harlow: Longman, 1989), p. 57.

[89] Samuel *et al.*, *Enemy Within*, p. 28. See also, *Daily Mail*, 9 July 1968.

[90] T. Mason, *Association Football and English Society 1863–1915* (Brighton: Harvester, 1981), Ch. 5;
J. Williams and R. Taylor, 'Boys Keep Swinging: Masculinity and Football Culture in England', in
T. Newburn and E.A. Stanko (eds), *Just Boys Doing Business?* (Routledge, 1994), p. 225. Also pp. 215–16.

[91] R. Holt, *Sport and the British: A Modern History* (Oxford: Oxford University Press, 1989), p. 330.

[92] Heidensohn, *Women and Crime*, p. 5.

[93] For the late nineteenth century, see L. Zedner, *Women, Crime, and Custody in Victorian England* (Oxford: Clarendon Press, 1991), pp. 20, 304–5.

during the second half of the century throw further light on the gendering of crime. They reveal, for example, that 34 per cent of men, but only 8 per cent of women, born in 1953 had been convicted of an offence by the time they reached the age of 40.[94] They confirm, once again, that it was men, not women, who behaved in ways that seemed likely to threaten the social order.

ETHNICITY, VISIBILITY AND PREJUDICE

If there was one group – of men and boys – that received particular attention from the forces of law and order, it was those from ethnic minorities. This, of course, is to enter highly contested terrain. Whether one accounts for the state's treatment of the Irish, Jews, Asians, Afro-Caribbeans and other non-white groups in terms of majority prejudices or minority failings seems to depend less upon the evidence that is available than upon the presuppositions that one brings to bear. The author of this book makes no claim to intellectual superiority or out-of-the-ordinary objectivity. He recognizes that he is as likely as anybody else to struggle to break free from the values and assumptions held by those of his particular age, gender, ethnic, generational, class and occupational background. Yet even when every allowance has been made for authorial subjectivity, it will probably not be easy to challenge the arguments that are put forward here about state coercion and ethnic minority alienation.

The state and its agents always saw immigrants as a problem.[95] They tended to regard nineteenth-century Irish enclaves as criminal, early twentieth-century Jewish districts as alien and impenetrable, and late twentieth-century Asian and Afro-Caribbean communities as a combustible mixture of criminality, impenetrability and disaffection.[96] Such attitudes became more pervasive and more prominent with the growth of non-white immigration and the concentration of ethnic minority communities in certain cities and certain parts of the country. Indeed, it will be recalled from Chapter 1 that during the second half of the century there emerged a powerful image of inner city areas as 'black enclaves', which threatened, it was commonly believed, the culture and way of life of white residents.[97] Stigmatized from the moment they set foot in the country, immigrants and their families faced extraordinary difficulties in their dealings with the state, its agencies and its agents. In fact, whatever the merits and demerits of the concept of institutional racism, there is little doubt that the police force, the prison service, the judiciary and the legal profession all had a long history of prejudicial attitudes and discriminatory behaviour.

There is evidence from the earliest years of the century that the police were racist in their dealings with the members of the small Chinese, West African and Afro-Caribbean communities that clustered in port cities.[98] Such attitudes surfaced, it seems, wherever and whenever there were visible minorities. A Metropolitan Police constable explained

---

[94] Walklate, *Gender*, p. 3. Also Briggs *et al., Crime and Punishment*, p. 185.

[95] C. Holmes, *A Tolerant Country? Immigrants, Refugees and Minorities in Britain* (Faber and Faber, 1991); P. Panayi, *Immigration, Ethnicity and Racism in Britain* (Manchester: Manchester University Press, 1994).

[96] Emsley, *English Police*, pp. 158–60.

[97] R. Miles and J. Solomos, 'Migration and the State in Britain: A Historical Overview', in C. Husband (ed.), *'Race' in Britain: Community and Change* (Hutchinson, 1987), p. 101.

[98] Emsley, *English Police*, pp. 159–60.

in the late 1930s that it was not only 'aliens' who needed to be watched. 'There's one fellow who runs half a dozen girls: a coloured fellow. I've never been able to understand how a white girl can fall for that sort of thing; but they do.' The trouble, he went on, was that, 'The coloured chaps are British subjects, so you can't deport them.'[99]

It was large-scale immigration from the 1950s onwards that brought matters to a head. The public furore that erupted over mugging in the early 1970s provides a telling test bed on which to examine the authorities' attitudes towards the ethnic minority population. The best known study of this 'moral panic' is *Policing the Crisis: Mugging, the State, and Law and Order*, which was published in 1978 by Stuart Hall and a team from the Centre for Contemporary Cultural Studies at Birmingham University.[100] They were, they stressed, by no means disinterested spectators, and their engagement and commitment drove them to a series of powerful and challenging conclusions. Mugging, they suggested, was a socially constructed phenomenon.

> It was introduced into public consciousness by media coverage of muggings in the United States and police anticipation of its appearance in Britain. Its 'discovery' in 1972 was followed by a crime control explosion. It received massive media coverage. Judges, politicians and moralists presented it as an index of the growing tide of violence, of the breakdown of public morality and of the collapse of law and order.[101]

Official views about the relationship between crime, race and anxiety were 'worked out', they suggested, in the courts. They cited the comments made by Judge Gwynn Morris in 1975 when sentencing five West Indian youths to lengthy periods of imprisonment and detention. 'Within memory', he observed, Brixton and Clapham 'were peaceful, safe and agreeable to live in.'

> But the immigrant resettlement which has occurred over the past 25 years has radically transformed the environment. Those concerned with the maintenance of law and order are confronted with immense difficulties. This case has highlighted and underlined the perils which confront honest, innocent, unaccompanied women who are in the street after nightfall. I notice that not a single West Indian woman was attacked.[102]

Public rhetoric, this book has stressed time and again, should not necessarily be taken as a guide either to private beliefs or to public behaviour. Neither judicial musings nor police officers' jokes necessarily manifested themselves in discriminatory sentencing and intimidatory policing.[103] Nevertheless, police prejudices were expressed so openly and policing practised so partially that ethnic minority alienation was all but inevitable. In 1983, for example, the Policy Studies Institute published a detailed, careful and balanced study of the *Police and People in London*. It revealed, *inter alia*,

---

[99] W. Greenwood, *How the Other Man Lives* (Labour Book Service, 1937), p. 113.

[100] Hall *et al.*, *Policing the Crisis*. See also M. Pratt, *Mugging as a Social Problem* (Routledge & Kegan Paul, 1980); and, more generally, Cashmore and McLaughlin (eds), *Out of Order?*

[101] Hall *et al.*, *Policing the Crisis*, pp. 1–3, back cover.

[102] Hall *et al.*, *Policing the Crisis*, p. 333. See also S. Patterson, *Dark Strangers: A Study of West Indians in London* (Pelican, 1965), p. 184.

[103] D.J. Smith and J. Gray, *Police and People in London: The PSI Report* (Gower, 1985), p. 402.

that racial prejudice and racial language were 'prominent and pervasive' among junior officers. The book's authors cite, for instance, the graffiti in a lavatory used only by officers and civilian staff.

> Fight racialism – smash a nigger in the gob today.

> Q: What's the difference between a nigger and a bucket of shit?
> A: The bucket.[104]

They cite too a police driver who attempted to draw a distinction between his beliefs and his behaviour. 'I freely admit that I hate, loathe and despise niggers. I can't stand them. I don't let it affect my job though. There are some decent ones, though, like that bloke we've just dealt with. Not the African cunt, the other one.'[105]

The Policy Studies Institute study revealed too that police officers tended to subscribe to a racist catch-22; they assumed that black people committed crimes, and assumed too that whoever committed crimes must be black. 'How does an experienced policeman decide who to stop?' one officer asked rhetorically. 'Well, the one that you stop is often wearing a woolly hat, he is dark in complexion, he has thick lips and he usually has dark fuzzy hair.'[106] Such stereotyping was not confined to London or to the lower ranks. In the late 1980s, for example, the Staffordshire police distributed a leaflet as part of its crime prevention initiatives: it asked residents of white areas to look out for cars with black drivers, and make a note of their numbers.[107] Nor indeed was stereotyping confined to the police. An inquiry carried out by the Commission for Racial Equality at the very end of the century revealed a prison system that was racked with racism. One senior manager at Brixton said 'that he regarded the term "Paki" as acceptable. Graffiti were found in the staff toilet that said: "Preserve wildlife, pickle a nigger". It was removed but reappeared two years later along with "KKK for ever in Brixton".'[108]

It will come as no great surprise therefore that those from minority ethnic communities always regarded the authorities with suspicion. In the 1890s, Charles Booth referred to an area of London's Limehouse which was known as the Fenian Barracks, and 'had a very bad name with the police for violence, sending, we are told more police to hospital than any other block in London … and being Irish if one of their number is taken by the police a rescue is attempted'.[109] In the early years of the new century, recalls Arthur Harding, 'The Jews were the best people in the world to get as witnesses against the police for this reason: that they remembered the brutality of the Russian and Polish authorities – they were only too glad of a chance to hit back at them.'[110] In fact, what trust there was fell into decline. When she arrived in Britain in

---

[104] Smith and Gray, *Police and People*, pp. 388, 392.

[105] F. Bresler, 'The law that puts hate into race relations', *Daily Mail*, 1 July 1980; Smith and Gray, *Police and People*, p. 403. Also N. Fielding, 'Cop Canteen Culture', in Newburn and Stanko (eds), *Just Boys Doing Business?*

[106] Smith and Gray, *Police and People*, p. 405.

[107] R. Chigwada, 'The Policing of Black Women', Cashmore and McLaughlin (eds), *Out of Order?*, p. 136.

[108] 'Prisons boss calls racism inquiry findings shameful', *The Guardian*, 17 December 2003.

[109] D. Woods, 'Community Violence', in J. Benson (ed.), *Working Class*, pp. 182–3.

[110] R. Samuel, *East End Underworld: Chapters in the Life of Arthur Harding* (Routledge & Kegan Paul, 1981), p. 193.

the late 1950s, recalled a Wolverhampton woman 30 years later, the police 'were so nice. They were. You could talk to them and you'd see 'em in the street and they'd tick their hats, say good morning.' But, she reflected, 'Now you don't see that.'[111]

The social surveys carried out during the second half of the century provide statistical confirmation of ethnic minority resentments and suspicions. The Policy Studies Institute research conducted in the early 1980s revealed starkly the jaundiced views held by West Indian informants about police behaviour in the capital. It showed that West Indians were twice as likely as white, Asian or other non-white respondents to believe that the police often used threats in the course of questioning. West Indians were three times as likely as these other respondents to believe that the police often falsified records of interviews, four times as likely to believe that they often fabricated evidence, and four times as likely to believe that they often used unreasonable violence at police stations. It did not follow, the compilers of the statistics were at pains to point out, that it was personal conflict/contact with the police that caused people to be critical of them. However, they conclude, reasonably enough, that in the circumstances, 'a change in police policy and behaviour would look like the best thing to try'.[112]

CLASS, SUSPICION AND SURVEILLANCE

One does not need to subscribe to a thoroughgoing class analysis of British society to recognize that the authorities viewed the working class as a greater threat than the upper class and the middle class. Indeed, such a conclusion follows more or less inescapably from the arguments that have been put forward already in this chapter. Strikers, hooligans and those from ethnic minorities, it needs scarcely be said, tended overwhelmingly to be working-class.

There were, of course, middle-class protestors and demonstrators. Indeed, there was a time, between, say, the 1930s and the 1970s, when sitting down during the national anthem, getting involved in political demonstrations and joining the Communist Party seemed to constitute a seemingly essential stage in the middle-class student's coming of age.[113] Dennis Healey recalls that his parents reacted 'without alarm' to the announcement that he had joined the Communists at Oxford University in the late 1930s.

> Mother was already a socialist, and my father, though I suppose he would have accepted the description of Asquithian liberal, took the familiar line that if I was not a Communist at twenty, there was something wrong with my heart; if I was still a Communist at thirty, there was something wrong with my head.[114]

There was a time, during the late 1950s and early 1960s when, according to the opinion polls, the Campaign for Nuclear Disarmament attracted the support of up to a third of all members of the public. 'Its leaders were largely upper class and upper-middle class', explains Arthur Marwick. The movement 'pointed the way towards the

---

[111] Black and Ethnic Minority Project, 92.DE-624/6/88, Pearl Gordon.

[112] Smith and Gray, *Police and People*, p. 248. Also T. Jefferson, 'Discrimination, Disadvantage and Police-Work', in Cashmore and McLaughlin (eds), *Out of Order?*, pp. 183–4.

[113] A. Marwick, *British Society since 1945* (Penguin, 1982), p. 172. Also personal recollection.

[114] D. Healey, *The Time of My Life* (Penguin, 1989), p. 36.

participatory sixties: it involved housewives (though usually middle-class ones).'[115] Then too there was a time, during the 1980s and 1990s, when middle-class, single-issue pressure groups appeared to pose a serious threat to some of the nation's entrenched economic, social and political interests. Such groups campaigned in favour of abortion law reform, gay rights, green issues and fox hunting; they protested against new airports, new motorways, new housing developments and (just after the turn of the century) the high price of petrol.[116]

Foreigners, Communists and peace protestors were always suspect. In 1909, for example, the Birmingham police were in contact with the Special Branch over a German teacher at the city's Berlitz School of Languages who was suspected of trying to subvert a young man working for the telegraphic section of the Post Office.[117] In 1924, the Chief Constable of Huntingdonshire wrote to the head of MI5 about a London firm planning to open a hosiery factory in the county: 'Do you know anything about these people … I do not like the sound of their names.'[118] In the late 1950s, MI5 agent Peter Wright helped to bug the headquarters of the Communist Party of Great Britain. 'The operation, known as TIEPIN, worked exactly as planned and for some months MI5 had full coverage of every important CPGB meeting.'[119] Twenty-five years later, the Minister of Defence Michael Hestletine campaigned ruthlessly against the Campaign for Nuclear Disarmament. 'He might be sensitive to hard-luck cases in Liverpool', observed Hugo Young, 'but he did not scruple to deploy foul means as well as fair against the enemies of the state, as he defined them to be, who constituted the one-sided disarmers of CND. If evidence was needed, he would get it from any source, including MI5.'[120]

But middle-class protestors and demonstrators were a minority within a minority. The authorities were always a great more anxious about the threat – whether real or imagined – that was posed by the working-class majority. It was their duty, they believed, to monitor the beliefs and allegiances of strikers and hooligans, but also of trade-union leaders, Labour Party politicians, the extreme right, the extreme left and (to some extent) the millions upon millions of working people who made up the mass of the population. Fear of the working-class 'enemy within' waxed and waned with changes in broader economic, social and political circumstances. The Special Branch provided the Cabinet with regular reports of revolutionary and industrial unrest from the earliest years of the century. Then, during the First World War, the intelligence branch of the general staff produced weekly summaries for the army's general head quarters. 'It would appear that if Military action has to be taken to suppress strikes or to maintain public order', explained Lord Willoughby de Broke in 1918, 'it must be

---

[115] Marwick, *British Society*, p. 122.

[116] R. Hattersley, *Fifty Years On: A Prejudiced History of Britain Since the War* (Abacus, 1997), p. 320; A. Rawnsley, *Servants of the People: The Inside Story of New Labour* (Penguin, 2001), pp. 396–414; personal recollection.

[117] Emsley, *English Police*, p. 107. See also Porter, 'Secrecy and the Special Branch'.

[118] Emsley, *English Police*, p. 139.

[119] P. Wright, *Spy Catcher: The Candid Autobiography of a Senior Intelligence Officer* (Toronto: Stoddart, 1987), p. 57.

[120] H. Young, *One of Us: A Biography of Margaret Thatcher* (Pan, 1989), p. 434.

efficacious and therefore ruthless to a degree not pleasant to contemplate. It might, therefore, be well to try to understand the point of view of the Working-Classes.'[121]

The industrial disputes of the 1920s and the hunger marches of the 1930s provoked further anxieties. In 1921, Sir Basil Thompson, the head of the Special Branch, addressed the annual general meeting of the chief constables' association on the subject of 'The Revolutionary Movement and the Third International'. He warned his listeners about the pressure that moderate labour leaders faced from 'younger and more irresponsible elements among their own men'.[122] When the chief constable of Staffordshire issued his orders for the policing of a march by the unemployed in 1936, he instructed his superintendents to collect 'the names of any known Communist among the marchers, or other persons likely to cause breaches of the peace'.[123]

The Second World War led, as would be expected, to a further, and much tighter, round of suspicion, surveillance and supervision.[124] Then too, the miners' strike of 1984–5 brought home to a new generation the intrusive power of the state. Anybody who read a newspaper or watched the television gained a sense of the weapons that the state had at its disposal. They could see that the government was well prepared. In the aftermath of the 'race' riots of 1981, it had seen to it that the police received new vehicles, weapons and body armour, and that the national reporting centre at Scotland Yard was permanently available. 'If we hadn't had the Toxteth riots,' Lord Whitelaw admitted, 'I doubt if we could have dealt with Arthur Scargill.'[125] The public could see too that the government was determined to defeat a group of workers which epitomized, for both right and left, working-class tradition, working-class organization and working-class solidarity. Four-and-a-half months into the dispute, Margaret Thatcher launched her vitriolic assault on the striking miners who, she claimed, were 'a scar across the face of the country. We had to fight an enemy without in the Falklands. We always have to be aware of the enemy within, which is more difficult to fight and more dangerous to liberty.'[126]

But what was the impact of such suspicion and surveillance? What did middle-class demonstrators and protestors – and those who did not demonstrate or protest – think about the state's attempts at control and regulation? What did working-class strikers – and the millions more who never even contemplated taking industrial action – make of the state's efforts to monitor their thinking and manage their behaviour? Such

---

[121] D. Englander, 'Military intelligence and the defence of the realm: The surveillance of soldiers and civilians during the First World War', *Bulletin of the Society for the Study of Labour History*, 52, 1987, p. 24.

[122] Emsley, *English Police*, p. 139.

[123] Emsley, *English Police*, p. 138.

[124] For general attitudes about, and treatment of, immigrants during the two world wars see, for example, D. Cesarani and T. Kushner (eds), *The Internment of Enemy Aliens in Twentieth Century Britain* (Frank Cass, 1993); F. Lafitte, *The Internment of Aliens* (Penguin, 1940); R. Stent, *A Bespattered Page? The Internment of His Majesty's 'Most Loyal Enemy Aliens'* (Deutsch, 1980); C. Holmes, *John Bull's Island: Immigration and Society, 1871–1971* (Basingstoke: Macmillan, 1988). Also C. Emsley, 'The Second World War and the Police in England and Wales', in C. Finnau (ed.), *The Impact of World War II in Policing in North-West Europe* (Leuven: Leuven University Press, 2003).

[125] Young, *One of Us*, p. 368.

[126] Young, *One of Us*, p. 371.

questions, it needs scarcely be said, are a good deal easier to pose than they are to answer. However, it does seem that during the course of the century, there occurred a significant convergence in the ways that the classes reacted to state intervention.

It was motoring, and to a lesser extent drug-taking, that provided the key to the changes taking place. Indeed, it has been suggested that the growth of motoring and drug-taking – and the offences to which they gave rise – revolutionized the relationship between the police, the middle class and the working class.

> The rise of the motor car dramatized a development that had not been so visible in the fields of drugs and homosexuality, if only because the prosecutions for them had been so much less frequent. When once the increase in behavioural policing had been a means of criminalizing the poor in the name of middle-class respectability, now the process was beginning to operate in reverse. And while the spread of car ownership after the Second World War brought more of the less prosperous into the courts, the later increase in drug taking further expanded the liability of the privileged, or at least of their children. The courts had scarcely become havens of social equality, but they could no longer be viewed simply as agencies of class control.[127]

The proponents of such views are certainly correct in suggesting that motoring, and later drug-taking, worsened the relationship between the police and the middle class. The judiciary and the police were perfectly well aware of what was happening. In 1920, at Nottinghamshire Assizes, the managing director of a large engineering firm was sentenced to nine months hard labour for manslaughter following a traffic accident on the Great Northern Road. 'You have not only been guilty of wicked negligence,' said the judge, 'but also of running away after you had done this fell work, and you have put up your servants to tell lies. It is a very bad case. If I were trying a chauffeur without your education I should pass a severe sentence, and I see no reason why I should be more lenient to you.'[128] Later in the decade, the chief constable of Staffordshire saw fit to warn his men against too rigorous an application of the traffic laws. Motoring offenders, he reminded them, 'may be persons of the utmost respectability of character and position, by accident brought, so to speak, into collision with the law: and common sense requires they should not be treated as possible criminals'.[129]

In fact, it has been claimed that the typical twentieth-century criminal was a motorist.[130] And there is no denying that the enormous growth in convictions for offences involving motor vehicles brought the middle class, in growing numbers, to the attention of the police. In 1900, there were fewer than 600 convictions for motoring in the whole of England and Wales. This figure had risen to 375,000 by 1952, and to 1.49 million by 1996 – a year, which also saw 188,000 written warnings, issued and

---

[127] Briggs *et al.*, *Crime and Punishment*, p. 208. Also F.M.L. Thompson, 'Social control in Victorian Britain', *Economic History Review*, xxxiv, 1981, p. 199.

[128] *Daily Mail*, 11 February 1920.

[129] Weinberger, *Best Police in the World*, p. 64. Also, Northumbria County Record Office, T/2/3, George Sparks; 'Doctor fined £20', *Observer*, 26 June 1927.

[130] Hood and Roddam, 'Crime, Sentencing and Punishment', p. 686.

3.35 million fixed penalties imposed.[131] By the end of the century, the authorities were dealing with just over 5 million motoring offences a year, a figure equivalent to one offence for every ten men, women and children in the country.[132]

The typical motorist, middle class or working class, felt, it seems, that they were being unfairly hounded.[133] A survey conducted for the government as part of the 1961 Royal Commission on the Police revealed that motorists were second only to young men in their criticism.[134] The investigation carried out by the Policy Studies Institute during the early 1980s confirmed that Londoners felt it less important for the police to pursue motoring offenders than it was for them to catch burglars, robbers and muggers – and less important indeed than getting to know local people and establishing contact with ethnic minority leaders.[135] How often have we heard it said – or said it ourselves – that the police should leave motorists alone, and get on with their proper job of catching criminals?

The claim that motoring, and to a lesser extent drug-taking, improved the relationship between the police and the working class is much less convincing. It is true, it must be conceded, that police–working-class relations improved during the course of the century. Working-class people benefited, sometimes more than the middle class, from the improvements in violence, lawlessness and public disorder that the police helped to bring about. Moreover, as working people became better off, they were probably more inclined to look favourably upon the forces' role as protectors of property.[136] But it is difficult to see that any improvement in police–working-class relations had much to do with working-class people welcoming the police as guardians of the highway.

Working-class suspicions of the state and its agents were long established, deep-seated and extremely difficult to shift. Again, it is not necessary to subscribe to an all-enveloping, class-based analysis of British society to recognize that many working-class people regarded the police, in Robert Storch's words, as 'unwelcome spectators into the very nexus of urban neighbourhood life'.[137] It is important to recognize too that working-class people were more likely than those from the middle class to drive for a living: taxi drivers were subject to a swathe of regulations,[138] and van and lorry drivers had to do their best to keep a clean licence.[139] Indeed, the spread of car ownership from the 1950s onwards had the effect of bringing drivers of all classes before the courts. Whatever the circumstances in which working-class people came to court, they were likely to find the experience dispiriting, demeaning and demoralizing. Richard Hoggart suggested in 1957 that there was perhaps no place that better illustrated class divisions, the differences between 'them' and 'us', than a north country magistrates' court.

---

[131] Hood and Roddam, 'Crime, Sentencing and Punishment', p. 687.

[132] See also Smith and Gray, *Police and People*, p. 282.

[133] 'Mr. Stephen Coleridge fined again', *Observer*, 8 April 1906.

[134] Weinberger, *Best Police in the World*, p. 74.

[135] Smith and Gray, *Police and People*, p. 202.

[136] Briggs *et al.*, *Crime and Punishment*, pp. 218–21.

[137] Cited in Briggs *et al.*, *Crime and Punishment*, p. 151.

[138] Greenwood, *Other Man*, pp. 245–6, 248–9.

[139] Greenwood, *Other Man*, pp. 9–10.

The policemen may themselves feel nervously under the eye of superior officials, but to the working-class people in the well of the court they look like the hired and menacing – the more menacing because now on their own ground, with their helmets off – assistants of that anonymous authority which the bench symbolizes. The magistrate's clerk may be one who likes to 'run people around a bit'; the figures on the bench seem to peer down from a distant world of middle-class security and local importance.[140]

THE STATE, OPPOSITION AND ACCEPTANCE

It will never be possible to judge precisely the impact that state initiatives had upon popular behaviour and popular attitudes. But it is necessary, at the very least, to distinguish between the initiatives directed at criminal activity and those intended to contain political opposition and to control personal morality. It is essential to recognize too that whereas the state persisted in – and sometimes intensified – its attempts to manage what it saw as criminal and political deviancy, it began to withdraw (it will be seen later) from many aspects of peoples' private lives. Indeed, even when the authorities remained resolute, what is striking is the modest – some might say pitiful – amount of overt opposition that state activity provoked among the mass of the population. It does not seem unreasonable to conclude therefore that insofar as the state attempted to direct popular behaviour and popular attitudes, it tended to promote, not hostility and resistance, but indifference, acceptance and acquiescence.

---

[140] Hoggart, *Uses of Literacy*, pp. 74–5.

5 THE MANIPULATIVE POWER OF RELIGION, EDUCATION AND THE MEDIA

MANIPULATION, POWER, POLITICS AND CULTURE

The study of power relations makes for curious intellectual and political bedfellows. It was seen in the previous chapter that however bitter their other disputes, scholars from across the political spectrum tend to agree both about the stability of British society and about the reasons for it. Those in power were able to maintain their authority, it is believed, not simply because of the coercive power of the state but also because of the manipulative skills that the country's political and cultural institutions were able to bring to bear. Religion, education and the mass media played a key role, it is suggested, in persuading the great majority of the population that there was no reason for them to attempt to dislodge, or even seriously challenge, the existing system of power relations.

There is nothing new, of course, about the suggestion that those in power might seek to use religion, education, the media – and anything else that came to hand – as a way of influencing attitudes and controlling behaviour. Such 'manufacturing of consent' had deep roots and produced, it is often claimed, the most profound consequences. Noam Chomsky argues that,

> In capitalist democracies there is certain tension with regard to the locus of power. In a democracy the people rule, in principle. But decision-making power over central areas of life resides in private hands, with large-scale effects throughout the social order … the problem is typically approached by a variety of measures to deprive democratic political structures of substantive content, while leaving them formally intact. A large part of this task is assumed by ideological institutions that channel thought and attitudes within acceptable bounds, deflecting any potential challenge to established privilege and authority before it can take form and gather strength.[1]

Thus it is a cliché to describe the Church of England as the Conservative Party at prayer; it is commonly accepted that schools exist to transmit values and attitudes from one generation to the next; and it has become a commonplace to comment, generally unfavourably, on the political partisanship of the press. Indeed, it was practically 40 years ago that A.J.P. Taylor claimed, in one of his acidly perceptive asides, that the Conservatives party relied mainly upon what he called its 'natural advantages':

> Most of the national press supported it: in 1929 seven daily newspapers out of ten, and all the Sunday newspapers except one … Universities … and

---

[1] N. Chomsky, *Necessary Illusions: Thought Control in Democratic Societies* (Pluto, 1989), p. vii.

to a great extent the Church of England, were pillars of Conservatism in thin disguise.[2]

What has happened during the past 25 years or so is that the concept of 'manufacturing consent' has been broadened in the attempt to explain a great deal more than the securing of party political advantage.[3] Dismay at the appeal of Thatcherite policies combined with dissatisfaction with coercive explanations of popular acquiescence to push scholars in a number of new directions. They began to ask new questions, mine untapped sources of evidence, and turn to concepts such as hegemony[4] and social control[5] which had rarely been employed by historians of twentieth-century Britain. Indeed, hegemony and social control seemed for a time almost to take on a life of their own.[6]

Whether or not such concepts were properly understood and rigorously applied, they suffused the scholarly – and not so scholarly – approaches adopted by those seeking to explain the maintenance of power and authority in terms of the messages transmitted by the country's political and cultural institutions. Education, religion and the media all came in for their share of opprobrium, with education, in particular, held to be enormously influential.

Feminist scholars blamed the school system for sustaining the subordination of women. So although Sara Delamont conceded that it would be ridiculous to suggest that schools create sex stereotyping, she was insistent that they 'develop and reinforce sex segregations, stereotypes, and even discrimination which exaggerate the negative aspects of sex roles in the outside world, when they could be trying to alleviate them'.[7] Left-wing scholars bemoaned the role that education played in perpetuating working-class people's acceptance of the disadvantaged position they occupied within capitalist society. So although Stephen Humphries recognized that the late nineteenth- and early twentieth-century educational system aimed to promote both meritocracy and social improvement, he believed that it did so in ways antipathetic to the long-term interests of the mass of the population:

> it sought to ameliorate important social problems – principally the
> demoralization and destitution of some sections of the working class, juvenile
> crime, street-gang violence, disease and drunkenness – through an infusion of
> bourgeois values such as hard work, discipline and thrift. Fundamentally, it
> attributed social deprivation to the ignorance and immorality of working-class

---

[2] A.J.P. Taylor, *English History* (Penguin, 1970 edition), p. 334.

[3] E.S. Herman and N. Chomsky, *Manufacturing Consent: The Political Economy of the Mass Media* (Vintage, 1994).

[4] A 'ceaseless endeavour to maintain control over the "hearts and minds" of subordinate classes'. P. Ransome, *Antonio Gramsci: A New Introduction* (Brighton: Harvester Wheatsheaf, 1992), p. 132.

[5] The 'imposition of opinions and habits by one class upon another'. F.M.L. Thompson, 'Social control in Victorian Britain,' *Economic History Review*, xxxiv, 1981, p. 190.

[6] J. Benson, *The Working Class in Britain, 1850–1939* (Harlow: Longman, 1989), p. 1.

[7] S. Delamont, *Sex Roles and the School* (Routledge, 1990), p. 2. See also S. Askew and C. Ross, *Boys Don't Cry: Boys and Sexism in Education* (Buckingham: Open University Press, 1988); V. Walkerdine, *Democracy in the Kitchen: Regulating Mothers and Socialising Daughters* (Virago, 1980).

culture rather than to capitalist structures and therefore proposed individual as opposed to political solutions to problems of class inequality.[8]

This is convincing as far as it goes. Indeed, one is tempted to say that almost any approach was likely to represent an improvement on the uncritical, Whiggish history of education that had been force-fed to generations of trainee teachers. It does not follow, however, that the social control approach should be welcomed unreservedly, and applied uncompromisingly to the study of religion, education and the media. The social control approach promises a great deal, but has been criticized from the left as well as the right, and presents a number of ideological, conceptual and empirical difficulties.[9] Clearly, it is tempting to believe that if clergymen, teachers and journalists advocated particular attitudes and actions, and if large numbers of people thought and behaved in these ways, then the former must have caused the latter. But this is both condescending and illogical. It is condescending in that it assumes that people were the passive victims of sources beyond their control. It is illogical insofar as it suggests that they did not have their own reasons for thinking and behaving in the ways that they did.[10]

Accordingly, it is the aim of this chapter to assess the extent to which manipulation should be set alongside coercion in explaining how those in power were able to maintain their authority during a century of unprecedented economic, technological, social and cultural change. It will be suggested that while it is easy enough to show that those active in religion, education and the media espoused particular values and ideas, it is exceptionally difficult to decide whether their efforts had anything like the impact that common sense – and proponents of the social control approach – would lead one to suppose.

It is not difficult to show that clerics, educators and those involved in the media often tended to promote assumptions, attitudes and behaviour that were likely to prove acceptable to those with power to exert and authority to maintain. But did they do so by design or by default? At certain times, in certain places, those involved in these attempts at shaping public opinion knew perfectly well that they were doing the authorities' bidding. However, in most circumstances the process seems to have been considerably less self-conscious. Thus Herman and Chomsky's analysis of media bias in the United States of America has a much more general applicability. Most biased choices, they believe, result from what they describe as

> the preselection of right-thinking people, internalized preconceptions and the adaption of personnel to the constraints of ownership, organization, market and political power. Censorship is largely self-censorship, by reporters and commentators who adjust to the realities of source and media organizational requirements, and by people at higher levels within media organizations who are chosen to implement, and have usually internalized, the constraints imposed by proprietary and other market and governmental centers of power.[11]

---

[8] S. Humphries, *Hooligans or Rebels? An Oral History of Working-Class Childhood and Youth 1889–1939* (Oxford: Blackwell, 1981), p. 31.

[9] G.S. Jones, 'Class expression *versus* social control', *History Workshop*, 4, 1977, pp. 163–70; Thompson, 'Social control'.

[10] J. Rose, *The Intellectual Life of the British Working Classes* (Yale University Press, 2001), pp. 1–11.

[11] Herman and Chomsky, *Manufacturing Consent*, p. xii.

CHURCH, CHAPEL, MOSQUE AND TEMPLE

Such market-based analysis seems, on the face of it, to have little to contribute to the attempt being made here to identify the role of religion in the maintenance of power relationships. Further reflection suggests, however, that 'the preselection of right-thinking people', 'internalized preconceptions', 'adaption' and 'self-censorship' are only too relevant to the task at hand.

Of course, not all churches and sects behaved in the same way. Indeed, one of the most striking developments occurring during the course of the century was the way in which religious organization, belief and practice became increasingly complex, heterogeneous – and resistant to generalization. When Paul Badham was asked to contribute a chapter on religious pluralism in modern Britain to a volume published in 1994, he explained that although the brief he was given excluded the Church of England, mainstream nonconformity and Roman Catholicism, it still included 'the Independent, the Afro-Caribbean and the Pentecostal churches, the sects and new religious movements, and the non-Christian religions represented in Britain, including Jews, Muslims, Sikhs, Hindus and Buddhists'.[12]

Nevertheless, for most of the century, the churches tended to sustain conventional patterns of power relations. This is not to say that church leaders were reluctant to criticize the economic and social circumstances presided over by those in authority. In 1926, for example, the bishops of the Church of England intervened, albeit reluctantly, to try to broker a solution to the General Strike, some of their number sympathizing publicly with the miners whom they considered to be the injured party in the dispute.[13] Sixty years later, the Church of England's report, *Faith in the City*, lambasted the Thatcher government for policies which, it claimed, had laid waste both the inner cities and to the housing estates surrounding them.[14] Indeed, the established church, led by Robert Runcie, the Archbishop of Canterbury, and David Jenkins, the Bishop of Durham, was widely perceived as providing a significant focus of opposition to the ambitions of successive Thatcher administrations.[15]

Yet even when religious leaders criticized those in power, they did so in terms that tended to reinforce, rather than undermine, the foundations upon which British society was organized. Sometimes members of the hierarchy appealed for common decency and common sense. At the beginning of the century, for instance, the Archdeacon of Worcester said he was confident that housing was an issue which, like so many others, involved – or ought to involve – 'fair dealing between man and man, class and class'.[16]

---

[12] P. Badham, 'Religious Pluralism in Modern Britain', in S. Gilley and W.J. Sheils (eds), *A History of Religion in Britain: Practice and Belief from Pre-Roman Times to the Present* (Oxford: Blackwell, 1994), p. 489. See also P. Brierley, 'Religion', in A.H. Halsey (ed.), *Twentieth-Century British Social Trends* (Basingstoke: Macmillan, 2000).

[13] E.R. Norman, *Church and Society in England, 1770–1970: A Historical Study* (Oxford: Clarendon, 1976), pp. 337–9; W.R. Garside, *The Durham Miners 1919–1960* (Allen & Unwin, 1971), pp. 210–12.

[14] G. Davie, *Religion in Britain since 1945: Believing without Belonging* (Oxford: Blackwell, 1994), pp. 151–4.

[15] Badham, 'Religious Pluralism', p. 499.

[16] Norman, *Church and Society*, p. 223. See P. Hastings, 'The General Strike in Kent', in N. Yates (ed.), *Kent in the Twentieth Century* (Woodbridge: Boydell Press/Kent County Council, 2001), p. 393; D. Childs, *Britain Since 1939: Progress and Decline* (Basingstoke: Palgrave, 2002), p. 7.

Sometimes church leaders appealed to free market economics. In his 1927 book, *Economics and Christianity*, the Bishop of Gloucester was scathing in his criticism of those who had attempted to intervene in the General Strike: 'There seems to be an idea that if you approach economic questions as a Christian you can alter or modify economic laws.' But, he thundered, 'That you cannot do.'[17]

Even when members of the hierarchy resisted the temptation to pontificate on the merits of common-sense morality and the wisdom of conventional economic analysis, the staffing, structures and activities of the country's religious institutions generally sustained, rather than challenged, existing gender and class relationships. However many women and working people became involved, and however great the contribution they made to the country's religious life, the leadership of churches, chapels, mosques and temples tended to remain what it always had been: male and middle class.[18]

It is not surprising therefore that they found proposals to admit women to the ministry contentious and divisive. The nonconformist churches were accommodating, but the Roman Catholic Church refused to countenance the idea, and Judaism's Orthodox and Reform branches adopted contradictory stances.[19] The Church of Scotland began to discuss the subject in the 1930s, admitted women to the ministry and the eldership in the late 1960s, but by 1996 had appointed women to just 15 per cent of its clerical positions.[20] The synod of the Church of England accepted in 1975 that there were 'no fundamental objections to the ordination of women to the priesthood',[21] but the first ordinations did not take place until 1994, and early in the new century a group of women clergy accused the church of continuing to behave in a prejudicial and discriminatory fashion. They did not pull their punches:

> There are a number of reasons – fear of conflict, misogyny, the bishops' wish
> to present a united front to the world, a devotion to the old boy network or,
> in some cases, to a closeted gay network, laziness, indifference, an excessive
> concern about what Rome thinks and a habitual stance of not taking women
> seriously.[22]

The ways in which the churches were staffed and organized certainly reflected prevailing class structures and relationships. This could be seen most clearly, of course, in the established church.[23] So although Edward Norman dismisses what he calls the 'vulgar' Marxist view that Church of England clergy propagated the morality and politics of the ruling class to which they belonged, he concedes that, 'most of the social attitudes and ideas adopted by churchmen were a reflection of

---

[17] Cited in Norman, *Church and Society*, p. 331. Also 'Husbands try more good will', *Daily Mail*, 2 January 1950.

[18] See, for example, P. Ackers, 'West End chapel, back street Bethel: Labour and capital in the Wigan Churches of Christ c. 1845–1945', *Journal of Ecclesiastical History*, 47, 1996.

[19] A.M. Suggate, 'The Christian Churches in England since 1945: Ecumenism and Social Concern', in Gilley and Sheils (eds), *History of Religion*, p. 485. Information from Leila Woolf.

[20] C.G. Brown, *Religion and Society in Scotland since 1707* (Edinburgh: Edinburgh University Press, 1997), p. 203.

[21] Davie, *Religion*, p. 181. See also 'Women win right to be reverend', *Daily Mail*, 3 July 1985.

[22] S. Bates, 'Church persists with sexual apartheid, say women priests', *The Guardian*, 25 October 2001.

[23] 'Mme. D'Arblay's great nephew', *Observer*, 30 December 1906.

class-consciousness – including the radical and critical ideas'. It is true, he continues, that the composition of the clergy changed during the course of the century:

> the strictly aristocratic element declined, but the landed and professional middle-class element filled the gap. Many clergymen were themselves the sons of clergymen. By the 1960s the pattern had altered surprisingly little. The general social tone of the ministry was by then still middle to upper class. The bishops tended to approximate more to the upper than to the middle class. The over-all background, especially of those who have risen to senior and influential positions in the Church, is public school and ancient University.[24]

NURSERY, SCHOOL, COLLEGE AND UNIVERSITY

Herman and Chomsky's analysis of the media is just as valuable when it comes to assessing the role that education played in the maintenance of conventional power relationships. Indeed, it is now more than 30 years since Richard Johnson challenged the Whiggish world of educational history with his claim that the nineteenth-century 'obsession' with working-class education was best understood as a concern about authority and power, about the assertion and re-assertion of control.

> This concern was expressed in an enormously ambitious attempt to determine, through the capture of educational means, the patterns of thought, sentiment and behaviour of the working class. Supervised by its trusty teacher, surrounded by its playground wall, the school was to raise a new race of working people – respectful, cheerful, hard-working, loyal, pacific and religious.[25]

What was true of the nineteenth century was true, by and large, of the twentieth. Those in authority knew that the underlying purpose of education was to transmit the values and attitudes of the generation in power to the generations that followed. 'The true aim of education,' it was claimed in 1909, 'it is now generally recognised, is something more than the mere training of the intelligence.' In physical education, for instance, 'The child unconsciously acquires habits of discipline and order and learns to respond cheerfully and promptly to the word of command.'[26] Those in authority ensured therefore that the state, at both national and local levels, made increasing efforts to control the financing of the system, the provision of the infrastructure, the training of teachers, the attendance of pupils, the contents of the curriculum, and the ways in which it was delivered. If this was the century of the child, it was also one that saw a major realignment in the relationship between children, their parents, their teachers and the state.[27]

---

[24] Norman, *Church and Society*, p. 9.

[25] R. Johnson, 'Educational policy and social control in early Victorian England', *Past and Present*, 49, 1970, p. 119. Cf. A. Green, *Education, Globalization and the Nation State* (Basingstoke: Macmillan, 1997), Ch. 5.

[26] 'Scientific leap-frog', *Observer*, 22 August 1909. See also 'Education of the future', *Observer*, 8 June 1930; M. Vlaeminke, *The English Higher Grade Schools: A Lost Opportunity* (Woburn Press, 2000), pp. 1–6.

[27] A.H. Halsey, *Change in British Society* (Oxford: Oxford University Press, 1989), p. 114. See 'Tragedy of teacher overcome by stress of Ofsted.' *Daily Mail*, 7 April 2000.

The educational system reflected, and sought to reinforce, the underlying structures and values of the society that it served. Neither economic growth, economic redistribution nor new patterns of spending and saving sealed the class fissures that existed within the system. There were state schools and private schools (with 5–8 per cent of the school-age population educated privately throughout the century).[28] There were, for many years, grammar schools, technical schools and secondary modern schools. There were private tutors, finishing schools and further education colleges; and by the end of the century, there were ancient universities, redbrick universities, 'plateglass' universities and polytechnics/'new' universities (though until the expansion of higher education in the 1960s, fewer than 5 per cent of 18–19-year-olds went on to university).[29] Everybody knew that there were differences between Cambridge and Wolverhampton, between Oxford and Hull, between Edinburgh and Paisley – and most people had a pretty good idea what the differences were.

Nor did economic growth, economic restructuring or new patterns of saving and spending do much to dilute the messages about gender that were embedded within the educational system.[30] There were boys' schools and girls' schools, there were boys' subjects and girls' subjects, and for many years even junior schools had separate boys' and girls' entrances and separate boys' and girls' playgrounds.[31] Teachers knew, and their students could scarcely fail to recognize, that although the profession attracted large numbers of women (and from the 1960s offered them equal pay), inequalities remained entrenched at all levels. Women often trained separately from men, they were more likely than their male colleagues to work with young children, they were less likely to gain promotion, and they were more likely therefore to remain in the classroom.[32]

Teachers knew, even if their students did not, that the curriculum, the ways it was planned and the ways it was delivered, tended to present a gendered view of the world. In fact, for most of the century, official policy demanded no less. London County Council stressed in 1920 that insofar as the education of working-class girls was vocational, 'the vocation should be domestic life rather than handicrafts'.[33] The White Paper on educational reconstruction published in 1943 reminded its readers that 'girls largely look to leaving factory, shop or office to get married and set up homes of their own'.[34] The Crowther Report of 1959 concurred: 'the broad distinction between boys'

---

[28] G. Smith. 'Schools', in Halsey (ed.), *British Social Trends*, p. 187; W.R. Niblett, *The Public Schools Today* (University of London Press, 1948).

[29] A.H. Halsey, 'Further and Higher Education', in Halsey (ed.), *British Social Trends*, p. 226.

[30] For an example from the second half of the century, see 'Boys will be boys', *Daily Mail*, 1 April 1965.

[31] Personal recollection; R. Glasser, *Growing up in the Gorbals* (Chatto & Windus, 1986), p. 38; M. Spring Rice, *Working Class Wives: Their Health and Conditions* (Pelican, 1939), pp. 204–5.

[32] Delamont, *Sex Roles*, Ch. 4; A. Oram, *Women Teachers and Feminist Politics 1900–1939* (Manchester: Manchester University Press, 1996), p. 33; R. Williams, I. Reid and M. Rayner, 'Her Majesty's Inspectorate in the 1980s', *Research in Education*, 45, 1991, pp. 15–16.

[33] London County Council, *Memorandum*, 1920, W. van der Eyken (ed.), *Education, the Child and Society: A Documentary History 1900–1973* (Penguin, 1973), p. 241. See also 'Domestic training in schools', *Observer*, 4 May 1930.

[34] *White Paper on Educational Reconstruction*, 1943, van der Eyken (ed.), *Education*, p. 391.

and girls' interests … is rightly reflected in curriculum planning … For a good many girls wage earning is likely to seem a temporary preoccupation'.[35]

Although policy makers began to abandon such stereotyping during the second half of the century, it would be naive to suppose that this resulted in the delivery of a non-gendered, non-discriminatory educational experience. In 1965, the principal of St Ninian Boys' Preparatory School, Canterbury, reminded parents that for the annual photograph, 'hairstyles are to be such that there can be no doubt that this is a single-sex school'.[36] The mixed-sex comprehensive schools that came into being during the 1960s permitted, and sometimes demanded, that boys and girls be taught differently. It was not just that boys played football and cricket, while girls were expected to play rounders and netball. It went much deeper than that. It was claimed in the early 1970s, for example, that something like half of all comprehensive schools provided their pupils with an openly gendered curriculum: 'There were about a dozen subjects altogether not open to boys, among them catering and clothes design. There were over a dozen subjects in mixed comprehensives that were not open to girls, among them engineering and gardening.'[37] Nor should it be forgotten that the curriculum constituted just one element of the gendered environment in which children were educated. It was reported in the early 1980s, for instance, that in one Newcastle comprehensive school, pupils were divided by gender some 20 times a day.

> Pupils were listed separately on the register, went into assembly in single-sex lines, waited outside classrooms in single-sex lines, had separate PE, used different cloakrooms, changing rooms and lavatories, ate lunch in different sittings, and so on.[38]

NEWSPAPERS, MAGAZINES, CINEMA, RADIO AND TELEVISION

Herman and Chomsky's 'propaganda model' of mass media behaviour can also be applied, with appropriate qualifications, to the analysis of the British media and the part they played in the reinforcement of conventional power relationships. The media, the model suggests, 'serve to mobilize support for the special interests that dominate the state and private activity'.[39] Newspapers, magazines, cinema, radio and television all served, in other words, to sustain the age, gender, ethnic and class assumptions upon which power was predicated and authority maintained.[40]

---

[35] R. Lowe, *Schooling and Social Change 1964–1990* (Routledge, 1997), p. 100. See also B. Williamson, *The Temper of the Times: British Society since World War II* (Oxford: Blackwell, 1990).

[36] 'Boys will be boys', *Daily Mail,* 1 April 1965. See also 'Your hair can be permanently waved for a guinea, sir', *Manchester Guardian,* 10 January 1951.

[37] Lowe, *Schooling and Social Change,* p. 103.

[38] Delamont, *Sex Roles,* p. 56. Also J.M. Stafford, *Homosexuality and Education* (Manchester: Manchester University Press, 1988), p. 44.

[39] Herman and Chomsky, *Manufacturing Consent,* p. xi.

[40] See, for example, J. Curran and J. Seaton, *Power without Responsibility: The Press and Broadcasting in Britain* (Routledge, 1991).

They did so partly by the support they offered to the parties of the right. A.J.P. Taylor claimed, it will be recalled, that during the 1920s, one of the Conservative Party's 'natural advantages' was the support it received from a large majority of the daily and Sunday press.[41] These so-called 'natural advantages' remained very much intact. Denis Healey claims that during the middle and late 1970s, for instance, the popular press, with the exception of the *Daily Mirror*, tended to react to whatever he did as Labour Chancellor of the Exchequer 'with the same knee-jerk vituperation'.[42] Indeed, there developed what James Curran and Jane Seaton describe as 'a yawning gap' between editorial opinion and electoral opinion. By 1987, they point out, 'the Conservative Party had the support of 72 per cent of national daily circulation but only 43 per cent of the vote'.[43]

It is not surprising therefore that it became common to attribute the electoral failings of the Liberal and Labour parties to the machinations of a hostile, right-wing press. Fleet Street was blamed, *inter alia*, for the fall of the Liberal leader Herbert Asquith in the 1920s, the humiliation of Labour leader Neil Kinnock during the 1980s, and the victory of John Major's Conservative Party in 1992. Indeed, it did not go unnoticed that during the first of her three premierships, Margaret Thatcher offered knighthoods to the editors of *The Sun*, the *Daily Mail* and the *Sunday Express* – and that each of them felt able to accept.[44]

It would be difficult then to overlook media support for right-wing political parties. It is a great deal easier to overlook – or at least to underestimate – the ways in which media ownership, structures and practices reflected the age, gender, ethnic and class assumptions upon which power was predicated in twentieth-century Britain. It should be recognized, suggests Stuart Hall, in an echo of Herman and Chomsky, that all branches of the media tend to 'reproduce the definition of the powerful, without being in a simple sense in their pay'.[45]

It is well known, of course, that press ownership became concentrated increasingly in the hands of a small number of powerful proprietors and unbending corporations. Between the wars, press barons like Beaverbrook, Kemsley, Northcliffe and Rothermere dominated Fleet Street. By the late 1940s, three press groups controlled 60 per cent and more of national newspaper circulation – with a further five chains controlling 44 per cent of regional evening circulation and 65 per cent of regional morning circulation.[46] Such integration and domination encouraged, and most certainly did nothing to discourage, a growing homogeneity of outlook among all major sections of the press. Even when individual papers eschewed the Conservatives, they offered their support to mainstream, establishment parties. The national press, explain Curran and Seaton, tended to bolster the forces of continuity and stability.

> It generally endorsed the basic tenets of the capitalist system – private enterprise, profit, the 'free market', and the rights of property ownership.

---

[41] Taylor, *English History*, p. 334.

[42] D. Healey, *The Time of My Life* (Penguin, 1990), p. 442.

[43] Curran and Seaton, *Power without Responsibility*, p. 124.

[44] H. Young, *One of Us: A Biography of Margaret Thatcher* (Pan, 1990), p. 510.

[45] Cited in Curran and Seaton, *Power without Responsibility*, p. 269.

[46] Curran and Seaton, *Power without Responsibility*, pp. 52–6, 91–2.

By frequently invoking the consensual framework of the national interest and by projecting positive symbols of nationhood (such as sporting heroes), the press fostered a national identity at the expense of class solidarity.[47]

What was true of the press was true, more or less, of magazines, cinema, radio and television. During the 1930s and 1940s, for instance, women's magazines urged their readers, in turn, to be homemakers, to engage wholeheartedly in the war effort, and then to return unquestioningly to their traditional role as full-time wives and mothers.[48] Indeed, we know that even at the very end of the century, women's magazines continued, many of them, to present a world in which nurses married doctors, secretaries their bosses, and love generally conquered all. Radio and television too tended to reflect established views concerning what to do and what to think, what was right and what was wrong. For many years, the 'authority figures' reporting the news, presenting light entertainment shows, commentating on sporting events – and appearing in commercial breaks – all tended to be middle-aged, male, white and middle class. Thus it was a matter of teenaged pleasure – and middle-aged concern – that in the 1960s, youthful disc jockeys on pirate radio stations began to play the music that the BBC declined to broadcast.[49] It was a matter of comment – and congratulation – that in the late 1980s, the Nationwide Building Society aired an advertisement featuring a woman who could be identified as Jewish. 'It didn't occur to us that we were being brave and the client didn't question the decision at all', recalls the president of the Institute of Practioners in Advertising. 'All the same, I don't think they would have agreed, at that time, to us casting a Caribbean woman to connect with the bulk of the population.'[50]

So it was that whatever their differences, the churches, the schools and the media all tended to offer a clear and consistent view of British society. On the one hand, they presented Britain as a country in which teenagers and old people, men and women, those from ethnic minorities, and those from the different classes knew – or were expected to know – their place, and behaved – or were expected to behave – in conventionally acceptable ways. On the other hand, they presented Britain as a country in which those with talent, determination – and a certain amount of luck – could rise to the very top. One is reminded, yet again, of Herman and Chomsky's analysis of media behaviour.

> In most cases ... media leaders do similar things because they see the world through the same lenses, are subject to similar constraints and incentives, and thus feature stories or maintain silence together in tacit collective action and leader-follower behavior.[51]

---

[47] Curran and Seaton, *Power without Responsibility*, p. 107. For press treatment of royal funerals, coronations and birthdays see, for example, *The Times*, 7 February 1952; *Manchester Guardian*, 2–4 June 1953; *News of the World*, 12 June 1960; *Daily Mail*, 20 July 2000.

[48] D. Philips and A. Tomlinson, 'Homeward Bound: Leisure, Popular Culture and Consumer Capitalism', D. Strinati and S. Wagg (eds), *Come on Down? Popular Media Culture in Post-War Britain* (Routledge, 1992), p. 33; M. Pugh, *Women and the Women's Movement in Britain, 1914–1999* (Basingstoke: Macmillan, 2000), pp. 82–7.

[49] Personal recollection. See also A. Bede's letter to *Daily Mail*, 2 April 1970.

[50] C. Alnot, 'Altered images', *The Guardian*, 31 October 2001.

[51] Herman and Chomsky, *Manufacturing Consent*, p. xii.

LEADER-FOLLOWER BEHAVIOUR

So far, so good. In fact, some readers might wonder why it has taken so long to reach this point in the analysis. For as F.M.L. Thompson pointed out more than 20 years ago, there is nothing 'particularly new in observing that those who have power, authority, and influence seek to use them to protect and preserve the state of things which gives them power, and to maintain the peaceful, and preferably contented, subordination of those less comfortable than themselves'.[52] Nevertheless, readers might also wonder whether Herman and Chomsky's division of the population into leaders and followers is perhaps not a touch too simple, and does not come a touch too close to assuming the very thing that is to be examined.

In all events, there is no denying that the next stage of the analysis is a good deal more challenging. It is all very well to show that those in power advocated attitudes and actions likely to preserve their authority. What then has to be demonstrated is that those without power were persuaded to accept – and act upon – the attitudes and actions that were urged upon them. For this to be done, it has to be shown that it was the advocacy of the powerful – and not anything else or anybody else – that persuaded those without power to think and behave in the ways that they did.

This is to demand a very high standard of proof. It has been decided therefore to pursue the investigation in two stages. The first, much briefer, step will involve the presentation of simple, but it is hoped telling, statistical information concerning church membership, school attendance and the licensing of radio and television receivers. The second, much more substantial, step will consist of the detailed analysis of the ways in which school children and teenagers, men and women, those from ethnic minorities, and those from the middle class and working class reacted to the messages that were directed towards them. It will be suggested that most of these groups responded more positively than one might imagine to the advocacy of their 'superiors'.

Statistics of church membership, school attendance and radio/television licences are readily available and, used with caution, can prove highly revealing. Of course, it is never sensible to assume that everything remained constant other than the particular development for which one happens to have evidence. However, if one is prepared to make the assumption – heroic though it may be – that the nature and effectiveness of the messages transmitted by the churches, the schools and the media changed little during the course of the century, then Figure 5.1, Table 5.1 and Figure 5.2 assume very considerable significance.

They suggest that, during the course of the century, religion's power to persuade declined in relation both to education and to the media. Indeed, even if one believes that the nature and effectiveness of the messages transmitted by religion, education and the media changed during the hundred years under investigation, it is difficult to see that they changed sufficiently to invalidate this broad generalization. Thus it will be assumed for the moment that the trends indicated were real rather than constructed: that religion steadily lost its capacity to shape popular attitudes, that education gradually increased its capacity to do so, and that radio – and then television – rapidly expanded the media's capacity to do so.[53] It is these three quantitatively-driven hypotheses that

---

[52] Thompson, 'Social control', p. 189.

[53] C. Morgan, 'Church agonises at baseness of children', *The Sunday Times*, 20 October 2002.

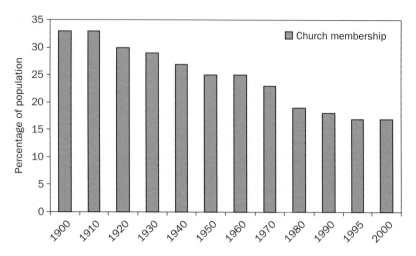

Figure 5.1 Church membership in the United Kingdom, 1900–2000
Source: Based on P. Brierley, 'Religion', in A.H. Halsey (ed.), *Twentieth-Century British Social Trends* (Basingstoke: Macmillan, 2000), pp. 654–5.

TABLE 5.1 SCHOOL ATTENDANCE OF CHILDREN AGED 5–11, UNITED KINGDOM, 1900/1–97

Year	School attendance percentage
1900/1	83
1938	89
1997	94

Source: G. Smith, 'Schools', in A.H. Halsey (ed.), *Twentieth-Century British Social Trends* (Basingstoke: Macmillan, 2000), p. 183.

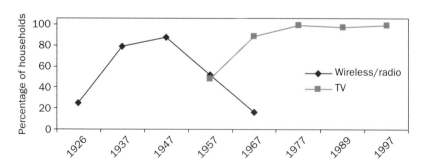

Figure 5.2 Radio and television licences per household, United Kingdom, 1926–97
Source: Based on J. Gershuny and K. Fisher, 'Leisure', in A.H. Halsey (ed.), *Twentieth-Century British Social Trends* (Basingstoke: Macmillan, 2000), p. 640.

will form the basis of the discussion to be undertaken in the remainder of the chapter. It will be shown that the evidence available suggests that insofar as manipulation took place, it was due less to the continuing impact of religion than to the growing influence of education and the burgeoning power of the media.

THE SUSCEPTIBILITY OF THE YOUNG

It was the young who were always most at risk from the machinations of those seeking to influence attitudes and behaviour. 'Give me a child for the first seven years,' ran the Jesuit maxim, 'and you may do what you like with him afterwards.' But it does not follow that religion, education and the media were effective in inoculating twentieth-century children with values and attitudes acceptable to those with power and position to protect. It is by no means self-evident that the state, its agencies and its agents were successful in producing, in Richard Johnson's memorable phrase, 'a new race of working people – respectful, cheerful, hard-working, loyal, pacific and religious'.[54]

In fact, there are reasons for doubting the effectiveness of such efforts. Scholars from both left and right stress the reluctance and/or the discrimination with which children – and their parents – approached the religious and educational provision offered to them. Historians like Carl Chinn and Stephen Humphries believe that during the first half of the century many poor families felt that work was more important than school, and resisted, sometimes fiercely, those aspects of classroom teaching and discipline that they did not like.[55] 'There was almost a stigma about attending school at all,' recalls Bill Naughton, 'an obligation that denied the family the dozen or so badly needed shillings that could be earned working in the mill.'[56] Even after the Second World War, concludes J.S. Hurt, there continued to be considerable resistance to the enforcement of compulsory school attendance:

> some parents still acquiesced in rather than accepted the legal requirements that had changed the pattern of a family life that dated back to a pre-industrial society. What to one social group had appeared to be remedial legislation had added a burden to another.[57]

During the second half of the century, there was wave upon wave of concern.[58] The combined efforts of the churches, a century or so of compulsory education and several decades of media innovation seemed to have resulted in a deterioration rather than an improvement in young people's attitudes and behaviour. 'What *can* we do about these bored, resentful, destructive rebels in our classrooms?', demanded the *Daily Mail*'s

---

[54] Johnson, 'Educational policy', p. 119.

[55] C. Chinn, *The Worked All Their Lives: Women of the Urban Poor in England, 1880–1939* (Manchester: Manchester University Press, 1988), pp. 68–9; Humphries, *Hooligans*, esp. Chs 2–4. See, for instance, 'Boys funeral stopped', *Observer*, 20 June 1909; 'Boys who will work', *Observer*, 15 May 1927.

[56] B. Naughton, *Neither Use Nor Ornament: A Memoir of Bolton, 1920* (Tanset: Bloodaxe Books, 1995), p. 62.

[57] J.S. Hurt, *Elementary Schooling and the Working Classes 1860–1918* (Routledge & Kegan Paul, 1979), p. 213.

[58] See for example, 'The lesson of Andy the boy from the back street', *Daily Mail*, 6 January 1965; 'Trap for born losers', *Daily Mail*, 6 July 1995.

education correspondent in 1975.[59] Those closer to the problem were apparently just as concerned. 'Sit for a while in a school staffroom and you are left in no doubt from snippets of conversation as to where disruption lies: it lies in the child. The child is disruptive, unco-operative, difficult, disturbed, aggressive, awkward and bloody-minded.'[60] One factor often put forward to explain such attitudes and behaviour was the declining popularity of religion. The sociologist Grace Davie emphasizes, for example, that, 'more and more young people opt[ed] out of active religiosity, not only temporarily but for the greater part of their lives'.[61] Sociological and Conservative Party thinking converged on this, if on little else. The party's mid-1960s crusade against permissiveness claimed that,

> the growth in the crime rate may be attributed in part to the breakdown of certain spontaneous agencies of social control which worked in the past. These controls operated through the family, the Church, through personal and local loyalties, and through a stable life in a stable society.[62]

Such pessimism was based only partly upon reality. Young people posed much less of a threat to the established order than newspaper correspondents, classroom teachers, Conservative Party politicians – or anybody else – were inclined to suppose.[63] The great majority of children and teenagers spent more time in their bedrooms or at church youth clubs than they did at rock festivals or on the football terraces. They managed, the overwhelming majority of them, to get through their teenage years without becoming embroiled in anything that could possibly be described as delinquent – let alone destabilizing – behaviour.[64]

Such conformity owed more than a little to the continuing power of religion, the growing power of education and the burgeoning power of the media. However much young people rejected scriptural teaching, misbehaved at school, ignored what they read in the press or criticized what they saw on television, they were unable – most of them – to insulate themselves from the assumptions and prescriptions that surrounded them. Religion, education and the media helped to provide the moral and intellectual framework within which, and against which, young people shaped the values, attitudes and preconceptions that remained with them, very often, for the remainder of their lives.[65]

Church and school combined for many years to instil – or at least to reinforce – notions of conformity, respectability and respect for authority. Indeed, when they look back to the first 30 years of the century, respondents sometimes remark how closely the teaching they received at home, in school and Sunday school complemented one another. The daughter of a north-east Lancashire fitter and turner who attended school soon after the First World War recalls that her teachers reinforced the discipline

---

[59] *Daily Mail*, 5 April 1975.

[60] J. Lawrence, D. Steed and P. Young, *Disruptive Children – Disruptive Schools?* (Croom Helm, 1984), p. 3.

[61] Davie, *Religion*, p. 122.

[62] Cited by G. Pearson, *Hooligan: A History of Respectable Fears* (Basingstoke: Macmillan, 1991), p. 235.

[63] G. Scott, 'My Childhood', 2004. I owe this reference to Samantha Badger.

[64] J. Benson, *The Rise of Consumer Society in Britain, 1880–1980* (Harlow: Longman, 1994), p. 168.

[65] R. Moore, *Pit-Men, Preachers and Politics: The Effects of Methodism in a Durham Mining Community* (Cambridge: Cambridge University Press, 1974), p. 25.

her parents taught her. 'You were terrified. No, not terrified, but the respect was there, you were held in awe. Everything they told us to do must be done. There was no laughing and grinning and giggling at the teachers as they do these days. But they had the respect, it was really respectful.'[66]

Sunday schools too did much more – and for much longer – to reinforce notions of authority and morality than those living in the early twenty-first century probably suspect. 'Sunday school', concludes Richard Sykes, 'was, to a large extent, a vehicle for the transmission of significant facets of the popular religious repertoire.'[67] It was a repertoire that was often both well received and well remembered.[68] 'Well I think it taught us standards that we have lived by ever since', recalls a West Midlands woman who attended a United Methodist chapel in the late 1920s. 'Right from wrong and do to others as you would they do to you, sort of thing.'[69] The son of a car worker-turned-small shopkeeper agrees. What he learned at the Primitive Methodist Sunday school he attended at much the same time, he remembers, was 'that you didn't swear, didn't fight, go drinking, get drunk, gamble […] Oh yes, you knew what was right and what wrong. My mum used to say – and I used to say it with my lad – "Badness leads to sadness", she'd say.'[70]

The handing down of such homilies from generation to generation suggests that considerable caution is required before associating the century-long decline in religious attendance with a comparable decline in religious influence. And such caution is most certainly justified. Schools, Sunday schools (and the uniformed youth organizations associated with them) continued to insist – with little obvious resistance – upon the importance of respect, obedience, the tenets of conventional morality, and the superiority of Britain and all that it stood for.[71]

Whenever they were young, the nation's children were subjected to a substantial, albeit declining, programme of patriotic, nationalistic and imperialist propaganda. They heard it at school and Sunday school, they read it in their comics, school books and library books, and they were likely to come across it again when they went to the cinema, listened to the radio or switched on the television.[72] George Orwell's analysis of the values and virtues espoused by films and radio programmes during the 1930s is well known and sharply apposite. They promoted, he believed, 'patriotism, religion, the Empire, the family, the sanctity of marriage, the old school tie, birth, breeding, honour and discipline'.[73] Orwell was right. The BBC, for example, established itself as

---

[66] E. Roberts, *A Woman's Place: An Oral History of Working-Class Women 1890–1940* (Oxford: Blackwell, 1984), pp. 26–7. Cf. F. Gresswell, *Bright Boots: An Autobiography and Anthology* (Robert Hale, 1956), p. 66.

[67] R.P.M. Sykes, 'Popular Religion in Dudley and the Gornals, c.1914–1965', University of Wolverhampton PhD, 1999, p. 123.

[68] Northumbria County Record Office, T/76 Miss Haywood; T/10 W. Hale; Museum of Edinburgh, Newhaven Community Group, T.305/95.

[69] Sykes, 'Popular Religion', p. 125.

[70] Sykes, 'Popular Religion', p. 125.

[71] T.P. Sykes cited in *Newcastle Evening Chronicle*, 10 September 1905; 'Empire education', *Observer*, 13 January 1924.

[72] M. Paris, *Warrior Nation: Images of War in British Popular Culture, 1850–2000* (Reaktion, 2000).

[73] J. Richards, 'Boy's Own Empire: Feature Films and Imperialism in the 1930s', in J.M. MacKenzie (ed.), *Imperialism and Popular Culture* (Manchester: Manchester University Press, 1986), pp. 140–1. See also J. Richards and A. Aldgate, *Best of British: Cinema and Society 1930–1970* (Oxford: Blackwell, 1983).

the 'reverent chronicler' of royal, patriotic and imperial occasions.[74] It is well known, for instance, that from its earliest days, it broadcast imperial events like the Empire Games, test matches and rugby internationals likely to be of interest to sports enthusiasts of all ages.[75] It was 'a happy coincidence', observed the *Manchester Guardian*, that just as the Coronation procession of 1937 had put television on the map, so the BBC resumed broadcasting in 1946 with 'the Victory march as the first big event of the new service'.[76] It is less widely appreciated, perhaps, that for many years the Corporation produced programmes designed explicitly to foster young people's interest in the British Empire. Thus the philosophy underpinning a series for sixth formers broadcast during the early 1940s was clear and unapologetic. England, it explained, 'is the single country in the world that, looking after its own interests with meticulous care, has at the same time something to give to others'.[77]

But what did the nation's young people make of this patriotic and imperial propaganda? It was not difficult for them to see, when they grew up, that efforts had been made to guide their thinking. 'Oh ah, you had that drummed into you' at school between the wars, confirms the son of a Bristol docker. 'The British Empire and all this, that and the other, you know. Britons never shall be slaves … and all this, that and the other.'[78] It is doubtful, however, whether young people were quite so perceptive at the time. When the author of this book was a child in the 1950s and early 1960s he was taught – and he accepted – that Britain was the best country in the world, its superiority epitomized by the royal family and the empire/commonwealth over which it ruled. When his daughters were children during the late 1970s and 1980s, they joined enthusiastically in the celebrations their schools organized for the silver jubilee of Queen Elizabeth in 1977 and the marriage of Prince Charles and Diana Spencer in 1981.[79]

BOYS AND GIRLS, MEN AND WOMEN

Whenever they were young, the nation's children were taught too that boys and girls were different, that they should behave differently and that they should – and undoubtedly would – grow up to perform different roles at home, at work and in the community. Indeed, it will be recalled from earlier in the chapter that the ways in which schools, churches and the media were staffed and organized, and the values that they espoused all tended to reflect prevailing attitudes towards gender and gender relations.

So too did the magazines young people read, the music they listened to and the films and television programmes they watched. Between the wars, for example, publications aimed at both boys and girls presented clearly delineated images of

---

[74] J.M. MacKenzie, ' "In Touch with the Infinite": The BBC and the Empire, 1923–53', in MacKenzie (ed.), *Imperialism*, p. 167.

[75] R. Holt, *Sport and the British: A Modern History* (Oxford: Oxford University Press, 1990), pp. 311–12.

[76] *Manchester Guardian*, 7 June 1946.

[77] MacKenzie, ' "In Touch with the Infinite" ', p. 177.

[78] Avon County Reference Library, Bristol People's Oral History Project, Transcript R008, p. 7; Benson, *Working Class*, pp. 148, 160–1. Also W. Woodruff, *The Road to Nab End: An Extraordinary Northern Childhood* (Abacus, 2002), p. 125.

[79] Personal recollection.

masculinity and femininity.[80] Boys' magazines suggested that manliness consisted of a combination of obedience, self-discipline, courage and leadership (with courage and leadership desirable, fortuitously, only when they involved an acceptance of society as it currently existed).[81] Girls' magazines promoted what feminist scholars describe as 'a domesticated heterosexuality, organized according to a specific career progression' from girlhood to womanhood.[82] In fact, such scholars make little effort to conceal their indignation when they consider the care and consistency with which these magazines reinforced dominant notions of patriarchy. In a book published at the very end of the century, Imelda Whelehan notes that although contemporary magazines *Mizz*, *Sugar* and *Minx*, like *Jackie* of her generation, refer to female friendships, their emphasis is firmly upon fashion, beauty and boys.

> In my reading of girls' magazines I would have to agree with Germaine Greer, who declares that 'the British girls' press trumpets the triumph of misogyny and the hopelessness of the cause of female pride'. All girls' magazines seem to do is prepare children for the world of glossy women's magazines which will open up further vistas of anxiety about one's body, one's boyfriend, one's lifestyle, one's attitude.[83]

It was never easy to withstand such pressures. Could one really expect the nation's boys and girls, men and women to stand out against the weight of these, and similar assumptions and exhortations? Could one realistically imagine the people of the country mounting a sustained and successful challenge to the deep-seated, gendered foundations upon which the whole of society was organized? None of this suggests, of course, that the nation's readers, listeners and viewers were empty receptacles to be filled by anybody with a spiritual, ideological or commercial agenda to impart.[84] It was a case less of coercion and passive acceptance than of persuasion and positive reinforcement. The messages about gender promoted by religion, education and the media were strikingly similar to those propagated by the politically powerful – and similar too, it should be remembered, to those held (for their own reasons) by the majority of people on the receiving end of such pressures. So it is that Penny Tinkler concludes her study of girls' magazines during the first half of the century with some telling reflections on the relationship between gender, ideology and power. Rejecting the view that girls were duped by their reading, her view is that,

> given the organisation and experiences of adolescent girlhood, many readers would have recognised the 'preferred meanings' embedded in girls' magazines

---

[80] See J. Richards and D. Sheridan, *Mass-Observation at the Movies* (Routledge & Kegan Paul, 1987), Ch.14.

[81] K. Boyd, 'Knowing Your Place: The Tensions of Manliness in Boys' Story Papers, 1918–39', in M. Roper and J. Tosh (eds), *Manful Assertions: Masculinities in Britain since 1800* (Routledge, 1991), p. 161. See also J. Bourke, *Dismembering the Male: Men's Bodies and the Great War* (Reaktion, 1996). For First World War literature, see G. Robb, *British Culture and the First World War* (Basingstoke: Palgrave, 2002), p. 36.

[82] P. Tinkler, *Constructing Girlhood: Popular Magazines for Girls Growing up in England, 1920–1950* (Taylor & Francis, 1995), p. 187.

[83] I. Whelehan, *Overloaded: Popular Culture and the Future of Feminism* (Women's Press, 2000), p. 53. See also P. Kirkham and J. Thumin (eds), *Me Jane: Masculinity, Movies and Women* (Lawrence & Wishart, 1995); Y. Tasker, *Working Girls: Gender and Sexuality in Popular Cinema* (Routledge, 1998).

[84] Whelehan, *Overloaded*, p. 54; Childs, *Britain Since 1939*, p. 5.

and would have learned the feminine lessons conveyed in their weekly and monthly papers, even if they subsequently rejected them.[85]

Valerie Walkerdine agrees. Brought up in a middle-class family in Derby during the 1950s, she trained as a primary school teacher in London but managed to avoid what she describes as the fate of so many would-be teachers, 'the engagement ring and return to the provinces to marry'. She went on to study for a PhD, teach and research at London University's Institute of Education, and become committed to radical politics, Marxism and feminism. When she looks back at her childhood, what she remembers – with something of a shudder – is its 'conservative and respectable ordinariness'. Gender and class stereotyping, she now believes, combined to reinforce one another. It was, she recalls,

> the church, the school, the Brownies, the Guides and the fêtes and competitions which helped provide the building blocks of my formation. Yet gazing further, looking through the window of the past, I glimpse the happiness of sunny days at the tea table. Laughter, hopes and fears and pain, pain of loss, pain of leaving, of wanting. Fear of the reproduction of that ordinariness inside myself. To be ordinary is to be a woman; to be ordinary is to be a worker: terror and desire.[86]

Neither the feminism of the 1960s, the new feminism of the 1970s (nor the Spice Girls' much vaunted 'girl power' of the late 1990s) did a great deal to undermine the assumptions about gender and gender relations that the churches, the schools and the media exemplified so closely and promulgated so assiduously. With even academic feminists finding it difficult to break free from the gendered assumptions and ideological categories they were seeking to undermine,[87] it is scarcely surprising that the rest of the population rarely made much effort to do so. As the Spice Girls' Emma Bunton pointed out, 'Of course I'm a feminist. But I could never burn my Wonderbra. I'm nothing without it.'[88] It is important therefore to distinguish between well-publicized flirtations with autonomy and openness, and the more deep-seated, and much more influential acceptance of, and commitment to, conventional gender roles:

> the focus on sexy young celebrities is reassuring for those who find self-proclaimed 'feminists' threatening, because although these stars represent success (often measured materially) and empowerment (often measured by the breadth of their fan-base), they also visually offer an adherence to and belief in traditional feminity.[89]

---

[85] Tinkler, *Constructing Girlhood*, p. 187.

[86] V. Walkerdine, 'Dreams from an Ordinary Childhood', in L. Heron (ed.), *Truth, Dare or Promise: Girls Growing up in the Fifties* (Virago, 1985), p. 65. See also pp. 70–1, 76–7.

[87] M. Barrett, *Women's Oppression Today: The Marxist/Feminist Encounter* (Verso, 1988 edition), p. 150.

[88] Whelehan, *Overloaded*, p. 10.

[89] Whelehan, *Overloaded*, pp. 56–7. See also G. Murphy, 'Media Influence on the Socialisation of Teenage Girls', in J. Curran, A. Smith and P. Wingate (eds), *Impacts and Influences: Essays on Media Power in the Twentieth Century* (Methuen, 1987).

BRITISH AND FOREIGN, WHITE AND BLACK

What then was the relationship between religious, educational and media pressures and ethnic minority subordination? In answering this question, the problem is no longer to distinguish between rhetoric and reality – there was never much likelihood, after all, of those from ethnic minorities confusing the rhetoric of equal opportunities with the day-to-day reality of demonization, discrimination and disadvantage. And demonization there was in abundance. Even the most reluctant critics of Britain's political and cultural institutions would be hard put to deny that the churches, the schools and the media – and the media in particular – marginalized members of Britain's ethnic minorities.[90] The problem rather is to distinguish between public representations of ethnic minorities and the public and private reactions of those being represented. This is a good deal more difficult. Even the most sensitive students of Britain's majority–minority relations will be hard placed to decide whether or not religion, education and the media persuaded immigrants and their families to accept as normal the economic, social and political disadvantages from which they suffered.

During the first half of the century, Britain's religious, educational and media institutions took it for granted that Britain provided the yardstick against which other nations, nationalities and ethnic groups should be judged. They found, almost invariably, that the rest of the world fell far short of the standards that Britain set. One is reminded inescapably of Ronald Robinson and John Gallagher's celebrated description of mid-Victorian Britain's outlook on the world:

> Upon the ladder of progress, nations and races seemed to stand higher or lower according to the proven capacity of each for freedom and enterprise: the British at the top, followed a few rungs below by the Americans, and other 'striving, go-ahead' Anglo-Saxons. The Latin peoples were thought to come next, though far behind. Much lower still stood the vast Oriental communities of Asia and North America where progess appeared unfortunately to have been crushed for centuries by military despotisms or smothered under passive religions. Lowest of all stood the 'aborigines' whom it was thought had never learned enough social discipline to pass from the family and tribe to the making of a state.[91]

This confidence in Britain's superiority survived long beyond the mid-Victorian years. By the beginning of the twentieth century, explains Penelope Summerfield, music hall songs had developed what she describes as a defensive celebration of British power:

> Sons of the Sea! All British born!
> Sailing in ev'ry ocean. Laughing foes to scorn.
> They may build their ships, my lads,

---

[90] L. Young, *Fear of the Dark: 'Race', Gender and Sexuality in the Cinema* (Routledge, 1996), pp. 53–4; 'You white hearted villain!', *Daily Mail*, 3 January 1970; 'The persecution of a good man', *Daily Mail*, 3 April 1985.

[91] R. Robinson and J. Gallagher with A. Denney, *Africa and the Victorians: The Official Mind of Imperialism* (Basingstoke: Macmillan, 1961), pp. 2–3. See too D. Cannadine, *Ornamentalism: How the British Saw their Empire* (Penguin, 2001), p. 5.

And think they know the game,
But they can't build boys of the bulldog breed
Who made old England's name.[92]

Defensive or aggressive, celebratory or cautionary, the message, reiterated time and time again, was that Britain was best. The world beyond its shores might be intriguingly colourful, but it could be alarmingly dangerous – and it was inevitably disturbingly different. Britain itself, was frequently presented through a bucolic, rose-tinted haze. Thus the characters selected by the BBC to represent Britain in its Christmas programmes during the 1930s were, it has been noted, 'statistically untypical: speakers of pure regional dialect, members of closed communities, practitioners of traditional crafts'.[93] Symbolically, however, they were exceptionally well chosen, their stereotypicality rendering them immediately recognizable. The rest of the world could not but pale by comparison. Even the white Dominions did not escape the condescension of the metropolitan media. In 1936, for example, the girls' magazine *Peg's Paper* launched four serials set against a foreign background. One of them, 'When a Man Sins', opened with words that made clear the stance it was adopting: 'Lawless love, unfettered hate, primitive passion, all awaited June when she went to the Backwoods of Canada to become a bride … she preferred the hero to most of the others – he was white.'[94]

The country's religious, educational and media institutions continued for many years to regard the world beyond Britain with the same, or a similar, sense of superiority. However, during the second half of the century, they also began to look inwards.[95] Faced with large-scale immigration and the establishment of substantial immigrant settlements, they turned their attention to minority ethnic communities within Britain. They assumed – reasonably enough – that the great majority of their congregations, pupils, readers, listeners and viewers were white. They assumed – unreasonably and in ways that tended to become self-fulfilling – that ethnic minority communities posed a threat to majority, white society.[96]

The media showed scant interest in the discrimination and disadvantage that shaped ethnic minority life, but paid an enormous amount of attention to the dislocation and disruption that such discrimination and disadvantage could produce.

---

[92] P. Summerfield, 'The Effingham Arms and the Empire: Deliberate Selection in the Evolution of Music Hall in London', in E. Yeo and S. Yeo (eds), *Popular Culture and Class Conflict 1590–1914: Explorations in the History of Labour and Leisure* (Brighton: Harvester, 1981), p. 236.

[93] D. Cardiff and P. Scannell, 'Broadcasting and National Unity', in Curran *et al.* (eds), *Impacts and Influences*, p. 164. See also *Express and Star*, 14 December 1936; A. Kirk-Greene, *Britain's Imperial Administrators, 1858–1966* (Basingstoke: Macmillan, 2000).

[94] G. Murphy, 'Media Influence on the Socialisation of Teenage Girls', in Curran *et al.* (eds), *Impacts and Influences*, p. 213.

[95] For the first half of the century see, for example, C. Volante, 'Identities and Perceptions: Gender, Generation and Ethnicity in the Italian Quarter, Birmingham, c1891–1938', University of Wolverhampton PhD, 2001, Ch. 6.

[96] P. Braham, 'How the Media Report Race', in M. Gurevitch, T. Bennett, J. Curran and J. Woollacott (eds), *Culture, Society and the Media* (Methuen, 1982), p. 273; J. Tulloch, 'Television and Black Britons', in A. Goodwin and G. Whannel (eds), *Understanding Television* (Routledge, 1990), pp. 143–6.

Stereotyping was rampant. 'The way of the Hun' was the headline *The Observer* gave to its 1915 report of an incident in which a German was the *victim* of a domestic shooting.[97] Race, colour, conflict and violence became intimately entwined, with newspaper headlines reporting the 'colour bar', 'race hate' and 'racial clashes'.[98] Indeed, long after Britain had acquired a substantial black population, the single most regular exposure of 'black' people on television was provided – almost unbelievably – by the *Black and White Minstrel Show*, a programme in which white entertainers 'blacked up'.[99]

The national and local press adopted a familiar line. According to the *Daily Express*, in 'Cities like Wolverhampton, Leicester, Bradford and Reading ... the whole character has undergone an astonishing transformation. They now bear a closer resemblance to Bombay or Johannesburg than they do to the rest of England.'[100] Enoch Powell's 'rivers of blood' speech in 1968 encouraged the press to report – perhaps we should say propagate – widely-held racist views. The editor of Wolverhampton's *Express and Star*, the local paper covering Powell's parliamentary constituency, put it like this:

> We cannot build up the sort of reader-editor relationship which establishes the local paper as a local ombudsman on matters like unemptied dustbins, uncut grass verges, unadopted roads, unlit streets, excessive council house rents, and all that sort of thing, and then snap it off shut on a major social issue like this. To do this would be to betray that faith which readers would have in us and the social function of newspaper production.[101]

'The persecution of a good man' was how the *Daily Mail* headed its editorial defending Bradford headmaster Ray Honeyford in 1985:

> A year ago in a high-flown journal of limited readership, he wrote his mind on the subject of ethnic education. He is opposed to it. He thinks it places white children who are in the minority at schools such as his, at disadvantage. He believes it makes coloured children less likely to adapt and succeed in Britain. To most people, whatever their colour, those views will seem no more than conventional common sense.[102]

Much of the press continued in the same, or similar, vein. 'We examine why thousands of Czech and Slovak gypsies are now claiming political asylum in Britain', announced the *Daily Mail* in 1997. 'Jarda says that in Britain, chickens cost just £1 and the

---

[97] 'The way of the Hun', *Observer*, 25 July 1915. See also 'The decrease of crime', *Observer*, 18 April 1915.

[98] Braham, 'Media', p. 273.

[99] Tulloch, 'Television', p. 144.

[100] Braham, 'Media', p. 272.

[101] Braham, 'Media', p. 282. See 'Smethwick widow "terrorised" says Tory', *Daily Mail*, 7 January 1965; 'Teacher quits over coloured children', *Daily Mail*, 2 July 1965; 'De Freitas ordered to keep quiet', *Daily Mail*, 1 September 1965.

[102] 'The persecution of a good man', *Daily Mail*, 3 April 1985. See also, 'Black power bar', *Daily Mail*, 5 September 1985; 'Race row head is backed by judge', *Daily Mail*, 6 September 1985; 'Fury of mother labelled "racist" in playground murder report', *Daily Mail*, 2 January 1990.

Government hands out money every week. So how long before the other million gypsies like him unburden their grinding poverty and head towards Dover?'[103]

The problem is to ascertain the impact of such stereotyping and positioning. The task, we know, can be extraordinarily difficult. It is necessary, naturally, to demonstrate, rather than assume, that there was a relationship between religious, educational and media manipulation and ethnic minority subordination. It is also necessary, we must remember, to avoid making the seemingly all-too-easy assumption that the 'black' minority (or indeed the white majority) was homogeneous in its beliefs, its attitudes and its assumptions.

Nevertheless, it is possible to delineate, in broad terms, the impact that the media had upon ethnic minority attitudes towards majority society, and the ways in which the leaders of the majority exercised their power. Jeffrey Richards draws our attention to the work of the anthropologist Hortense Powdermaker which suggests, he explains, 'that on the whole people will accept depictions of something they know nothing about. But they will reject as inaccurate faulty depictions of things they know about at first hand.'[104] If Powdermaker is correct – and common sense suggests that he may well be – it will help us to understand minority (and majority) attitudes towards media treatment of ethnicity.

Those from ethnic minorities knew at first hand about demonization, discrimination and disadvantage. And certainly it is easy enough to show that the leaders of ethnic minority communities, and the bodies on which they sat, were highly critical of the ways in which the white media – and the white majority they represented – chose to exercise their power. Ethnic minority spokespeople demanded, for example, that the media should employ more ethnic minority journalists, broadcasters and production workers, and that radio, television and the press should reflect more accurately ethnic minority needs and experiences. The Commission for Racial Equality pointed out, for example, that,

> The portrayal of ethnic minorities in Drama, Light Entertainment and other programme areas depends to a large extent on the employment opportunities open to ethnic minority artists. Any difficulties they face will have a two-fold effect: first on employment prospects, secondly on the 'visibility' and roles which television gives to those of ethnic minority origin.[105]

It is more difficult to know how representative such 'official' views were of 'mainstream' minority opinion.[106] Privately, no doubt, people's day-to-day concerns often tended to be a good deal more personal and parochial. A Punjabi girl attending a predominantly white, rural secondary school during the late 1980s reported that her education taught her to deny her ethnic identity: 'I say I'm British when I come to school, but if I was like with my family or relations it would be Sikh.'[107] A

---

[103] *Daily Mail*, 20 October 1997. See also 'Minister warns Slovak gypsies keep out', *Daily Mail*, 22 October 1997; S. Heffer, 'Rivers of blood?', *Daily Mail*, 7 February 1999.

[104] Richards, 'Boy's Own Empire', pp. 160–1.

[105] Tulloch, 'Television', p. 147.

[106] J. Downing, *The Media Machine* (Pluto, 1980), p. 82.

[107] M.J. Taylor, 'Learning Fairness through Empathy: Pupils' Perspectives on Putting Policy into Practice', in M. Lancaster and M. Taylor (eds), *Ethics, Ethnicity and Education* (Kogan Page, 1992), p. 163. See also V.K. Edwards, *The West Indian Language Issue in British Schools: Challenges and Responses* (Routledge & Kegan Paul, 1979).

Wolverhampton man, who arrived from Jamaica during the 1960s, insists that he has not forgotten his roots.

> I took my kids back ... because there is so much TV news ... I felt that it was important for them to see what Jamaica is about. Whilst peoples got their own impression and their own idea insofar as ... coloured people ... all [are] Rastafarian, drug smoking. That is not the case. That is the misapprehension people 'as, and to a degree they haven't let us live that down.[108]

Often, the reporting of overseas wars and indigenous riots brought matters to a head. The Gulf War of 1991, for example, forced young Punjabis in the Southall area of west London to face up to the gender and generational divisions within what outsiders tended to consider an opaquely homogenous community. Kashif, a young Muslim, was only too aware of the need to balance public, western-based views of the social order with the private, Islam-based demands of the family. At school, he took the Allies' side in the war: 'Like here when I say "we" I mean the Allies but at home I say "them".' The contradictions he and his Muslim schoolmates had to negotiate were substantial and deep-seated.

> The news talks about the anger of British Muslims and their loyalty to Islam but what is a British Muslim? Is he more British or more Muslim? You can't exactly have an equal choice of both, it's difficult to say but I think I'm more westernised, I wouldn't say I'm British because we're in two societies at the same time, one is Islamic society, but not to the true extent, and the other is westernised society, but bearing away from it. If you look at the small things in these societies they are totally different, like your behaviour, your duties and your role in the family.[109]

Ten years later, on the very day that I drafted the first version of this passage, the Home Office published its report into the riots that had broken out in Oldham, Burnley and Bradford in the summer of 2001. Neither local schools nor the local press escaped their share of criticism. The former were condemned for operating a Eurocentric curriculum and providing predominantly Christian worship, the latter for publishing anonymous and inflammatory letters.[110] A few days before the appearance of the report, the Labour Home Secretary, David Blunkett, issued a call for new immigrants and their children to do more to adopt British 'norms of acceptability', and went on to hint at the introduction of 'light touch' naturalization tests.[111] It provoked the sort of response in ethnic minority communities that one would expect. 'I'm not sure what I would have to do to fit into Mr Blunkett's definition of Britishness', complained Suman Singh, a young woman interviewed while shopping at an Asian sweet centre in Glasgow:

> I wear saris or salwar kameez, the food I eat is Indian – the sweets here are the kind I grew up with and I like them more than Cadbury's things. Does that mean

---

[108] Black and Ethnic Minority Project, 71.DX-624/6/69, Mr McPherson.

[109] Cited in M. Gillespie, *Television, Ethnicity and Cultural Change* (Routledge, 1995), p. 138. See also *The Guardian*, 28 September 1993.

[110] *The Guardian*, 11 December 2001.

[111] *The Guardian*, 10 December 2001.

I'm not British or patriotic enough? I speak perfect English, as do my family, and I have O grade history so I would pass his 'whiteness test'. But I wouldn't want to. I can define my own nationality, I don't need Mr Blunkett to do it for me.[112]

ASSURANCE AND REASSURANCE, THE MIDDLE CLASS AND THE WORKING CLASS

It follows from the discussion to this point that religion, education and the media tended to present the existing system of power relationships – and class relationships – as natural, advantageous and unassailable. The middle class were assured that their values, attitudes and assumptions were not only intrinsically desirable but also ideally attuned to the demands of exercising power. The working class were reassured that however inequitable the distribution of power might appear, the middle class's control of the nation's economic, social, cultural and political capital was just as much to their advantage as it was it to those responsible for exercising authority over them.

Religion, education and the media all tended to reinforce the middle class's own view of the world. The public schools were more influential than one might imagine. The leading schools, it is widely recognized, allowed the upper and better-off middle class to retain their domination of such centres of power and influence as the episcopate, the judiciary and the civil service.[113] The less well-known schools, it is not always appreciated, prepared boys from a variety of middle-class backgrounds for employment in a range of more modest, but locally powerful and prestigious professional occupations.[114] Christine Heward has made a detailed study of Ellesmere College in Shropshire, an institution which she describes as being 'in the lower echelons of the public school hierarchy'. She concludes that during the 1930s and 1940s parents who sent their sons to the school were generally well satisfied with the success with which it prepared them for entry into acceptable middle-class occupations. 'The school's effectiveness was based on the rigour of the regime, every aspect of which was harnessed towards the end of producing successful career men.'[115]

Most branches of the media also tended to reinforce a middle-class view of the world. Children's television, it was claimed in the 1960s, suffered from the same deficiencies as women's television: 'a certain detachment from life, a middle-class assumption that everyone is interested in ponies and lives in the Surrey Hills'.[116] Even the satire boom of the 1960s, it has been suggested, was 'a long-overdue mutiny within the ruling middle class'.[117] But no section of the media was more active than

---

[112] *The Guardian*, 11 December 2001.

[113] 'The new Principal of King's College', *Observer*, 27 November 1927.

[114] H. Perkin, *The Rise of Professional Society: England since 1880* (Routledge, 1989), pp. 258–66; C. Heward, *Making a Man of Him: Parents and their Sons' Education at an English Public School 1929–50* (Routledge, 1988), p. 198.

[115] Heward, *Making a Man*, pp. 199–200.

[116] Stuart Hood cited by J. Critchley, 'Fit for the Surrey hills,' *The Times*, 9 December 1967.

[117] N. Acherson, 'It's beyond parody', *The Observer*, 6 August 2000; A. Crisell, 'Filth, Sedition and Blasphemy: The Rise and Fall of Television Satire', in J. Corner (ed.), *Popular Television in Britain* (BFI Publishing, 1991).

the *Daily Mail* in reinforcing a middle-class view of the world. Throughout the century the paper was associated, particularly in the eyes of its detractors, with clerical drudgery, suburban taste and lower middle-class pretensions.[118] During the 1920s, explain Tom Jeffery and Keith McClelland, the *Mail* took it as axiomatic that, 'the middle class and the nation were one'. Recognizing that the retired, the unorganized and those on fixed incomes found it exceptionally difficult to manage, it responded by 'massaging the self-concern of the middle class and, in a longer perspective, by delivering a world fit for the middle class to live in'.[119] It proved a winning formula. The paper's circulation increased from some 1.4 million in 1940, to about 1.9 million in 1970 and nearly 2.4 million by the end of the century. Its secret, complained the paper's critics, was the way in which it cosseted and cajoled its middle-class readership. At the turn of the millennium, a *Guardian* journalist reported on the paper's success with a mixture of personal distaste and professional admiration. He noted that it flattered middle-class 'aspirations and crystallised their fears, helped form their values and fanned their discontents'.[120]

> The *Mail* sees good people threatened by bad. By criminals, by people pushing dangerous ideas, by people setting a poor example, whether living off benefits on a council estate or being over-indulgent and rich. The job of the paper is to describe this ceaseless battle, while drawing the lessons from it which will enable the good people – assumed to be the majority of the British population – to win … It calls itself the straightforward voice of Middle England – and seeks to impose that imagined community's values on everyone else …[121]

The use of the term 'Middle England' is intriguing. It suggests, *inter alia*, that one should be careful about associating any newspaper exclusively with a single social class. A survey carried out in 1928 revealed that in London, for example, 15 per cent of working-class families saw the *Daily Mail*, while a surprising 33 per cent of middle-class and lower middle-class families had access to the *Daily Mirror*.[122] But this common readership serves only to strengthen the argument that is being propounded in this section of the chapter. The press tended always to reinforce a middle-class view of the world. Thus even though Richard Hoggart pointed out in the mid-1950s that the middle class and working class often read the same papers, he went on immediately to emphasize that he found 'the dailies aimed particularly at middle-class people more unpleasant than those for working-class people. They tend to have an intellectual smugness, a spiritual chauvinism and snobbery, and a cocktail-party polish which makes their atmosphere quite peculiarly stifling'.[123]

---

[118] J. Carey, The *Intellectuals and the Masses: Pride and Prejudice among the Literary Intelligentsia, 1880–1939* (Faber and Faber, 1992), pp. 6–8; 'Whip 'em says a town', *Daily Mail*, 1 April, 1950.

[119] T. Jeffery and K. McClelland, 'A World Fit to Live In: The *Daily Mail* and the Middle Classes 1918–39', in Curran *et al.* (eds), *Impacts and Influences*, p. 41.

[120] A. Beckett, 'Mail order', *The Guardian*, 22 February 2001.

[121] Beckett, 'Mail order'.

[122] Jeffery and McClelland, 'World Fit to Live In', pp. 34–5. Also Mass-Observation, A 2410, 'Battersea Bye-Election', 1946, p. 22.

[123] R. Hoggart, *The Uses of Literacy: Aspects of Working-Class Life with Special Reference to Publications and Entertainments* (Penguin, 1957), pp. 244–5.

Not everybody, of course, accepted what they were told. But it was never easy for those brought up as middle class to shake themselves free of the values and assumptions urged on them by the families they grew up in, the friends they socialized with, the churches they visited, the schools they attended, the papers they read and the television programmes they watched. As a young, female, white-collar worker explained in the late 1940s,

> I like the *News* the best, it's mostly pictorial and it's a small paper. I think most women like small papers. I like to read Around The Town and Reader's Views, and the Woman's section is very good, they give the latest fashions. They have a lady who writes who goes about the shops and she gives advice about what's going on. I don't bother about the other papers.[124]

As the novelist and playwright Rachel Billington complained in the mid-1990s, 'The BBC has announced it intends to re-examine its guidelines on taste and decency and obscene language. Some people may be surprised to hear there *are* still guidelines.'[125]

It was not easy either for working-class people to escape the reassuring, class conciliatory embrace that was thrown around them. Whether they were singing hymns, doing their homework, reading the paper, or watching the television, they were reminded time and again that they lived in a society which, though not perfect, possibly came as close to perfection as could reasonably be hoped for. Sometimes, working-class people too rebelled against such anodyne reassurances. However, when they did so it was often with small, almost private gestures rather than by publicizing their grievances, engaging in left-wing politics or leaping to the barricades. Happily, there have been a number of interesting studies of working-class people's attitudes during the first half of the century.[126] Stephen Humphries, for instance, interprets working-class children's refusal to take their school work seriously as evidence, not of ignorance and laziness, but of 'a widespread disassociation from, and rejection of, the bourgeois ethic of rational and methodical striving for personal achievement and advancement'.[127] H.L. Beales and R.S. Lambert's *Memoirs of the Unemployed*, published in 1934, included the comment by an East Anglian carpenter that, 'If there is one thing that makes me "see red" it is the pictures and descriptions of such things as society weddings, court functions, and so on.'[128] Richard Hoggart puts it rather differently. Stressing the marginalization of the working-class autodidact, he recalls that, the 'minority who became conscious of their class-limitations, and take up some educational activity – so as to "work for their class" or "improve themselves" – tend to be ambiguously regarded'.[129]

Those brought up in religious families were sometimes dismayed by the snobbery and petty jealousies that seemed to animate the congregations they encountered. A Dudley man recalls that in the early 1940s his father refused to attend church after he

---

[124] Mass-Observation, 3089, 'Attitudes Towards Local Newspapers in Glasgow', 1949, p. 13.

[125] R. Billington, 'Does our TV have to be so coarse?', *Daily Mail*, 7 July 1995.

[126] For example, Rose, *Intellectual Life*, p. 172.

[127] Humphries, *Hooligans*, p. 45.

[128] A. Marwick, *Class: Image and Reality in Britain, France and the USA since 1930* (Fontana, 1981), p. 82.

[129] Hoggart, *Uses of Literacy*, p. 84. See also Museum of Edinburgh, T/12/87.

saw a workman in overalls turned away by a sidesman. A woman from nearby Gornal became disillusioned ten years or so later when her chapel began to attract a wealthier congregation.

> They'd got to have the biggest hats, they'd got to have the biggest, and they'd shopped at this particular shop. And you'd think, well hang on a minute, that's got nothing to do with it. It dain't matter if you come in your carpet slippers really ... That's when I decided to come out. But I've always been a strong believer.[130]

If resentment was common, rebellion was virtually unheard of. Whether or not the working people were persuaded by what their economic and social 'betters' told them, they found that it coincided pretty closely with their own view of the world. They knew that they were working class, they took increasing pride in their working-class identity and they accepted, the great majority of them, that the class system in which they found themselves was entrenched, pervasive and immutable.

During the first half of the century, therefore, working people were as likely to joke about the middle class, as they were to engage them in any kind of proletarian struggle. 'Rather than chafe at their supposed "betters",' admits Standish Meacham, 'they turned their backs on them.'[131] The factory worker, for example, was 'neither deeply involved with his workmates nor deeply antagonistic to his employer; on the whole his attitude to both more nearly approximates one of indifference'.[132] According to Robert Roberts, resignation was a great deal more usual than resistance in the Salford slum where he grew up.

> The class struggle, as manual workers in general knew it, was apolitical and had place entirely within their own society. They looked upon it not in any way as a war against the employers but as a perpetual series of engagements in the battle of life itself ... Marxist 'ranters' from the Hall who paid fleeting visits to our street insisted that we, the proletariat, stood locked in titanic struggle with some wicked master class. We were battling, they told us (from a vinegar barrel borrowed from our corner shop) to cast off our chains and win a whole world. Most people passed by; a few stood to listen, but not for long; the problems of the 'proletariat', they felt, had little to do with them.[133]

Between the 1940s and the 1970s, suggested Arthur Marwick in the early 1980s, 'a certain optimism and sense of confidence in the former period has now been replaced by a sense of bloody-minded resignation and a feeling of "once a worker always a worker" and why, anyway, aspire to anything better?'[134] Thereafter, however, the growth of prosperity seemed, not surprisingly, to take the edge off working-class

---

[130] Sykes, 'Popular Religion', p. 241. See also p. 259.

[131] S. Meacham, *A Life Apart: The English Working Class 1890–1914* (Thames & Hudson, 1977), p. 20.

[132] D. Lockwood, 'Sources of variation in working class images of society', *Sociological Review*, 14, 1966, p. 257.

[133] R. Roberts, *The Classic Slum: Salford Life in the First Quarter of the Century* (Manchester: Manchester University Press), p. 28.

[134] A. Marwick, *British Society since 1945* (Penguin, 1982), p. 208.

discontent. 'You know it's hard to say,' reflected a Preston man, 'but you have everything that the middle class had before you. Television, fridges, cars, holidays you know. Paid holidays of course, which you didn't used to get at one time ... we are still working class but we are certainly better off working class.'[135]

COERCION, MANIPULATION AND WORK

It is difficult then to weigh the coercive power of the state against the manipulative power of education, religion and the media. However, there seems little doubt that the country's political and cultural institutions played a part in confirming the majority of the population in the view that they had no reason to seek to undermine the existing system of power relationships. It is also difficult, as will be seen in the following chapter, to weigh the coercive power of the state and the manipulative power of education, religion and the media against the iron disciplines of work. However, it will be suggested that although the state, religion, education and the media all played a part in reinforcing existing power relationships, they did not have the same impact as the simple, but seemingly easily overlooked, need to earn a living.

---

[135] Lancaster, Mr RIP, p. 72.

6 THE IRON DISCIPLINES OF WORK

COERCION, MANIPULATION AND POWER

What, then, was the relationship between power and work? It is the aim of this chapter to examine the extent to which the stability of British society can be explained by people's day-to-day need to earn a living. It is an approach that has been adopted at various times by scholars of both right and left. According to F.M.L. Thompson, for example, 'Work was the supreme instrument of social control.'[1] According to Stephen Marglin, 'Wage advances were to the capitalist what free samples of heroin are to the pusher: a means of creating dependence.'[2] Whatever their rhetorical flourishes, such views have a great deal to commend them. It can certainly be shown that Britain's employers made sustained, and largely successful, efforts to increase the control that they were able to exercise over their employees. It also seems likely, though it cannot be proved, that such efforts played a crucial role in persuading employees to accept more broadly based structures of domination and subordination. The thrust of this chapter will therefore be to argue that employers' control at the workplace was doubly important. It encouraged an acceptance of workplace subordination, and an acceptance, more widely, of the authority wielded by those who exercised the political, economic, social and cultural leadership of the country.

This chapter will suggest, in other words, that one of the most fruitful ways of studying power relations in twentieth-century Britain is by examining what have been described as the 'iron disciplines of waged labour'.[3] It will argue that the iron disciplines of waged labour – or rather of work, whether waged or salaried – were of crucial and continuing importance. This chapter, like the others in the book, begins with a discussion of developments affecting the population as a whole, before moving on to examine the experiences of different social groups: the young, middle-aged and elderly; men and women; members of ethnic minorities; and those from the middle class and the working class. It will suggest that no matter what resistance they put up, no major section of the population seemed able to escape the ideologically controlling clutches of having to work for a living.

---

[1] F.M.L. Thompson, 'Social control in Victorian Britain', *Economic History Review*, xxxiv, 1981, p. 205.

[2] S. Marglin, 'What do bosses do? The origins and functions of capitalist production', *Review of Radical Political Economy*, 6, 1974, p. 26.

[3] See, for instance, P. Joyce, 'The Historical Meanings of Work: An Introduction', in P. Joyce (ed.), *The Historical Meanings of Work* (Cambridge: Cambridge University Press, 1987); A.J. McIvor, *A History of Work in Britain, 1880–1950* (Basingstoke: Palgrave, 2001), introduction; Thompson, 'Social control'.

EMPLOYERS, COERCION AND MANIPULATION

There is no doubt that in the twentieth century, as in the nineteenth, Britain's employers made determined attempts to maintain and extend the control that they were able to exercise over their employees. It is well known that the owners of many large, capital-intensive industries adopted a range of strategies in their attempts to ensure employee compliance with the demands of factory labour and other forms of mass production. In cotton and coal, in engineering and motor manufacturing, and later in mail order and financial services, they tightened supervision, introduced new technology, encouraged internal promotion, paid relatively high wages, adopted piece-rate systems of payment, and sometimes established company welfare schemes.[4]

If the cotton industry stood as a symbol of the first generation of factory discipline, the motor industry did the same with respect to the so-called 'new' industries that developed between the two world wars. The scale and severity of work in the car industry grew prodigiously. In 1914, Oxford, for example, 'was still a pre-industrial town', with Morris Motors employing fewer than a hundred people. By 1939, almost a third of the city's workforce was engaged in motorcar manufacture: 4,670 at Morris Motors, 1,190 at Morris Radiators, and 5,250 at Pressed Steel. After the First World War,

> a production line was organized with the chassis being pushed from one group of workers to the next. It was at this point that improving the organization of work by subdividing operations, by using single-purpose machines to drill the chassis frame, and by synchronizing the work of various assembly lines began to have serious effect. By 1926 each worker was engaged in a task of about 2½ minutes' duration.[5]

It was the call centre, no matter which industry it served, that came to epitomize the extension and brutalization of employers' control towards the end of the century.[6] The scale and severity of work in this new environment became widely recognized, widely resented, and widely condemned. Meeting service targets was bad enough. 'We have targets for everything', explained a Credcard worker in 1999: 'for how long the calls take, how long you take to type up the call, anything you can measure statistically. If it moves they'll measure it including how long you take to go the toilet.' Meeting sales targets was even worse. 'Travel insurance, that's a complete nightmare', complained a union representative. 'When somebody phones in for a balance you have to try to get a sale or get them interested as well as turning the call round in 155 seconds.'[7] Management could be almost unbelievably insensitive. Those in

---

[4] R. Fitzgerald, *British Labour Management and Industrial Welfare 1846–1939* (Croom Helm, 1988); H. Freidman and S. Meredeen, *The Dynamics of Industrial Conflict: Lessons from Ford* (Croom Helm, 1986).

[5] R.C. Whiting, *The View from Cowley: The Impact of Industrialization upon Oxford, 1918–1939* (Oxford: Clarendon Press, 1983), p. 30. See also J. Benson, *The Working Class in Britain, 1850–1939* (Harlow: Longman, 1989), p. 13.

[6] For late-century surveillance at Nissan and Peugeot, see G. Sewell and B. Wilkinson, ' "Someone to watch over me": Surveillance, discipline and the Just-in-Time labour process', *Sociology*, 26, 1992.

[7] P. Taylor and P. Bain, 'Trade unions, workers' rights and the frontier of control in UK call centres', *Economic and Industrial Democracy*, 22, 2001, pp. 52–3. I owe this reference to Matthew Brannan.

charge of a British Telecom call centre in Cardiff, for instance, refused to allow a husband to tell his wife that their son had been taken to hospital.[8]

Nevertheless, it is easy to be misled. Despite the attention they attracted, relatively few firms attempted to impose such intensive, centrally managed systems of control. And those that did attempt to do so never employed more than a minority of those working in twentieth-century Britain. It is tempting, as so often, to mistake the controversial for the commonplace.

Even so, the majority of firms employing the majority of employees wished to ensure the malleability of their workers. However, they set about extending their authority in ways that were less intrusive, less confrontational – and a good deal less likely to provoke resentment and resistance. Whether or not they established centrally managed systems of control, the owners of large, capital-intensive firms often relied upon family recruitment and the establishment of company welfare schemes. Such schemes, their organizers believed, reduced the economic insecurity that encouraged industrial unrest, provided a manageable forum for worker participation, and thus moderated the conflict that was inherent in the employer–employee relationship.[9]

Firms looked first to their salaried employees. 'Their loyalty was essential to the running of the firm, and, with the creation of large managerial bureaucracies from the turn of the century, companies needed to increase their investment in their staff.'[10] They turned later to their weekly paid workers. The civil service, local government, brewers, shoe makers, carpet firms, food manufacturers, railway companies and many other large employers provided their employees with benefits over and beyond their take-home pay. Indeed, the late-century development of human resource management was grounded, like welfare capitalism before it, in the belief that 'short-term conflict-management and relations with the union should take second place behind the longer-term task of nurturing employee commitment *en route* to the optimum utilization of human capital'.[11]

When small firms, owner-proprietors and individual householders took on labour, they did not introduce new technology, pay high wages, establish formal welfare schemes or adopt any of the other commonly recognized means of imposing workplace control. Farmers, shopkeepers, small manufacturers and those employing domestic help relied – whether deliberately or not – upon the bonds of obligation that they were able to create by means of family recruitment, employer–employee propinquity, and the provision of non-wage benefits on a personal and/or an ad hoc basis.[12] A farm labourer reported in the late 1930s, for instance, that his wages were 32 shillings a

---

[8] *Express and Star*, 17 August 2001. See also 'A call for charge', *The Guardian*, 19 February 2001. Cf. D. Jack, 'Spend-a-penny Ministry check', *Daily Mail*, 1 September 1965.

[9] Fitzgerald, *British Labour Management*, p. 19. Also J. Turner, 'Labour and business in modern Britain', *Business History*, xxxi, 1989, p. 5; D. Montgomery, 'Introduction: Workers' choices, company policies, and loyalties', *International Labor and Working-Class History*, 53, 1998.

[10] Fitzgerald, *British Labour Management*, p. 3.

[11] P. Ackers and J, Black, 'Paternalist Capitalism: An Organization Culture in Transition', in M. Cross and G. Payne (eds), *Work and the Enterprise Culture* (Falmer Press, 1991), pp. 54–5. See also Fitzgerald, *British Labour Management*; R. Fitzgerald, 'Employers' labour strategies, industrial welfare, and the response to New Unionism at Bryant and May, 1888–1930', *Business History*, xxxi, 1989.

[12] See J.C. Carrier, *Gifts and Commodities: Exchange and Western Capitalism since 1700* (Routledge, 1995).

week plus 'privileges'. By privileges, he explained, he meant such benefits as 'milk and vegetables and a small plot of ground on the farm where he could grow things and keep a pig and fowls'. The whole point of such privileges, he stressed, was that they were voluntary. 'The farmer's no need to give you vegetables and milk if he doesn't want to.'[13] Fifty years later, a Black Country personnel manager explained that the lock firm where he worked encouraged company loyalty by a combination of local recruitment, internal promotion and the avoidance of redundancy.

> We advertise all jobs in town, and we take the view that if you can get a good quality person from a family contact [that is ideal]. There was a time when no matter how bad you were, if your Dad worked here you got a job.[14]

EMPLOYEES, RESENTMENT AND RESISTANCE

However carefully such strategies were planned and executed, they sometimes provoked resentment and resistance rather than compliance and acceptance. The problem for the historian is that whereas overt forms of opposition like trade-union membership and strike action are reasonably easy to quantify, more covert forms of dissatisfaction such as absenteeism, restriction of output, petty pilfering and 'taking it easy' remain impossible to assess with anything remotely approaching statistical precision.[15]

Nor is this all. Although statistical evidence of trade-union membership and strike activity is easy enough to assemble, it remains exceptionally difficult to interpret. Indeed, it suggests that the twentieth century saw signs both of growing and of declining resentment. Of course, trade-union density (the proportion of potential members who were unionized) was not the function solely of workplace resentment and resistance. Resentful workers might be scared of joining a union, and contented workers might be scared of not joining.[16] Nonetheless, trade-union density does at least provide an indication of the extent to which employees felt it sensible to deal with their employers on a collective, rather than an individual, basis. It suggests that employees' tendency to deal collectively with their employers grew until about 1920, declined until the early 1930s, grew again between the mid-1930s and the late 1970s, before declining precipitously during the 1980s and 1990s.[17]

Nor, of course, was the propensity to strike the function solely of workplace resentment and resistance. Resentful workers might be scared of taking industrial action, just as contented workers might feel fearful of failing to join their colleagues in a strike or lockout.[18] Nonetheless, strike propensity provides an indication of the extent to which employees felt it sensible to resist the demands of their employers by

---

[13] W. Greenwood, *How the Other Man Lives* (Labour Book Services, 1937), pp. 73–4. See also Northumbria County Record Office, T/84, Mrs Kearnley.

[14] Ackers and Black, 'Paternalist Capitalism', p. 43.

[15] 'Football absentees', *Manchester Guardian*, 27 February 1946.

[16] 'Miss Bondfield's Labour Notes', *Daily Mail*, 11 February 1920. Benson, *Working Class*, Ch. 7.

[17] Membership was highest, and strikes most frequent, in industries such as coal, iron and engineering where employers were most assertive.

[18] R. Church and Q. Outram, *Strikes and Solidarity: Coalfield Conflict in Britain 1889–1966* (Cambridge: Cambridge University Press, 1998), Ch. 1.

the collective withdrawal of labour. It suggests that the number of working days lost per worker grew just before the First World War, grew again in the early 1920s, peaked in the late 1920s, and thereafter fell to a very low level, where it remained, with the exception of the late 1970s and early 1980s, until the end of the century and beyond.

It does not follow, obviously, that a decline in strike propensity was synonymous with the disappearance of workplace recalcitrance.[19] The trouble is that the empirical difficulties of studying covert forms of workplace behaviour demand an unusually high degree of imaginative historical reconstruction. This allows those on the right to stress the disruptive effects of workplace obstruction, and those on the left to see in such disruption signs of militant, working-class consciousness. These are difficult and elusive issues. Nevertheless, it will be suggested that covert forms of resentment and resistance probably became less common between the beginning and the end of the century. During the late 1940s, Ferdynand Zweig interviewed some 400 industrial workers with a view to discovering whether restrictive practices were becoming more or less widespread in British industry. 'When I started my inquiry', he admitted, 'I was under the impression that restrictive practices were increasing, because of the strengthened bargaining power of the Unions.' However, he soon changed his mind, concluding that 'the reverse is true'.[20] Fifty years later, two management experts from the University of Keele sought to show that even under total quality management the workforce was able to retain a degree of control over working life. However, they had to cast round rather desperately for evidence in support of their argument. For instance, they cited a worker from a major retail bank who told them how employee autonomy enabled his team to solve a problem that had been annoying them.

> We've got this notice board that we leave with the memos on, and people initial them when they've read them. But then you get a great big stockpile of memos because people haven't read them. So what we've decided to do is to leave them in there for a week so that they don't go missing. We've got separate box files now, so that someone can just go in the room and say like, 'I haven't read a memo in a week' and they [the memos] are in week order, and they can pick up that week's memos.[21]

This may have been workplace control, but it was not control that many early century activists would probably have recognized.

EMPLOYERS, PERSUASION AND COMPLIANCE

It can also be suggested, more broadly, that employers' coercion and manipulation proved increasingly effective in persuading the population as a whole of the benefits to

[19] P. Thompson and S. Ackroyd, 'All quiet on the workplace front? A critique of recent trends in British industrial sociology', *Sociology*, 29, 1995, p. 619; ' No-strike promises help to win new engine plant', *Daily Mail*, 6 April 1990.

[20] N. Tiratsoo and J. Tomlinson, 'Restrictive practices on the shopfloor in Britain, 1945–60: Myth and reality', *Business History*, 36, 1994, p. 70.

[21] D. Knights and D. McCabe, ' "Ain't misbehavin"? Opportunities for resistance under new forms of "Quality" Management', *Sociology*, 34, 2000, pp. 429–30.

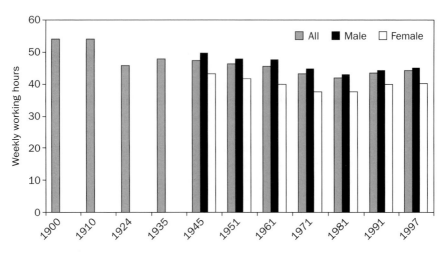

Figure 6.1 Working hours of manual workers in manufacturing, Great Britain, 1900–97

Source: Based on D. Gallie, 'The Labour Force', in A.H. Halsey (ed.), *Twentieth-Century British Social Trends* (Basingstoke: Macmillan, 2000), p. 306.

be derived from an acceptance of conventional sources of authority. However, this represents a dauntingly difficult step in the process of explaining why it was that the twentieth century saw so little challenge to the existing economic, social and political order. Indeed, it hardly needs saying that monocausal explanations of complex developments should always be approached with an enormous amount of scepticism.

There are certainly a priori reasons for questioning whether the country's economic, social and political stability can be explained in terms of employer coercion and manipulation. The causes for doubt lie most obviously in the lack of access that employers had to those whom they did not employ, and the declining access that they had even to those whom they did employ.

The labour force participation rate hovered just above and just below the 60 per cent level.[22] This was far too low a figure, one might suppose, for employer control to provide a convincing explanation for the consent and compliance of the 40 per cent of the population who were not in employment at any particular time. Working hours too are central to the argument, and Figure 6.1 provides an indication of the way in which they fell during the course of the century. It shows that in manufacturing industry, for instance, working hours declined by nearly 20 per cent between 1900 and 1997. It is difficult to see, on the face of it, that even within the workplace declining employee hours can be used to sustain an argument in favour of increasing employer control and manipulation.[23]

Nevertheless, it is believed that employer control and manipulation probably did become increasingly important in engaging the consent and compliance of the population. Unfortunately, the evidence, by its very nature, will almost certainly prove too imprecise and ambiguous for many readers' tastes – especially when it is applied to

---

[22] Not that all 60 per cent attended as assiduously as they should.

[23] McIvor, *Work*, p. 241.

considering employer influence beyond the workplace. There seems little doubt, however, that employers in large, capital-intensive industries managed to ensure day-to-day compliance with the demands of factory production. They did so partly by fear. 'You kept wiping the perspiration off,' recalls a Preston girl who began weaving in 1911, 'and you daren't stop, there was no stopping.'[24] They did so partly by inspiring respect and admiration. 'In those days the bosses did not live far and wide', recalls an Accrington weaver. 'The bosses were people who were men who had come from the rank and file of the industry.'[25]

More and more, however, employers in large, capital-intensive industries ensured compliance by the provision of financial incentives. 'There's been a rush on lately and it's been overtime every night for the past two weeks', complained a man working the line in a car factory during the late 1930s. 'Eleven hours a day I've been putting in. Eight's bad enough, but that extra three is just about getting me down.' However, he had no intention of leaving: 'The money's the only thing that keeps me here.'[26] One is reminded of Luton's 'affluent' car workers who were immortalized by John Goldthorpe and his collaborators in the classic study they published almost exactly three decades later. They reported that, 'the reason that our respondents by far most frequently gave for remaining in their present jobs – and most appeared to be quite firmly attached – was in fact the high level of pay that they could earn'.[27]

Employers in large, non-factory industries also seemed to secure the compliance of their employees. A Post Office clerk with 30 years' experience reported in the 1930s that the most attractive aspect of her job was its security. 'I am well paid, I get good holidays and when I'm due for retirement there's a pension for me on which I can live.'[28] Fifty years later, the personnel manager of a West Midlands carpet firm was certain that its policy of internal promotion was the key to the company's success in retaining and controlling the workforce:

> it provides a career structure to people in fairly low levels of jobs. It has enabled us to keep labour where we might otherwise have lost it … they know that if they stay two or three years, they can get a weaving position. That has really helped us in times when labour was difficult to get hold of, if you go back to 1970.[29]

Those employed by small firms, owner-proprietors and individual householders appeared to accept more readily still the authority that they encountered at the workplace. Small work groups, low wages and economic insecurity all tended to heighten workers'

---

[24] S. Meacham, *A Life Apart: The English Working Class 1890–1914* (Thames & Hudson, 1977), p. 110.

[25] Manchester Polytechnic/Manchester Metropolitan University, Manchester Studies, Transcript 630, p. 7. See also A. Fowler, *Lancashire Cotton Operatives and Work, 1900–1950: A Social History of Lancashire Cotton Operatives in the Twentieth Century* (Aldershot: Ashgate, 2003), Ch. 1.

[26] However, he went on, 'I'm beginning to ask myself is it worth it?' Greenwood, *Other Man*, p. 93. For a valuable brief discussion, see McIvor, *Work*, pp. 64–6. Also, '2,500,000 houses to be built', *Observer*, 6 April 1924.

[27] J.H. Goldthorpe, D. Lockwood, F. Bechhofer and J. Platt, *The Affluent Worker in the Class Structure* (Cambridge: Cambridge University Press, 1969), p. 56.

[28] Greenwood, *Other Man*, p. 66. Cf. 'Punished enough', *Observer*, 18 December 1927.

[29] Ackers and Black, 'Paternalist Capitalism', p. 43.

sense of dependence upon their employers. Farmers were adept, it was seen earlier in the chapter, at manipulating wages and perquisites in their pursuit of farmworker compliance. A Shropshire man recalls, for instance, that when he started work as a 14-year-old in the early 1920s, 'The farmer and his wife treated me right; food and bedding and did my washing … We played table tennis in the evenings and I even learnt to dance.'[30]

Other employers too were aware of the importance of providing non-wage benefits. A lorry driver working for a small haulage firm just before the Second World War reported that his boss was 'a first rate chap'. The reason he gave was revealing:

> he doesn't put any limit to our expenses providing they're reasonable … Well, if we were in a town away from home and we couldn't get ordinary digs he'd pay whatever we spent providing we brought the receipt back. I've known us to spend thirty shillings on one night's expenses between us – me and my mate. And we've had as much as £6 expenses on the week. When a boss treats you like that you always want to play the game with him.[31]

Cleaners working in private homes sometimes regarded themselves as 'helping out' rather than as being employed. Others went further still: 'I'd probably clean for Barbara even if she didn't pay me because she's so good', explained one employee towards the end of the century. 'We're really good friends now.' Nicky Gregson and Michelle Law are quick to point out where this could lead:

> In a sense then, cleaners who construct their employment in terms of false kinship and/or friendship are caught in an unintentional pay [and ideological] trap of their own making. They become entirely dependent on their employers for pay rises, yet many convey the impression to their employers (through the existence of favour and gifts) that pay is a minor concern to them.[32]

But surely, it will be objected, the iron disciplines of work did not operate in anything like the simple, straightforward fashion that the analysis so far has tended to suggest. Has not the empirical basis of the discussion been far too thin and selective? Is it not the case that the relationship between material causes and ideological consequences has been assumed rather than tested (let alone proved)? And can it not be argued that the decision to explore the relationship between work and ideology in terms of the population as a whole has impeded, rather then facilitated, the attempt to explain why there occurred so little effective challenge to existing patterns of power and authority?

Such criticisms, it must be admitted, carry considerable weight. Accordingly, the remainder of the chapter will attempt to consider the relationship between work and ideology in a good deal more detail, and with a good deal more rigour. The result, it is hoped, will be that the arguments put forward will prove still more persuasive than

---

[30] N. Mansfield, 'Agricultural Trades Unionism in Shropshire 1900–1930', University of Wolverhampton PhD, 1997, p. 176.

[31] Greenwood, *Other Man*, p. 11.

[32] N. Gregson and M. Lowe, *Servicing the Middle Classes: Class, Gender and Waged Domestic Labour in Contemporary Britain* (Routledge, 1994), pp. 222–4.

those that have been set out so far. The analysis will be conducted, as in previous chapters, by focusing upon the experiences of some of the most important groups within Britain's diverse and growing population: the young, adults and the middle-aged; men and women; members of ethnic minorities; and those from the middle class and the working class.

AGE, ACCEPTANCE AND REJECTION

Age, once again, was of considerable significance. It will be shown that young people, adults and the middle-aged tended to experience work in different ways; and it will be suggested that they tended therefore to draw different conclusions as to the nature and legitimacy of the economic, social and political order in which they found themselves. The life course, it will be argued, is as central to the study of ideology as it is to so many other features of economic, social, cultural and political experience.

Adolescence was crucial. Whether or not parents and teachers taught children specifically about the relationship between work, power and authority, young people learned soon enough that such a relationship existed, and that it was likely to affect many, if not most, aspects of their lives. Those aspiring to professional careers were taught, *inter alia*, the need for planning, judgement and independence of mind. Those destined for clerical or manual jobs were taught the need for respect, obedience and good timekeeping. Whatever their hopes, fears and expectations, adolescence inducted young people into the rudiments – and sometimes more than the rudiments – of super-iority and inferiority, of domination and subordination.[33]

As soon as they started their first job, young people were taught the importance of deferring to their employers, their supervisors and their more experienced colleagues. However, working-class boys, it must be admitted, frequently found it difficult to react in the ways expected of them. Down the pit, on the shop floor, in the workshop and at the building site, young workers caused a disproportionate amount of disruption and trouble.[34] Indeed, Stephen Humphries concludes from his study, *Hooligans or Rebels? An Oral History of Working-Class Childhood and Youth 1889–1939*, that neither boys nor girls were anywhere near as deferential and conformist as many historians – myself included – are inclined to believe.

> Just as larking about in school, in youth organisations and in free leisure time generated excitement and created freedom from authoritarian demands and restrictions, so at work it helped to reduce tension and frustration and to assert informal control over repetitive and depersonalised production processes.[35]

Nevertheless, many – perhaps most – young workers tended to accept pretty much what they were taught. When 15-year-old Louis Heren began work as a messenger at

[33] H. Perkin, *The Rise of Professional Society: England since 1880* (Routledge, 1989), pp. 366–74; P. Willis, *Learning to Labour: How Working Class Kids Get Working Class Jobs* (Gower, 1977), Ch. 3.

[34] For example, 'The Boy in Industry', *Ministry of Munitions Report, 1917*, pp. 5–6; J. Benson, *British Coalminers in the Nineteenth Century: A Social History* (Harlow: Longman, 1989), pp. 36, 49.

[35] S. Humphries, *Hooligans or Rebels? An Oral History of Working-Class Childhood and Youth 1889–1939* (Oxford: Blackwell, 1981), p. 142. Also pp. 143–9.

The Times in 1934, he found himself under the military-style supervision of the chief commissionaire, Mr McCluskie. 'We were always addressed as Gentlemen Cadets, but discipline was stricter than in fighting regiments. Some found it irksome, but with the cadets from superior public schools I accepted it as normal because of Mr McCluskie.'[36] When the author of this book, a young teenager in the late 1950s, took a holiday job at a branch of Home and Colonial Stores in the outer suburbs of London, he was taught, and remembers accepting, the need to be polite and respectful, and to do as he was told.[37]

In fact, even the most recalcitrant of teenagers appeared to accept the disciplines of the workplace more readily than those of the schoolroom. In his classic 1977 study, *Learning to Labour: How Working Class Kids Get Working Class Jobs*, Paul Willis explains how this came about. Asked about the differences between school and work, a bricklayer's mate pointed out that at work, 'You can get the sack, you know what I mean, it's different from school. You couldn't really get the sack at school, apart from being expelled and you don't fucking mind that.' But there was more to it than this. Boys with negative attitudes towards school often found work discipline much more acceptable.

> They treat you different, don't they. They know if they say anything to you,
> that you don't like, that it's, you'll put one on 'im like ... but at school the
> teachers, they say things to you, which disheartens you like and everything.[38]

The disciplinary power of the first job was thrown into relief when youth unemployment prevented such socialization and social control taking place.[39] There were concerns during the 1920s and 1930s, and again during the 1980s and 1990s, that teenagers adapted more readily than older workers to long-term unemployment.[40] These concerns were often linked, either explicitly or implicitly, with anxieties about the breakdown of youth discipline and the collapse, more generally, of such 'traditional British' virtues as decency, integrity and hard work. 'I never knew any school-girl that had a baby' in the 1950s, claimed a West Midlands woman at the turn of the millennium. It 'was unthinkable. Today there must be thousands. Everywhere you go there are pushchairs and prams and the mothers are so young one expects to see a doll instead of a baby.'[41] It is not necessary to subscribe to this apocalyptic vision of late twentieth-century developments to recognize that youth unemployment might stunt – or sever – the link between work, ideology and behaviour. 'I don't know what the dole will do to you, but I used to be a really good-tempered and friendly chap', reported a young Bristolian in the early 1980s:

> but while on the dole someone just says something I don't like and I'll have a
> good go to give them a fat lip ... When my parents and I had rows all the time

---

[36] L. Heren, *Growing up Poor in London* (Hamish Hamilton, 1973), p. 141.

[37] Personal recollection.

[38] Willis, *Learning to Labour*, p. 110.

[39] Those returning from war also sometimes found it difficult to adjust to contemporary work discipline. Imperial War Museum, 22575/3/3, F. Newhouse.

[40] W. Hannington, *The Problem of the Distressed Areas* (Gollancz, 1937), Ch. vi; S. Constantine, *Unemployment in Britain between the Wars* (Harlow: Longman, 1980), p. 39.

[41] 'CS' to Wolverhampton *Express and Star*, 23 June 2001.

they just used to get on my wick. They used to be shouting at me that I had to get a job or go and live elsewhere ... So I used to just walk out, slam the door, and be ready to set on the first person who spoke to me.[42]

By the time they reached their twenties and thirties, the overwhelming majority of men, and an increasing minority of women, were in paid employment. Experience and expediency persuaded all but the most independently minded that there were few, if any, alternatives to the economic – and political – system in which they found themselves. Robert Roberts recalls the acquiescence of those living in the Salford slum where he was brought up at the beginning of the century: 'general apathy stemmed not from despair at the unions in chains nor the failure of such political action as there was; it sprang from mass ignorance: the millions did not know and did not want to know.'[43]

Those in their twenties and thirties found unemployment a terrible burden.[44] Married men hated having to look to their wives, sons and daughters for support – one South Wales miner describing himself during the Depression as 'a pauper through having to depend upon my children for a living'.[45] However, even the high levels of unemployment pertaining in the 1920s and 1930s, and again in the 1980s and 1990s, did not undermine the importance that young adults attached to paid work. John Burnett puts it like this:

the man still sees himself as the provider, having a public profile in his search for work, attending job interviews, engaging in informal work outside the home, and this role was still accepted by wives, even when reduced income leads to an enlargement of their own domestic work.[46]

It was credit that provided one of the key links between work, ideology and behaviour. Those with loans to repay recognized the restraining effect that debt imposed upon their freedom of action. It was said, for example, that in the 1950s and 1960s, Oxford car workers remained out on strike until the bills pushed the clock off the mantelpiece.[47] Those with mortgage repayments to meet could not easily contemplate going on strike, giving up work, questioning the private possession of property, let alone attempting to overthrow the economic and political basis upon which society was organized.[48] In 1927, a leading building society figure claimed that,

the man who has something to protect and improve – a stake of some sort in the country – naturally turns his thoughts in the direction of sane, ordered, and perforce economical government. The thrifty is seldom or never an extremist

---

[42] J. Burnett, *Idle Hands: The Experience of Unemployment, 1790–1990* (Routledge, 1994), p. 290. See also 'Seventies kids: The blues generation', *The Times*, 28 November 2002.

[43] R. Roberts, *The Classic Slum: Salford Life in the First Quarter of the Century* (Manchester: Manchester University Press, 1971), p. 90.

[44] 'The right to work', *Observer*, 4 March 1906.

[45] Constantine, *Unemployment*, p. 40. See also W. Woodruff, *The Road to Nab End: An Extraordinary Childhood* (Abacus, 2002), p. 44.

[46] Burnett, *Idle Hands*, p. 292.

[47] Information from Steve Tolliday.

[48] 'We queued for Union vegetables', *Daily Mail*, 1 April 1980.

agitator. To him revolution is anathema; and, as in the earliest days Building Societies acted as a stabilising force, so today they stand, in the words of the Rt. Hon. G.N. Barnes, as 'a bulwark against Bolshevism and all that Bolshevism stands for'.[49]

Although home ownership was presented increasingly in terms of choice, citizenship and individual control, the relationship between work, ideology and behaviour was more complicated than such rhetoric suggested. By the time of the miners' strike of 1984–5, it was commonly believed that younger miners, 'who had the big mortgage and the new car and video', would find it difficult to participate in industrial action even if they wished to do so. In the event, their mortgages served to reinforce, rather than undermine, existing ties of occupation, community and class. If the strike failed, their homes would be unsaleable.

> Home-ownership may have given the new purchasers a 'stake in the country' as Conservatives had always believed, but it was one which pit closures threatened as much as they did the miner's job. 'No way could we sell the houses we had bought.'[50]

Then in the 1990s, the growth of unemployment, the spread of flexible and part-time working, and the withdrawal of mortgage tax relief combined to reinforce the controlling power of the relationship between work, ideology and behaviour. 'Without the certainty of appreciating values of property, the homeowner in the 1990s was in a more precarious and powerless position than at any stage since the 1950s.'[51] Even with the near-certainty of appreciating values towards the end of the century, few homeowners gave up work for a life of individualism, anarchy or rebellion.

The relationship between middle age, work and ideology was just as contradictory.[52] On the one hand, those in their forties and fifties seemingly confounded their reputation for passivity and conservatism by expressing more dissatisfaction than younger workers with the iron disciplines of work. On the other hand, they tended to confirm their reputation for care and caution by recognizing more readily than young workers the difficulty of challenging the controls that employers exercised, and by displaying less willingness than younger colleagues to translate workplace dissatisfaction into more fundamental criticism of the way in which society was organized.

Middle-aged workers sometimes expressed their dissatisfaction with the restraints of factory and other forms of work discipline by moving into self-employment. A minority of skilled men in their forties and fifties obtained smallholdings, started small building firms, ran taxis, began selling in the streets and, with their wives, took

---

[49] A. Murie, 'Secure and Contented Citizens? Home Ownership in Britain', in A. Marsh and D. Mullins (eds), *Housing and Public Policy: Citizenship, Choice and Control* (Buckingham: Open University Press, 1998), p. 83. See also M. Swenarton, *Homes Fit for Heroes: The Politics and Architecture of Early State Housing in Britain* (Heinemann, 1981), pp. 81–7.

[50] R. Samuel, 'Introduction', in R. Samuel, B. Bloomfield and G. Boanas (eds), *The Enemy Within: Pit Villages and the Miners' Strike of 1984–5* (Routledge & Kegan Paul, 1986), pp. 13, 25.

[51] Murie, 'Secure and Contented Citizens', p. 95. See also, 'We prayed for an end to it', *Daily Mail*, 1 April 1980.

[52] Mrs E. Parson in *Daily Mail*, 7 April 1970.

over pubs or opened corner shops.[53] But these were the exceptions that proved the rule. However dissatisfied they were, the vast majority of middle-aged workers remained constrained by fear of the unknown and concern to protect themselves, so far as they could, against the vicissitudes of illness and old age. Indeed, the anxieties of middle age seemed almost to transcend gender, ethnicity and class. Whoever they were and whatever their circumstances, the middle-aged tended to be more anxious than younger workers about holding on to their jobs. They dyed their hair, stopped wearing their glasses – and started working out at the gym.[54] Yet whatever they did, they faced particular difficulties in retaining, let alone obtaining, jobs in mining, heavy industry, dock work and general labouring where physical strength was regarded as more important than skill or experience.[55] Indeed, by the end of the century, the *Daily Mail*, along with many other sections of the media, had become concerned about the prospects even of those with jobs where skill and experience were more important than physical strength. 'At 45, these men used to think: "How do I prepare myself for the next promotion?" Now they have to think: "How do I prepare myself to make a fresh start if I'm made redundant?" '[56]

GENDER, MARRIAGE AND COMPLIANCE

The fact that such anxieties seemed to transcend gender, ethnicity and class does not mean that gender was unimportant. There is no doubt that men and women experienced work in different ways, and no doubt either that this encouraged them to approach the legitimacy of power relationships somewhat differently. Gender, it must be stressed, is as important as the life course when attempting to unravel the relationship between work and ideology, between labour discipline, workplace responses and popular attitudes.

Women were always less involved than men in full-time, permanent, paid employment. Figure 6.2 shows clearly the changes taking place. 'Whereas at the beginning of the century women were much less likely to be economically active than men and formed only a minority of those in work, as the century progressed their participation rates increased sharply and so did their share of employment.'[57] However, what is most pertinent to the present analysis is that even at the very end of the

---

[53] *Daily Mirror*, 28 July 1995. J. Benson, *The Penny Capitalists: A Study of Nineteenth-Century Working-Class Entrepreneurs* (Dublin: Gill & Macmillan, 1983), p. 131; Benson, *Working Class*, p. 29.

[54] Article by J. Gillott, *Daily Mail*, 2 January 1965.

[55] Wolverhampton Oral History Project, Inverview 25, pp. 4–5. See also Burnett, *Idle Hands*, pp. 217–18; J. Benson, *Prime Time: A History of the Middle Aged in Twentieth-Century Britain* (Harlow: Longman, 1997), p. 88.

[56] *Daily Mail*, 4 May 1996. Also N. Cohen and R. Mckie, 'Ring in the wrinklies', *Observer*, 18 January 1995; Benson, *Prime Time*, p. 91.

[57] D. Gallie, 'The Labour Force', in A.H. Halsey (ed.), *Twentieth-Century British Social Trends* (Basingstoke: Macmillan, 2000), p. 291. It is not always realized how common the marriage bar was in inter-war Britain. M. Savage 'Trade unionism, sex segregation, and the State: Women's employment in "new industries" in inter-war Britain', *Social History*, 13, 1988, p. 226. See also 'The schoolmaster's grievances', *Observer*, 15 May 1921.

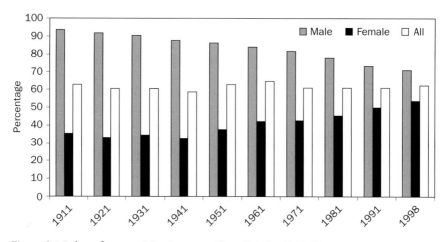

Figure 6.2 Labour force participation rates, Great Britain, 1911–98

Source: Based on D. Gallie, 'The Labour Force', in A.H. Halsey (ed.), *Twentieth-Century British Social Trends* (Basingstoke: Macmillan, 2000), p. 292.

century, fewer than 54 per cent of women were recorded as economically active, a figure which represented less than 45 per cent of all those in paid employment. Thus Figure 6.2 provides powerful support for the contention that women were less affected than men by the iron disciplines of work.

However, considerable caution is necessary. It has been seen in previous chapters how easy it is to slip from generalization to stereotyping when attempting to incorporate gender into the analysis. Women, it has been stressed, were as homogeneous as men or the members of any other large social group. Thus the growth of women's participation in the labour market was the consequence overwhelmingly of the increasing involvement of married women. Single women had always worked; married women began to work in growing numbers during the final three decades of the century.[58] It will obviously be necessary, therefore, to attempt to take account of marital status when investigating the relationship between work, gender and ideology.

The investigation is complicated by the fact that most women worked not in manufacturing but in the tertiary sector where, it has been seen, employers were more successful than elsewhere in the economy at persuading employees of the validity of workplace – and more broadly based – power relationships.[59] But even the tertiary sector sometimes threw up cases of occupational – and class – opposition. Domestic servants, it has been seen, are commonly held to be among the most deferential and compliant of all workers. Yet there were some who displayed sharp resentment at their subordination. In the late 1920s, Winifred Foley was sacked from her post as a kitchen maid at a teachers' training college for speaking to one of the students:

> After my previous jobs I thought perhaps I had cut off my nose to spite my
> face, but I felt a kind of glory in my rebellion. I sang *The Red Flag* as loud as

---

[58] 'How to be a top girl', *The Times*, 18 July 1968; 'Half our wives go to work', *Daily Mail*, 3 January 1980.

[59] For examples of resistance in manufacturing, see S. Brompton, 'The women who are running out of miracles', *Daily Mail*, 7 April 1975; Friedman and Meredeen, *Dynamics*, p. 192.

I dared among the clatter of the pots and pans, and thought of my Dad and all the downtrodden workers in the world, and nearly cried.[60]

Nonetheless, there is evidence from all parts of the economy that women tended to regard their employers with indifference or respect rather than with indignation and resentment. In a recent discussion of 'women, gender relations and inequalities at work' during the first half of the century, Arthur McIvor claims that, 'work was a source of identity, camaraderie, job satisfaction, pride and self-respect for women as well as men. Female shop assistants, clerical workers, domestic servants, seamstresses, teachers, nurses, print and textile workers have all articulated an intense commitment to their paid jobs.'[61] Elizabeth Roberts draws a different, but complementary, conclusion from her study of working-class women in Barrow-in-Furness, Lancaster and Preston during the 1940s, 1950s and 1960s. It is difficult, she stresses, to generalize about women's attitudes towards their work, their employers and their supervisors. However, she finds that, 'When young women disliked a job, for whatever reason, they were much more likely to leave than to have a dispute with the management or owners, either in person or via a union.'[62] Married women, she concludes, regarded themselves as mothers first and workers second.

> These had always been characteristics of women's paid work. But despite their greater participation in the labour market, women appeared to be curiously more marginalized and less powerful than in pre-war days.[63]

It is scarcely surprising therefore that the subject of women and trade unionism has fascinated – and infuriated – generations of labour historians. James Hinton's analysis of the unions' failure to recruit women at the beginning of the century is typical of the genre. Pointing out that fewer than one working woman in 30 was unionized, compared to one working man in six, he maintains that the explanation was structural rather than ideological. 'The main reason for this difference was not that women were intrinsically less clubbable, but that they were concentrated in those occupations most difficult to organise whatever the sex of the workforce.'[64]

It is not in the least surprising that the relationship between gender and class has also fascinated – and infuriated – recent generations of feminist scholars. They are scathing in their criticism of conventional approaches to class analysis, whether Marxist or non-Marxist, which conspire, they believe, to deny women a class position

---

[60] W. Foley, *A Child in the Forest* (British Broadcasting Corporation, 1974), p. 230. See also P. Taylor, 'Daughters and Mothers – Maids and Mistresses: Domestic Service between the Wars', in J. Clarke, C. Critcher and R. Johnson (eds), *Working-Class Culture: Studies in History and Theory* (Hutchinson, 1979).

[61] McIvor, *Work*, pp. 197–8.

[62] E. Roberts, *Women and Families: An Oral History 1940–1970* (Oxford: Blackwell, 1995), p. 56.

[63] Roberts, *Women and Families*, p. 139.

[64] J. Hinton, *Labour and Socialism: A History of the British Labour Movement 1867–1974* (Brighton: Wheatsheaf, 1983), p. 31. Also Savage, 'Trade unionism, sex segregation and the State', pp. 211–14; Benson, *Working Class*, pp. 177, 191; 'Women's labour day', *Observer*, 18 July 1909. Importantly, many trade unionists were bitterly opposed to equal pay for women: J. Roeber, 'The pitfalls of equal pay', *The Times*, 18 July 1968; Friedman and Meredeen, *Dynamics*, pp. 139, 151–2.

in their own right.[65] Miriam Glucksmann uses her study of women workers in the new industries of inter-war Britain to develop a new model of the connection between gender relations and class relations. She argues that,

> The sexual division of labour enmeshed with the technical division of labour in such a way that women's labour power was used in a quite distinct manner from men's. Their relation to capital was unique and so too were their conflicts with it. Since some male workers acted as functionaries of capital, were in charge of the production process and had authority over its workers, their immediate interests and conflicts with capital were quite likely to be very different from those of women.[66]

So whatever one's ideological predispositions, it is impossible to escape the conclusion that men and women experienced work in different ways, and that these differences probably encouraged them to take different views about the way in which the country's economy and society were organized. Women were more likely than men to regard their employers' power as immutable, more likely than men to find that power acceptable, and more likely than men to accede to broadly based patterns of power and authority, domination and subordination.

ETHNICITY, EXCLUSION AND ACCEPTANCE

The relationship between ethnicity, work and ideology has not received anything like the same amount of attention. And there is no doubt that unravelling the relationship is likely to prove a daunting and contentious task. It has been emphasized several times already that members of ethnic minorities were a great deal more heterogeneous than popular stereotyping allows. It needs to be added, of course, that any discussion of ethnic minority work habits, work attitudes and responses to authority should be approached with considerable sensitivity since these are among the aspects of minority life where popular stereotyping often tends to run offensively amok.

It will be suggested that the key to understanding the relationship between ethnicity, work and ideology lay in the nature of minority employment. 'Ethnic minorities', explains Andrew Godley, 'are often trapped at the periphery of the labour market.'[67] When they arrived in the country, Irish, Chinese, New Commonwealth

---

[65] M. Glucksmann, 'In a class of their own? Women workers in the new industries in inter-war Britain', *Feminist Review*, 24, 1986.

[66] M. Glucksmann, *Women Assemble: Women Workers and the New Industries in Inter-War Britain* (Routledge, 1990), pp. 263–4. See too L. Morley, 'A Class of One's Own: Women, Social Class and the Academy', in P. Mahony and C. Zmruczek (eds), *Class Matters: 'Working Class' Women's Perspectives on Social Class* (Taylor & Francis, 1997).

[67] A. Godley, 'Leaving the East End: Regional Mobility Among Eastern European Jews in London', in A.J. Kershen (ed.), *London: The Promised Land? The Migrant Experience in a Capital City* (Aldershot: Avebury Press, 1997), pp. 52–3. K. Gardner, *Age, Narrative and Migration: The Life Course and Life Histories of Bengali Elders in London* (Oxford: Berg, 2002), p. 96; C. Wilson, 'Liverpool's Black population during World War II', *Black and Asian Studies Association Newsletter* 20, 1998, p. 8; 'Finding jobs for young migrants', *The Times*, 11 July 1968; 'Chinese teacher upset by race row', *Daily Mail*, 5 July 1985. For Anti-Welsh prejudice, see Museum of Welsh Life, No. 14, RS1, Mary, K.

and other non-white immigrants tended to gravitate, as might be expected, towards low paid, low status, low skilled employment. However, even when they and their children had been in the country for many years, they found it difficult to break free from this occupational ghettoization.[68]

> Successive pieces of research conducted from the 1960s through into the 1980s have revealed a pattern of continuing disadvantage, with people from minority ethnic groups clustered in particular industries and occupations, and over-represented in semi-skilled and unskilled jobs.[69]

The impact of such persistent, structural disadvantage upon ethnic minority ideology can scarcely be overestimated. Those forced to take jobs for which they felt overqualified found it particularly difficult to cope with their occupational ghettoization. Bhajan Devsi came to Britain from India during the 1960s. 'I thought I was gonna get a job like that, straightaway, see draughtsman, but I couldn't', he recalls. 'That's when I found the discrimination again. With all my qualifications I couldn't get a job … So I had to take a job in a machine shop.'[70] Two studies carried out in Bristol between the mid-1960s and the mid-1970s reveal more of the relationship between work and ideology. Anthony Richmond questioned respondents in the St Paul-Montpelier area of the city about whether, in the light of their qualifications, they were satisfied with the work they were doing. He discovered that there were substantial differences between minority and majority responses. 'Whereas 41 per cent of the English-born were very satisfied, this was characteristic of 32 per cent of the Irish, and only 19 per cent of the foreign-born. By the same token, 13 per cent of the foreign-born said they were *very* dissatisfied, compared with 6 per cent of the Irish and 3 per cent of the English.'[71] Those forced to take jobs for which they were culturally ill-prepared also found it difficult to adjust. Ken Pryce's 1979 book *Endless Pressure* attempted to analyse the lifestyles of members of the city's West Indian community in terms of their responses to 'shit-work' and 'slave-labour'. One respondent reported how he had tried working as a semi-skilled machine and capstan operator:

> At the last place where a guy is the son of the man who owned the place – he was trying to be funny again, to show me that he was the boss there – for I came in late, he don't talk to me properly, he was trying to shout at me and him telling me if I just come there one more morning late, I had it! I didn't like the way he was putting it to me, because I wasn't used to that attitude. In Jamaica, we never tolerate that.[72]

Some of those unwilling to accept the disciplines of wage labour moved into begging, street selling and petty crime. The Irish community of Sparkbrook in Birmingham

---

[68] 'Black in Britain', *The Guardian*, 21 March 1995.

[69] D. Mason, *Race and Ethnicity in Modern Britain* (Oxford: Oxford University Press, 1995), p. 44.

[70] Black and Ethnic Minority Experience Project, DX-624/6/1-2, B. Devsi. See also Gardner, *Age, Narrative and Migration*, pp. 79–80, 96.

[71] A.H. Richmond, *Migration and Race Relations in an English City: A Study in Bristol* (Oxford: Oxford University Press, 1973), p. 95.

[72] K. Pryce, *Endless Pressure: A Study of West Indian Lifestyles in Bristol* (Duckworth, 1979), pp. xi, 52.

contained, it was reported in the mid-1960s, a 'small sub-group' that made its living 'mainly by petty thieving (usually from shops) and/or by finding various ways of living off a combination of casual earnings, Unemployment Benefit and National Assistance'.[73] The West Indian respondent above who fell out with his boss's son began making a living by a combination of stealing and pimping. Indeed, Pryce concludes that the 'hustlers' he interviewed in Bristol during the early 1970s all depended, *inter alia*, upon immoral earnings, and all refused 'to be bogged down by a set way of life on the nine-to-five pattern'.[74]

However, the great majority of those unwilling to accept the demands of wage labour adopted more conventional – and more acceptable – forms of self-employment. According to the 1901 census, 7.7 per cent of all full-time costermongers, hucksters and street sellers in the country were foreign-born, compared to less than 1 per cent of the population as a whole.[75] In the next few years, there developed in Leeds tailoring what were known as 'bedroom workshops'; indeed, the *Jewish Chronicle* reported in 1906 that, 'the majority of the Jewish men are tailors and they work very largely in their own homes'.[76] In mid-century Sparkbrook, there emerged a 'distinct class' of Pakistani entrepreneurs. 'Their shops are meeting-places and gossip exchanges for immigrants. They advertise the films at the local Asiatic film clubs and distribute the Urdu newspapers.'[77] In Bristol too, many immigrants expressed the wish to set up a business of their own. 'This ambition was also found among the English-born, but to a lesser extent: approximately a quarter of the English and the Irish males, compared with 42 per cent of the West Indian, Indian, and Pakistani males.'[78] The reason that South Asians were more likely than Afro-Caribbeans to be self-employed, concluded a report by the Small Businesses Research Trust in 1998, was not because the former were more entrepreneurial, but because, 'The influence of socio-economic context, or opportunity structure, continue to affect the life chances of Britain's ethnic minorities, and its impact can rarely be detached.'[79]

It was easy enough to voice entrepreneurial aspirations, but a good deal more difficult to translate them into action. Thus it is important, as so often, to avoid mistaking rhetoric for reality, the colourful for the commonplace. The fact is that however much they disliked the demands of wage labour (and however much they resented their occupational ghettoization), those from ethnic minorities, like those from the majority population, relied overwhelmingly upon wage labour when it came to supporting themselves and their families.

---

[73] J. Rex and R. Moore, *Race, Community and Conflict: A Study of Sparkbrook* (Oxford: Oxford University Press, 1967), p. 85. See also J. White, *The Worst Street in North London: Campbell Bunk, Islington, Between the Wars* (Routledge & Kegan Paul, 1986), p. 55.

[74] Pryce, *Endless Pressure*, p. 54. Also Mason, *Race and Ethnicity*, pp. 56–7.

[75] Benson, *Working Class*, p. 46.

[76] J. Buckman, *Immigrants and the Class Struggle: The Jewish Immigrant in Leeds 1880–1914* (Manchester: Manchester University Press, 1983), p. 29.

[77] Rex and Moore, *Race, Community and Conflict*, p. 124. For early twentieth-century Birmingham, see C. Volante, 'Identities and Perceptions: Gender, Generation and Ethnicity in the Italian Quarter, Birmingham, c1891–1938', University of Wolverhampton PhD, 2001, Ch. 4.

[78] Richmond, *Migration and Race Relations*, p. 97.

[79] 'Black businesses break out', *The Guardian*, 20 January 1998.

The best evidence comes, yet again, from the studies that were carried out in Bristol during the early 1970s. Even though Pryce's study *Endless Pressure* took as its subject West Indian 'hustlers' (and 'teenyboppers'), he was at pains to point out that the majority of West Indians in the city found ways of coping with 'the alienating effect menial work tasks have on the typical industrial worker'.[80] He identified, in particular, a 'black, conventional working class that is politically apathetic but hard working and God-fearing … In this group is to be found, too, almost the entire female West Indian population – the mothers, the daughters, the sisters and the wives – which is another reason why it is the single biggest working group.'[81]

Patricia Jeffery's concern, it will be recalled, was with the Pakistani community of the city. She agrees with Rashmi Desai that there were two broad ways in which immigrants responded to their participation in the labour market. There was assimilation, by which they came to share the values, attitudes and behaviour of the majority population; and there was accommodation, by which they accepted the relationships available to them without sharing the values and attitudes of the majority population. Pakistani workers, she stresses, accommodated, rather than assimilated, the demands that work made upon them. They regarded their work instrumentally, many Muslim men not eating in works canteens – and not having much contact of any kind with their British workmates. 'The men are usually union members, but largely because their places of work are union shops, and they are not involved in union work.'[82]

There is no doubt then that members of Britain's minority ethnic communities recognized, and resented, the disadvantages – the so-called 'ethnic penalty' – from which they suffered in the labour market. However, they did not feel, most of them, that there was a great deal that could be done.[83] Unknown, unassuming and unthreatening, generation upon generation of ethnic minority men got on with their employers and workmates as best they could; generation upon generation of their wives and partners put up with tedious and demeaning work in order, they hoped, to give their children and grandchildren a better chance in life. Their experience of work confirmed – and no doubt contributed to – their belief that Britain's system of authority relations was pretty much inviolable.

CLASS, AUTHORITY AND IDEOLOGY

It was class, it must be clear by now, that bound together, and helps to explain, the relationship between experiences of work and attitudes towards authority. There was a time, not so long ago, when such a claim would have been regarded, by scholars from both left and right, as a statement more or less of the obvious. But not any more. The bitterly acrimonious debate concerning the merits and demerits of postmodernism has led a number of historians to abandon class-based analysis, and has encouraged

---

[80] Pryce, *Endless Pressure*, p. 55.

[81] Pryce, *Endless Pressure*, pp. 188–9.

[82] P. Jeffery, *Migrants and Refugees: Muslim and Christian Pakistani Families in Bristol* (Cambridge: Cambridge University Press, 1976), pp. 74–5, 103.

[83] Equal opportunities initiatives only achieved so much. See 'Red Ken may break with Kit Kat', *Daily Mail*, 4 April 1985.

many many more to exercise considerable caution about making claims that class divisions remain fundamental to the proper analysis of twentieth-century social history.

What then has this chapter achieved so far? It has shown that Britain's employers made sustained, and largely successful, efforts to increase the control that they were able to exercise over their employees. It has gone on to suggest that although such efforts provoked resentment and resistance, they proved increasingly effective in persuading employees (and non-employees) of the inevitability – not to say the desirability – of accepting the ways in which power and authority were exercised in twentieth-century Britain.

It is difficult to understand employers' strategies – be they the introduction of centrally managed systems of control, the reliance on family recruitment and company welfare, or the creation of personal bonds of obligation – if one does not do so in class terms. It is just as difficult to understand employees' responses – be they moving into self-employment, joining a trade union and going on strike, or working as hard as possible and seeing one's employer as a friend – without the adoption of some form of class perspective. There is no need to adopt a crude, unnuanced Marxist stance to believe that people's position in the labour market (and the class structure) influenced, and often influenced very strongly, the views they took concerning the legitimacy of the economic, social and political order in which they lived and worked.

However, these are remarkably complex issues, and class consciousness remains one of the most contentious topics with which the social historian ever has to deal. The complications are both conceptual and empirical. It difficult to decide which definition of class consciousness to use; and even when the decision has been made, it is not easy to know which evidence to use to show what employers and employees thought about their own, and other people's position within society. As E.P. Thompson pointed out many years ago when discussing late eighteenth- and early nineteenth-century rural life, 'The same man who touches his forelock to the squire by day – and who goes down to history as an example of deference – may kill his sheep, snare his pheasants or poison his dogs at night.'[84]

It is important to distinguish, if nothing else, between class identity (the definition of oneself as upper class, middle class or working class) and class opposition (the perception that those from the other classes were one's opponents).[85] When this is done, it can be seen that employers across the economy – whether in mining, engineering or retailing – analysed developments in terms of class identity and class opposition. In 1911, a commentator sympathetic to the coal owners published what he described as an 'authentic narrative' of the recent Cambrian Combine strike in South Wales, a coalfield notorious for the bitterness of its industrial relations. He explained:

> The causes were no less personal and political than they were industrial and
> economic. For over 18 months prior to the outbreak at the mid-Rhondda
> collieries of the Cambrian colliery Combine a severe test for supremacy had
> been waged between the younger and the older leaders of the South Wales
> Miners' Federation. The younger leaders were Socialists imbued with

---

[84] E.P. Thompson, 'Patrician society, plebeian culture', *Journal of Social History*, vii, 1974, p. 399.

[85] See M. Mann, *Consciousness and Action Among the Western Working Class* (Basingstoke: Macmillan, 1973). Mann's four-tier model of class consciousness also includes 'class totality' and 'class alternative'.

Communistic theories concerning the relations of Capital and Labour, and the older leaders were orthodox trade unionists.[86]

Domestic service and retailing were about as far removed from mining as it was possible to get. Yet here too employers analysed their problems in the terms – if not the language – of class identity. Sometimes they did so almost unwittingly. A debutante brought up in a Scottish castle between the wars recalls that, 'All of our footmen were called John, irrespective of the name the parson had bestowed on them at baptism. My father announced firmly that he couldn't be bothered to learn a new name every time the footman changed.'[87]

In 1963, the former chairman of Brown's of Chester ('one of the oldest retail concerns in the country') published a guide on *How to Prepare for the New Era in Retailing*. One of the industry's major failings, he believed, lay in the poor quality of its employees. 'The hours that they work are generally regarded as bad and their pay is usually too low. In other words, the retail trade is, with a very few notable exceptions, recruiting only what is left after other and in many cases less exacting trades have taken their pick.' Class, age and gender stereotyping coalesced as he went on to amplify what he meant.

> It is an exaggeration but nearly true to say that those who serve in shops today are doing so either because they have failed to make the grade in some more interesting profession or because they are so lacking in ambition that they are content to do the job in a desultory way pending a more exciting adventure such as marriage.[88]

Children learned early in life to tailor their aspirations to the realities of their class identity. 'I'd love to have been a bank manager,' recalled a boy brought up in Tipton during the 1940s and early 1950s, 'but how could you with holes in your trousers?'[89] Once they were in work, employees routinely analysed their experiences in terms of class identity and, to a lesser extent, of class opposition. Those subjected to strict supervision by powerful employers in large, capital-intensive industries were the most likely to think of themselves as working class, the most likely to join a trade union and the most likely to go out on strike. 'Opposition was a consequence of economic fact', explains Standish Meacham: 'as long as even a skilled workman with a large family remained condemned to a graceless life of semi-poverty, there would be a consciousness of "them" and "us".'[90] Nor, of course, were those employed in the service sector of the economy in any position to overlook the differences that marked them out from their

---

[86] D. Evans, *Labour Strife in the South Wales Coalfield, 1910–1911* (Cardiff: Cymric Federation Press, 1963), preface, p. 1. See also R.P. Arnot, *South Wales Miners Glowyr de Cymru: A History of the South Wales Miners' Federation (1898–1914)* (Allen & Unwin, 1967), p. 175. Cf. 'South Wales', *Observer*, 3 April 1921.

[87] C. Miller, *A Childhood in Scotland* (John Murray, 1981), p. 21.

[88] L.M. Harris, *Buyer's Market: How to Prepare for the New Era in Retailing* (Business Publications, 1963), pp. 141–2.

[89] A. Watkiss, Old Habits …?: An Examination of Working-Class Survival Strategies in Tipton, 1945–70, University of Wolverhampton MA, 1999, p. 54.

[90] Meacham, *Life Apart*, p. 14. See also Benson, *Working Class*, p. 164.

employers and very often their customers. Cleaners, domestic servants and shop workers were reminded time, time and time again that they were different from, and inferior to, both those who employed them and those whom they served. Indeed, in some cases, the ways in which they were treated almost beggars belief. The 12-year-old daughter of a Barrow-in-Furness maintenance man began work as a domestic servant on a farm in the very early years of the century:

> Christmas Day come and I was a bit home sick. Got our Christmas Day dinner and washed up and all that and she said, 'Ista finished now?' Said, 'Yes madam.' She said, 'If thou gets all that paper there, a big needle and a ball of string, go down to the paddock.' The toilet was the paddock, a long way out. She said, 'Sit there and take the scissors and cut some paper up and thread it for the lavatory,' and I sat there all Christmas Day and I cried nearly a bucketful of tears'.[91]

Nonetheless, class identity developed only uncertainly into class opposition. Even when working people defined themselves as working class and regarded their employers as class opponents, they were as likely to ignore them, or joke about them, as they were to get involved in any kind of class struggle. 'Rather than chafe at their supposed "betters",' admits Meacham, 'they turned their backs on them.'[92] As the music hall comedian 'Little Tich' put it in his late nineteenth-century sketch about the gas-meter collector, 'My brother's in the gas trade too, you know. In fact he travels on gas. He's a socialist orator.'[93] But class symbols were never far away. A Scottish servant, born in 1920, recalls:

> I had this little black dress which I hated … I said one day, 'can I change that black dress to a grey one?' Oh, that was OK, 'but you still have to wear your apron'. Your apron was your badge of servitude, I suppose, or I suppose it was just, 'we have a maid'.[94]

Even trade-union activists often found it hard to make the jump from class identity to class opposition. It is clear, for example, that during the inter-war years, trade-union leaders became less and less willing to engage in strike action. The executive of the small Eastern Counties Agricultural and Small Holders' Union, for instance, opposed strikes, advocating instead political activity, the establishment of smallholdings and the creation of an Agricultural Wages Board where representatives of both sides of the industry could sit down together and resolve their differences.[95] Although the executive of the giant Transport and General Workers' Union had no desire to relinquish the strike weapon, it developed the machinery with which to pursue the

---

[91] E.A.M. Roberts, *Working Class Barrow and Lancaster 1890 to 1930* (Lancaster: University of Lancaster, 1976), pp. 15–16.

[92] Meacham, *Life Apart*, p. 20.

[93] G.S. Jones, 'Working-class culture and working-class politics in London, 1870–1900: Notes on the remaking of a working class', *Journal of Social History*, 7, 1974, p. 493.

[94] Museum of Edinburgh, T/12/87.

[95] A. Howkins, *Poor Labouring Men: Rural Radicalism in Norfolk 1872–1923* (Routledge & Kegan Paul, 1985), pp. 13, 37, 95, 104, 178.

peaceful settlement of disputes.[96] It is equally clear that such attitudes persisted – and probably intensified – during the second half of the century. As a shop steward from the lock industry argued in the late 1970s, 'I think the management and the union should work together … I don't believe in strikes, I don't think it achieves anything.'[97] As the historian of the North Wales Miners has pointed out recently, in the five years following the miners' strike of 1984–5, more than 100 pits closed with the loss of more than 100,000 jobs. 'The NUM had lost half its membership and was rapidly losing its wider influence in the TUC and the Labour Party … In all areas of the NUM an increasing number of activists continued to opt for redundancy rather than gamble on an uncertain future.'[98]

WORK, ATTITUDES AND AUTHORITY

The relationship between work, attitudes and authority will never be susceptible to the sort of analysis likely to persuade those suspicious of material explanations of ideological developments. The relationship becomes more difficult still to disentangle when one attempts to take a broader view, comparing the impact of work with the impact of policing, the law and law enforcement, let alone the impact of religion, education and the media. Nonetheless, it is plausible, it is believed, to suggest that work played a role in persuading all major sections of the population that there was no realistic alternative to the way in which British society was organized.

---

[96] V.L. Allen, *Trade Union Leadership: Based on a Study of Arthur Deakin* (Longman, Green & Co., 1957), pp. 77, 90, 103.

[97] Ackers and Black, 'Paternalist Capitalism', p. 28.

[98] K. Gildart, *North Wales Miners: A Fragile Unity, 1945–1996* (Cardiff: University of Wales Press, 2001), pp. 202–3.

PART THREE
THE ACCOMMODATION
OF CHANGE

7 MEN AND WOMEN, PARENTS AND CHILDREN

FAMILIES, FEELINGS AND RELATIONSHIPS

The study of personal relationships – like the study of health, the study of consumption and the study of power relationships – has attracted increasing interest in recent years. Encouraged and emboldened by the preoccupations of feminist theory and the potentialities of oral methodology, those interested in the history of personal relationships have become more and more ambitious. No longer content with examining family structure and household formation, they have begun to pose a series of new, challenging and important questions. Did the material, ideological, political and legal changes taking place during the twentieth century reinforce or compromise the institution of marriage? Was there a weakening of family ties in the face of growing prosperity, increasing longevity, rising expectations, feminist criticisms and a burgeoning youth culture? Is it true that moral values collapsed and promiscuous behaviour intensified so that the very foundations of modern British society began to be undermined?

In answering such questions, historians have discovered more common ground than they probably expected. Indeed, the study of personal relationships, like the study of health, the study of consumption and the study of power relationships, can make for oddly assorted intellectual and ideological bedfellows. It seems to be agreed by commentators of every persuasion that the twentieth century witnessed a truly remarkable transformation in people's family, emotional and sexual lives. This is how one of the leading scholars in the field, Lesley Hall, describes the changes that, it is agreed, occurred between the 1880s and the millennium:

> No longer is heterosexual marriage the only acceptable form of sexual
> relationship with all others stigmatized and marginalized. Family structure and
> size have undergone considerable mutation. Marriages were then terminated
> (except in a very small proportion of cases) only by death or desertion,
> sometimes followed by remarriage, in the first case, or bigamy, in the second.
> Now there may be one or more sequential unions, either remarriage or
> cohabitation, and the maintenance of some kind of relationship with former
> spouses.[1]

---

[1] L.A. Hall, *Sex, Gender and Social Change in Britain Since 1880* (Basingstoke: Macmillan, 2000), p. 1. See also P. Laslett, 'Foreword', to British Family Research Committee, *Families in Britain* (Routledge & Kegan Paul, 1982).

The consensus collapses, however, as soon as historians (and non-historians for that matter) switch their attention from what happened, to whether what happened was desirable or undesirable. These are matters that give rise, we are all aware, to deeply felt, intense and often acrimonious differences of opinion. Those on the left tend to be enthusiastic about many of the changes that have taken place. They welcome women's growing economic, social and sexual independence. They are inclined to share in society's growing acceptance of pre-marital (and extramarital) sex, the increasing use of divorce as a way of ending unsatisfactory marriages, and the more widespread toleration of homosexuality and other so-called 'alternative' lifestyles. By the 1960s, points out Jeffrey Weeks, 'There was an important shift towards privatisation of decision making, towards a legal acceptance of moral pluralism.'[2] Almost anything, some seem to suggest, had to be better than what had gone before. When Erica Jong looks back at her mother's life (in the United States of America) around the middle of the century, she concludes that, 'It was not that my mother gave up. It was just that she chose a more acceptable female path: outer capitulation, inner resentment – the old, old story.'[3]

Those on the right tend to despair at much of what they see going on around them. They feel, for example, that women's newly won 'independence' not only epitomizes, but also probably helped to cause, many of the ills afflicting Britain at the end of the twentieth century. They believe that society's growing acceptance of pre-marital sex, cohabitation, extramarital affairs, separation, divorce and homosexuality has led, inevitably and catastrophically, to the erosion of the nation's core values, the undermining of family life, the neglect of the elderly, and an upsurge in sexual and psychological dysfunction. By the end of the century, there was anxiety, bordering on disbelief.

> What's gone wrong with marriage? In one generation, the number of people getting married has halved, the number divorcing has trebled, and the proportion of children born outside marriage had quadrupled.[4]

It is not difficult to understand why the study of family, emotional and sexual history arouses such disagreements and such passions. It involves dealing with intensely personal issues that are virtually impossible to analyse dispassionately, can sometimes be

---

[2] J. Weeks, *Sex, Politics and Sexuality: The Regulation of Sexuality since 1800* (Harlow: Longman, 1989), p. 273. There has been, for instance, a growing toleration of, and interest in, homosexuality and lesbianism. See for example, F. Mort, *Dangerous Sexualities: Medico-moral Politics in England since 1830* (Routledge, 1987); S. Jeffery-Poulter, *Peers, Queers and Commons: The Struggle for Gay Law Reform from 1950 to the Present* (Routledge, 1991); National Lesbian and Gay Survey, *What a Lesbian Looks Like: Writings by Lesbians on Their Lives and Lifestyle* (Routledge, 1992); K. Plummer (ed.), *Modern Homosexualities: Fragments of Lesbian and Gay Experience* (Routledge, 1992); K. Weeks, *Invented Moralities: Sexual Values in an Age of Uncertainty* (Polity Press, 1995).

[3] E. Jong, *Fear of Fifty: A Midlife Memoir* (Glasgow: Chatto & Windus, 1994), p. 53.

[4] C. Dyer, 'Let's stay together', *The Guardian*, 25 October 1999. See also Ann Temple column in *Daily Mail*, 6 July 1960; R. Miles, 'Plastic values for a fragile generation', *Observer*, 18 June 1995; S. Pinker, 'How science has proved that marriage really is bliss', *Daily Mail*, 17 January 1998; E. Hopkins, *The Rise and Decline of the English Working Classes, 1918–1990* (Weidenfeld & Nicolson, 1991), pp. 275–6.

embarrassing to discuss openly, and almost always prove difficult to substantiate empirically. Certainly, it is a daunting task to bring together, and try to make sense of, the mass of material that is available. There is statistical evidence of family structure and household formation, social survey investigation into personal behaviour and individual attitudes, not to mention a seemingly unending stream of contemporary commentary about what was happening to the domestic, emotional and sexual lives of people in Britain.

ISOLATION, PROMISCUITY AND SELFISHNESS

It has been decided to approach these issues by concentrating upon three of the most important, most discussed and most contentious aspects of Britain's twentieth-century family, emotional and sexual history. The first is the growing isolation in which people supposedly lived, the second is the increase in the promiscuous behaviour in which they allegedly indulged, and the third is the ever more selfish ways in which, many believe, they lived out many aspects of their lives.

Even setting the agenda in such stark terms points to the difficulties ahead. After all, one person's isolation, promiscuity and selfishness are another's independence, freedom and self-reliance. Can one really understand other people's personal lives? How is one to balance the pleasures of some against the miseries of others? Will it ever be possible to judge the happiness and unhappiness of millions of people, some of them born in the early to middle years of the nineteenth century, others entering the twenty-first century as children and teenagers?

However, writing a study such as this demands a willingness to generalize – some would say pontificate – on the basis of imperfect conceptualization and inadequate empirical foundations. Thus it will be argued that the family remained of critical significance, materially, emotionally and symbolically, in the life of the nation. There is no denying that family relationships have changed profoundly during the course of the century. However, it will be suggested that the claims so commonly made about the weakening of family ties in the face of increasing longevity, growing prosperity, rising expectations and new assumptions about age and gender, need to be treated with the greatest possible caution.

The statistical evidence provided by the census at ten-yearly intervals (with the exception of 1941) makes it possible to delineate, in broad terms, the changes taking place in family formation and family structure. Such evidence also provides some basis at least for identifying the major changes that were taking place in people's emotional and sexual lives. It must be conceded, however, that in no part of the book is it more important to warn against the perils of generalization, or more important to urge the value of disaggregating the analysis on the basis of age, gender, ethnicity and social class. Nevertheless, national statistics provide a natural starting point for the more detailed analysis that is to follow. Accordingly, it is the purpose of this section of the chapter to present the statistical information that bears best upon the three issues that have been selected for particular attention: isolation, promiscuity and selfishness.

ISOLATION, LONELINESS AND INDEPENDENCE

Isolation is the most amenable of the three to statistical investigation. The data collected by the census on household formation and household structure is extremely informative,

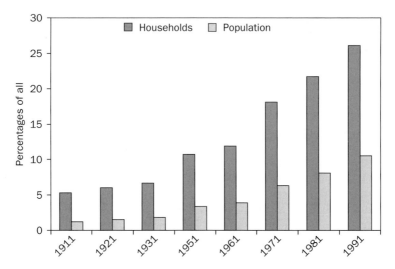

Figure 7.1 Single-person households, England and Wales, 1911–91

Source: Based on D. Coleman, 'Population and Family', in A.H. Halsey (ed.), *Twentieth-Century British Social Trends* (Basingstoke: Macmillan, 2000), p. 77.

revealing beyond any doubt that it became increasingly common for people in Britain to live alone. Figure 7.1 presents the evidence concerning single-person households in two ways. It shows first that the number of such households in England and Wales increased practically five times in 80 years, from just over 5 per cent of all households in 1911, to a fraction more than 26 per cent in 1991.[5] It shows too that the number of people living in single-person households increased nearly nine times, from barely 1 per cent of the population in 1911 to over 10 per cent in 1991. By the end of the century, 6.5 million people in Britain lived on their own. 'Are we turning into a nation of loners?', wondered *The Guardian*.[6]

The answer, almost certainly, was no. It needs to be stressed how difficult it is to use household structure as a measure of social isolation and social integration. For, as a moment's thought will confirm, those who lived alone were not necessarily socially isolated, any more than those who lived with other people were necessarily socially integrated. Yet, insofar as census evidence can be used as a measure of isolation and integration, it refutes many of the more alarmist concerns that have been sounded. The fact that at the end of the century 26 per cent of households contained only one person means, naturally, that 74 per cent of households contained two or more people. The fact that by the end of the century just over 10 per cent of the population lived on their own means, equally obviously, that just under 90 per cent of the population lived with other people.

There are other reasons too for challenging the view that Britain had become a nation of loners. These will be considered in detail later in the chapter when attention switches to some of the major groups that made up society: the young, middle-aged and

---

[5] See Mass-Observation , 3089, 'Notes on the Cost of Living', 1949, p. 2.

[6] W. Woodward, 'Are we turning into a nation of loners?', *The Guardian*, 27 March 2000.

elderly; the two sexes; those from ethnic minorities; and those from the upper class, the middle class and the working class. For the moment, what needs to be stressed is that the mass of social survey, oral and other qualitative evidence attests strongly to the continuing resilience, flexibility and importance of family and other social networks. As longevity increased, husbands and wives tended – unless they separated – to spend more years in each other's company. Indeed, for much of the century it remained relatively unusual for married couples to spend more than a few days apart. When Mass-Observation questioned 100 husbands and wives (from all classes) in 1947, it discovered that nearly half had never been separated from their spouse for more than a week at a time, and that only 22 had been separated for as long as a month (although the war of course had been hugely disruptive).[7] Even when people lived alone, they often – in fact very often – remained integrated into the families in which they had been brought up. A report published by the Family Policy Studies Centre at the very end of the century attempted, *inter alia*, to dispel the myth that those living alone were necessarily isolated. In fact, it concluded, the family remained 'the key social network and primary source of informal care and support for most people'.[8]

PROMISCUITY, SHAME AND LIBERATION

Promiscuity is much less amenable to the combination of quantitative and qualitative analysis that has been employed – helpfully, it is hoped – in attempting to assess changes in isolation and integration. The problems once again are both conceptual and methodological. What is promiscuity? If one person's isolation is another's loneliness and another's independence, then what some think of as promiscuous and shaming others will most certainly regard as natural and liberating. But even if promiscuity can be defined, how is it to be measured and interpreted? What does under-age sex tell us about sexual attitudes? Are teenage pregnancies evidence of sexual precocity or sexual ignorance? Is cohabitation a sign of emotional caution or sexual abandon? Is extramarital sex a symptom of functional or dysfunctional marriages, of a healthy or unhealthy society? Three statistical indicators have been selected for the light they throw on the 'promiscuity' which distinguished – some would say disfigured – the second half of the century. They are the age of first intercourse, the illegitimacy rate and the cohabitation rate. It will be suggested that although the term promiscuity is far too subjective to be helpful, there is not the slightest doubt that the second half of the century saw distinctive changes in both sexual behaviour and sexual attitudes.

There was a significant decline in the age at which both men and women first had (heterosexual) sexual intercourse. Figure 7.2 is drawn from the British National Survey of Sexual Attitudes and Lifestyles, a controversial enquiry involving over 18,000 men and women that was carried out at the beginning of the 1990s. It suggests that the age of first intercourse had declined by 15 per cent during the previous 40 years. Those born in the early 1930s (aged 55–59) typically first had intercourse at the age of 20 or 21, whereas those born between the mid-1960s and the mid-1970s (aged 16–24) probably did so when they were no older than 17.

[7] Mass-Observation, 2495, 'State of Marriage', 1947, p. 2a.
[8] Woodward, 'Loners'. Also A. Phillips, 'Friends are the new family', *The Guardian*, 12 December 2003.

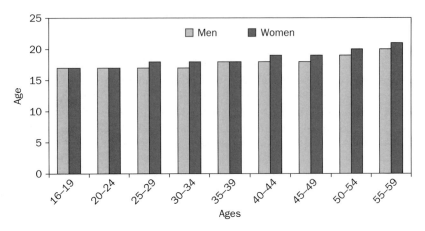

Figure 7.2 Age of first heterosexual sexual intercourse, Great Britain, c.1990

Source: Based on K. Wellings, J. Field, A. Johnson and J. Wadsworth, *Sexual Behaviour in Britain: The National Survey of Sexual Attitudes and Lifestyles* (Penguin, 1994), p. 38.

It is easy enough to plot this decline, a great deal more difficult to know what to make of it. There are a number of anomalies. On the one hand, the generation coming of age at the end of the century had sex at a younger age than those from earlier generations; on the other hand, they were more likely than their parents and grandparents to use contraception when doing so. On the one hand, they were less likely than their parents and grandparents to have their first experience of sexual intercourse within marriage; on the other hand, men brought up towards the end of the century were less likely than their fathers and grandfathers to have their first experience with a prostitute.[9]

The illegitimacy rate poses similar difficulties. Illegitimacy statistics are reasonably easy to plot but remarkably difficult to interpret.[10] It is widely recognized, however, that the decades following the Second World War witnessed an enormous increase in the number of children born to unmarried parents. Nonetheless, the scale of the change may still come as something of a surprise. Certainly, it is not always appreciated quite how unusual illegitimacy was during the first half of the century.[11] During practically the whole of this period, fewer than one child in 20 was born 'out of wedlock'. In fact, even in 1945, amidst the promiscuity supposedly engendered by the war, the illegitimacy rate had increased only to one child in 16.[12]

---

[9] K. Wellings, J. Field, A. Johnson and J. Wadsworth, *Sexual Behaviour in Britain: The National Survey of Sexual Attitudes and Lifestyles* (Penguin, 1994), p. 85. See J. Bourke, *Working-Class Cultures in Britain, 1890–1960: Gender, Class and Ethnicity* (Routledge, 1994), Ch. 2; R. Glasser, *Growing Up in the Gorbals* (Glasgow: Chatto & Windus, 1986), p. 131.

[10] Weeks, *Sex*, p. 253. P. Thane, 'The Real Sexual Revolution: Birth, Marriage and Death in Britain, 1920s–1950s', Rethinking Britain 1918–1959, Institute of Historical Research Conference, March 2004.

[11] G. Frost, ' "The black lamb of the black sheep": Illegitimacy in the English working class, 1850–1939', *Journal of Social History*, 37, 2003, p. 295. Monica Furlong in *Daily Mail*, 6 April 1965.

[12] D. Coleman, 'Population and Family', in A.H. Halsey (ed.), *Twentieth-Century British Social Trends* (Basingstoke: Macmillan, 2000), p. 51.

Thereafter, the situation changed, and changed dramatically. By the mid-1990s, more than one child in three was born outside marriage: a total of 233,000 children a year in England and Wales alone.[13] It was a change of genuine profundity, and one that led observers of all ideological persuasions to wonder what had happened to the nation's morals, and what was likely to happen to the family life of the nation.[14] They were right to be puzzled. It is clear, however, that the figures reflect, if nothing else, the fact that marriage was being supplemented – and to some extent replaced – by cohabitation. Many more couples than ever before lived together, stayed together, bought a house together, had children together and brought them up together – but saw little material, moral or legal reason for getting married.

Cohabitation did not begin to attract serious statistical attention until the 1970s. There is no doubting, however, that during the first half of the century it was highly unusual for lovers and engaged couples even to consider setting up home with one another. It is striking, for instance, that the index to Elizabeth Roberts's comprehensive examination of working-class family life between 1890 and 1940 does not even include an entry for cohabitation.[15] Indeed, it has been estimated that as late as the 1950s and early 1960s fewer than 5 per cent of all women lived with a man before they married.[16]

It was during the late 1960s, as one might expect, that attitudes and behaviour began to change.[17] By the late 1970s and early 1980s, cohabitation was anything but unusual. Practically a quarter of couples marrying for the first time (and 65 per cent of those remarrying) had lived together previously, a practice which delayed, but did not replace, their subsequent marriage.[18] Thereafter, the incidence and impact of cohabitation grew yet again. By the end of the century, some 60 per cent of those marrying for the first time (and over 75 per cent of those remarrying) had lived together previously. However, what was also new was that cohabitation was now likely to delay subsequent marriage plans more or less indefinitely.[19]

It does not follow, of course, that cohabitation – even when it replaced marriage – represented a decline in couples' commitment to one another. Two studies published at the very end of the century epitomize the complexities of the debate. The first, the Family Policy Studies Centre report, was used earlier in the chapter when discussing isolation. It claimed, for example, that couples who lived together without getting married were three or four time more likely than married couples to separate (and claimed too that the presence of children did not appear to reduce significantly the breakdown rate).[20] The second of the studies, an investigation carried out by Nottingham

---

[13] Coleman, 'Population and Family', p. 51.

[14] For a pioneering – many would say flawed – investigation published in the 1970s, see Edward Shorter, *The Making of the Modern Family* (Fontana/Collins, 1977), Ch. 3.

[15] E. Roberts, *A Woman's Place: An Oral History of Working-Class Women 1890–1940* (Oxford: Blackwell, 1984).

[16] Dyer, 'Let's stay together'.

[17] J. Lewis, *Women in Britain Since 1945* (Oxford: Blackwell, 1992), Ch. 2.

[18] 'Adultery: It's still the number one reason', *Daily Mail*, 1 July 1980.

[19] A. Barlow, S. Duncan, G. Evans and A. Park, *Just a Piece of Paper? Marriage and Cohabitation in Britain*, www.scpr.ac.uk/news bsa pr2001.htm; Coleman, 'Population and Family', pp. 59–60.

[20] Woodward, 'Loners'.

University's School of Sociology and Social Policy, was designed to reveal, *inter alia*, whether cohabitants with children were 'less committed and more individualistic than married couples'. The answer, they found, was that they were not. Commitment, they believed, took different forms among cohabiting and married couples, but 'it is not clear that one form is superior to the other, or that the commitment to children is different'. The only substantial difference between the two groups, they concluded, was that the former preferred to keep their commitment to each other private, while the latter wished to make a public declaration affirming the importance of their relationship.[21]

SELFISHNESS, SELF-ABSORPTION AND INDEPENDENCE

If it is difficult to uncover convincing statistical indicators of isolation and promiscuity, it will be well nigh impossible, one would think, to come up with acceptable, quantifiable measures for something as intangible and subjective as selfishness. One person's selfishness and self-absorption is all but certain, we have seen, to be another's independence, freedom and self-reliance. Nonetheless, it will be suggested, and with some confidence, that the accusations of selfishness levelled so cavalierly at those living towards the end of the century need to be leavened by a healthy dose of historical perspective.

It has been decided to use three measures of selfishness: the divorce rate, the number of children in care, and the number of old people in care. It will be objected, no doubt, that all three measures are imperfect, as likely to reflect contemporary legal, economic and demographic circumstances as they are prevailing levels of selfishness. How is it possible, it will be asked, to separate the wish to divorce from the ability to do so, the desire to care for one's children and parents from the material conditions pertaining, the family structures in place and the welfare services available? When Kathleen Dayus's husband died in 1931, she decided she had no choice but to place her four children in care:

> It was a bitterly cold day when I took my children to Moseley Village Home, and left them there in the charge of the matron. I hugged and kissed them and after giving them a few sweets I'd saved I walked away before they saw my tears. I don't remember anything about walking back alone to my mother's house that day. I only remember that when I climbed those dark, narrow attic stairs, and entered that room with so many memories, I broke down completely.[22]

Nevertheless, it is believed that divorce, child care and care of the elderly provide plausible – or anyway not implausible – guides to individual and family selfishness. The number of petitions filed for divorce increased exponentially. Figure 7.3 reveals the enormity of the change. It can be seen that during the first half of the century and beyond, those who married stayed married. The statistics are startling. Ninety-eight per cent of those marrying in 1926 were still married two decades later, as were 93 per cent of those marrying in 1951. Over 90 per cent of couples married at mid-century could reasonably look forward to celebrating their silver wedding anniversary. Thereafter,

---

[21] Dyer, 'Let's stay together'.

[22] K. Dayus, *All My Days* (Virago, 1988), p. 74.

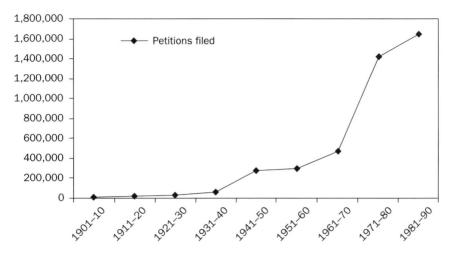

Figure 7.3 Petitions filed for divorce, England and Wales, 1901–90
Source: Based on D. Coleman, 'Population and Family', in A.H. Halsey (ed.), *Twentieth-Century British Social Trends* (Basingstoke: Macmillan, 2000), p. 62.

the divorce rate doubled and doubled again, with the result that well over a quarter of couples who married in 1971 were no longer married 20 years later. But even this was not the end of it. What the figure does not show is that 29 per cent of those marrying in 1978 divorced within 15 years, or that 24 per cent of those marrying in 1983 divorced within ten years.[23]

These were prodigious changes. But do they indicate a new selfishness, a new-found determination to live for oneself, no matter what the consequences for one's family and friends? Surely not. And certainly not in the simple, unambiguous way that some commentators suggest. When using divorce statistics to examine selfishness – or anything else – it is essential to keep the broader context constantly in mind. The growing vulnerability of marriages, it bears repeating, was a reflection, in large degree, of growing prosperity, the reordering of domestic responsibilities, the increase in women's earnings and, most crucially, the fact that changes in the divorce laws made it a great deal easier for couples who were unhappy to bring their legal relationship to an end.[24]

Those who regard marriage as a patriarchal device for the subjugation of women are in no doubt that the growth of divorce was the consequence, less of new-found selfishness, than of new found honesty. 'Forty per cent of marriages end in divorce',

[23] Coleman, 'Population and Family', p. 64. See also D. Leonard and M.A. Speakman, 'Women in the Family: Companions or Caretakers?', V. Beechey and E. Whitelegg (eds), *Women in Britain Today* (Buckingham: Open University Press, 1986), pp. 44–6.

[24] J.R. Gillis, *For Better, For Worse: British Marriages 1600 to the Present* (Oxford: Oxford University Press, 1985), part III; R. Phillips, *Untying the Knot: A Short History of Divorce* (Cambridge: Cambridge University Press, 1991), Ch. 9. Also 'Divorce law reform', *Observer*, 14 February 1909; 'After it all, that champagne feeling', *Daily Mail*, 3 July 1980.

confirmed one late-century critic of conventional family life. But this figure, she insisted, should not be interpreted as 'an indicator of moral decline':

> in the past divorce has been either impossible or difficult. Women who divorced were either socially humiliated or avoided as predatory femmes fatales. Those lifetime marriages we were all supposed to admire were often built on hypocrisy and double standards. Tories and mistresses are a standing joke.[25]

Such views were shared more widely than one might imagine. Indeed, in this respect, if few others, feminist theory and popular opinion tended to coalesce. When Mass-Observation conducted its so-called 'Little Kinsey' inquiry in 1949, it discovered that most of those interviewed preferred broken marriages to unhappy marriages.[26] 'Take my sister,' explained a 34-year-old shop assistant, 'anything would be better than the hell she has to put up with from her husband.'[27] When John R. Gillis came towards the end of his study of British marriages from the seventeenth century to the 1980s, he made much of the tension that existed between individualism and domesticity/egalitarianism.

> For most of the twentieth century both sexes have been torn between the potent force of modern individualism and the equally strong desire to have a home and family ... There is no question that with respect to values both men and women are more libertarian and egalitarian than twenty years ago. Today, there is a tendency for younger women to postpone marriage and older women to abandon it.[28]

What then of the number of children in care, and the number of elderly people being looked after institutionally? Once again, the figures are difficult to interpret, reflecting, *inter alia*, changing ideological, political and professional views about the best ways of balancing the rights of families against the needs of the vulnerable.[29] It is widely believed, of course, that families in the past used to look after parents and elderly relatives much better than they do now: you didn't 'cast them on one side like they would today'.[30] However, it is difficult to see that either set of statistics offers support for the view that family life was collapsing, and self-interest intensifying.[31]

Figure 7.4 shows that during the first 40 years of the century, parents were decreasingly likely to place – or have placed – their children in care. It reveals that although the number of children in (Poor Law institutional) care in England and Wales rose from just over 57,000 at the beginning of the century to more than 70,000 a decade later, it declined thereafter so that by the late 1930s the figure was down to

---

[25] J. Winterson, 'If marriage is going to survive, it's got to include everyone – regardless of their sexuality', *The Guardian*, 29 January 2002.

[26] L. Stanley, *Sex Surveyed 1949–1994: From Mass-Observation's 'Little Kinsey' to the National Survey and the Hite Reports* (Taylor & Francis, 1995), p. 131.

[27] Stanley, *Sex Surveyed*, p. 126. See also, E. Goodman, 'The 40 year itch', *Daily Mail*, 4 September 1975.

[28] Gillis, *For Better, For Worse*, p. 319.

[29] J. Parker and J. Webb, 'Social Services', in Halsey (ed.), *British Social Trends*, pp. 530–4.

[30] Wolverhampton Oral History Project, Interview 19, p. 19. Also, P. Thane, *Old Age in English History: Past Experiences, Present Issues* (Oxford: Oxford University Press, 2000), pp. 430–1.

[31] Women's Group on Public Welfare, *The Neglected Child and His Family: A Study Made in 1946–7* (Oxford: Oxford University Press, 1948).

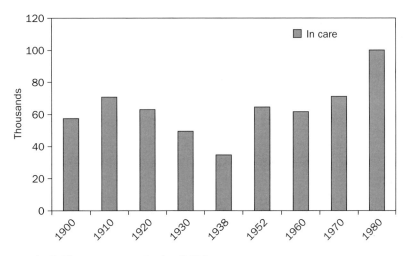

Figure 7.4 Children in care, England and Wales, 1900–80
Source: Based on J. Parker and J. Webb, 'Social Services', in A.H. Halsey (ed.), *Twentieth-Century British Social Trends* (Basingstoke: Macmillan, 2000), pp. 531–2.

under 35,000. It suggests too that during the second half of the century, the number of children in (local authority) care fluctuated in line, not with individual and family selfishness, but with prevailing political imperatives. The number of such children increased from 64,000 to 100,000 between 1952 and 1980 (a period during which the emphasis was upon statutory intervention). Their numbers then declined, in England and Wales, from 95,000 to 54,000 between 1980 and 1998 (a period during which the emphasis tended to be upon reducing public expenditure).[32]

Figure 7.5 is equally interesting. It shows that during the course of the century children were less and less likely to place – or have placed – their parents in institutional care. Although the number of elderly people looked after in this way increased from barely 25,000 in 1900 to just over 97,000 90 years later, this represented a significantly declining proportion of the elderly population: 28 per cent at the beginning of the century, 16 per cent in 1920, 17 per cent in 1970, and 12 per cent in 1990. Whether this decline was the result of the declining poverty of the elderly, decreasing public and private provision or increasing individual and family commitment is impossible to say. Anyway, it requires a considerable leap of faith to believe that a decline in institutional care provides evidence of an increase in individual and family selfishness.[33]

It has been seen in previous chapters how helpful it can be to narrow the focus from the population as a whole to some of the major groups within it. Nowhere, it must be stressed, is this reorientation more necessary than when attempting to understand personal and family relationships in all their multiplicity, diversity and complexity. In

---

[32] Parker and Webb, 'Social Services', pp. 530–2. It must not be forgotten, of course, that between 1901 and 1996/7 the population of England and Wales increased from under 33 million to over 52 million.

[33] See J. Benson, *Prime Time: A History of the Middle Aged in Twentieth-Century Britain* (Harlow: Longman, 1997), pp. 105–7.

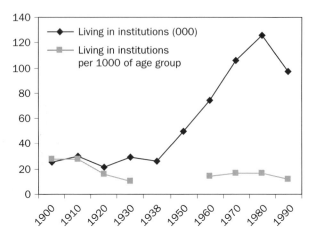

Figure 7.5 Elderly in care, England and Wales, 1900–90

Source: Based on J. Parker and J. Webb, 'Social Services', in A.H. Halsey (ed.), *Twentieth-Century British Social Trends* (Basingstoke: Macmillan, 2000), p. 515.

fact, when this narrower focus is applied, it can be seen once again how dangerous it is to hazard linear, monocausal models of long-term, nationwide developments.

ADOLESCENCE, MIDDLE AGE AND OLD AGE

No aspect of personal and family relationships can possibly be understood without recognizing age differences, and their impact over the life course. However, there is space here to consider just three age-related issues: the supposed promiscuity of the young, the alleged selfishness of the middle-aged, and the widely deplored isolation of the elderly. These three issues have been selected not just because of their intrinsic interest but because of the impact that they exerted, many believe, upon the moral and material fabric of the nation's life.

The examination of young people's sexual behaviour and attitudes is both helped and hindered by the attention they attracted. There was always a great deal of interest – much of it highly prurient – in what adolescents were getting up to. Such concerns reached a crescendo during the First and Second World Wars, during the 1960s and again towards the end of the century. 'In late 1914', explains Angela Woollacott, 'an epidemic of khaki fever broke out across Britain. Young women, it seemed, were so attracted to men in military uniform that they behaved in immodest and even dangerous ways.'[34] During the Second World War, 'Government Departments were concerned that there were no satisfactory means of bringing under treatment a number of girls and women who were responsible for much inefficiency of Servicemen through their infection with venereal disease.'[35] In late 1961 and early 1962, the Central

---

[34] A. Woollacroft, '"Khaki fever" and its control: Gender, class, age and sexual morality on the British homefront in the First World War', *Journal of Contemporary History*, 29, 1994, p. 325. See also J. Paxman, *The English: A Portrait of a People* (Penguin, 1999), p. 229; Bourke, *Working-Class Cultures*, pp. 37–8; 'Girls who turn from love', *Daily Mail*, 16 February 1920.

[35] H. Jones, *Health and Society in Twentieth-Century Britain* (Harlow: Longman, 1994), p. 95.

Council for Health Education discovered that the press carried over 400 items on teenage sexual behaviour in just four months – an average of more than three a day.[36]

Whatever the difficulties of using such evidence, it alerts us to the possibility that young people's sexual behaviour and attitudes changed less than contemporary commentators were inclined to believe. It is easy, it seems, to exaggerate both the modesty of early twentieth-century adolescents and the recklessness of their late twentieth-century counterparts. Victorian and Edwardian children were not necessarily as innocent as we imagine.[37] They knew many ways of having fun. 'I was in this gang of six boys and three girls', recalls a Bristol woman born in 1904. 'We used to go up the quarry an' we 'ad this old bath that we flattened out, an' we used to take it in turns, with a boy on the front an' a girl on the back, to slide down the quarry. I did come 'ome most nights with me drawers broke.'[38] As they grew older, courting couples, engaged couples – and others – went on to experiment more adventurously. The Registrar-General reported in the late 1930s, for example, that nearly 30 per cent of mothers conceived their first child before they were married.[39] Indeed, it has been estimated, more generally, that almost 20 per cent of married women born before 1904 had pre-marital sex, a figure that rose to practically 40 per cent of those born between 1914 and 1924, and 43 per cent of those born between 1924 and 1934.[40]

Nor should it be assumed that young people during the second half of the century were necessarily well informed, experienced and promiscuous. 'My life is jazz and sex', confided 16-year-old Coventry schoolboy Peter Bailey to his diary in 1954. 'I get a fair amount of one but more of the other.'[41] Thirteen years later, even *The Sun* conceded that, 'It is tempting but fallacious for middle-aged authority to equate automatically long-haired boys, mini-skirted girls, and both sexes when mysteriously dressed as Red Indians, with sexual depravity, drug-taking, political instability and a criminal outlook.'[42] Indeed, the National Survey of Sexual Attitudes and Lifestyles carried out in the early 1990s discovered that fewer than 30 per cent of young men, and fewer than 20 per cent of young women, had experienced sexual intercourse before the age of 16. The 'Higher proportions of sexually active teenagers sometimes cited', the Survey's authors warned sternly, 'may result from estimates based on non-random samples, or calculations using a different denominator.'[43] The truth, one contraceptive manufacturer concluded

[36] M. Schofield, *The Sexual Behaviour of Young People* (Harlow: Longman, 1965), p. 7.

[37] But they were probably as ignorant as we imagine.

[38] S. Humphries, *Hooligans or Rebels? An Oral History of Working-Class Childhood and Youth 1889–1939* (Oxford: Blackwell, 1981), p. 136.

[39] Hall, *Sex, Gender and Social Change*, p. 122.

[40] M. Plant and M. Plant, *Risk-takers: Alcohol, Drugs, Sex and Youth* (Tavistock/Routledge, 1992), p. 88. See also Schofield, *Sexual Behaviour*, pp. 25–37; P. Summerfield, 'Women in Britain since 1945: Companionate Marriage and the Double Burden', in J. Obelkevich and P. Catterall (eds), *Understanding Post-War British Society* (Routledge, 1994), p. 68.

[41] P. Bailey, 'Jazz at the Spirella: Coming of Age in Coventry in the 1950s,' p. 34. Courtesy of Peter Bailey.

[42] 'You're never too old to be young', *Sun*, 14 October 1967. Also, Weeks, *Sex*, pp. 254–5.

[43] Wellings *et al.*, *Sexual Behaviour*, p. 42.

in 1990, was that, 'Many young people are not sexually active. However, those who are having sexual intercourse are likely to have multiple partners.'[44]

The middle-aged were just as heterogeneous in outlook and behaviour. There were some who were selfish and some who were selfless – and many no doubt who were both according to inclination, mood and circumstance. However, public perceptions of those in their forties and fifties were a good deal less nuanced – and a good deal less complimentary. It was widely held in the late 1940s, for instance, that 'parents today are not as willing to sacrifice personal comfort and pleasure in the interests of their children'. It was commonly believed, 'that the sense of family responsibility and unity is weakening, and that people in this country are less interested than they were in the fate of their elderly and disabled relatives'.[45] By the 1980s, unfaithful husbands were blaming their behaviour on the male menopause.[46] By the end of the century, feminism, according to both its supporters and its detractors, had substantially affected family life. The ageing of the so-called baby-boom generation meant, claimed Angela Nenstalter, that 'women are refusing to play their time-honoured roles and those roles are breaking down'.[47] According to the *Daily Mail,*

> It is one of the abiding images of the great British family: Mum, Dad and the children sitting round the table for dinner … More working women with less time to cook has led to a rise in microwaveable meals, snack food and other dinners which are less formal. Even the traditional Sunday roast is less of an event as it now has to compete with sporting events and seven-day shopping.[48]

The examination of such claims enables us to explore both the alleged selfishness of the middle-aged and the supposed isolation of the elderly. Such age-related stereotyping, it transpires, is considerably exaggerated. For, as has been seen already, it is impossible to use the number of old people in institutional care as evidence of a long-term increase in middle-aged selfishness.[49] It was not that only a tiny minority of old people were ever in public institutional care – it was also that those in care received regular visits from their middle-aged sons and daughters. A 1949 report on elderly patients in a Birmingham infirmary revealed, for instance, that even after four years in care, 40 per cent of men, and 46 per cent of women, still received at least one visit a week.[50]

Indeed, during the first three-quarters of the century, a surprisingly large number of middle-aged children shared their homes with one or both of their parents. It was estimated in 1951, for example, that 60 per cent of the over-sixties with surviving

[44] Plant and Plant, *Risk-takers*, p. 91.

[45] A.P. Thompson, 'Problems of ageing and chronic sickness', *British Medical Journal*, 30 July 1949.
'Peter, 12, lived by himself 4 months', *Daily Mail*, 6 January 1950.

[46] 'The final fling of a worried man', *Daily Mail*, 5 September 1985.

[47] A. Nenstalter, 'The time of our lives', *The Guardian*, 19 April 1999. See also *Radio Times*,
15 June 1967, p. 11.

[48] 'Why there's no longer a place for the family meal', *Daily Mail*, 4 April 2000. See also 'Trap for born losers', *Daily Mail*, 6 July 1995; H. Kennard in *Daily Mail*, 31 October 2003.

[49] For a more detailed discussion, see Benson, *Prime Time*, pp. 105–18.

[50] Thompson, 'Problems'.

children were living with a son or daughter;[51] and it has been calculated that as late as 1971, 13 per cent of men, and 29 per cent of women, over the age of 65 were living with relatives.[52] Even when the middle-aged did not share their homes with their parents, they continued, many of them, to offer interest and support. A 1957 study of a 'typical' general practice in the suburbs of London reported that 86 per cent of those in their eighties maintained 'regular contact with their families'.[53] The authors of a late 1980s' study of the very old (those aged 90 and over) concluded that the members of their sample, 'despite their great age, were, for the most part, still firmly enmeshed, at least in a kinship network. Spouses … had mostly died but other kin, even though partially depleted, were strongly in evidence.'[54] As Pat Thane observes laconically, 'Family support for older people was not a negligible feature of the British welfare state in the late twentieth century.'[55]

MEN, WOMEN AND DOUBLE STANDARDS

Even the most cursory examination of family support for older people shows the need for gender to be inserted into the analysis. 'How often have you seen the fifty-year-old woman guiding the seventy-five-year-old around the hospital, the supermarket, the theatre foyer?', demanded Germaine Greer: 'middle-aged women are the only ones free to do it, and the whole responsibility tends to fall on them.'[56] It was a common view. Among the reasons a Glaswegian – female – social worker gave for the growing problem of geriatric care was the fact that there were no longer 'enough daughters in the family that they could take their turn in looking after the elderly people'.[57]

Women, it must be remembered, were sometimes more isolated than men. It was seen in Chapter 1 that the single, widowed and divorced constituted a declining, but substantial, proportion of adult women: 47 per cent in 1931, 36 per cent in 1961. Many women too lived with a child (or children), but without any adult companionship. The number of lone parents (the vast majority of them women) trebled from just over 500,000 in the early 1970s to 1.6 million in the mid-1990s. 'Within that 1.6 million, the fastest growing group is single, never-married lone mothers. Their proportion, 42% in 1997, is nearly double the proportion of 24% for 1984.'[58]

---

[51] P. Townsend, *The Family Life of Old People: An Inquiry in East London* (Routledge & Kegan Paul, 1957), pp. 21–2. See also J. Fry, 'Care of the elderly in General Practice: A socio-medical reassessment', *British Medical Journal*, 21 September 1957.

[52] E. Grundy, 'Longitudinal Perspectives on the Living Arrangements of the Elderly', in M. Jefferys (ed.), *Growing Old in the Twentieth Century* (Routledge, 1989), p. 131.

[53] Fry, 'Care of the elderly'. See also J. Macnicol, *The Politics of Retirement in Britain, 1878–1948* (Cambridge: Cambridge University Press, 1998), pp. 283–4.

[54] M. Bury and A. Holme, *Life After Ninety* (Routledge, 1991), p. 134.

[55] Thane, *Old Age*, p. 433. See also Woodward, 'Loners'; Leonard and Speakman, 'Women in the Family', p. 65.

[56] G. Greer, *The Change: Women, Ageing and the Menopause* (Penguin, 1992), p. 315. See also Museum of Edinburgh, The Newhaven Group, T.232/93, Betty Hepburn.

[57] Museum of Edinburgh, T.68/97.

[58] Woodward, 'Loners'. See also Women's Group on Public Welfare, *Neglected Child*, pp. ix, 26.

Even married women could feel isolated, a problem that probably reached its peak around the middle of the century. It is no coincidence, for example, that Ann Oakley published her classic study of the sociology of housework in 1974. Loneliness, she maintained, was 'an occupational hazard for the modern housewife, who is often cut off not only from community life but from family life – in the wider sense – also'.[59] The growth of prosperity, the decline in family size, the spread of suburbanization, the desire for better housing, and the demand for higher standards of domestic comfort all had the effect, *inter alia*, of tying wives and mothers to the home, and distancing them from their family, friends and neighbours.[60] 'Few who have not worked or lived in the suburbs can realise the intense loneliness of their unhappy inhabitants', claimed a neurological consultant from a London teaching hospital in 1938.[61]

Hyperbole aside, there is no doubt that many mid-century housewives, both middle-class and working class, found their lack of social contact extremely unsettling. 'The last couple of months it's been dragging', explained the wife of a London supermarket manager in the early 1970s: 'you feel "I wish I could talk to somebody" … not knowing anybody else you tend to get this feeling unless you go out and talk to someone you'll go stark raving mad.'[62] A lorry driver's wife agreed: 'I could be murdered here and no one would know. When the milkman comes, it's an event.'[63] In the final analysis, it has been suggested, during the third quarter of the century working-class women's 'aspiration towards better accommodation for themselves and their families was stronger than their attachment to a friendly and supportive neighbourhood'.[64]

In many respects, too, women were less selfish than men. Of course, putting the argument as starkly as this points immediately to problems ahead. Indeed, however carefully one qualifies propositions of this sort, one knows only too well that one is stepping into a political, ideological and empirical minefield. Nevertheless, there have been hints already that women behaved less selfishly than men. It was women, it has been seen, who tended to assume responsibility for the care of elderly relatives; it was women who made up the vast majority of lone parents. In fact, there is available a seemingly unending and persuasive supply of oral and autobiographical material attesting to the selflessness of women as wives, mothers, daughters, relatives, neighbours and workmates.

Such evidence, for all its consistency, must be treated very carefully indeed. The difficulty is that the oral and autobiographical sources used by students of twentieth-century social history tends to under-record, and thus misrepresent, key aspects of

---

[59] A. Oakley, *The Sociology of Housework* (Oxford: Blackwell, 1985), p. 88. Cf. E. Ross, ' "Not the sort that would sit on the doorstep": Respectability in pre-World War I London neighbourhoods', *International Labor and Working Class History*, 27, 1985.

[60] E. Roberts, *Women and Families: An Oral History, 1940–1970* (Oxford: Blackwell, 1995).

[61] J. Giles, *Women, Identity and Private Life in Britain, 1900–50* (Basingstoke: Macmillan, 1995), p. 96.

[62] Oakley, *Housework*, p. 91. See also E. Ross, 'Survival networks: Women's neighbourhood sharing in London before World War One', *History Workshop Journal*, 15, 1983.

[63] Oakley, *Housework*, p. 91

[64] Roberts, *Women and Families*, p. 230. Also A. Myrdal and V. Klein, *Women's Two Roles: Home and Work* (Routledge & Kegan Paul, 1956), pp. 146–9. Cf. S. Gunn and R. Bell, *Middle Classes: Their Rise and Sprawl* (Cassell, 2002), pp. 66–71.

men's personal relationships. Autobiographers and those interviewed by oral historians are invariably adults looking back over their lives, and they tend to pay greater attention to the home-based sacrifices of their mothers than to the work-based efforts of their fathers.[65] Many husbands and fathers, it must not be forgotten, made their fundamental contribution to family relationships by working, often for decades on end, in jobs that were poorly remunerated, intellectually or physically demanding and, most crucially of all, carried out completely out of sight of their wives and children.[66] Moreover, many husbands helped more – and cared more – than either their own rhetoric or conventional stereotyping would suggest.[67]

The reassessment of men's commitment to family life does not mean that we should revise downwards the contribution that women made. We need to avoid both gender stereotyping and gender hagiography. Yet whatever men's contribution to family life, the fact remains that women of all ages, of all ethnic backgrounds, of all classes normally did more than the men in their lives to support their partners, raise their children, stay in touch with their relatives and help their neighbours.[68]

Elizabeth Roberts concluded *A Woman's Place*, her study of Lancashire working-class women during the first half of the century, with the warning that the oral evidence she used was complex and revealed, as one would expect, 'a mass of individual differences'. However, this did not inhibit her from generalizing about those she was studying. They were, she discovered, 'disciplined, inhibited, conforming and ... placed perceived familial and social needs before those of the individual'. The conclusion was inescapable. 'Women's considerable powers were all exercised, firmly, in the perceived interests of their families – that is how they saw their "place".'[69] Roberts returned to these issues in *Women and Families*, a book that took her study of Lancashire working-class women to the beginning of the 1970s. A great deal, she discovered, had changed between 1940 and 1970, but a great deal remained the same. 'It is an irony', she concluded, 'that in a time when there was a growing interest in individual rights, women continued to place others' interests before their own, whether it was those of their husbands, their parents or their children.'[70]

Statistical enquiry confirms what oral and newspaper evidence suggests. Just a few months into the new millennium, the Office for National Statistics published the largest ever statistical study of the United Kingdom's 23 million men. It revealed, as might be anticipated, that although men's behaviour was changing, it was likely to be many years before men and women assumed anything like equal responsibility for housework,

[65] J. Dash, *Good Morning Brothers!* (Lawrence & Wishart, 1969), p. 14.

[66] The difficulty has never been fully recognized. But see, for example, Roberts, *Woman's Place in Britain, 1850–1939* (Harlow: Longman, 1989), p. 11.

[67] J. Benson, *The Working Class in Britain, 1850–1939* (Harlow: Longman, 1989), p. 102; *Bourke, Working-Class Cultures*, pp. 84–5.

[68] Leonard and Speakman, 'Women in the Family', pp. 65–6.

[69] Roberts, *Woman's Place*, p. 203.

[70] 'The interesting exception to this generalization', she noted, 'was a group of grandmothers for whom personal interests and pleasures were more important than family obligations.' Roberts, *Women and Families*, pp. 238–9.

cooking and child care. The lead author of the study explained, for example, that,

> Childcare was once regarded as the primary preserve of women. Today men
> with children living in the household report spending three-quarters of an hour
> a day caring for and playing with their children. This is just under half the
> amount reported by women.[71]

Double standards abounded, and never more than when sexual behaviour and sexual attitudes were under discussion. For it was a fundamental paradox of personal relationships that there tended to be an inverse relationship between individual promiscuity and public disapproval. Women were less likely than men to experiment sexually, but a great deal more likely to be castigated for doing so.[72]

There is no denying that at the beginning of the century, a sexual double standard operated powerfully at all levels of society. It meant, as one historian puts it, that 'unchastity for men was understandable and even necessary for health, but for women it was unforgivable'.[73] Thus the furore over 'khaki fever' that erupted during the First World War was concerned, it will be recalled, with the social and sexual behaviour of young women, not the behaviour of their male partners. The fever, explains Angela Woollacott, 'seemed a flagrant challenge to the belief that sexual chastity was integral to respectable femininity'.[74] So it was that when *The Englishwoman* discussed the issue in 1916, it did so in outspoken terms:

> Headstrong, impressionable, undisciplined girls, hardly more than children,
> have made themselves a nuisance by running after soldiers without any thought
> of more than silly or perhaps vulgar flirtation, and, by turn tempters and
> tempted, have often ended by entangling themselves and their soldier friends
> in actually vicious conduct.[75]

Such attitudes never entirely disappeared. Those seeking to examine sexual behaviour and sexual morality at mid-century rely heavily upon surveys such as Geoffrey Gorer's *Exploring English Character* which was published in 1951. Arthur Marwick, for example, uses it to show both the existence of the sexual double standard and the fact that it found more favour with women than it did with men. He cites Gorer's claim that just over half the men, but nearly two-thirds of the women, interviewed in his investigation disapproved of pre-marital sex. He goes on to quote Gorer's interview with a teenage Liverpool girl who was asked if a man should have sexual experience before marriage. 'I think yes,' she replied, 'because until a man has such an experience he really cannot define LOVE as anything particular, because men fall victim to their

---

[71] J. Carvel, 'Old habits die hard for new man', *The Guardian*, 12 July 2001.

[72] 'Boys will be boys', *Daily Mail*, 4 April 1990; 'How science has proved that marriage really is bliss', *Daily Mail*, 17 January 1998.

[73] S. Bruley, *Women in Britain since 1900* (Basingstoke: Macmillan, 1999), p. 13.

[74] Woollacott, 'Khaki fever', p. 327. See also Hall, *Sex, Gender and Social Change*, pp. 92–8; L.A. Hall, 'Impotent ghosts from No Man's Land: Flappers' boyfriends, or crypto-patriarchs? Men, sex and social change in 1920s Britain', *Social History*, 21, 1996, pp. 57–8.

[75] Woollacott, 'Khaki fever', p. 331. See also 'War babies', *Observer*, 18 April 1915; G. Robb, *British Culture and the First World War* (Basingstoke: Palgrave, 2002), p. 50.

emotions much more easily than women.' However, she did not think that women should engage in pre-marital sex, 'because although I am a woman and believe in equality of the sexes, I am still old-fashioned enough to believe a woman should be perfectly pure before she enters into matrimony'.[76]

Those examining the double standard towards the end of the century are able to turn not only to social surveys but also, of course, to their own day-to-day experiences and those of their friends, acquaintances and workmates.[77] The National Survey of Sexual Attitudes and Lifestyles discovered, for example, that by the early 1990s the gap between men's and women's attitudes had narrowed but not disappeared: nearly three-quarters of men, but only two-thirds of women, said that they condoned sex before marriage.[78] However, it was not necessary to consult many surveys, watch much television, listen to much radio, read many newspapers, or talk to many people to realize that the double standard retained considerable potency. One has only to think back to the controversy that erupted in the wake of Charles Murray's campaign in the late 1980s and early 1990s to popularize the concept of the 'underclass'. Illegitimacy, he maintained, 'is the best predictor of an underclass in the making'.[79] Murray's critics were furious. 'I would be a rich woman', retorted the Director of the National Council for One Parent Families, 'if I had a pound for every time I have heard a man talk about "these girls who make themselves pregnant".'[80]

MINORITIES, DOUBLE STANDARDS AND STEREOTYPING

The stereotyping of single mothers represented one of the late twentieth-century's less appealing political and ideological developments. But it pales almost into insignificance when set alongside the abuse that for decades had been heaped upon the personal relationships and domestic arrangements of those from ethnic minorities. Such issues remain, of course, among the most sensitive with which historians – or any other scholars – ever have to deal. But in dismantling the demonization that continued to exert so powerful a hold, it is important not to erect in its place some politically correct abstraction that conceals all differences and eschews anything that might be construed as moral judgement or ideological disapproval.[81]

It has been decided that the most helpful approach is to concentrate upon two of the country's most visible minorities: Afro-Caribbeans and those from South Asia. These two groups displayed, we are told, not just different attitudes towards entrepreneurship but almost diametrically opposed patterns of personal and family relationships. It is

---

[76] A. Marwick, *British Society since 1945* (Penguin, 1990), p. 66. He notes in a characteristic aside that, 'Expressed attitudes towards sex are notoriously hard to disentangle from actual sexual behaviour. Loudmouths may be the shortest in actual performance; the discreet may be living it up.'

[77] See, for example, 'They're single, successful, so why are they still available?' *Daily Mail*, 4 January 1985; 'Women having more fun between the sheets', *Express and Star*, 30 April 2003.

[78] Wellings *et al.*, *Sexual Behaviour*, p. 248.

[79] C. Murray, 'The Emerging British Underclass', in Institute of Economic Affairs, *Charles Murray and the Underclass: The Developing Debate* (IEA Health and Welfare Unit, 1996), p. 25.

[80] S. Slipman, 'Would You Take One Home with You?', Institute of Economic Affairs, *Charles Murray*, p. 164.

[81] S. Duncan, *Mothers, Care and Employment: Values and Theories* (Leeds: CAVA and University of Bradford, 2003), pp. 13, 24–30.

said, for instance, that, 'The West Indian population had never absorbed the ethos of the male breadwinner ... Pakistani and Bangladeshi households, on the other hand, tend to contain extended family groups rather than nuclear or single-parent families.'[82] One should always be suspicious of such stereotyping. Eunice Chambers came to Britain from Jamaica in 1960, and his wife stayed at home to look after their children. 'Well, I wouldn't allow her to go out to work, because I didn't like the idea that she ... leave the kids ... An' that was one of the reasons why I had it so hard.'[83]

Nevertheless, conventional stereotyping is closer to the truth than many would like to believe. In all events, it will be suggested that Afro-Caribbeans were more likely than South Asians to find themselves isolated, and that Afro-Caribbean men were more likely to place their own needs above those of the family, and more likely to experiment sexually.[84] It can certainly be demonstrated that Afro-Caribbeans were more likely than South Asians – and more likely than the indigenous population – to live alone, or to live as lone parents. (This does not mean, one must stress, that those who lived on their own or with only children for company felt isolated and lonely, or that those who lived with other people felt integrated and fulfilled.) However, the differences between the domestic arrangements of the two groups were highly significant. It has been found, for instance, that in the early 1980s, 'only 5 per cent of Asian households consisted of one adult alone compared with 13 per cent of West Indian and 20 per cent of white households'.[85]

There were differences too between seemingly similar one-adult households. For, as was pointed out in 1989, 'West Indians have as high an incidence of households consisting of one adult with or without children as whites – one quarter of all households. However, these white households consist mainly of pensioners while the West Indian households contain many more young single adults and lone-parent families.'[86] What statistics cannot show are the material and emotional consequences of lone motherhood. A 13-year-old London boy complained in the 1970s,

> You get a black guy from Brixton like me with everything in the world going
> against him, and his family too. Maybe that part of it isn't so bad for me, but
> I have to worry about my brothers too. What's going to happen to *them*? They
> need a family; my youngest brother he needs a father. I can't be a father to him.
> What the hell, I'm only a couple of years older than him.[87]

---

[82] Bruley, *Women*, pp. 175–7. See also, R. Oakley, 'Cypriot families', British Family Research Committee, *Families in Britain* (1982); E. Goody and C.M. Groothues, 'Stress in Marriage', in V.S. Khan (ed.), *Minority Families in Britain: Support and Stress* (Basingstoke: Macmillan, 1979).

[83] Black and Ethnic Minority Project, 76DX-624/6/72. See also 49DX-624/6/48 and DX-624/6/29; L. Christie, *To Be Honest With You* (Penguin, 1996), p. 42.

[84] Duncan, *Mothers, Care and Employment*, p. 26.

[85] I. Diamond and S. Clarke, 'Demographic Patterns among Britain's Ethnic Groups', in H. Joshi (ed.), *The Changing Population of Britain* (Oxford: Blackwell, 1989), p. 185. See also R. Berthoud and S. Beishon, 'People, Families and Households', T. Modood and R. Berthoud (eds), *Ethnic Minorities in Britain: Diversity and Disadvantage* (Policy Studies Institute, 1997), pp. 23–4.

[86] Diamond and Clarke, 'Demographic Patterns', p. 185. Also, G. Driver, 'West Indian Families: An Anthropological Perspective', in British Family Research Committee, *Families in Britain*.

[87] T.J. Cottle, *Black Testimony: The Voices of Britain's West Indians* (Aldershot: Wildwood House, 1978), p. 28. Also, 'The myth and the mister', *The Guardian*, 21 March 1995.

It also seems that Afro-Caribbean men were more likely than South Asians to place individual needs ahead of those of the family. Indeed, it has been seen already that young people from Pakistani and Bangladeshi backgrounds struggled more than other adolescents to reconcile their desire for autonomy with their parents' demands for family based, culturally acceptable attitudes and behaviour. It was a struggle which, as generation upon generation of young Asians discovered, often had only one outcome. 'I've had loads of girlfriends, some English, some Indian,' explained a Leeds mechanic in the 1970s, 'but I've always known that in the end I'd do what the family expected and marry the girl they choose. I'm quite happy about that, in fact it's quite a relief.'[88] By the end of the century, concludes Tariq Modood, even when young South Asians made their own marriage plans, 'parents are closely involved (perhaps in even introducing the prospective partner)'.[89]

It can be suggested finally that Afro-Caribbean men were more likely than South Asians to experiment sexually. The qualitative and statistical evidence is mutually reinforcing. 'All the girls at work talk about is boys and sex and their figures', remarked a Yorkshire machinist of South Asian descent, in the 1970s. 'Sometimes I'm quite jealous of them being able to do whatever they want and I do enjoy their jokes. But I think they've got too much freedom and they just go and fall pregnant and have to marry lads who won't really care for them. There's not much happiness in that.'[90] The Fourth National Survey of Ethnic Minorities, published in 1997, revealed that 18 per cent of Caribbean couples described themselves as 'living as married', compared with 11 per cent of white couples and fewer than 4 per cent of Asian couples.[91] The survey revealed too stark differences in what it described as patterns of parenting and partnership. It did so in a passage which is worth quoting at some length:

> Nine out of ten South Asian families with children had two formally married parents. For white families, there were important groups where the parents were living as married, had separated or divorced, or had never married at all, but three quarters were still in the 'traditional' pattern with two married parents. For Caribbean families, on the other hand, one third had single, never-married mothers. Once the numbers living as married, or no longer married, have been added in, fewer than half of Caribbean families with children were headed by a couple in a formal marriage.[92]

---

[88] C. Ballard, 'Conflict, Continuity and Change: Second-Generation South Asians', in Khan (ed.), *Minority Families*, p. 124. See also *Between Two Cultures: A Study of Relationships between Generations in the Asian Community in Britain* (Community Relations Commission, 1976). For Imran Khan's marriage to Jemima Goldsmith, see *The Sunday Times*, 14 May 1995.

[89] T. Modood, 'Culture and Identity', in Modood and Berthoud (eds), *Ethnic Minorities*, p. 319. See also, K. Gardner, *Age, Narrative and Migration: The Life Course and Life Histories of Bengali Elders in London* (Oxford: Berg, 2000), pp. 148, 151. See also D. Murphy, *Tales from Two Cities: Travel of Another Sort* (Penguin, 1987), Ch. 3.

[90] Ballard, 'Conflict, Continuity and Change', p. 115. See also D. Coleman and J. Salt, *The British Population: Patterns, Trends, and Processes* (Oxford: Oxford University Press, 1992), p. 512.

[91] Berthoud and Beishon, 'People, Families and Households', p. 28.

[92] Berthoud and Beishon, 'People, Families and Households', p. 39.

Those from ethnic minorities were damned if they did, and damned if they didn't. Afro-Caribbeans were castigated for their selfishness and exploitation of women, Pakistanis and Bangladeshis for their clannishness and oppression of women. Ethnic minority personal relationships were all tarred, one way or another, with being different from, and inferior to, those of the indigenous population.[93]

CLASSES, DIFFERENCES AND PERCEPTIONS

None of this is to suggest, of course, that it is easy to generalize about Britain's minority populations. Indeed, it will be clear from the discussion so far how necessary it is to take account of class differences and class attitudes in any attempt to understand personal relationships and the ways in which contemporaries interpreted them.

During the first half of the century, most middle-class adults subscribed, more or less conscientiously, to a strict and sometimes repressive regime of respectability. Upper middle-class girls were warned, like their Victorian forebears, that when they married, they 'might not at first like the thing men wanted to do'.[94] Lower middle-class girls continued to be imbued with a dread of pregnancy, one of the most terrible catastrophes that could befall a respectable girl and her family.[95] 'It is difficult to convey the fear of pregnancy women felt', recalls Miriam Stoppard. As late as the 1960s, 'fearless sex was beyond imagination'.[96] Boys from the middle class were encouraged to place a low value on caring and nurturing, and bear constantly in mind the rigidity of the boundaries separating the sexes. Public schools taught, it has been pointed out, that, 'men and masculinity were important and in charge, women were insignificant, subordinate, their purpose to enable men to realise their aims and ambitions, through docile, domestic service'.[97] Such values and attitudes, it needs scarcely be said, were not always likely to produce happy and fulfilling personal relationships.[98]

The second half of the century saw major changes.[99] It was shown earlier in the chapter that the spread of suburbia sometimes led to a more isolated and restricted existence than those moving onto new estates anticipated.[100] But this was not always the case. 'The fact was', concludes John Burnett, 'that for all its limitations and failings, the suburb represented a kind of utopian ideal, an arena for a new and better life for family and children, based on a house with substantially improved space and amenity

---

[93] 'In through the back door', *The Times Higher Education Supplement*, 10 October 1997.

[94] D. Athill, *Yesterday Morning* (Granta, 2001).

[95] R. Samuel, ' Suburbs under siege', *New Socialist*, May/June 1983.

[96] M. Stoppard, 'Pills, polygamy and Nobel lust', *The Times Higher Education Supplement*, 28 September 2001.

[97] C. Heward, *Making a Man of Him: Parents and their Sons' Education at an English Public School 1929–50* (Routledge, 1988), pp. 157–8. Also J. Bourke, *Dismembering the Male: Men's Bodies, Britain and the Great War* (Reaktion, 1996).

[98] But see, for instance, E. Jones (ed.), *The Memoirs of Edwin Waterhouse: A Founder of Price Waterhouse* (Batsford, 1988), p. 200; 'Tribute to a wife and mother', *Observer*, 19 January 1930.

[99] R. Hattersley, *Fifty Years On: A Prejudiced History of Britain Since the War* (Abacus, 1997), p. 174.

[100] L. Davidoff, M. Doolittle, J. Fink and K. Holden, *The Family Story: Blood, Contract and Intimacy 1830–1960* (Harlow: Longman, 1999), p. 200.

standards.'[101] A Lancaster man remembers moving into a council house during the 1920s. 'It had a bathroom that was another luxury ... and what my mother particularly enjoyed was hot water from the boiler, just open the tap and that was it, smashing. And there was an open space at the back and a garden to sit in. You could see some green grass instead of flags and cobbles.'[102]

Other developments were equally emancipating. Middle-class adolescents were always more likely than their working-class counterparts to go away to school, move away from home and thus make more choices about how they wished to live their lives. The hippies of the 1960s were a case in point. Although there were probably fewer than 60 serious communal groups in existence at the end of the decade, their rejection of conventional society involved, it was widely understood, alternative ways of growing up: 'play not work, drugs not drink, communes not marriage'.[103] The student population was larger, growing fast and playing a much greater role in the shaping of middle-class – and later working-class – personal relationships. During the first 40 years of the century, fewer than 3 per cent of 18–21-year-olds went on to full-time higher education. But thereafter, numbers grew apace. The Robbins Report of 1963, the expansion of teacher training, and the creation of the polytechnics (later the new universities) had a remarkable effect upon student numbers. The proportion of 18–21-year-olds studying full time leapt from 8.5 per cent in the early 1960s, to over 13 per cent in the early 1980s, and 33 per cent by the late 1990s.[104] Although more of these students lived at home than had previously been the case, universities and colleges provided increasing numbers of young people (and mature students) with opportunities for independence, experimentation and self-indulgence. It reminds us that what statistically-minded historians might regard as separation, promiscuity and selfishness, those involved in higher education might well think of in a much more positive light.

It is also easy to misinterpret the relationship between class and contraception. There are those who blame the introduction of the oral contraceptive pill for many of the evils of the modern world, and others who praise it as an invention that freed women from fear, ill health and unhappy marriages.[105] It is tempting, for example, to exaggerate the pill's short-term impact. When the first Brook Centre began offering contraceptive advice to unmarried students from London University in 1963, there was a storm of criticism at its 'official sanction for premarital intercourse'.[106] In 1970, fewer than 20 per cent of married couples under the age of 45 were using the pill, and even in the early 1990s only a quarter of women were employing it as their contraception of choice.[107]

---

[101] J. Burnett, *A Social History of Housing 1815–1985* (Methuen, 1986), pp. 256–7.

[102] E. Roberts, *Working Class Barrow and Lancaster, 1890–1930* (Lancaster: University of Lancaster, 1976), p. 35. Also P. Willmott, *The Evolution of a Community: A Study of Dagenham after Forty Years* (Routledge & Kegan Paul, 1963), pp. 6–7.

[103] M. Drake, *The Sociology of Youth Culture and Youth Subcultures: Sex and Drugs and Rock 'n' Roll* (Routledge & Kegan Paul, 1980), p. 16.

[104] A.H. Halsey, 'Further and Higher Education', in Halsey (ed.), *British Social Trends*, pp. 226–7.

[105] C. Fitzherbert, 'When intercourse began', *Daily Telegraph*, 23 June 2001. See L.V. Marks, *Sexual Chemistry: A History of the Contraceptive Pill* (Yale University Press, 2001).

[106] Hall, *Sex, Gender and Social Change*, p. 171.

[107] Marwick, *British Society*, p. 113; Wellings *et al.*, *Sexual Behaviour*, p. 331.

As the National Survey of Sexual Attitudes and Lifestyles reported in 1994, studies of women's contraceptive behaviour 'show the association with social class to be more marked for whether a method is used at all than for specific choice of method'.[108] In other words, it was not middle-class use of the pill that was significant. It was the fact that the middle class (whether male or female, married or single) were more likely than the working class to control their fertility in some way. 'French letters were not cheap', recalls Ralph Glasser of early twentieth-century Glasgow. 'Some fellows carried them around all the time, or said they did. I didn't.'[109] In time, though, the pill contributed, along with other forms of contraception – and a host of broader political, social and economic developments – to changing the material, emotional and sexual relationships of the middle class. It is difficult, after all, to envisage late twentieth-century, middle-class cohabitation, deferment of childbearing and multiplication of dual-career families developing in the ways they did without the spur, direct or indirect, of the so-called contraceptive revolution.

Middle-class observers rarely valued working-class relationships very highly. Their anxiety has been seen already in, for example, the concern expressed about the behaviour of working-class girls during the First and Second World Wars. It was visible too in many other ways. Late nineteenth- and early twentieth-century intellectuals agreed that suburbia was dreadful, but differed as to what precisely made it so awful. Some regarded it as dull and soulless, others as a hotbed of illicit sex. In *The Secret Glory*, published in 1922, the hero, Ambrose Meyrick, is particularly offended by what he sees as suburban pretensions to virtue:

> I suppose that, by nature, these people would not be so very much more
> depraved than the ordinary African black fellow. Their essential hideousness
> comes, I take it, from their essential and abominable hypocrisy.[110]

Social reformers and social workers were always concerned about working-class relationships. It was seen in Chapter 4 that the authorities viewed the working class as a greater threat than the middle class to economic, social and political stability. It was not just that strikers, hooligans and those from ethnic minorities were overwhelmingly working class; it was also that for many years those in power tended to pathologize anything that deviated from conventional, bourgeois assumptions about what was right and proper.

It was common to associate large families with irresponsibility, working mothers with neglect, the multiple occupancy of bedrooms with incest, and adolescent experimentation with prostitution. 'It is really a form of pastime', explained the superintendent of a Scottish girls' school in 1925. 'They don't do it for money but they get boxes of chocolates and things of that kind, fish dinners and nights at the theatre and bits of

---

[108] Wellings *et al.*, *Sexual Behaviour*, p. 338. For the first half of the century, see D. Gittins, *Fair Sex: Family Size and Structure, 1900–39* (Hutchinson, 1982), esp. Ch. 6. For middle-class women's concern about the health risks of the pill, see Marks, *Sexual Chemistry*, p. 201.

[109] Glasser, *Growing Up*, p. 109.

[110] Cited in J. Carey, *The Intellectuals and the Masses: Pride and Prejudice among the Literary Intelligentsia, 1880–1939* (Faber and Faber, 1992), pp. 51–2. See also 'Now the unwed mothers are office girls', *Daily Mail*, 7 July 1960.

finery and that sort.'[111] Middle-class women married for love, suggested Mass-Observation in 1947. Working-class women did so in order to get a home of their own.[112] The 'flight' of working-class women 'into marriage', Hannah Gavron claimed in 1968, 'is perhaps their only way of acquiring the outward signs of adulthood and a limited and temporary limelight'.[113] John Gillis agreed:

> Working-class women begin to think of marriage earlier than do their middle-class counterparts, who are more involved in school and career, more likely to have left home for the university or their own apartment, and thus less subject to parental control. Living at home, working-class women are more likely to have experienced tensions with their parents. For them, early marriage and motherhood are the means to independence.[114]

Gavron and Gillis are right. One does not need to sympathize with middle-class notions of superiority – still less subscribe to a thoroughgoing class-based analysis of society – to recognize that material circumstances exerted a powerful impact upon personal relationships. For a good deal of the century, truncated educational opportunities, traditional work patterns, low and uncertain incomes, poor accommodation, and limited geographical and social mobility restricted working-class horizons, constrained their choices and undermined the health and energy required to develop rich, humane and companionable family lives.[115] Working-class men and women tended to choose their partners from a narrow geographical and social circle.[116] Once married, hard work, tiredness, money worries, inadequate accommodation, lack of privacy, large families and fear of pregnancy inhibited them, more than their middle-class contemporaries, from developing companionable marriages and satisfying sexual relationships.[117] Mr and Mrs 'L' lived with her parents in London at the middle of the century. 'His in-laws are quite nice and well meaning, but ... he doesn't feel at home. They have only their bedroom to retire to, and everyone knows what is going on.'[118]

The poorer the family, the more likely it was that the problems confronting it would drive its members apart and, when they brought them together, generate

---

[111] L. Mahood, *Policing Gender, Class and Family: Britain, 1850–1940* (UCL Press, 1995), pp. 140–1. See also 'Labelled children', *Birmingham Mail*, 27 September 1927; E. Showalter, *The Female Malady: Women, Madness and English Culture, 1830–1980* (Virago, 1993), p. 224.

[112] Mass-Observation, 2495, 'The State of Matrimony', 1947, p. 16.

[113] Cited in Gillis, *For Better, For Worse*, p. 316.

[114] Gillis, *For Better, For Worse*, p. 316.

[115] The following section is based largely upon Benson, *Working Class*, Ch. 4. See also 'Ethics of married life', *Westminster Gazette*, 21 September 1905; 'Starving man dies, wife accused', *Daily Mail*, 5 April 1950; 'Sad life that led a girl to jail', *Daily Mail*, 4 January 1990.

[116] E. Slater and M. Woodside, *Patterns of Marriage: A Study of Marriage Relationships in the Urban Working Classes* (Cassell, 1951), pp. 198–9.

[117] 'Overcrowding in Bethnal Green', *Observer*, 20 April 1930; Glasser, *Growing Up*, p. 77.

[118] Slater and Woodside, *Patterns of Marriage*, p. 170. Also Mass-Observation, A 2495, 'The State of Matrimony', 1947, p. 13.

domestic tension. The son of a Bristol building worker recalls that his mother, a part-time cleaner, 'was kind but she was hard, if you understand, but she had to be hard because of so many children'.[119] It has been seen that living with in-laws was stressful. It goes without saying that taking in lodgers was difficult, and even when families lived alone, there was always something to argue about. Eliot Slater and Moya Woodside, for instance, presented a bleak view of working-class marriages in London between the wars:

> Seen through the eyes of children, it is open discord between the parents which is impressive and remembered in after-years – 'fights over everything', 'always at logger-heads', 'life was a lot of squabbles', 'not too good if Father was in beer', 'I wouldn't like to get on like them in my later life'.[120]

It was prosperity that was the key to the development of closer, more companionable, more fulfilling personal relationships.[121] As families became better off, smaller, healthier and more comfortably housed, husbands and wives were more likely to enjoy spending time together. They read, talked, gardened, tackled odd jobs, did the crossword, listened to the radio, filled out their pools coupon, went out with the children and took trips to the seaside.[122] For many years, these developments were epitomized by that shrine to late nineteenth- and early to mid-twentieth-century working-class domesticity, the front parlour. Used only at weekends or when entertaining visitors, it demonstrated, for all to see, the availability of resources surplus to immediate requirements. It represented, as Martin Daunton has pointed out, a transitional stage in working-class achievements and aspirations, a stage that 'permitted the purchase of furniture and fittings but which did not sanction their frequent use'.[123]

It was the prosperity of the second half of the century that laid the foundation for the transformation of working-class aspirations, achievements – and relationships. When Peter Willmott and his team interviewed East London boys born during the 1940s, they confirmed that theirs was the first generation 'to grow up without malnutrition and poverty'. As a tailor's cutter explained, 'You can have a lot more things than they would, the previous generation, television and things like that. And a working man can own a motor-car, and go out at week-ends … What some people call the good old days were really the bad old days.'[124]

---

[119] Avon County Reference Library, *Bristol People's Oral History Project*, Transcript R059, p. 9.

[120] Slater and Woodside, *Patterns of Marriage*, p. 43.

[121] And poverty continued to stunt them. D. Vincent, 'Love and death and the nineteenth-century working class', *Social History*, 5, 1980, p. 247.

[122] Roberts, *Woman's Place*, pp. 122–3; S. Constantine, 'Amateur gardening and popular recreation in the 19th and 20th centuries', *Journal of Social History*, xiv, 1981; R. McKibbin, 'Work and Hobbies in Britain, 1880–1950', in J.M. Winter (ed.), *The Working Class in Modern British History: Essays in Honour of Henry Pelling* (Cambridge: Cambridge University Press, 1983).

[123] M.J. Daunton, *House and Home in the Victorian City: Working-Class Housing 1850–1914* (Arnold, 1983), p. 280.

[124] P. Willmott, *Adolescent Boys of East London* (Penguin, 1975), p. 20.

POVERTY, PROSPERITY AND RELATIONSHIPS

Whether or not the generations growing up during the second half of the century used their new-found prosperity to purchase television sets and motorcars, the fact that they grew up without malnutrition and poverty was of absolutely fundamental importance. Only those who have never had to worry about the size of their next pay packet or where their next meal was coming from would deny the deleterious effects of poverty, or the liberating impact that financial security, let alone financial prosperity, had upon relationships between men and women, between parents and their children.

8 THE POWER OF CLASS, THE POWER OF THE NATION

FASHIONS, CLAIMS AND CAUTIONS

The study of 'identity' has become increasingly fashionable in recent years. Indeed, it sometimes seems that one cannot open a history journal, browse through a publisher's catalogue or cast an eye over an academic conference programme without being inundated with studies of identity in every imaginable form. A recent issue of the *Social History Society Newsletter*, for example, carried a call for papers for an international conference on 'Tourisms: Identities, Environments, Conflicts and Histories', which was intended to examine, *inter alia*, the 'relationships between tourism and cultural imperialism, and the concepts of "touring cultures" and "travelling identities"'. The *Newsletter* also contained a review of Eric Hopkins's book, *Industrialisation and Society: A Social History, 1830–1951* that criticized it on the grounds, among others, that 'Questions of national identity are ignored entirely.'[1]

Certainly, most historians of nineteenth- and twentieth-century Britain now make at least passing reference to issues of national identity. Intrigued by nationalist developments in Wales, Scotland and Ireland since the 1970s, shocked (very often) by popular enthusiasm for the Falklands War of 1982, and conscious of recurring anxieties about Britain's place in the world, the historical profession has moved questions of nationalism, national character and national identity towards the top of its agenda.[2] When he was Director of the Centre for Contemporary Cultural Studies at Birmingham University and Professor of Sociology at the Open University, Stuart Hall played a leading part in this reformulation of what was worthy of serious academic investigation. When he reflects on the changes he witnessed, he remarks that,

> One of the most important debates over the last 20 years has been what does it mean to be English, and the relationship to declining imperial power: what is it to have been master of the world, and now second-rate, underpins so many social events – from the Falklands to football hooliganism.[3]

This burgeoning preoccupation with nationhood and national identity has been accompanied by a sharply declining interest in class and class identity. Spurred on by

---

[1] *Social History Society Bulletin*, 25, 2000, pp. 25–6, 32, 49. See also the Economic and Social Research Council's Thematic Priorities, 2000: Governance and Citizenship.

[2] R. Samuel, 'Introduction: Exciting to be English', in R. Samuel (ed.), *Patriotism: The Making and Unmaking of British National Identity, Volume I History and Politics* (Routledge, 1989); J. Richards, *Films and British National Identity: From Dickens to Dad's Army* (Manchester: Manchester University Press, 1997), p. xi.

[3] M. Jaggi, 'Prophet at the margins', *The Guardian*, 8 July 2000.

domestic prosperity, the collapse of communism, the rise of Thatcherism and the dominance of the new right, many historians – of all political persuasions – began to question the significance of economic and social factors in explaining cultural and political change. 'There is a powerful sense in which class may be said to have "fallen"', explains Patrick Joyce, one of postmodernism's leading critics of class-based analysis. 'Instead of being a master category of historical explanation, it has become one turn among many, sharing a rough equality with these others.'[4]

Whatever view one takes of such historiographical developments, it is clear that neither class identity nor national identity can any longer be ignored or taken for granted. Accordingly, it is the aim of this chapter in the book to examine the ways in which class identity and national identity have developed during the course of the century. This is a truly daunting task. It is far from easy to define class or national identity. Indeed, even when they have been defined, it remains difficult to choose, collect and interpret the empirical evidence required to enable one to pursue the analysis. The challenge, it is worth emphasizing, is to plot developments in the class and national identities of millions upon millions of people, across every part of Britain during a hundred years of deep-seated economic, political, social and cultural change.

There is no point then concealing the complexities of disentangling the relationship between material conditions, systems of authority, patterns of behaviour and class and national identities. However, progress can certainly be made. And because class is at the core of the inquiry, the structure of the chapter will be different from those that have gone before. Rather than being relegated to the end of the analysis, class identity and class pride will be examined at every stage of the investigation. It will be stressed how important it is to distinguish between different forms of class consciousness, between nationalism, nationality and national identity, and between developments in England, Scotland, Wales and Great Britain as a whole. It will be suggested that when this is done, the picture becomes a good deal clearer. It will be argued that class identity and national identity did not cut across one another to the extent that is often supposed. More people than one might imagine continued to identify with, and be proud of, *both* the social class and the country to which they belonged.

CLASS CONSCIOUSNESS, CLASS IDENTITY AND CLASS PRIDE

The term 'class consciousness' tends to be bandied about with little concern for precisely what it means. It was possible, after all, for people to adopt a number of contradictory stances towards the way in which society was organized. They might deny the existence of class, recognize and welcome its existence, recognize and accept its existence, recognize and resent its existence, or so resent its existence that they seek

---

[4] P. Joyce, *Democratic Subjects: The Self and the Social in Nineteenth-Century England* (Cambridge: Cambridge University Press, 1994), p. 2. See also K. Jenkins, *Rethinking History* (Routledge, 1991); K. Jenkins, *On 'What is History?': From Carr and Elton to Rorty and White* (Routledge, 1997); A. Munslow, *Deconstructing History* (Routledge, 1997). For criticisms, see R.J. Evans, *In Defence of History* (Granta, 1997), and G.W. Bernard, 'History and Postmodernism', in G.W. Bernard, *Power and Politics in Tudor England* (Aldershot: Ashgate, 2000).

to overthrow the very economic and social foundations upon which it depended. Then too, people might well adopt different stances at different times, in different places, in different circumstances. For, as we have already seen, E.P. Thompson pointed out (of a much earlier period), that 'The same man who touches his forelock to the squire by day – and who goes down to history as an example of deference – may kill his sheep, snare his pheasants or poison his dogs at night.'[5]

Happily, a number of scholars have suggested ways through the impasse. Michael Mann, for instance, proposes a four-tier model of class consciousness, and it is a modified version of his framework that forms the basis of the discussion in this chapter.[6] It will be suggested that the most helpful approach is to distinguish between two broad tiers of consciousness: class identity, the identification of oneself as upper class, middle class or working class; and class pride, the pride that one feels in one's upper-class, middle-class or working-class identity.

UPPER-CLASS IDENTITY AND PRIDE

The upper class were only too well aware of the class to which they belonged. Indeed, it could be said that almost everything they did was designed with class identity and class pride in mind. Struggling to survive in a world where so much (they felt) seemed to be against them, they set enormous store by the distinctiveness of the aristocratic lifestyle.[7] They knew that their sources of income, the houses in which they lived, the way they spoke, the clothes they wore, their love of blood sports, their trips abroad and their commitment to the London 'season' all served to emphasize their physical, economic, social and cultural distance from the mass of the population.[8] 'In any case,' as F.M.L. Thompson explains, even 'those who were forced to sell up everything were rarely put out onto the street with nothing but the clothes they stood up in. There was usually enough capital left to live in a villa in the Channel Islands or the south of France, or to start again in Rhodesia, Kenya, Canada, Australia, or New Zealand.'[9] As Ken Roberts points out, the upper class 'retained the status and many of the privileges

---

[5] E.P. Thompson, 'Patrician society, plebeian culture', *Journal of Social History*, vii, 1974, p. 399.

[6] M. Mann, *Consciousness and Action among the Western Working Class* (Basingstoke: Macmillan, 1973). For attempts to apply the model, see M. Haynes, 'Strikes', in J. Benson (ed.), *The Working Class in England 1875–1914* (Croom Helm, 1984), pp. 112–14; J. Benson, *The Working Class in Britain, 1850–1939* (Harlow: Longman, 1989), pp. 151–5, 163–6.

[7] F.M.L. Thompson, 'English landed society in the twentieth century: I, Property: Collapse and survival', *Transactions of the Royal Historical Society*, 40, 1990.

[8] J. Benson, *The Rise of Consumer Society in Britain, 1880–1990* (Harlow: Longman, 1994), p. 205. R. Dahrendorf, *On Britain* (BBC, 1982), pp. 56–7. For aristocratic 'inconspicuous' consumption, see R. Perrott, *The Aristocrats: A Portrait of Britain's Nobility and their Way of Life* (Weidenfeld & Nicolson), 1968, pp. 255–72.

[9] F.M.L. Thompson, 'English landed society in the twentieth century: II, New poor and new rich', *Transactions of the Royal Historical Society*, I, 1991, p. 13. See also 'Decayed royalty', *Birmingham Evening Despatch*, 4 November 1919; P. Clarke, *Hope and Glory: Britain 1900–1990* (Penguin, 1996), p. 121; *To War with Whitaker: The Wartime Diaries of the Countess of Ranfurly, 1939–45* (Mandarin, 1995), pp. 8–18.

of its predecessor. Hereditary lords retained their right to sit and vote in parliament (in the House of Lords) until the very end of the twentieth century.'[10]

MIDDLE-CLASS IDENTITY, PRIDE AND ANXIETY

It has been seen in previous chapters that the state, education, religion and the media, and work all tended to reinforce middle-class identity and middle-class pride. But they were less successful, it seems, in allaying middle-class anxieties. Although – and no doubt because – the middle class were far from homogeneous, they knew that the way in which they earned their living, the way they spoke, the way they dressed, the houses they owned, the shops they patronized, the food they ate, the friends they made, the holidays they took and the sports they enjoyed all sent out powerful, and immediately recognizable, signals about their class identity.[11]

They recognized the importance of having a proper career.[12] They took care, for example, to shop in ways that befitted their identity, or at any rate the identity they wished to protect – or to which they aspired. For many years, they tended to avoid mail order, and regarded chain stores with considerable suspicion. They demanded their due. '[I]f there was anybody being served' when a colonel's sister from Newcastle went shopping during the early decades of the century, 'she expected them to stand on one side and let her go first.'[13] Department stores did their best to be reassuring. A representative from Denson's of Chester explained in 1939, for instance, that, 'People in this city are rather particular, and they do not like it to be known that they buy cheap stuff from the chains.'[14] But it was not just in provincial cities that stores sought to satisfy middle-class aspirations and soothe middle-class anxieties.[15] The author of this book was brought up in suburban Essex during the 1950s and early 1960s, and when he looks back he can see that one of the main reasons his mother joined the Consumers' Association and shopped at stores like Stones of Romford and Roomes of Upminster was because it helped to confirm the family's highly prized lower middle-class identity.[16] In one of Alan Bennett's dramas, somebody exposes himself in a branch of Sainsbury's. 'Tesco's you could understand', remarks an elderly woman.[17]

---

[10] K. Roberts, *Class in Modern Britain* (Basingstoke: Palgrave, 2001), p. 170.

[11] See, for example, D. Lockwood, *The Blackcoated Worker: A Study in Class Consciousness* (Oxford: Clarendon, 1989); A. Light, *Forever England: Femininity, Literature and Conservatism Between the Wars* (Routledge, 1991), pp. 12–13; R. Samuel, 'Suburbs under siege', *New Socialist*, May/June 1983; S. Gunn and R. Bell, *Middle Classes: Their Rise and Sprawl* (Cassell, 2002).

[12] Gunn and Bell, *Middle Classes*, pp. 152–4.

[13] Northumbria County Record Office, T/84/Mrs Kearnley.

[14] *Smallware and Accessories*, March 1939.

[15] W. Lancaster, 'British Department Stores and Society since 1850', unpublished paper, University of Warwick, November 1989.

[16] Personal recollection. See also G. Davies, 'Positioning, image and the marketing of multiple retailers', *International Review of Retail, Distribution and Consumer Research*, 2, 1992; M. Hilton, 'The fable of the sheep, or private virtues, public vices: The consumer revolution of the twentieth century', *Past and Present*, 176, 2002.

[17] S. Jeffries, 'What your supermarket says about you', *The Guardian*, 12 March 2004.

The middle class knew too that sport had a vital role to play in distinguishing them from the working class. Even when they were interested in games like cricket that were popular with all classes of society, middle-class participants took pains to retain their social and physical distance.[18] They batted rather than bowled, they captained the teams in which they played, and when they watched league, county or test matches, they liked to do so from the members' pavilion or other segregated parts of the ground.[19] Often, of course, middle-class enthusiasts turned to sports like squash, tennis and golf that were too expensive, time-consuming or socially exclusive to attract significant working-class involvement. 'Tennis and golf clubs were worlds within worlds,' explains Richard Holt, 'business contacts and mutual reassurance for the reasonably well off, islands of sociability within the unfathomable seas of domestic privacy.' He goes on to paint an evocative picture of club life: 'Comfortably ensconced behind a gin and tonic at the "nineteenth hole" or lining up a vital putt in the monthly medal, the golfer could forget the troublesome outside world and settle down to enjoy his or her modest affluence.'[20]

Whether or not they played golf, the middle class were proud, many of them, of their prosperity, their taste and their refinement.[21] But some, it must be conceded, were racked with guilt. Try as he might, George Orwell could never shake himself free from his childhood conditioning. He recalls, for example, that when he was 13 years old during the First World War, he found himself in a third-class railway compartment with a group of farmworkers returning home from market. He was almost sick when a bottle of beer was passed round, and he thought that he would have to drink from it 'after all those lower-class male mouths'.[22] When Jean Bernard joined the ATS (Auxiliary Territorial Service) during the Second World War, she had to make certain adjustments. 'I'd been used to having my own room and I remember being pitched in with twenty-seven others, many of whom, it semed, didn't take off their day clothes at night. I found this a bit of a sea-change.'[23] Other commentators made almost no effort to question their class assumptions. 'Why should I feel ashamed of the indisputable fact that we, the middle classes, fill the better schools with our children and the theatres with ourselves', demanded the novelist Lynne Reid Banks in 1980.[24] Those less in the public eye were prepared to speak even more bluntly. 'I can't understand people who feel guilty about the working classes', explained a woman from one of London's more expensive suburbs in the mid-1970s. 'People will always be different, even if everyone has the same houses and the same money. We would

---

[18] 'Snobbery in sport', *Observer*, 2 January 1927.

[19] R. Holt, *Sport and the British: A Modern History* (Oxford: Oxford University Press, 1990), pp. 291–2. Also T. Mason, *Sport in Britain* (Faber and Faber, 1988), pp. 78–9.

[20] Holt, *Sport*, p. 133. Also J. Hill, *Sport, Leisure and Culture in Twentieth-Century Britain* (Basingstoke: Palgrave, 2002), p. 35.

[21] R. Lewis and A. Maude, *The English Middle Classes* (Penguin, 1953), Ch. 3; 'Families start village war', *Daily Mail*, 3 September 1960.

[22] J. Carey, *The Intellectuals and the Masses: Pride and Prejudice among the Literary Intelligentsia, 1880–1939* (Faber and Faber, 1992), p. 40. Mass-Observation, A10, p. 2.

[23] Imperial War Museum, 18001/6/1–2, J.C. Bernard.

[24] A. Marwick, *British Society Since 1945* (Penguin, 1990), p. 202.

always be richer in our minds than the working classes, just by reading books.' But her arrogance was tinged with anxiety:

> Labourers can earn a lot of money these days; God, they must have money the prices they charge! But all they are concerned with is revenge, in the petty ways of their minds. Jealousy and bitching is their main occupation.[25]

This mixture of arrogance and anxiety remained characteristic of many middle-class responses. 'How many times do we hear stories of footballers revelling the night away in some nightclub?' wondered a Nottingham man at the end of the century. 'The majority of English footballers are paid grotesque salaries and many of them have a working-class mentality: a fatal combination.'[26] The 1960s' housing estates, concluded a Professor of Criminology at Loughborough University, 'that's where everything awful resides. You find large numbers of criminals there. They burgle each other and they assault each other.'[27]

WORKING-CLASS AWARENESS AND RESENTMENT

Working-class people were no less aware. They recognized the sharp material differences that separated the skilled from the unskilled, the employed from the unemployed, the respectable from the rough. But they understood too that however much such heterogeneity camouflaged their common class identity, it was rarely sufficiently powerful enough to destroy it. Indeed, it has been seen in previous chapters that while the state, education, religion and the media, and work reinforced working-class identity and sometimes encouraged working-class pride, they also generated working-class resentment.

Working people, like those from the middle class, took care to shop in ways consistent with their class identity (as well as their class aspirations and anxieties). They tended to avoid specialist shops, and for many years regarded department stores and even supermarkets with a certain amount of suspicion. Almost anything, many seemed to feel, was preferable to the condescension of shop assistants in middle-class stores.[28]

Working-class shoppers preferred, for much of the century, to patronize the corner shop, the Co-op and the branches of national chain stores. Corner shops, everybody knew, were generally run by people of modest means, and as Peter Mathias has pointed out, in these circumstances, 'a working-class background and consciousness could be a precious asset. Such men knew their future markets instinctively and innately.'[29] The Co-operative Movement too was established by, and for, working-class people – and even after the Second World War 60 per cent of skilled workers in

---

[25] Marwick, *British Society*, p. 207.

[26] *Observer*, 29 September 2002. I owe this reference to Kristina Bennert.

[27] 'Crime', *The Sunday Times Magazine*, 8 October 2000, p. 55.

[28] M. Tebbutt, *Making Ends Meet: Pawnbroking and Working-Class Credit* (Leicester: Leicester University Press, 1983), p. 194. P. Scott, 'The twilight world of interwar British hire purchase', *Past and Present*, 177, 2002.

[29] P. Mathias, *Retailing Revolution: A History of Multiple Retailing in the Food Trades Based Upon the Allied Suppliers Group of Companies* (Longman, Green and Co., 1967), p. 106. Cf. W. Woodruff, *The Road to Nab End: An Extraordinary Northern Childhood* (Abacus, 2002), p. 50.

London used the stores on a regular basis.[30] The chain store took over where the Co-operative Movement left off. For, as an interviewee explained to Mass-Observation in the early 1940s, 'They are a good system for the working class pocket. Their stuff is not for rich people's standards, but for the working man's family they make the money go further.'[31] Class identity slipped easily into class resentment. 'Clothes? I can't afford to buy clothes', complained a middle-aged 'artisan' a few years later:

> I need a new suit of clothes but I can't pay £15 for a suit. I know they have been cheaper but the utility suits are no good at all. It takes nearly three weeks wages to buy a suit of clothes – that's the way I have to reckon it. I suppose we ought to be getting used to it by now, but it's getting worse instead of better.[32]

Nor were working-class enthusiasts likely to overlook the relationship between sport, class identity and class pride. Sports such as angling, billiards, boxing, darts, rugby league, snooker and soccer became associated closely – and sometimes almost exclusively – with working-class (male) culture.[33] During the late nineteenth and early twentieth centuries, suggests Tony Mason, football played its part in encouraging 'the idea among working men that they were part of a group with similar experiences and interests which were not shared by the bulk of another group, the middle classes'. Indeed, he goes on to argue that, 'The widespread experience which working men had of playing and watching association football probably aided the formation of a more general consciousness of class.'[34]

During the early years of the twentieth century, newspaper, survey and oral evidence suggests, the relationship between sport, class identity and class pride began to solidify. The billiards' correspondent of the *Daily Herald* insisted in 1919 that he wanted 'no narrow class prejudices' in the sport. 'With the game becoming more democratic every day, I am hoping to see in the very near future representatives from working-men's clubs throw down the gage to the best players in the amateur world for title honours.'[35] Thirty years later, Mass-Observation reported on working-class concern that class barriers were inhibiting British sporting success. 'There is plenty of talent', claimed an Edinburgh paper worker, 'but working children don't get the opportunity – it's not tapped.'[36] It was when she moved from primary to grammar

---

[30] Mass-Observation, 2460, 'A Report on People and the Co-op', 1947, pp. 3, 5, 40. See also J. Birchall, *The International Co-operative Movement* (Manchester: Manchester University Press, 1997), p. 86; L. Sparks, 'Consumer Co-operation in the UK 1945–93', in J. Benson and G. Shaw (eds), *The Retailing Industry, Volume 3 Post 1945 – Retail Revolutions* (Tauris, 1999).

[31] Mass-Observation, 1532 'Report on Shopping Habits (Part III), 1942, p. 20. See also S.R. Davey, *Recollections* (Sheffield Women's Printing Co-op, n.d.), p. 25.

[32] Mass-Observation, 3089, 'Notes on the Cost of Living', 1949, p. 8.

[33] J. Lowerson, 'Brothers of the Angle: Coarse Fishing and English Working-Class Culture, 1850–1914', in J. Mangan (ed.), *Pleasure, Profit, Proselytism: British Culture and Sport at Home and Abroad 1700–1914* (Cass, 1988); S. Shipley, 'Tom Causer of Bermondsey: A boxer hero of the 1890s', *History Workshop*, 15, 1983.

[34] T. Mason, *Association Football and English Society 1863–1915* (Brighton: Harvester, 1981), pp. 242, 256.

[35] *Daily Herald*, 2 April 1919.

[36] Mass-Observation, 3045, 'A Report on British Sport', 1948, p. 15.

school in the 1960s that a working-class girl from Barrow-in-Furness first realized the basis of such resentment. Her classmates 'had their own tennis racquets and their own brand new leather satchels and all the hockey gear with them, and mine was all from my cousin'.[37]

Such class awareness and resentment proved difficult to dislodge. Whatever the unifying impact of the two world wars, they certainly did not eliminate class differences, class identity or class pride. Carmarthenshire solicitor Cecil Phillips was sent to fight in Gallipoli in 1915. Watching his troopship re-coal in Malta en route to the campaign, he was fascinated, he recalled, by 'the ceaseless chatter of the lower class Maltese which likened them to monkeys'. Depressed about the conditions in which he and his colleagues had to exist once in Turkey, he was incensed to learn a few months later that, 'the Welsh miners are out again. The men are mad about it, and they would soon deal with them if they had the opportunity.'[38]

Trade-union representatives saw things rather differently. Soon after the war, a national organizer for the farmworkers' union attempted to draw upon his members' class awareness and resentment when addressing a strike meeting in Staffordshire.

> During the war they were told that they, the labourers, were really the people that mattered, and the workers believed it ... The cause of the unrest was that the eyes of the working man had been opened during the war, by being told that they were of the greatest importance to the life of the nation – they believed it. They were promised that if they went forth to the battlefields they would come back to a land that was a fit place for heroes to live in ... Now the working class were asking the Government to cash the IOU, which they had failed to do.[39]

Whatever the tensions revealed (or exacerbated) by the First World War, the Second World War tends to be remembered in a much more positive light. It was the 'people's war', 'our finest hour', the time when the people of the country pulled together to defeat the common enemy. It revealed, it is said, a sense of national purpose that transcended the age, gender, ethnic, class and other divisions that normally segmented British society. The early years of the war are imbued with particular

---

[37] University of Lancaster, Social and Family Life in Preston, Lancaster and Barrow, 1940–70, Mrs P5B, p. 32.

[38] R. Barlow, 'The Gallipoli Campaign 1915: Experiences of two Carmarthenshire men', *Carmarthenshire Antiquary*, xxvii, 1992, pp. 80, 82. I am grateful to Huw Bowen for this reference. For the dispute, see A. Mor-O'Brien, 'Patriotism on trial: The strike of the South Wales Mines, July 1915', *Welsh History Review*, 12, 1984. See also 'What Welsh soldiers think of the strike', *Observer*, 18 July 1915; *Daily Express*, 30 September 1915; N. Ferguson, *The Pity of War* (Penguin, 1999), pp. 206–7. For industrial relations during the Second World War, see A. Tyndall, 'Patriotism and principles: Order 1305 and the Betteshanger Strike of 1942', *Historical Studies in Industrial Relations*, 12, 2001.

[39] N. Mansfield, 'Class conflict and village war memorials, 1914–24', *Rural History*, 6, 1995, p. 74. See also M. Swenarton, *Homes Fit for Heroes: The Politics and Architecture of Early State Housing in Britain* (Heinemann, 1981); M. Petter, ' "Temporary Gentlemen" in the aftermath of the Great War: Rank, status and the ex-officer problem', *Historical Journal*, 37, 1994. Also '250,000 women on the farms', *Observer*, 24 February 1918.

significance. The evacuation of British troops from Dunkirk, the 'Battle of Britain' fought by Fighter Command, and the population's dogged resistance to the 'Blitz' on London and other cities by the German *Luftwaffe* all epitomized, it is believed, the 'bulldog spirit' of the island race. This was 'British or English moral pre-eminence, buttressed by British unity'.[40]

Contemporaries began to explain the stoical reaction of London's East Enders to the authorities' failure to plan properly for the Blitz in terms of the 'myth of the Cockney wisecracking over the ruins of his world'.[41] It was an analysis that found its way into both the historical canon and the national consciousness. The attack on Buckingham Palace in September 1940 (and the Queen's remark that, 'I'm glad we've been bombed. It makes me feel I can look the East End in the face') has assumed almost iconic status. 'Nothing', concluded Angus Calder in 1969, 'was more calculated to arouse a feeling of solidarity across the classes.'[42]

However, Calder and others interested in the shaping of national ideology have begun to reconsider.[43] At the turn of the millennium, Channel 4 produced a programme in its *Secret History* series about the Battle of Britain. Even those critical of the programme conceded the fundamental validity of its argument. 'It is not that I'm pretending that there wasn't a class divide', conceded the *Daily Telegraph*'s television reviewer: 'the Auxiliary Air Force attracted the flying-helmeted upper classes, while, as war approached, the lower social echelons joined the Volunteer Reserve. It was when the two sides were thrown together that the problems started – different living quarters, segregated messes (if only divided by a curtain) and the fact that auxiliary pilots became Pilot Officers while those from the Volunteer Reserve became Sergeant Pilots.' It could not be otherwise, he concluded. That 'is the sort of society pre-war Britain was.'[44]

Those wishing to challenge the conventional, class-collaborative view of British society during the war have further ammunition at their disposal. They can point, for example, to the study *War Factory* that Mass-Observation published in the autumn of 1943. The trouble in the machine shop, it emphasized, was 'not that the girls do not realise that their work is important to the war, but that the majority of them are so little *interested in the war that they do not care whether their work is important to it or not*'.[45] Critics of the class-collaborative view of British society can also draw upon evidence such as that contained in a Home Office intelligence report, two years earlier, on labour problems on Merseyside. 'The workers' idea (possibly distorted) of the employers' attitude to the war effort appears important. It seems that their patriotism is over-shadowed by their unwillingness to make profits for employers

---

[40] A. Calder, *The Myth of the Blitz* (Pimlico, 1992), pp. 1–2.

[41] A. Calder, *The People's War: Britain 1939–1945* (Pimlico, 1969), p. 165.

[42] Calder, *People's War*, p. 168. The Queen's remark was cited admiringly in her obituaries 60 years later: *Sunday Times*, 31 March 2002; *Daily Mail*, 1 April 2002; *Daily Mirror*, 1 April 2002.

[43] Calder, *Myth*, p. xiii. J. Bourne, 'Goodbye to all that? Recent writing on the Great War', *Twentieth Century British History*, 1, 1990.

[44] *Daily Telegraph*, 26 July 2000. Also Imperial War Museum, 004634/6, Reel 4/5, D.A. Nicholls; *Guardian*, 26 July 2000.

[45] Mass-Observation, *War Factory: A Report* (Gollancz, 1943), p. 45.

whom they regard as their natural enemies.'[46] Indeed, Harold L. Smith suggests that while there were signs of reduced 'class feeling' in the months following Dunkirk, such 'feeling' continued to be important throughout the war, and possibly contributed to the Labour Party's victory in the general election of 1945.[47]

The more astute scholars of Britain's twentieth-century social history have always recognized the co-existence of class identity alongside national identity.[48] Sometimes they reinforced one another, sometimes they cut across one another, and sometimes they appeared to exercise no discernible effect upon one another. In all events, class was neither an ideological construction to be explained away by postmodernist theorizing nor a backward-looking barrier to modernization to be eradicated by growing national prosperity. A survey conducted in 1972 by Richard Scase revealed that 70 per cent of manual workers regarded themselves as working-class.[49] An opinion poll carried out by the *Guardian/ICM* in 1999 repeated some of the questions put by Geoffrey Gorer in 1955. It concluded that,

> Britain is as class-ridden as ever it was in the mid 1950s, but we now see ourselves as overwhelmingly middle class rather than working class ... The number of people describing themselves as working class has shrunk from fifty-four percent to forty-one percent.[50]

NATION, NATIONALITY AND NATIONAL IDENTITY

What then was the relationship between class identity and national identity? It will come as no surprise at this stage of the book to discover that this is another of those questions that are easier to ask than they are to answer. Indeed, it will be recalled from the beginning of the chapter that when considering such issues it is important to distinguish clearly between developments in Great Britain, England, Wales and Scotland, and to be clear what is meant by nation, nationality and national identity.

Nation, nationality and national identity are often confused. Thus at the risk of infuriating specialists in the field, it has been decided to adopt three working definitions which, it is hoped, will expedite the analysis that follows. The terms nation

---

[46] H.L. Smith (ed.), *Britain in the Second World War: A Social History* (Manchester: Manchester University Press, 1996), p. 45.

[47] Smith, *Britain*, p. 41. S. Fielding, P. Thompson and N. Tiratsoo, *"England Arise": The Labour Party and Popular Politics in 1940s Britain* (Manchester: Manchester University Press, 1995); M. Waller, *London 1945: Life in the Debris of War* (John Murray, 2004).

[48] See, for example, P. Dodd, 'Englishness and the National Culture', in R. Colls and P. Dodd (eds), *Englishness: Politics and Culture 1880–1920* (Croom Helm, 1987); P. Mandler, 'Against "Englishness": English culture and the limits to rural nostalgia, 1850–1940', *Transactions of the Royal Historical Society*, 5, 1997; Richards, *Films and British National Identity*; J. Springhall, *Youth, Empire and Society: British Youth Movements, 1883–1940* (Croom Helm, 1977). Cf. L. Colley, 'Whose nation? Class and national consciousness in Britain 1750–1830', *Past and Present*, 113, 1986.

[49] Marwick, *British Society*, p. 208.

[50] A. Travis, 'How we left the working class and joined the middle class,' *The Guardian*, 29 December 1999. See also, R. Hattersley, 'Class war will always be with us', *The Guardian*, 25 March 2002; M. Savage and A. Miles, *The Remaking of the British Working Class, 1840–1940* (Routledge, 1994), pp. 89–90.

and nationality can be dealt with quickly since they are not the direct concern of this investigation. The nation, many now agree, is best understood as an ideological construction, an 'imagined community'.[51] This is less opaque than it may appear. 'As an initial working assumption', explains Eric Hobsbawm, 'any sufficiently large body of people whose members regard themselves as members of a "nation" will be treated as such.'[52] Nationality, on the other hand, is a legal term. It means, and there is no disagreement about this, the nation to which one officially belongs, the nation that issues one with a passport.

It is national identity, rather than the nation or nationality, that is the concern of this chapter.[53] And national identity, like the nation, is an ideological construction: it is the nation to which one believes that one belongs. It is here that the complications begin to mount. It is important to recognize, for instance, that one can believe that one belongs to more than one nation. It is important to recognize too that the nation (or nations) to which one believes one belongs may or may not be the same as that to which one officially belongs. And it is important to recognize that it is possible to adopt a number of different stances towards the nation (or nations) to which one believes one belongs: one can be proud of one's nationality, ashamed of it, or indifferent towards it.

BRITISH NATIONAL IDENTITY AND NATIONAL PRIDE

The children of Britain were subjected, it was seen in Chapter 5, to a substantial, albeit declining, programme of patriotic, nationalistic and imperial propaganda. Defensive or aggressive, celebratory or cautionary, the message reiterated time and again was that Britain was different – and that Britain was best. The debate that erupted in the 1980s and early 1990s over the type of history that should be taught as part of the *national* curriculum demonstrates the importance that many continued to attach to the inculcation of shared national values and beliefs.[54]

The people of Britain, whatever their age, gender, ethnicity and class, were reminded of British national identity whenever there was a discussion about the British constitution, the British army, or the British Empire.[55] They were reminded again whenever they went shopping, chose a holiday, followed their favourite sport, read the paper, listened to the radio or watched the television. Shopkeepers focused on the British/non-British origins of their products as they thought best. Those selling

[51] B. Anderson, *Imagined Communities: Reflections on the Origin and Spread of Nationalism* (Verso, 1983).

[52] E.J. Hobsbawm, *Nations and Nationalism since 1870: Programme, Myth, Reality* (Cambridge: Cambridge University Press, 1990), p. 8.

[53] B. Williamson, *The Temper of the Times: British Society since World War II* (Oxford: Blackwell, 1990), pp. 89–93; European Science Foundation, *Representations of the Past: National Histories in Europe* (Strasbourg: ESF, 2004).

[54] My italics. A. Howkins, 'A Defence of National History', in R. Samuel (ed.), *Patriotism*, Vol. 1, p. 19. 'The imperial inheritance', *Observer*, 13 June 1909; 'New works at Luton', *Observer*, 22 May 1927. M. Halcrow, *Keith Joseph: A Single Mind* (Basingstoke: Macmillan, 1989), Ch. 20; S. Berger, 'British and German Socialism Between Class and National Identity', in S. Berger and A. Smith (eds), *Nationalism, Labour and Ethnicity, 1870–1939* (Manchester: Manchester University Press, 1999), p. 42.

[55] Richards, *Films and British National Identity*, pp. 7–8.

high-class goods stressed, for example, that their cigars came from Cuba, their leather from Spain, their fashions from France. Those catering for the mass market (fashion shops and hairdressers aside) tended to emphasize the indigenous origins of their products. During the 1930s, Cadbury's explained that it used 'Milk from British farms only', Aspro traded under the slogan 'British to the Core', while Vauxhall Motors claimed to embody, 'All That Is Best in British Motoring'.[56] Even the producers of British sherry got into the act. 'Whiteway's British sherry is of the same high standard of quality as their Port style wines. The reasonable price at which it is sold now brings a Sherry type wine within the reach of all, and not just a drink for the well-to-do. It is also most excellent and economical.'[57] Indeed, a Gallup poll survey of 1939 revealed that 46 per cent of respondents did their best to discover whether or not the products they were considering purchasing had been made in Britain, and used the information to boycott goods produced in Germany, Italy and Japan.[58]

During the second half of the century, the British became, in some respects at least, less proud of their British identity. Relative economic decline, poor industrial relations, the withdrawal from Empire, and the Suez débâcle provided few opportunities for national rejoicing (albeit plenty of opportunities for racist stereotyping).[59] A Consumer Council report of 1980 revealed a typically ambivalent approach. It concluded that,

> several mothers recognise that T-shirts and cheap clothing from Hong Kong will probably be of inferior quality and will not wear/wash as well as the UK equivalent … Consumers feel that if there is a choice between two identical products – one Foreign and one British – they will select the latter, but that is as far as Patriotism goes … 'Buying British', if not a thing of the past, is being regarded now as a luxury that not all can afford to indulge in.[60]

However, the media continued to reinforce notions of British identity and British superiority. The most popular television comedy of the 1970s and 1980s, for example, was reputed to be *Dad's Army*, a series about a group of elderly men in a wartime Home Guard unit in an out-of-season seaside resort. It encapsulated, mocked – and celebrated – what many felt it was to be British. The butcher, Corporal Jones, constantly recalls his service under Kitchener in the Sudan, where he fought in the battle of Omdurman. The bank manager, Captain Mainwairing, 'maintains the typically British disdain for the French. He thinks them not much use after lunch: "All that wine and garlic – it's very debilitating. All they know how to do is chase women." '[61]

---

[56] Benson, *Consumer Society*, pp. 144–6.

[57] *Express and Star*, 15 December 1936.

[58] G.H. Gallup, *The Gallup International Public Opinion Polls: Great Britain 1937–1975* (Random House, 1976), p. 19. See also R. Glasser, *Growing Up in the Gorbals* (Glasgow: Chatto & Windus, 1986), p. 70.

[59] R. Hattersley, *Fifty Years On: A Prejudiced History of Britain since the War* (Abacus, 1997), p. 114; Marwick, *British Society*, pp. 101–2.

[60] A. Foster, 'Country of Origin Marking: The Consumer's View', *Retail and Distribution Management*, March–April 1980, p. 48.

[61] Richards, *Films and British National Identity*, p. 362. See G. McCann, *Dad's Army: The Story of a Classic Television Show* (Fourth Estate, 2001). Cf. ' "True Brit" replies to the burning of the flag', *Daily Mail*, 1 April 1980.

The relationship between advertising, the media, national identity and national pride is exceptionally difficult to disentangle. It is easy enough to describe advertising and media strategies, a great deal more difficult to ascertain their impact upon popular attitudes. In all events, by the turn of the millennium sections of the media revealed a widespread, and apparently deep-seated, nostalgia for a time when, they believed, British national identity had been unchanging and unchallenged. 'In the Fifties,' recalls a *Mail on Sunday* columnist, 'we knew what Britishness was ... Our footballers had unmistakably English names like Tom Finney or Stanley Matthews or Sam Bartram. If there were men around called Gianfranco Zola, you tended to find them selling ice cream'.[62]

However powerful (or offensive) such nostalgia might be, it points to the potency, rather than the powerlessness, of late-century notions about what it was to be British. Indeed, any belief in the demise of British national identity was laid firmly to rest by the public response to the Falklands War of 1982, the death of Diana, Princess of Wales in 1997 and the funeral, five years later, of Queen Elizabeth, the Queen Mother. 'Everybody's trying to understand the reaction to the Queen Mum's death, with the four-mile queues, people waiting in the cold for six hours to pay their respects', noted Tessa Jowell, the Secretary of State for Culture, Media and Sport. But she did not find the public response surprising. The crowds gathered, she believed, because people were yearning to express a sense of British national identity, 'a number of common values about decency, about solidarity, about the degree to which we are interdependent'.[63] Others drew less reassuring conclusions. There was no doubt, confirmed Sir Terence Conran, that nobody could touch the British when it came to organizing royal pageantry. But pride jostled with dismay.

> It is in such sharp contrast to the public services that we receive during our daily lives – chaos on our roads and railways, delays at our airports, disruptions at our schools, dismay in our National Health Service – and perhaps most depressingly, our inability to manufacture anything in this country any longer.[64]

ENGLISH NATIONAL IDENTITY AND NATIONAL PRIDE

The discussion of British national identity and national pride in no way exhausts the question of national awareness in twentieth-century Britain.[65] The English, the Welsh and the Scots, like the British, were always aware of their national identity. Indeed, the Welsh and Scots, unlike the British and the English, became increasingly proud of – or at least increasingly confident in – the national identities that helped to define them.[66]

---

[62] S. Steven, 'Why reality is a foreign land to Mr Hague', *Mail on Sunday*, 11 March 2001.

[63] J. Ashley, 'New Labour's nanny takes on the boys', *The Guardian*, 15 April 2002.

[64] T. Conran, 'Our perfectly paradoxical pomp', *The Sunday Times*, 14 April 2002.

[65] Only a minority of Britons saw themselves as European. J.R. Llobera, 'What Unites Europeans', in N. Guibernau (ed.), *Governing European Diversity* (Sage, 2001), p. 175;

[66] R. Weight, *Patriots: National Identity in Britain, 1940–2000* (Basingstoke: Macmillan, 2002); R. Colls *Identity of England* (Oxford: Oxford University Press, 2002).

Surprisingly perhaps, English national identity and national pride are the most difficult of the three to disentangle, and the least likely of the three to attract scholarly or other interest. 'The test', claimed Bernard Crick, in 1991, 'is bibliographic. Look at the subject catalogue in any major library under "nationalism". One will discover references to shelves of books on nationalism, whether analytical, polemical and celebratory, under American, French, German, Italian, etc., and certainly Irish, Welsh and Scottish, but often none, or astoundingly few, under "English".' All one might find, he concluded, is 'a handful of right rubbish written for the Public School prize-giving market of a generation ago'.[67]

The English tended to use the terms England and Englishness, Britain and Britishness more or less interchangeably. What was needed was more British stories, claimed the editor of the *London Magazine* in 1920. 'A fairly long editorial experience has satisfied me that the average Briton would rather read about English people in an English town than about Americans in America.'[68] Indeed, it was just a page or so ago that the *Daily Mail* columnist lamenting contemporary uncertainty about the meaning of *Britishness*, recalled the time when footballers had unmistakably *English* names.[69] The English knew that they were represented in sport by English football, rugby and cricket teams.[70] The English (together, confusingly, with the Welsh and Scots) knew too that they were taught English history at school, that they spoke the English language, and that England and Englishness were part of the national vocabulary.[71] 'England expects every man will do his duty', proclaimed Horatio Nelson; 'England is the mother of Parliaments', maintained John Bright; only 'Mad dogs and Englishmen go out in the midday sun', explained Noel Coward.[72]

Other public figures were not slow to elaborate. When the Bishop of London addressed a 'recruiting concert' in 1915, he told his audience, 'If you want to defend your wives and mothers, just slip across the silver streak and fight battles over there, so that an invader's foot may never stain the soil of England.'[73] One of Prime Minister Stanley Baldwin's recurring oratorical themes was the unchanging character of English rural life. His rhetoric reached its apogee, claims his biographer, in a speech that he delivered in 1924: 'The sounds of England, the tinkle of the hammer on the anvil in the country smithy, the corncrake on a dewy morning, the sound of the scythe against the whetstone, and the sight of a plough team coming over the brow of a hill …'[74] Urban life too was regarded as distinctive. 'The gentleness of English civilisation is perhaps its most marked characteristic', observed George Orwell in 1941. 'You notice it the instant you set foot on English soil. It is a land where the bus-conductors are

---

[67] B. Crick, 'The English and the British', in B. Crick (ed.), *National Identities: The Constitution of the United Kingdom* (Oxford: Blackwell, 1991), p. 92. But see, for example, Colls and Dodd (eds), *Englishness*.

[68] E. Middleton, 'More British stories wanted', *Daily Mail*, 17 February 1920.

[69] Steven, 'Reality'.

[70] Benson, *Consumer Society*, p. 155.

[71] A.H. Birch, *Political Integration and Disintegration in the British Isles* (Allen & Unwin, 1977), p. 135.

[72] J.M. and M.J. Cohen, *The Penguin Dictionary of Quotations* (Penguin, 1960), pp. 66, 121, 269.

[73] 'Bishop of London's appeal for recruits', *Observer*, 14 February 1915.

[74] R. Jenkins, *Baldwin* (Collins, 1987), p. 31. See also 'The future of the countryside', *Observer*, 19 January 1930.

good-tempered and the policemen carry no revolvers.'[75] Nearly 50 years later, on St George's Day 1987, Prime Minister John Major took up the theme in an evocation of Englishness/Britishness that attracted an enormous amount of attention – and derision:

> Fifty years from now, Britain will still be the country of long shadows on county grounds, warm beer, invincible green suburbs, dog lovers and pools fillers and – as George Orwell said – 'old maids cycling to holy communion through the morning mist'.[76]

Popular sentiment was at once more hard-edged and more difficult to disentangle. It seems, however, that English people's pride in their national identity, pretty much universal during the first half of the century, dipped thereafter, only to revive again with the approach of the millennium.[77] In the years before, during and after the Second World War, there was – in England at least – widespread acceptance of, and admiration for, English values and English identity. In 1938, for instance, an East End docker bumped into a Mass-Observation worker, and launched into a diatribe against the Jews. 'Well, cheerio,' he concluded, 'I don't know who you are and I don't care, I'm an Englishman and I'm not afraid of anyone.'[78]

Thereafter, however, there was a growing feeling that England was failing to adapt to the new world order and so forfeiting the traditional economic, military, imperial and political foundations on which the country's national pride had been based.[79] There were further pressures to contend with by the end of the century. The drive for closer European integration, the 'troubles' in Northern Ireland, the talk about regional assemblies, the demand for devolution in Wales and Scotland – and the resurgence of football hooliganism – all bred uncertainty about national identity.[80] But the uncertainty seemed to stimulate, rather than inhibit, pride in being English. A survey carried out at the turn of the millennium by the National Centre for Social Research revealed that the proportion of English people saying they owed allegiance to England, rather than Britain, had increased from 7 to 17 per cent in just two years. The conclusions of the report were clear and rather disturbing:

> We have found that those who feel English are indeed different from those who feel British, being consistently more inclined to want to shut out the outside world. Indeed 'Little Englanders' appear to be alive and well, if not yet very thick on the ground.[81]

---

[75] G. Orwell, *The Lion and the Unicorn: Socialism and the English Genius* (Penguin, 1982), p. 41.

[76] J. Paxman, *The English: A Portrait of a People* (Penguin, 1999), p. 142.

[77] Cf. Light, *Forever England*, pp. 8–9.

[78] Mass-Observation, 'A12, Anti-Semitism Survey', 1938, p. 3. Also, 2466, 'State of Undergraduate Opinion in Oxford', 1947, p. 2.

[79] Birch, *Political Integration*, p. 137.

[80] See, for example, C. Harvey, 'English Regionalism: The Dog that Never Barked', in Crick (ed.), *National Identities*; R. Colls and B. Lancaster (eds), *Geordies: Roots of Regionalism* (Edinburgh: Edinburgh University Press, 1992), Preface.

[81] J. Carvel, 'The rise of the Little Englanders', *The Guardian*, 28 November 2000.

The press picked up on the uncertainty. 'History, pride and England's crisis of identity', ran the headline over a *Daily Mail* feature by its editor Max Hastings. 'As memories of Empire and World War II recede, and immigration changes the nature of our society – in some important respects for the better – we have lost our way.'[82]

WELSH NATIONAL IDENTITY AND NATIONAL PRIDE

The Welsh became, if anything, increasingly confident in their Welshness. Resentment at English economic, social and cultural domination reinforced awareness of Welsh national identity, and thus provided the mainspring of modern Welsh nationalism.[83] Welsh cultural awareness manifested itself in many ways. Gervase Phillips claims, for example, that although more than 20 per cent of the male population of the Principality enlisted in the British army between 1914 and 1918, the experience did not overwhelm the distinctively Welsh character of those participating in the hostilities.[84] Hugh Bowen believes that during the 1920s, the choral outpourings of Swansea Town football club supporters 'allowed many spectators to give vocal expression to their identity and celebrate their Welshness – in Welsh naturally – if only for ninety minutes on a Saturday afternoon'. Visiting English teams, he concluded, 'often felt that they were playing in an unfamiliar foreign land'.[85] The Second World War, like the First, brought the Welsh and English together: 'there was frictions there between the Welsh boys and the English troops ... The Welsh boys was speaking their own language and we didn't like the fact that we didn't have many [Welsh] NCOs.'[86]

It was the Welsh language that provided the bridge – for both men and women – between cultural awareness and political assertiveness. Plaid Cymru (the Welsh Party) was founded in the mid-1920s to defend and promote the Welsh language, with the Welsh Language Society established in the early 1960s with similar aims – but a more militant approach. Neither made much headway initially: Plaid Cymru, for instance, had fewer than 4,000 members in the mid-1960s.[87] Thereafter, however, economic restructuring, long-term unemployment, English exploitation of Welsh water, and English people's purchasing of second homes in the Principality combined to stimulate a revival in nationalist support. When the Welsh Assembly met finally in 1999, Plaid Cymru secured 28 per cent both of the direct vote and of the 60 seats that were available.[88] Indeed, even in areas of North Wales such as Denbighshire and

---

[82] M. Hastings, 'History, pride and England's crisis of identity', *Daily Mail*, 4 May 2002.

[83] Birch, *Political Integration*, p. 118. Also Museum of Welsh Life, 8203/1, P. Barrett.

[84] G. Phillips, 'Dai Bach Y Soldiwr: Welsh soldiers in the British Army 1914–1918', *Llafur*, 6, 1993, p. 94.

[85] H. Bowen, 'Jack Fowler', in P. Stead and H. Richards (eds), *For Club and Country: Welsh Football Greats* (Cardiff: University of Wales Press, 2000), p. xx. I owe this reference to Hugh Bowen.

[86] Imperial War Museum, 11484/1, I. Duxberry.

[87] Birch, *Political Integration*, p. 128. Also Hobsbawm, *Nations*, p. 139. In fact, the proportion of the Welsh population speaking Welsh declined from 44 per cent in 1911 to 19 per cent in 1981 (information from Sally Smith).

[88] D. Butler, 'Electors and Elected', in A.H. Halsey (ed.), *Twentieth-Century British Social Trends* (Basingstoke: Macmillan, 2000), p. 400.

Flintshire where nationalism failed to become a clearly defined movement, Welshness, it seems, remained a key component of communal identity.[89]

SCOTTISH NATIONAL IDENTITY AND NATIONAL PRIDE

The Scots too became more assertive. It was Scottish social and cultural independence – unlike Welsh social and cultural subordination – that fuelled the Scots' sense of national identity. The Scottish religious, legal and educational systems were different from, and thought by Scots to be superior to, those operating south of the border. The Scots tended to see themselves as Scottish first, and British second. This was true literally as well as metaphorically. Scottish children, it was found, identified Scotland as 'their country', acknowledging that they were British only when they were older.[90] The Scots also tended to attach enormous importance, sports enthusiasts will know, to beating the 'auld enemy' at football. Over 149,000 people packed into Hampden Park to watch the first all-ticket England–Scotland game in 1937, and 50 years later millions of television viewers were able to watch Scottish supporters swinging from the goalposts and digging up the Wembley turf.[91]

It was not until the 1960s and 1970s, however, that nationalist politicians began to draw effectively upon the Scots' sense of national identity. Formed in the early 1930s, the Scottish National Party (SNP), like Plaid Cymru, took a considerable time to make its presence felt.[92] As in Wales, it was central government's management of the economy that fuelled nationalist assertiveness. Economic restructuring, long-term unemployment and disputes over the extraction of 'Scottish' oil all had their effect.[93] SNP membership reached 55,000 in 1967; the party won its first parliamentary seat three years later; and in the two general elections of 1974 it increased its share of the vote to not far short of 25 per cent.[94] When the Scottish Parliament (like the Welsh Assembly) met for the first time in 1999, the SNP (like Plaid Cymru) secured just under 30 per cent both of the direct vote and of the seats that were available.[95] Between 1992 and 2002, the proportion of those in Scotland describing themselves as Scottish increased from 72 per cent to 80 per cent while the proportion describing themselves as British declined from 25 per cent to 13 per cent.[96]

It is clear then that national identity and national pride need to be disaggregated on a national basis, in the same way that class identity and class pride can be understood

---

[89] K. Gildart, North Wales Miners : A Fragile Unity, 1945–1996 (Cardiff: University of Wales Press, 2001), p. 13. For English views of the Welsh, see J. Thomas, ' "Taffy was a Welshman, Taffy was a thief": Anti-Welshness, the press and Neil Kinnock', Llafur, 7, 1997.

[90] Birch, Political Integration, pp. 98–9; R. McCreadie, 'Scottish Identity and the Constitution', in Crick (ed.), National Identities, p. 39.

[91] Holt, Sport, pp. 259–60.

[92] T.M. Devine, The Scottish Nation, 1700–2000 (Basingstoke: Palgrave, 1999), p. 325.

[93] J. Mercer, Scotland: The Devolution of Power (John Calder, 1978), Chs x–xii; R. Levy, Scottish Nationalism at the Crossroads (Edinburgh: Scottish Academic Press, 1990), Ch. 3; C. Harvie, Scotland and Nationalism: Scottish Society and Politics 1707 to the Present (Routledge, 1998), pp. 183–7.

[94] Birch, Political Integration, pp. 108–9.

[95] Halsey (ed.), British Social Trends, p. 400.

[96] www.scpr.ac.uk/news/news bsa pr 2001.htm.

only when disaggregated on a class basis. Moreover, it is necessary to bear in mind the possibility that class identity and class pride were different in different parts of the country, and that national identity and national pride manifested themselves differently among the upper class, the middle class and the working class. And it is most certainly the case that class identity, class pride, national identity and national pride can be understood properly only when age, gender and ethnicity are inserted into the analysis.

AGE, CLASS AND NATION

The relationship between age, class, nation, identity and pride remains curiously neglected. However, it is widely accepted that as people grow older, they begin to hanker after stability and security, to grow increasingly censorious and conservative. 'In terms of any general definition of conservatism,' concludes Barrie Stacey, 'elderly people as a whole tend to be more conservative than middle-aged people and the latter tend to be more conservative than young adults.'[97] The argument here is somewhat different. It will be accepted that there was a relationship between age, class identity and national identity. But it will be suggested that as they grew older, people continued to identify with, and be proud of, their class identity; but that they became less inclined to identify with, and take pride in, their national identity.

Such claims may appear bizarre. We all know, do we not, that it is the young who are most likely to strike and join left-wing political parties, that it is the elderly who are most likely to deplore disruption, dislike foreigners, revere the royal family and oppose European integration? The key to unravelling this seeming contradiction lies in the distinction between age and generation.[98] The argument here is not that old people were more or less aware/proud of their class and nation than old people of previous generations. It is that as they grew older, people remained aware/proud of their class, but became less aware/proud of their nation.

What then was the relationship between age, class, class identity and class pride?It is not just Marxist historians inclined to homogenize intra-class differences who overlook the relationship between age and identity. Few scholars, whatever their ideological persuasion, seem to recognize the possibility of class identity and class pride changing over the life course.

It has been seen that for more than half the century, religion and education combined to instil and/or reinforce parental injunctions about the need for conformity, respectability and obedience to authority. However, it has been seen too that throughout the century it was the transition to work that taught young people the realities of class-based power and authority. Chafe though they might, most young people appeared to accept the disciplines of the workplace and absorb the lessons about class relationships

---

[97] B. Stacey, *Political Socialization in Western Society: An Analysis From a Life-span Perspective* (Arnold, 1978), pp. 143–4. Also Mass-Observation, A7, 'Report on West Fulham By-Election', 1938, p. 21; N.D. Glenn and T. Hefner, 'Further evidence on ageing and party identification', *Public Opinion Quarterly*, 36, 1972.

[98] See, for example, I. Benson, *Prime Time: A History of the Middle Aged in Twentieth-Century Britain* (Harlow: Longman, 1997), pp. 125–6; M.N. Franklin, *The Decline of Class Voting in Britain: Changes in the Basis of Electoral Choice, 1964–1983* (Oxford: Clarendon Press, 1985), pp. 22–3.

that employment laid before them.[99] They sometimes learned these lessons all over again when they began going out with the opposite sex. In 1965, 17-year-old Michael Escott, a postman's son from Devizes, eloped to Gretna Green with Jill Glover, the daughter of a major: 'Michael, a sixth-former at Devizes Grammar School, was wearing his school blazer when he left.'[100]

By the time they reached their twenties and thirties, experience and expediency had persuaded all but the most independently minded that there were few, if any, alternatives to the economic and political system in which they found themselves. But acceptance had many roots, and reluctance to complain was not necessarily the consequence of inter-class rapprochement. Although middle-aged workers were less likely than young workers to challenge their employers or criticize the class foundations of society, they probably expressed more dissatisfaction than their younger colleagues with the disciplines of the workplace. Ferdynand Zweig, one of the few scholars to explore such issues, found it difficult to decide which age group was the more class conscious. He concluded in the early 1950s,

> Outwardly at any rate, the impression I got was that a feeling of bitterness is much stronger among young men than it is among older men. But it must be taken into account that they can express themselves the more freely because they have a 'couldn't care less' spirit about their jobs, especially where the jobs are not particularly worthwhile, anyway.[101]

The middle class began to learn what the working class had always known, that there was no such thing as a job for life. Graham Sargeant reported in 1994:

> This year, many of my friends are reaching 50. One or two, riding high in affluence and achievement, are holding good parties. But their guests reveal a different story. For many more, the half century is bringing an end to careers they thought would go on a lot longer and, they hoped, further. To their amazement, they are cast as the fat being shed in the latest corporate diet plan.[102]

The evidence, it must be conceded, is far from strong. Nonetheless, there do appear to be some grounds for believing that the association so commonly made between youth, class identity and class pride is potentially misleading. The middle-aged and elderly, it seems, continued to identify with, and be proud of (or frustrated by) the positions they occupied within Britain's class structure.

There has been more interest in the relationship between age, national identity and national pride. But the findings are no easier to interpret. The studies that have been carried out tend to concentrate upon young people, upon the first half of the century and, despite their authors' best efforts, upon behaviour rather than attitudes.

---

[99] P. Rudd and K. Evans, 'Structure and agency in youth transitions: Student experiences of vocational further education', *Journal of Youth Studies*, 1, 1998, pp. 52–3.

[100] 'Schoolboy elopes with the major's daughter', *Daily Mail*, 6 January 1965. See also 'Pools heir elopes with store girl', *Daily Mail*, 1 September 1960.

[101] F. Zweig, *The British Worker* (Penguin, 1952), p. 60. Also R. Hoggart, *The Uses of Literacy: Aspects of Working-Class Life with Special Reference to Publications and Entertainments* (Penguin, 1957), p. 76.

[102] *The Times*, 26 September 1994.

Nonetheless, they do seem to suggest that as people grew older, their attachment to, and pride in, their nation tended to diminish, rather than increase.

These studies present a good deal of evidence attesting to young people's attachment to, and pride in, the nation state. John Springhall concludes from his examination of uniformed youth movements during the first 40 years of the century that they 'ensured the continuity of certain broadly conservative, conformist attitudes, particularly towards the British Empire'.[103] He cites, for instance, a claim made by the Scout Commissioner for Scotland during the 1920s. He was chiefly concerned with imparting, 'what we called the Scout spirit, something of what we call the public school spirit, which makes a boy play up and play the game for his side: something of what we call *esprit de corps*, which makes men do great deeds for their Regiment, forgetting themselves – and very much of what we call patriotism.'[104] Staffordshire schoolboy Roger Leese remembers his headmaster telling his class about the death of King George VI in 1952. Perhaps, he said to his friend, they had better not play football that evening.[105] A.H. Birch draws upon a combination of impressionistic and statistical evidence from the 1970s. He is struck by the fervour with which young promenaders sang 'Rule, Britannia' and 'Land of Hope and Glory' at the last night of the Proms, and he cites a survey published early in the decade which revealed that 48 per cent of young people between the ages of 14 and 17 agreed with the proposition that 'Britain is the best country in the world'.[106]

The lack of comparable interest in the attitudes of the middle-aged and elderly makes it difficult to sustain or refute the proposition that as people grew older, they became less aware, and less proud, of their national identity. However, there does exist certain – very limited – evidence challenging the view that people's political attitudes veered to the right as they grew older. It is generation, not age, that provides the key. Mark N. Franklin explains, for instance, that those first entitled to vote in the general election of 1929, 'will have been socialized during the years of Labour's rise to major party status'. This meant that they 'first had the chance to express a political preference in the election that saw this status confirmed (at the previous election Labour had won only 151 seats). It is not surprising', he concludes, 'that they and their successors provided the core of the class-based vote for that party.'[107]

The evidence, once again, is sketchy, and relates primarily to the middle of the century. However, there do seem some grounds for doubting the association conventionally made between age, national awareness and national pride. It may well be – one cannot put it more strongly – that some old people at least were less conservative and less aware/proud of their national identity than they had been when they were younger.

GENDER, CLASS AND NATION

The relationship between gender, class, nation, identity and pride has attracted a great deal more attention. The feminist movement has shown, if nothing else, how absurd it

---

[103] Springhall, *Youth*, p. 18.

[104] Springhall, *Youth*, p. 122. See also 'The pit-boy's boots', *Observer*, 11 September 1927.

[105] Information from Roger Leese.

[106] Birch, *Political Integration*, pp. 137–8.

[107] Franklin, *Decline of Class Voting*, p. 169.

is to assume that men and women felt the same, behaved the same or took the same view about the world in which they lived. Indeed, it will be shown here that women were less likely than men to be active politically, and that when they were active they were less likely to support parties of the left than the right. It will be suggested too that although women were less likely than men to join military and quasi-military organizations, they were probably more likely to adopt a broadly conservative view of the world.

However, very great care is required. The terms in which the debate is conducted are riven with – masculine – assumptions.[108] We might as well ask why men were enthusiastically class conscious and imperfectly patriotic, rather than why women were imperfectly class conscious and enthusiastically patriotic. All that can be said with any confidence is that men and women differed in their attitudes towards class and nation – and that these differences probably had their roots in the contrasting ideological, material – and class – circumstances in which they lived their lives.

There is no denying that the indicators normally used to measure class identity and class pride all point to women's 'failure' to define themselves and the world around them in class terms. Women, for instance, were much less likely than men to become involved in left-wing politics. Indeed, historians' attempts to rehabilitate women's activist credentials sometimes smack rather of desperation. Mike Savage and Andrew Miles claim, for example, that, 'The significance of women's involvement in the inter-war Labour Parties is rarely appreciated, but the figures are impressive. There were around 200,000 members of the women's section in the mid-1920s, and 155,000 individual women members in 1933, about 40 per cent of the total individual membership.'[109] But these figures look much less impressive when set alongside the membership of right-wing groups and women's 'non-political' organizations. The Tory Primrose League claimed a membership of 2 million in 1910. The Mothers' Union had over 5 million members in 1930, while the National Federation of Women's Institutes boasted a combined membership of almost 4.5 million in 1950 – and more than 3 million 40 years later.[110] Women were not expected to achieve much politically. When Prime Minister John Major promoted five women MPs in 1995, it was reported as 'Women's first step on the road to the top'.

> Bright, witty and with sharp political antennae, Mrs Knight, 44, is appointed Economic Secretary to the Treasury. She formerly ran her own chemical engineering firm and was a councillor in Sheffield with a Boadicea-like reputation for taking on ruling socialists.[111]

[108] B. Campbell, *The Iron Ladies: Why Do Women Vote Tory?* (Virago, 1987) pp. 1–4; M. Glucksmann, 'In a class of their own? Women workers in the new industries in inter-war Britain', *Feminist Review*, 24, 1986.

[109] Savage and Miles, *Remaking*, pp. 83–4. See also A. Bingham, ' "An era of domesticity"? Histories of women and gender in interwar Britain', *Cultural and Social History*, 1, 2004.

[110] Campbell, *Iron Ladies*, Chs 1–2; M. Pugh, *The Tories and the People 1880–1935* (Oxford: Blackwell, 1985), p. 27; B. Harrison and J. Webb, 'Volunteers and Voluntarism', in Halsey (ed.), *British Social Trends*, p. 597.

[111] 'Women's first step on the road to the top', *Daily Mail*, 7 July 1995.

Women were always less likely than their male colleagues to join a trade union.[112] Even unions that did not discriminate against female workers found it difficult to get them actively involved. During the first half of the century, for instance, many Preston women joined the town's Weavers, Winders and Warpers Association. However, 'most appear to have been concerned only with their wages and their domestic affairs; they simply paid their small subscription as a kind of insurance against the day when they might find themselves in dispute with the management'.[113] Mid-century retailing unions found themselves in something of a double-bind: 'Union administrators looked to women members to instigate action on their own behalf, while women members looked to the union to acknowledge their difficulties and create venues for action that would fit easily with family and other responsibilities.'[114]

However, the evidence is more ambiguous than conventional analysis allows. For, as Selina Todd has stressed recently, trade-union membership is neither the only nor perhaps the best measure of political participation and workplace militancy.[115] The textile workers of Preston identified themselves as working class, but displayed few obvious signs of working-class pride. What was true of Preston's textile unionists was probably true of working-class women generally. They were less likely than men to be in paid employment; and when they were, they were more likely to work in the tertiary sector where, it has been seen, employers found it easiest to persuade employees of the inevitability of existing power relationships. Indeed, it was argued earlier in the book that women across all sectors of the economy tended to regard their employers with indifference or respect rather than with indignation and resentment. But as the case of the Preston textile workers suggests, this does not mean that working-class women were unaware of their class identity. It means that although they were conscious of their class identity, they – like many men – displayed few obvious signs of class pride. When the Halewood sewing machinists went on strike in 1968, they repeatedly sought reassurance that the issue was grading rather than equal pay: 'Mention Equal Pay to the women up there (Halewood) and they don't want to know. They've got a different way of life up there. Up there the man is the boss.'[116]

Women, it seems to be accepted, were as enthusiastically patriotic as they were 'imperfectly' class conscious. Their contrasting stances can be interpreted, of course, as two sides of the same coin. Class identity and class pride, national identity and national pride are believed to cut across one another in ways inimical to the development of working-class patriotism. However, such assumptions are based upon unbalanced empirical and conceptual foundations. The trouble is that whereas we

---

[112] D. Gallie, 'The Labour Force', in Halsey (ed.), *British Social Trends*, pp. 309–10. Also, Mass-Observation, 2424, 'Trades Unions and Closed Shop', 1946, p. 7.

[113] E. Roberts, *A Woman's Place: An Oral History of Working-Class Women 1890–1940* (Oxford: Blackwell, 1984), p. 147.

[114] J. Cushman, 'Negotiating the Shop Floor: Employee and Union Loyalties in British and American Retail, 1939–1970', Glasgow University PhD, 2004.

[115] S. Todd, ' "Boisterous workers": Young women, industrial rationalisation and workplace militancy in interwar England,' *Labour History Review*, 68, 2003, p. 301.

[116] H. Friedman and S. Meredeen, *The Dynamics of Industrial Conflict. Lessons from Ford* (Croom Helm, 1986), pp. 151–2.

know a good deal about boys' and young men's membership of uniformed youth movements, about young men's experience of national service, and about adult men's participation in the two world wars, these were activities which, by definition, tell us nothing at all about women's behaviour and attitudes.[117]

In fact, it may be objected, institutional indicators are inherently unhelpful when adopting a gendered approach to the study of national identity and national pride. Nonetheless, the indicators which are available provide considerable support for the conventional view of women's conservatism. Let us look again at the popularity of such 'conservative' organizations as Townswomen's Guilds, the Mothers' Union and the National Federation of Women's Institutes.[118] In 1930, the Mothers' Union and Women's Institutes had 7 million members (a figure equivalent – almost unbelievably – to practically a third of the entire female population). Twenty years later, the two groups had well over 9 million members (a figure equivalent – still more unbelievably – to over a third of the entire female population). And even towards the end of the century, after decade upon decade of feminist struggle, the Mothers' Union and Women's Institutes boasted 4 million members (a figure greater than the entire population, male and female, of the Merseyside and West Midlands conurbations).[119] The statistical indicators, for what they are worth, offer no comfort at all to those seeking to challenge the conventional view of women's attachment to the 'traditional' values of hearth, home and nation.[120]

ETHNICITY, CLASS AND NATION

The debate about the relationship between ethnicity, class and nation may be less complex but it is certainly a great deal more sensitive.[121] Traduced almost beyond repair by the assumptions brought to bear upon it, it revolves around the argument that those from ethnic minorities can never be truly British (English, Welsh or Scottish). Many of the indigenous population believed that even when those from ethnic minorities were born and brought up in the country, they remained a race apart. They were regarded as unable to compete economically, unwilling to integrate socially, and incapable of identifying properly with the values and symbols of the country in which they lived.[122] When Norman Tebbitt promulgated his so-called 'cricket test' in 1990, it was castigated by some as offensive – but welcomed by others as little more than common sense.[123]

---

[117] Clarke, *Hope and Glory*, p. 232; Benson, *Working Class in Britain*, pp. 150–1.

[118] See also 'Ideal Homes Parliament', *Daily Mail*, 10 February 1920.

[119] B. Harrison and J. Webb, 'Volunteers and Voluntarism', in Halsey (ed.), *British Social Trends*, p. 597; B. Wood and J. Carter, 'Towns, Urban Change and Local Government', in Halsey (ed.), *British Social Trends*, p. 419.

[120] N. Yates (ed.), *Kent in the Twentieth Century* (Woodbridge: Boydell Press/Kent County Council, 2001), pp. 87–9, 392.

[121] K. Gardner, *Age, Narrative and Migration: The Life Course and Life Histories of Bengali Elders in London* (Oxford: Berg, 2002), p. 94.

[122] Northumbria County Record Office , T/76, Miss Haywood; 'Secret invasion', *Birmingham Mail*, 3 July 1926; 'Hospitals soon to have foreign doctors only', *Daily Mail*, 1 April 1975; 'White is wrong colour for job', *Daily Mail*, 4 April 1990.

[123] See Mac's cartoon in *Daily Mail*, 6 April 1990.

The class consciousness of those from ethnic minorities has never come in for the same condemnation. But immigrants and their children were perfectly well aware of their class position. From the time they set foot in the country, they realized, the great majority of them, that they did working-class jobs, that they lived in working-class areas, that they faced class – and other – discrimination, and that they were likely to be regarded, however they might think of themselves, as unambiguously and irredeemably working class.[124] Lilian Bader, for instance, was born in Liverpool in 1918, the daughter of an English mother and a West Indian father. She always wanted to work at something other than domestic service.

> I was rather naive and rather truthful, so that when I worked for the doctor and his wife, I went and found out about evening classes, and she just stopped me from having the evening off at that time. They were determined, and this applied to most working class kids (not just coloured kids) you had to know your place.[125]

But class identity rarely developed into class pride. The reason was, as Lilian Bader implies, that any form of class consciousness had to compete with ethnic identity and ethnic pride. And it was ethnic identity and ethnic pride that tended to emerge victorious. Insofar as those from ethnic minorities sought to challenge unappealing material and ideological aspects of British society, they did so through ethnic, rather than class-based, organization, activity and agitation.[126]

Moreover, ethnic identity and ethnic pride had to compete with national identity and national pride. 'I've been to Barbados 4 times', explained the 13-year-old granddaughter of a Barbadian immigrant, 'and I think it's boring. There's nothing to do and the animals are horrible – lots of lizards and stray dogs. I would never live there. I'm English really. I just go there to see family.'[127] Usually however, it was ethnic identity and ethnic pride that tended to emerge the winner. It was the hostility of the majority population that provides the key to understanding minority attitudes.[128] In the mid-1960s, a mathematics, biology and English teacher resigned from his secondary modern school

---

[124] It was often said that immigrants automatically dropped a social class. D. Pearson, *Race, Class and Political Activism: A Study of West Indians in Britain* (Gower, 1981), p. 159; S. Patterson, *Dark Strangers: A Study of West Indians in London* (Penguin, 1963), pp. 34–5. See also C. Volante, 'Identities and Perceptions: Gender, Generation and Ethnicity in the Italian Quarter, Birmingham, c1891–1938', University of Wolverhampton PhD, 2001, Ch. 7. It may be, however, that European immigrants were regarded as 'outside' the British class system. I owe this point to Laura Ugolini.

[125] B. Bousquet and C. Douglas, *West Indian Women at War: British Racism in World War II* (Lawrence & Wishart, 1991), p. 131. See D. Frost, 'Ambiguous Identities: Constructing and De-Constructing Black and White "Scouse" Identities in Twentieth-Century Liverpool', in N. Kirk (ed.), *Northern Identities: Historical Interpretations of 'The North' and 'Northerners'* (Aldershot: Ashgate, 2000).

[126] They did, however, favour the Labour Party over the Conservative Party. See Marwick, *British Society*, p. 216.

[127] 'Black in Britain', *The Guardian*, 20 March 1995.

[128] For class differences in majority population attitudes, see Mass-Observation , 2411, 'Anti-Semitism and Free Speech', 1946.

in Birmingham because, he claimed, immigrant children were slowing the progress of their white classmates.[129] Thirty years later, a correspondent to the local paper in nearby Wolverhampton maintained that it was the 'attitude' of some young blacks in court that might explain the longer sentences they received.[130]

From the time they arrived in the country, the first generation of post-war Afro-Caribbean immigrants responded in kind to the prejudice that they faced. The 'whole experience of living in a white racist society has helped to forge a black identity where in many cases such an identity did not previously exist, or not consciously thought about'.[131] Sarah Thompson came to Brixton from Jamaica in the mid-1950s. 'It's my heart's desire to say bye bye Britain … I never felt I belonged here. It's not my home. Jamaica is my home, it's in my blood.'[132] A Wolverhampton man found it difficult to understand majority attitudes: 'there is good an' bad in all cultures. Yet, so why is it that we are stigmatised as being violent, ill-mannered, and things like that?'[133]

By the end of the 1970s, according to John Rex and Sally Tomlinson, the revolutionary black consciousness of groups like the Rastafarians had effectively displaced 'simple working-class consciousness' among Afro-Caribbeans in the Handsworth area of Birmingham.[134] Subsequent generations of Afro-Caribbean and other minority groups responded forcibly to the hostility they faced. Many regarded themselves as belonging to an oppressed minority. 'When you're in school you all get harassed together, and see yourself as one – *all a we is one*.'[135] They identified weakly, if at all, with the values and symbols of majority society. In 1981, reporters from the magazine *New Society* compared majority and minority responses to the marriage of Prince Charles and Lady Diana Spencer. Their report is intriguing both for the language it uses and for what it reveals about young people's responses. In Trafalgar Square, they found bunting, crowds and good-humoured banter about the wedding. There was 'a battalion' of skinheads arm in arm. 'Two of them are draped in union jacks. One has a face decorated with red, white and blue greasepaint.' In Brixton, on the other hand, they discerned few, if any, signs of celebration:

> Gaggles of young blacks hang around a wire enclosure, their fingers looped
> through the holes like prisoners. The air inside the fence – a kids' playground –
> is thick with marijuana smoke. A monotonous reggae beat pulses from a couple
> of giant speakers near the entrance. There is an air of repressed hostility. I feel
> my presence is barely tolerated …[136]

---

[129] *Daily Mail*, 2 July 1965.

[130] 'Anglo Saxon', *Express and Star*, 5 January 1993.

[131] W. James, 'The Making of Black Identities', in R. Samuel (ed.), *Patriotism: The Making and Unmaking of British National Identity, Volume II Minorities and Outsiders* (Routledge, 1989), p. 237.

[132] W. Webster, *Imagining Home: Gender, 'Race' and National Identity, 1945–64* (UCL Press, 1998), p. 41. Cf. Williamson, *Temper of the Times*, p. 49.

[133] Black and Ethnic Minority Project, 71. DX-624/6/69, Mr McPhearson.

[134] J. Rex and S. Tomlinson, *Colonial Immigrants in British Society: A Class Analysis* (Routledge & Kegan Paul, 1979), p. 292. See also R. Ramadin, *The Making of the Black Working Class in Britain* (Aldershot: Wildwood House, 1987), pp. 482–3.

[135] James, 'Black Identities', p. 239.

[136] Williamson, *Temper of the Times*, p. 236.

The relationship between ethnicity, class and nation seems then to be more easily unravelled than that between gender, class and nation. Members of minority communities had a great deal in common. It was not just that many shared a working-class identity. It was that whether or not they shared such an identity, they were often thought to do so by members of the majority population unable, or unwilling, to move beyond the crudest form of colour stereotyping. In such circumstances, it is not surprising that many members of Britain's ethnic minorities identified themselves only very weakly as British, English, Welsh or Scottish; and that even when they did so they displayed few signs of pride in their Britishness, Englishness, Welshness or Scottishness. At the end of the century, just 6 per cent of those describing themselves as black, and 7 per cent of those describing themselves as Asian, classified themselves as English.[137]

CLASS IDENTITY AND CLASS PRIDE, NATIONAL IDENTITY AND NATIONAL PRIDE

It is fitting that this, the final chapter, should deal with some of the most intractable issues discussed in the book. And intractable they are. Attitudes leave less evidence than behaviour, and attitudes towards class and nation place particular demands upon the historian. It is important to stress therefore that the arguments put forward in this chapter, still more than those propounded elsewhere in the book, are propositions to be examined rather than conclusions to be accepted. Nevertheless, it would be wrong to end on a note of indecision and uncertainty. It is clear that more people than one might expect identified with, and were proud of, both their class and their nation. Class identity, class pride, national identity and national pride intersected in ways that belie easy generalization and confirm the importance, yet again, of considering economic circumstances, age, gender, ethnicity and class when examining the social history of twentieth-century Britain.

---

[137] *The Guardian*, 28 November 2000. However, more than a third classified themselves as British. See also 'Black in Britain', *The Guardian*, 20 March 1995.

CONCLUSION

Fashions come and fashions go, in history as in everything else. Circumstances change, perspectives alter, empirical evidence accumulates and theoretical approaches move in and out of favour. Indeed, anybody reading this book knows perfectly well from their own experience that the way in which we perceive the past depends, in large measure, upon our vantage point as we look back. The childhood we recall as teenagers is unlikely to be the same as the one we think back to when we are adult, middle-aged or elderly. The memories we have of our education, our first love and our first job will depend, almost certainly, upon the ways in which our subsequent economic, emotional and professional lives have developed.

What is true of the personal is true of the public. Even a few years into the new millennium, the world looks very different from the way it did in 2000. We saw in the introduction to the book that turn-of-the-century reflections, retrospectives and reassessments revealed a paradox in the way in which the people of Britain viewed the world. There was a deep-seated concern that the economic successes of the twentieth century had not been accompanied by corresponding advances in other aspects of national life. Economic gains, it was felt, had not been matched by social improvements. Those on the right lamented the decline of Britain's economic, military and diplomatic power, the disintegration of national unity and what they saw as the decline of traditional family life. Those on the left bemoaned the persistence of Britain's great-power pretensions, and the economic, social and cultural inequalities that blighted, they believed, so many aspects of life in twentieth-century Britain.

Within just two to three years, these anxieties were compounded by new fears and uncertainties. The collapse of the stock market, the events of September 11, the threat from global terrorism, the growth of American isolationism and the volatility of international relations all seemed to herald unparalleled, and seemingly insoluble, threats to the economic, physical and psychological well-being of those living in the West. Whatever their roots and whether or not they were exaggerated, such anxieties undermined any lingering optimism as to the probability – let alone the inevitability – of economic, social, political and cultural progress.

We must accept therefore that historical judgements are necessarily provisional. But this does not mean that we can hide between claims of authorial objectivity or fears of readers' displeasure to avoid interpreting the evidence at our disposal and making clear exactly what we think. It is a fundamental part of the historian's task to explain, as well as describe, what happened in the past. And it is surely only sensible to use our interpretation of what happened in the past to inform our understanding of what is happening in the present – and even, dare one say, of what is likely to happen in the future.[1]

What view should we take then of the twentieth century as we look back from our vantage point early in the twenty-first century? It is never easy generalize in this way.

---

[1] R.J. Evans, *In Defence of History* (Granta, 1997).

I remarked towards the end of an earlier book that, 'Any attempt to encapsulate 90 years of working-class history in a single volume may well seem unduly ambitious, and any attempt to summarise the results of that undertaking in a few hundred words will no doubt seem foolhardy in the extreme.'[2] If that attempt seemed excessively foolhardy, what is one to make of this effort at generalization and interpretation? It appears almost recklessly ambitious to attempt to present a hundred years of a country's social history in one volume, *and* to claim to interpret that history in the light of broader economic, political, cultural, demographic and ideological developments, *and* to try to capture the experiences of all the major social groupings in the country. Hubris, one might think, has a good deal to answer for.

But although specialization has its place, so too does generalization. If historians are to avoid talking exclusively to one another, we must risk the wrath – and contempt – of our professional colleagues. This means being prepared to tackle big questions, pose broad generalizations, and draw upon theoretical approaches, methodological insights and empirical evidence over which we are able to claim little, if any, specialist expertise. Sometimes, perhaps, the outsider really does see more of the game. In all events, this author, like most historians who write 'big' books on 'big' subjects, can claim research experience in several of the major topics considered, a teaching background in many of the others, and a good knowledge of the scholarly literature on all of the rest. It is therefore in a spirit of cautious confidence – of restrained recklessness – that it has been decided to bring the book to a close with three conclusions that emerge, it is believed, from the analysis presented in the preceding eight chapters.

If there is one argument at the core of *Affluence and Authority* it is that in seeking to understand social (and political, cultural, demographic and ideological) developments, primacy should most often be afforded to the material circumstances of day-to-day life. It is true, of course, that we must be wary of advancing simplistic models of cause and effect, and wary too of ascribing a spurious prosperity to the whole of the population. Nonetheless, wariness must not descend into paralysis. And that means affirming that it was the long-term improvement in the standard of living that provides the single most important key to understanding the social history of twentieth-century Britain.

It has been seen in virtually every chapter of the book that there was a close, and causal, relationship between material, social, political, cultural, demographic and ideological developments. It was the growth of prosperity (and the persistence of poverty) that did much to determine the stance that people took towards consumption and class, and the health (or ill health) that they enjoyed (or endured). It was the need to earn a living that accounted, in large measure, for the underlying stability of society which constituted, as so many have remarked, one of the most striking features of the country's twentieth-century history. It was the growth of prosperity, changing attitudes towards consumption, and the need to earn a living that, along with other material circumstances, provided the context within which people lived their lives. It is only when one has a firm sense of this material context that one can begin to make sense of people's personal, class and other relationships. The ways in which men and

---

[2] J. Benson, *The Working Class in Britain, 1850–1939* (Harlow: Longman, 1989), p. 207.

women, parents and children, the upper class, the middle class and the working class, immigrants and the native-born, the English, the Welsh and the Scots felt about themselves, thought about one another and dealt with one another tended most often to reinforce conventional notions of gender, age, class, ethnic and national identity.

The second issue addressed in the book is the balance between economic and social developments. Indeed, it will be recalled from the introduction to the volume that one of its central purposes was to challenge, or at least modify, the view that economic gains were undermined by social losses, that the British people failed to respond as constructively as they should have to the economic improvements that they enjoyed. 'Economic gains, but social losses.' It is one of the most weary of all the clichés in the historical lexicon. But is it accurate? Does it really provide a helpful way of capturing the complexity and contradictions of a hundred years of social, economic (and other) change?

This is a case where personal values and personal attitudes intrude in particularly disruptive fashion. We all know, and have seen time and again in this book, that what some people regard as a loss, others regard as a gain – and others no doubt regard as neither loss nor gain. Nonetheless, most of us would surely agree that some of the changes occurring in Britain during the course of the century must be counted as social losses rather than social gains. How else is one to characterize the proliferation of so-called diseases of prosperity such as cancer, strokes, heart disease – and health-related anxiety? What else is one to make of so many people's conviction that community spirit was waning, interpersonal relationships deteriorating, and crime and violence spiralling out of control?

However, the majority of the social and ideological changes taking place are a great deal harder to characterize. There is no agreement, for example, over whether the extension of state regulation, the growth of sexual experimentation and the multiplication of single person households should be welcomed as the expansion of personal freedom or condemned as the debilitating erosion of family relationships. There is no agreement either as to whether the growth of Welsh and Scottish national pride constituted the long overdue expression of indigenous identities or the dangerous emergence of a threatening xenophobia.

But some of the changes that took place must surely be interpreted in a positive light. Only the most perversely nostalgic curmudgeon would wish to go back to the days when one child in eight died in infancy, and those that survived went out to work at the age of 14. Only those far removed from day-to-day realities would regret the passing of a time when a visit to the doctor was a matter of careful financial calculation, when there was no radio, cinema or television, when most people never went away on holiday, when both men and women could expect to die before they reached the age of 50. One does not have to be a naïve believer in unfettered progress to recognize that many, probably most, of the changes discussed in this book benefited more people than they harmed. If the complexity and contradictions of a hundred years of economic and social change really need to be summarized in a five-word epithet, it should not be 'economic gains, but social losses'. It should be 'economic gains *and* social gains'.

There is one further issue that has surfaced time, time and time again in the course of the book. This is the question of whether or not the concept of class is a help or a hindrance in seeking to unravel the social history of twentieth-century Britain (or the history, one is tempted to add, of other Western countries). This is a particularly fraught question for scholars of my generation, background and interests. During the first 20 years of my career, I, along with the overwhelming majority of my social and labour history colleagues, took it for granted that class existed, and that class was important.[3] Although we knew that the classes could be difficult to define, and difficult therefore to identify with precision, we were prepared, most of us, to use the term descriptively, and we were happy, some of us, to afford it explanatory power as well.

In the past 15 years or so, such confidence has come in for the most scathing of criticism. A new generation of scholars has launched a savage and relentless attack on the most basic tenets of historical conceptualization, methodology and analysis.[4] As part of the postmodernist onslaught, they questioned the existence, and thus significance, of social class. Class existed, they claimed, only when it was clearly and explicitly articulated in the 'texts' being consulted. We have seen that according to Patrick Joyce, one of the doyens of this putative new orthodoxy, there had emerged, even ten years ago, 'a powerful sense in which class may be said to have fallen. Instead of being a master category of historical explanation, it has become one term among many, sharing a rough equality with these others.'[5]

It is undeniably true – and indisputably welcome – that social class has no a priori claim to be 'a master category of historical explanation' – or a master category, for that matter, of historical description. No category does. Nevertheless, the evidence presented in this book confirms the danger of throwing the baby out with the bath water. *Affluence and Authority* has one final – rather unfashionable – lesson to impart. It teaches us, whether we like it or not, that we should not think of abandoning class-based analysis. Class needs to be set alongside – sometimes above, and sometimes below – categories such as age, gender and ethnicity when attempting to describe and explain the ways in which British social history developed during the course of the twentieth century. When this is done, it can be seen that there was a close, and causal, relationship between class developments, and material, social, political, cultural, demographic and ideological developments.

---

[3] J. Benson, *The Working Class in Britain, 1850–1939* (Tauris, 2003), p. 2.

[4] See, for example, K. Jenkins, *Rethinking History* (Routledge, 1991); K. Jenkins, *On 'What is History?':
From Carr and Elton to Rorty and White* (Routledge, 1995); A. Munslow, *Deconstructing History*
(Routledge, 1997). Those wishing to pursue the debate between postmodernist scholars and their critics
should consult *Social History* between, for example, 1991 and 1996.

[5] P. Joyce, *Democratic Subjects: The Self and the Social in Nineteenth-Century England* (Cambridge:
Cambridge University Press, 1994), p. 2.

FURTHER READING

Place of publication is London unless otherwise noted.

INTRODUCTION

There is no shortage of guides to the history of twentieth-century Britain. J. Black, *Modern British History since 1900* (Basingstoke: Macmillan, 2000) and E. Royle, *Modern Britain: A Social History, 1750–1985* (Arnold, 1987) offer useful introductions; P. Clarke, *Hope and Glory: Britain 1900–1990* (Penguin, 1996) provides, *inter alia*, a challenge to the commonly held view that the century is best seen in terms of decline. For Wales, see K.O. Morgan, *Rebirth of a Nation: Wales, 1880–1980* (Oxford: Oxford University Press, 1982) and for Scotland, T.M. Devine, *The Scottish Nation, 1700–2000* (Basingstoke: Palgrave, 1999). An indispensable statistical guide, upon which this book draws heavily, is A.H. Halsey (ed.), *Twentieth-Century British Social Trends* (Basingstoke: Macmillan, 2000).

There are also a number of studies focusing on particular parts of the century. For the years between 1900 and 1950, see J. Stevenson's wide-ranging and accessible *British Society, 1914–45* (Penguin, 1984) and A.J.P. Taylor's brilliantly acerbic *English History, 1914–1945* (Penguin, 1975). For the years following the Second World War, see in particular, A. Marwick, *British Society since 1945* (Penguin, 1982), B. Williamson, *The Temper of the Times: British Society since World War II* (Oxford: Blackwell, 1990), D. Childs, *Britain Since 1939: Progress and Decline* (Basingstoke: Palgrave, 2002) and A. Rosen's short, and slightly idiosyncratic, *The Transformation of British Life 1950–2000: A Social History* (Manchester: Manchester University Press, 2003). Also useful are the collection edited by J. Obelkevich and P. Catterall, *Understanding Post-War British Society* (Routledge, 1994), and a volume by Roy Hattersley, the former deputy leader of the Labour Party, *Fifty Years On: A Prejudiced History of Britain since the War* (Abacus, 1997).

WEALTH, COMFORT AND POVERTY

There are many studies of wealth, income and the cost of living. Among the best known are J. Burnett, *A History of the Cost of Living* (Penguin, 1969), S. Pollard, *The Development of the British Economy 1914–1980* (Arnold, 1983), C. More, *The Industrial Age: Economy and Society in Britain 1750–1985* (Harlow: Longman, 1989), and R. Floud and D. McCloskey (eds), *The Economic History of Britain since 1700*, 3 volumes (Cambridge: Cambridge University Press, 1994). For the less well-known human development approach, see S. Horrell, 'Living standards in Britain, 1900–2000: Women's century?' *National Institute Economic Review*, 172, 2000.

The growth of adolescent economic power is examined, in different ways, by K.D. Brown, *The British Toy Business: A History since 1700* (Hambledon Press, 1996) and D. Fowler, *The First Teenagers: The Lifestyle of Young Wage-Earners in Interwar Britain* (Woburn Press, 1995). There has been less interest in the material circumstances of the middle-aged and elderly, but see J. Benson, *Prime Time: A History of the Middle Aged in Twentieth-Century Britain* (Harlow: Longman, 1997) and P. Thane, *Old Age in English History: Past Experiences, Present Issues* (Oxford: Oxford University Press, 2000).

Gender, ethnic and class inequalities have come in, naturally enough, for a good deal of attention. C. Glendinning and J. Millar (eds), *Women and Poverty in Britain* (Brighton: Wheatsheaf, 1987) and S. Horrell, 'Living standards in Britain, 1900–2000: Women's century?', *National Institute Economic Review*, 172, 2000 explore key aspects of women's economic well-being. R. Berthoud, 'Income and Standards of Living', in T. Modood and R. Berthoud (eds), *Ethnic Minorities in Britain: Diversity and Disadvantage* (Policy Studies Institute, 1997) provides one of the few detailed studies of ethnic minority living standards. There is a much more extensive literature on the relationship between class, prosperity and poverty. See, for example, D. Cannadine, *The Decline and Fall of the British Aristocracy* (Yale University Press, 1989), S. Gunn and R. Bell, *Middle Classes: Their Rise and Sprawl* (Cassell, 2002), J. Benson, *The Working Class in Britain, 1850–1939* (Harlow: Longman, 1989) and J.C. Brown, 'Poverty in Post-War Britain', in J. Obelkevich and P. Catterall (eds), *Understanding Post-War British Society* (Routledge, 1994). The interaction of age, gender, ethnicity and class has generated some fascinating studies. See, for instance, J. Bourke, *Working Class Cultures in Britain, 1890–1960: Gender, Class and Ethnicity* (Routledge, 1994), C. Chinn, *They Worked all their Lives: Women of the Urban Poor in England, 1880–1939* (Manchester: Manchester University Press, 1988), E. Roberts, *A Woman's Place: An Oral History of Working-Class Women 1890–1940* (Oxford: Blackwell, 1984) and K. Gardner, *Age, Narrative and Migration: The Life Course and Life Histories of Bengali Elders in London* (Oxford: Berg, 2002).

SPENDING AND SAVING

Historians have never shown a great deal of interest in saving. However, research into working-class strategies of poverty has helped to enhance our understanding of late nineteenth- and early twentieth-century developments. P. Johnson's outstanding *Saving and Spending: The Working-Class Economy in Britain 1870–1939* (Oxford: Clarendon Press, 1985) can be supplemented by M. Tebbutt, *Making Ends Meet: Pawnbroking and Working-Class Credit* (Leicester: Leicester University Press, 1983) and J. Benson, 'Working-class consumption, saving, and investment in England and Wales, 1851–1911', *Journal of Design History*, 9, 1996.

There has always been much more interest in spending, a tendency that has been reinforced in recent years by the surge of interest in consumption, consumerism and consumer society. J. Benson, 'Consumption and the consumer revolution', *Refresh*, 23, 1996, provides a simple starting point, and D. Miller (ed.), *Acknowledging Consumption: A Review of New Studies* (Routledge, 1995) a much richer and broader introduction. There are also a growing number of full-length studies. Among the most useful and original are P.K. Lunt and S.M. Livingstone, *Mass Consumption and Personal Identity: Everyday Economic Experience* (Buckingham: Open University Press, 1992) and G. Cross, *Time and Money: The Making of Consumer Culture* (Routledge, 1993). See also J. Benson, *The Rise of Consumer Society in Britain, 1880–1980* (Harlow: Longman, 1994).

There are also important studies of age, gender, ethnicity and class-related spending, many of them concerned as much with mainstream anxieties as with minority practices. For teenagers, see G. Pearson, *Hooligan: A History of Respectable Fears* (Basingstoke: Macmillan, 1983), S. Chibnall, 'Whistle and zoot: The changing meaning of a suit of clothes', *History Workshop*, 20, 1985, and J. White, *The Worst Street in North London: Campbell Bunk, Islington, Between the Wars* (Routledge & Kegan Paul, 1986). For the middle-aged, see J. Benson, *Prime Time: A History of the Middle Aged in Twentieth-Century Britain* (Harlow: Longman, 1997).

Although women's spending has received less attention than one would expect, there are a number of useful studies: R. Scott, *The Female Consumer* (Associated Business Programmes, 1976), E. Roberts, *A Woman's Place: An Oral History of Working-Class Women 1890–1940* (Oxford: Blackwell, 1984) and J. Obelkevich, 'Consumption', in J. Obelkevich and P. Catterall (eds), *Understanding Post-War British Society* (Routledge, 1994). Working-class spending attracted a great deal of anxiety. Two classic studies continue to repay careful attention: R. Hoggart, *The Uses of Literacy: Aspects of Working-Class Life with Special Reference to Publications and Entertainments* (Penguin, 1957) and J.H. Goldthorpe, D. Lockwood, F. Bechhofer and J. Platt, *The Affluent Worker in the Class Structure* (Cambridge: Cambridge University Press, 1969). Among more recent studies, see P. Johnson, 'Conspicuous consumption and working-class culture in late Victorian and Edwardian Britain', *Transactions of the Royal Historical Society*, 38, 1988 and J. Carey, *The Intellectuals and the Masses: Pride and Prejudice among the Literary Intelligentsia, 1880–1939* (Faber and Faber, 1992).

HEALTH, ILL HEALTH AND GOOD HEALTH

The study of health has changed substantially in recent years. Happily, there are two very well-informed synoptic studies: H. Jones, *Health and Society in Twentieth-Century Britain* (Harlow: Longman, 1994) and A. Handy, *Health and Medicine in Britain since 1860* (Basingstoke: Palgrave, 2001). Life expectancy is approached best through R. Fitzpatrick and T. Chandola, 'Health', in A.H. Halsey (ed.), *Twentieth-Century British Social Trends* (Basingstoke: Macmillan, 2000). Sickness statistics are less amenable to easy identification, but J.C. Riley makes an important contribution in *Sick, Not Dead: The Health of British Workingmen during the Mortality Decline* (Baltimore, MD: Johns Hopkins University Press, 1997).

There is a great deal of debate as to the causes of changes in sickness and life expectancy (T. McKeown, *The Modern Rise of Population* (Arnold, 1976)). The way to understand developments, many now believe, lies less in public health and medical intervention than in economic circumstances and patterns of consumption. See therefore A. Digby and N. Bosanquet, 'Doctors and patients in an era of National Health Insurance and private practice, 1913–38', *Economic History Review*, xli, 1988, D.J. Oddy and D.S. Miller (eds), *Diet and Health in Modern Britain* (Croom Helm, 1985) and J. Burnett, *Plenty and Want: A Social History of Food in England from 1815 to the Present Day* (Routledge, 1989).

Young people were notorious, of course, for indulging in activities injurious to their health. For early-century smoking, see R. Elliot, 'Growing up and giving up: Smoking in Paul Thompson's "100 Families"', *Oral History*, 29, 2001. For late-century drug-taking and sexual behaviour, see M. Plant and M. Plant, *Risk-Takers: Alcohol, Drugs, Sex and Youth* (Tavistock/Routledge, 1992) and K. Wellings, J. Field, A. Johnson and

J. Wadsworth, *Sexual Behaviour in Britain: The National Survey of Sexual Attitudes and Lifestyles* (Penguin, 1994). Old people, by contrast, were known for their vulnerability: M. Pelling and R.M. Smith (eds), *Life, Death and the Elderly: Historical Perspectives* (Routledge, 1991) and M. Sidell, *Health in Old Age: Myth, Mystery and Management* (Buckingham: Open University Press, 1995).

Women's health became a cause of increasing concern. For a sense of the scholarship now available, see S. Wilkinson and C. Kitzinger (eds), *Women and Health: Feminist Perspectives* (Taylor & Francis, 1994) which explores, as its title suggests, gender differences in health and health care. E. Showalter, *The Female Malady: Women, Madness and English Culture, 1830–1980* (Virago, 1993) considers how ideas about feminine behaviour shaped views of female insanity. M. Blaxter and E. Paterson, *Mothers and Daughters: A Three-Generational Study of Health Attitudes and Behaviour* (Aldershot: Avebury, 1982) reports the results of an important longitudinal investigation.

The relationship between ethnicity and health has attracted little detailed research. But two useful studies were published towards the end of the century: L. Marks and M. Worboys (eds), *Migrants, Minorities and Health: Historical and Contemporary Studies* (Routledge, 1997) and J.Y. Nazroo, *The Health of Britain's Ethnic Minorities: Findings from a National Survey* (Policy Studies Institute, 1997). The relationship between class and health has long attracted interest, with the first half of the century served better than the second. C. Webster, 'Healthy or hungry thirties?', *History Workshop*, 13, 1982 should be read in conjunction with N. Whiteside, 'Counting the cost: Sickness and disability among working people in an era of industrial recession, 1920–39', *Economic History Review*, xl, 1987. There are also a number of thought-provoking contemporary studies: B.S. Rowntree, *Poverty: A Study of Town Life* (Macmillan, 1902), M.S. Rice, *Working-Class Wives: Their Health and Conditions* (Penguin, 1939) and D. Black, J. Norris, C. Smith and P. Townsend, *Report of the Working Group on Inequalities in Health* (Department of Health and Social Security, 1980).

THE COERCIVE POWER OF THE STATE

There are two excellent, broad studies of twentieth-century policing: C. Emsley, *The English Police: A Political and Social History* (Harlow: Longman, 1991) and B. Weinberger, *The Best Police in the World: An Oral History of English Policing from the 1930s to the 1960s* (Aldershot: Scolar, 1995). See also D. Garland, *The Culture of Control: Crime and Social Order in Contemporary Society* (Oxford: Oxford University Press, 2001). For the policing of industrial disputes, see R. Geary, *Policing Industrial Disputes: 1893–1985* (Methuen, 1985), B. Fine and R. Millar (eds), *Policing the Miners' Strike* (Lawrence & Wishart, 1985) and R. Samuel, B. Bloomfield and G. Boanas (eds), *The Enemy Within: Pit Villages and the Miners' Strike of 1984–5* (Routledge & Kegan Paul, 1986).

There has been interest too in teenagers' anti-social behaviour. G. Pearson, *Hooligan: A History of Respectable Fears* (Basingstoke: Macmillan, 1983) examines public anxieties, S. Humphries, *Hooligans or Rebels? An Oral History of Working-Class Childhood and Youth 1889–1939* (Oxford: Blackwell, 1981) young people's resistance to attempts to control them. The authorities' dealings with black teenagers are considered – highly critically – by S. Hall, C. Critcher, T. Jefferson, J. Clarke and

B. Roberts, *Policing the Crisis: Mugging, the State, and Law and Order* (Basingstoke: Macmillan, 1978), and by M. Pratt, *Mugging as a Social Problem* (Routledge & Kegan Paul, 1980) and E. Cashmore and E. McLaughlin (eds), *Out of Order? Policing Black People* (Routledge, 1991).

Although mothers were frequently blamed for their children's failings, women themselves were rarely regarded as prone to criminality (F. Heidensohn, *Women and Crime* (Basingstoke: Macmillan, 1985) and S. Walklate, *Gender, Crime and Criminal Justice* (Cullompton: Willan, 2001)). The authorities were always much more concerned about male (generally working-class) intransigence and incorrigibility. The *Bulletin of the Society for the Study of Labour History* (and its successor the *Labour History Review*) has published a number of interesting articles as part of their long-running campaign against government secrecy. See, for example, D. Englander, 'Military intelligence and the defence of the realm: The surveillance of soldiers and civilians during the First World War', *Bulletin of the Society for the Study of Labour History*, 52, 1987, J. Callaghan and M. Phythian, 'State surveillance of the CPGB leadership, 1920s–1950s', *Labour History Review*, 69, 2004. Fascinating still is P. Wright, *Spy Catcher: The Candid Autobiography of a Senior Intelligence Officer* (Toronto: Stoddart, 1987).

THE MANIPULATIVE POWER OF RELIGION, EDUCATION AND THE MEDIA

Although R. Johnson, 'Educational policy and social control in early Victorian England', *Past and Present*, 49, 1970, and F.M.L. Thompson, 'Social control in Victorian Britain', *Economic History Review*, xxxiv, 1981, deal with the nineteenth rather than the twentieth century, they serve as thought-provoking introductions to the discussion in this chapter. The issues they raise are explored further in N. Chomsky, *Necessary Illusions: Thought Control in Democratic Societies* (Pluto, 1989) and E.S. Herman and N. Chomsky, *Manufacturing Consent: The Political Economy of the Mass Media* (Vintage, 1994).

The role that religion played in maintaining social order is contextualized in a number of wide-ranging studies: E.R. Norman, *Church and Society in England, 1770–1970: A Historical Study* (Oxford: Clarendon Press, 1976), C.G. Brown, *Religion and Society in Scotland since 1707* (Edinburgh: Edinburgh University Press, 1997) and G. Davie, *Religion in Britain since 1945: Believing Without Belonging* (Oxford: Blackwell, 1994). Historians of education pay less attention than one would expect to the maintenance of social order. But see, for example, A. Oram, *Women Teachers and Feminist Politics 1900–1939* (Manchester: Manchester University Press, 1996) and R. Lowe, *Schooling and Social Change 1964–1990* (Routledge, 1997). Historians of the media are much more alert to such issues. Particularly worth reading are J. Curran, A. Smith and P. Wingate (eds), *Impacts and Influences: Essays on Media Power in the Twentieth Century* (Methuen, 1987), J. Curran and J. Seaton, *Power without Responsibility: The Press and Broadcasting in Britain* (Routledge, 1991) and D. Strinati and S. Wagg (eds), *Come on Down? Popular Media Culture in Post-War Britain 1914–1999* (Basingstoke: Macmillan, 2000).

The supposed susceptibility of the young has stimulated a number of important contributions. Best known perhaps is S. Humphries, *Hooligans or Rebels? An Oral History of Working-Class Childhood and Youth 1889–1939* (Oxford: Blackwell, 1981). This can be supplemented by K. Boyd, 'Knowing Your Place: The Tensions of Manliness in Boys' Story Papers, 1918–39', in M. Roper and J. Tosh (eds), *Manful Assertions: Masculinities in Britain since 1800* (Routledge, 1991), J. Richards, 'Boy's Own Empire: Feature Films and Imperialism in the 1930s', in J.M. MacKenzie (ed.), *Imperialism and Popular Culture* (Manchester: Manchester University Press, 1986) and P. Tinkler, *Constructing Childhood: Popular Magazines for Girls Growing Up in England, 1920–1950* (Taylor & Francis, 1995). Girls grew up, but stereotyping persisted. See V. Walkerdine, *Democracy in the Kitchen: Regulating Mothers and Socialising Daughters* (Virago, 1980) and P. Kirkham and J. Thumin (eds), *Me Jane: Masculinity, Movies and Women* (Lawrence & Wishart, 1995).

The demonization of foreigners and immigrants also produced a scholarly reaction. The media have come in for particular opprobrium. See, for example, P. Braham, 'How the Media Report Race', in M. Gurevitch, T. Bennett, J. Curran and J. Woollacott (eds), *Culture, Society and the Media* (Methuen, 1982) and J. Tulloch, 'Television and Black Britons', in A. Goodwin and G. Whannel (eds), *Understanding Television* (Routledge, 1990). Also M. Gillespie, *Television, Ethnicity and Cultural Change* (Routledge, 1995) and L. Young, *Fear of the Dark: 'Race', Gender and Sexuality in the Cinema* (Routledge, 1996).

The relationship between class, religion, education and the media has been highly productive in terms of historical scholarship. The first half of the century is particularly well served. For religion, see R. Moore, *Pit-Men, Preachers & Politics: The Effects of Methodism in a Durham Mining Community* (Cambridge: Cambridge University Press, 1974); for education, see C. Heward, *Making a Man of Him: Parents and their Sons' Education at an English Public School 1929–50* (Routledge, 1988); and for the press, see T. Jeffery and K. McClelland, 'A World Fit to Live In: The *Daily Mail* and the Middle Classes 1918–39', in J. Curran, A. Smith and P. Wingate (eds), *Impacts and Influences: Essays on Media Power in the Twentieth Century* (Methuen, 1987). The classic study remains R. Hoggart, *The Uses of Literacy: Aspects of Working-Class Life with Special Reference to Publications and Entertainments* (Penguin, 1957). Destined perhaps to become a classic is J. Carey, *The Intellectuals and the Masses: Pride and Prejudice among the Literary Intelligentsia, 1880–1939* (Faber and Faber, 1992).

THE IRON DISCIPLINES OF WORK

There has always been a good deal of interest in the ways that large-scale employers exerted control over their employees. For the great nineteenth-century 'staples' of coal and cotton, see J. Benson, *British Coalminers in the Nineteenth Century: A Social History* (Harlow: Longman, 1989) and A. Fowler, *Lancashire Cotton Operatives and Work, 1900–1950: A Social History of Lancashire Cotton Operatives in the Twentieth Century* (Aldershot: Ashgate, 2003). For the 'new' industries established during the 1920s and 1930s, see R.C. Whiting, *The View from Cowley: The Impact of Industrialization upon Oxford, 1918–1939* (Oxford: Clarendon Press, 1983) and H. Friedman and S. Meredeen, *The Dynamics of Industrial Conflict: Lessons from Ford*

(Croom Helm, 1986). It is too soon to have a fully rounded study of late twentieth-century call centres, but P. Taylor and P. Bain lay some of the foundations with 'Trade unions, workers' rights and the frontier of control in UK call centres', *Economic and Industrial Democracy*, 22, 2001.

Although the control of unmechanized, casual and part-time work has never excited the same interest, there exist valuable studies, *inter alia*, of developments in building, agriculture and domestic service. See, for instance, J. McKenna and R.C. Rodger, 'Control by coercion: Employers' associations and the establishment of industrial order in the building industry of England and Wales, 1860–1914', *Business History Review*, 59, 1985, N. Mansfield, *English Farmworkers and Local Patriotism, 1900–1930* (Aldershot: Ashgate, 2001) and N. Gregson and M. Lowe, *Servicing the Middle Classes: Class, Gender and Waged Domestic Labour in Contemporary Britain* (Routledge, 1994).

Employee reactions to employer attempts to discipline them are a good deal more difficult to disentangle. For responses, formal and informal, see R. Church and Q. Outram, *Strikes and Solidarity: Coalfield Conflict in Britain 1889–1966* (Cambridge: Cambridge University Press, 1998), N. Tiratsoo and J. Tomlinson, 'Restrictive practices on the shopfloor in Britain, 1945–60: Myth and reality', *Business History*, 36, 1994 and P. Thompson and S. Ackroyd, 'All quiet on the workplace front? A critique of recent trends in industrial sociology', *Sociology*, 29, 1995.

The best guide to the ways in which young people learned about, and reacted to, work discipline is still P. Willis, *Learning to Labour: How Working Class Kids Get Working Class Jobs* (Gower, 1977). This should be read in conjunction with studies such as M. Glucksmann, *Women Assemble: Women Workers and the New Industries in Inter-War Britain* (Routledge, 1990) and two volumes by Elizabeth Roberts: *A Woman's Place: An Oral History of Working-Class Women 1890–1914* (Oxford: Blackwell, 1984), and *Women and Families: An Oral History 1940–1970* (Oxford: Blackwell, 1995).

The ways in which those from ethnic minorities responded to work and work discipline is best approached through studies of Birmingham and Bristol published during the 1960s and 1970s. See therefore, J. Rex and R. Moore, *Race, Community and Conflict: A Study of Sparkbrook* (Oxford: Oxford University Press, 1967), A.H. Richmond, *Migration and Race Relations in an English City: A Study in Bristol* (Oxford: Oxford University Press, 1973) and K. Pryce, *Endless Pressure: A Study of West Indian Lifestyles in Bristol* (Duckworth, 1979).

The relationship between class, work and authority is considered, of course, in many of the works recommended above. For middle-class responses, see R. Lewis and A. Maude, *The English Middle Classes* (Penguin, 1953) and S. Gunn and R. Bell, *Middle Classes: Their Rise and Sprawl* (Cassell, 2002). There exists, not surprisingly, a much more extensive literature on working-class reactions. For a recent guide to the first half of the century, see A. McIvor, *A History of Work in Britain 1880–1950* (Basingstoke: Palgrave, 2001). Other important studies include F. Zweig, *The British Worker* (Penguin, 1952) and J.H. Goldthorpe, D. Lockwood, F. Bechhofer and J. Platt, *The Affluent Worker in the Class Structure* (Cambridge: Cambridge University Press, 1969). For the impact of not working, it is instructive to read the final chapters of J. Burnett, *Idle Hands: The Experience of Unemployment, 1790–1990* (Routledge, 1994).

MEN AND WOMEN, PARENTS AND CHILDREN

Feminist scholarship has transformed our understanding of family life. The two chapters in E. Roberts, *The Changing Lives of Women since 1940* (Oxford: Blackwell, 1996) provide a concise introduction to historiographical (and structural) developments. J. Weeks, *Politics and Sexuality: The Regulation of Sexuality since 1800* (Harlow: Longman, 1989) and L.A. Hall, *Gender and Social Change in Britain since 1880* (Basingstoke: Macmillan, 2000) extend the analysis both conceptually and empirically.

Not everything discussed in this chapter is dealt with adequately in the literature: there are few detailed studies, for instance, of maternal selfishness, paternal selflessness, or adolescent compliance and conformity. Nevertheless, the last two decades have seen major advances on many fronts. We know a good deal more than we used to about courtship, marriage and divorce thanks to books such as J.R. Gillis, *For Better, For Worse: British Marriages 1600 to the Present* (Oxford: Oxford University Press, 1985), R. Phillips, *Untying the Knot: A Short History of Divorce* (Cambridge: Cambridge University Press, 1991) and L. Davidoff, M. Doolittle, J. Fink and K. Holden, *The Family Story: Blood, Contract and Intimacy 1830–1960* (Harlow: Longman, 1999).

Of all the stages of the life course, it was adolescence that provoked the greatest interest – and greatest anxiety. Compare, for example, A. Woollacroft, ' "Khaki fever" and its control: Gender, class, age and sexual morality on the British homefront in the First World War', *Journal of Contemporary History*, 29, 1994 with M. Schofield, *The Sexual Behaviour of Young People* (Harlow: Longman, 1965) and M. Plant and M. Plant, *Risk-Takers: Alcohol, Drugs, Sex and Youth* (Tavistock/Routledge, 1992). For the middle-aged and elderly, see J. Benson, *Prime Time: A History of the Middle Aged in Twentieth-Century Britain* (Harlow: Longman, 1997) and E. Grundy, 'Longitudional perspectives on the living arrangements of the elderly', in M. Jefferys (ed.), *Growing Old in the Twentieth Century* (Routledge, 1989).

There have been particular advances in the study of women's domestic lives. A. Oakley, *The Sociology of Housework* (Oxford: Blackwell, 1985) set the agenda, and scholars like E. Malos (ed.), *The Politics of Housework* (New Clarion Press, 1980) and J. Giles, *Women, Identity and Private Life in Britain, 1900–50* (Basingstoke: Macmillan, 1995) developed it further. Women's experiences and relationships can be understood, of course, only in conjunction with men's. This may seem little more than a statement of the obvious, but it has helped to revitalize the study of family relationships. For recent interpretations, see S. Bruley, *Women in Britain since 1900* (Basingstoke: Macmillan, 1999), T. Roper and J. Tosh, *Manful Assertions: Masculinities in Britain since 1800* (Routledge, 1991), L.A. Hall, 'Impotent ghosts from No Man's Land, flappers' boyfriends, or crypto-patriarchs? Men, sex and social change in 1920s Britain', *Social History*, 21, 1996 and J. Lewis, *Women in Britain since 1945: Women, Family, Work and the State in the Post-War Years* (Oxford: Blackwell, 1992).

There is more published on ethnic minority families than one might expect. Among the most useful are V.S. Khan, *Minority Families in Britain: Support and Stress* (Basingstoke: Macmillan, 1979) and S. Beishon, 'People, Families and Households', in T. Modood and R. Berthoud (eds), *Ethnic Minorities in Britain: Diversity and Disadvantage* (Policy Studies Institute, 1997).

However, it was the working-class family that always attracted the greatest attention. Some of the research produced is of exceptional interest. Contemporary works include E. Slater and M. Woodside, *Patterns of Marriage: A Study of Marriage Relationships in the Urban Working Classes* (Cassell, 1951), and K. Wellings, J. Field, A. Johnson and J. Wadsworth, *Sexual Behaviour in Britain: The National Survey of Sexual Attitudes and Lifestyles* (Penguin, 1994). For late-century interpretations, see C. Chinn, *They Worked All Their Lives: Women of the Urban Poor in England, 1880–1939* (Manchester: Manchester University Press, 1988), and two books by Elizabeth Roberts: *A Woman's Place: An Oral History of Working-Class Women 1890–1940* (Oxford: Blackwell, 1984) and *Women and Families: An Oral History 1940–1970* (Oxford: Blackwell, 1995). More specialized studies include G. Frost, '"The black lamb of the black sheep": Illegitimacy in the English working class, 1850–1939', *Journal of Social History*, 37, 2003, and P. Summerfield, 'Women in Britain since 1945: Companionate Marriage and the Double Burden', in J. Obelkevich and P. Catterall (eds), *Understanding Post-War British Society* (Routledge, 1994).

THE POWER OF CLASS, THE POWER OF THE NATION

Recent attacks on the concept of social class challenge the foundations upon which this chapter – indeed this entire book – are based. Postmodernist criticisms of class-based analysis are often disconcertingly opaque, but K. Jenkins, *Rethinking History* (Routledge, 1991), K. Jenkins, *On 'What is History?': From Carr and Elton to Rorty and White* (Routledge, 1997) and A. Munslow, *Deconstructing History* (Routledge, 1997) provide accessible introductions. R.J. Evans, *In Defence of History* (Granta, 1997) mounts a spirited defence, and G.W. Bernard, 'History and Postmodernism', in G.W. Bernard (ed.), *Power and Politics in Tudor England* (Aldershot: Ashgate, 2000) deserves more attention than historians of the twentieth century are likely to give it. M. Savage and A. Miles, *The Remaking of the British Working Class, 1840–1940* (Routledge, 1994) argue stoutly – and in my view correctly – for a class analysis of late nineteenth- and early twentieth-century developments.

F.M.L. Thompson's unparalleled research into the aristocracy can be approached through two papers he read to the Royal Historical Society: 'English landed society in the twentieth century: I Property: Collapse and survival', *Transactions of the Royal Historical Society*, 40, 1990 and 'English landed society in the twentieth century: II New poor and new rich', *Transactions of the Royal Historical Society*, 1, 1991.

Social historians have generally shown less interest in their own class than in the working class. But there are a number of valuable exceptions. R. Lewis and A. Maude, *The English Middle Classes* (Penguin, 1953) was described by its publisher as 'A critical survey of the history, present conditions and prospects of the middle classes, from whom come most of the nation's brains, leadership and organizing ability.' This should be compared, if one can get hold of it, with R. Samuel, 'Suburbs under siege: The middle-class between the wars Part III', *New Socialist*, May/June 1983. Much more accessible will be S. Gunn and R. Bell, *Middle Classes: Their Rise and Sprawl* (Cassell, 2002), the book of the BBC2 television series of the same name.

Any guide to the literature on working-class attitudes, experiences and behaviour must be extremely selective. Autobiographies like R. Roberts, *The Classic Slum: Salford Life in the First Quarter of the Century* (Penguin, 1973) and B.L. Coombes,

These Poor Hands: The Autobiography of a Miner Working in South Wales (Gollancz, 1939) provide an engaging starting point. Contemporary studies such as B.S. Rowntree, *Poverty: A Study of Town Life* (Macmillan, 1902), F. Zweig, *The British Worker* (Pelican, 1952) and D. Black, J. Norris, C. Smith and P. Townsend, *Report of the Working Group on Inequalities in Health* (Department of Health and Social Security, 1980) are also illuminating. Among the book-length histories I value most highly are S. Meacham, *A Life Apart: The English Working Class, 1890–1914* (Thames & Hudson, 1977), E. Roberts, *A Woman's Place: An Oral History of Working-Class Women 1890–1940* (Oxford: Blackwell, 1984), J. White, *The Worst Street in North London: Campbell Bunk, Islington, Between the Wars* (Routledge & Kegan Paul, 1986), J. Bourke, *Working Class Cultures in Britain, 1890–1960: Gender, Class and Ethnicity* (Routledge, 1994) and N. Mansfield, *English Farmworkers and Local Patriotism, 1900–1930* (Aldershot: Ashgate, 2001). Useful too, I hope, is J. Benson, *The Working Class in Britain, 1850–1939* (Harlow: Longman, 1989/Tauris, 2003).

The literature on nationality and national identity is smaller, but growing fast. There are two fine studies examining national and class identities during and after the First World War: N. Mansfield, 'Class conflict and village war memorials, 1914–24', [...] in the aftermath of [...] *Historical Journal*, 37, 1994. [...] Second World War. A. Calder, *The People's* [...] 1991 and A. Calder, *The Myth of the Blitz* (Pimlico, 1992) should be read together with H.L. Smith (ed.), *Britain in the Second World War: A Social History* (Manchester: Manchester University Press, 1996).

Britain, England, Wales and Scotland each has its own history, and to varying degree its own historiography: see, for example, B. Crick, 'The English and the British', in B. Crick (ed.), *National Identities: The Constitution of the United Kingdom* (Oxford: Blackwell, 1991). For Britain, see J. Springhall, *Youth, Empire and Society: British Youth Movements, 1883–1940* (Croom Helm, 1977). For England, see R. Colls and P. Dodd (eds), *Englishness: Politics and Culture: 1880–1920* (Croom Helm, 1987) and J. Paxman, *The English: A Portrait of a People* (Penguin, 1999), a book that attempts 'to discover the roots of the present English anxiety about themselves by travelling back into the past'.

There has been less interest in the relationship between age, gender, class identities and national identities. However, J. Springhall, *Youth, Empire and Society: British Youth Movements, 1883–1940* (Croom Helm, 1977) and M.N. Franklin, *The Decline of Class Voting in Britain: Changes in the Basis of Electoral Choice, 1964–1983* (Oxford: Clarendon Press, 1985) are thought-provoking. So too is S. Todd, ' "Boisterous workers": Young women, industrial rationalization and workplace militancy in interwar England', *Labour History Review*, 68, 2003. B. Campbell, *The Iron Ladies: Why Do Women Vote Tory?* (Virago, 1987) also raises important issues – not least perhaps the assumption embedded in its title. P. Bartley, *Emmeline Pankhurst* (Routledge, 2002) explores, *inter alia*, the way in which a socialist and leading militant suffragette ended up as a Conservative Party candidate. Hugo Young's study of Britain's first female (Conservative) prime minister, *One of Us: A Biography of Margaret Thatcher* (Pan, 1990), remains unsurpassed.

There are, finally, a number of challenging studies of the relationship between ethnicity, class identity and national identity. W. James, 'The making of black identities', in R. Samuel (ed.), *Patriotism: The Making and Unmaking of British National Identity, Volume II Minorities and Outsiders* (Routledge, 1989) provided an early impetus to the debate. For more recent contributions, see W. Webster, *Imagining Home: Gender, 'Race' and National Identity, 1945–64* (UCL Press, 1998) and D. Frost, 'Ambiguous identities: Constructing and de-constructing black and white "Scouse" identities in twentieth-century Liverpool', in N. Kirk (ed.), *Northern Identities: Historical Interpretations of 'The North' and 'Northerners'* (Aldershot: Ashgate, 2000). R. Winder, *Bloody Foreigners: The Story of Immigration to Britain* (Little, Brown, 2004) was published just as I was finishing the book.